Dimensions of Personhood

Edited by

Heikki Ikäheimo & Arto Laitinen

imprint-academic.com

Copyright © Imprint Academic, 2007

No part of this publication may be reproduced in any form without permission, except for the quotation of brief passages in criticism and discussion.

Published in the UK by Imprint Academic
PO Box 200, Exeter EX5 5YX, UK

Published in the USA by Imprint Academic
Philosophy Documentation Center
PO Box 7147, Charlottesville, VA 22906-7147, USA

ISBN 9 781845 400866

A CIP catalogue record for this book is available from the British Library and US Library of Congress

COVER ILLUSTRATION
'Wondering' by James Lane

This painting was created in response to the Tsunami that wreaked havoc throughout Asia. It was exhibited at 'Artists for Tsunami Relief', an event that included artwork created by over 40 artists from all over the world. It is the first panel of a triptych that depicts a Thai family throughout the Tsunami experience and shows the family looking out to sea after the initial earthquake has struck. The painting now hangs in the home of an Indonesian family. For the use of the image on this cover, a donation has been made to Tsunami relief in place of the customary artist's fee. For more information and details of how to order a print of the painting, see:

http://www.yessy.com/moai

Contents

About Authors	4
Editors' Introduction, *Heikki Ikäheimo & Arto Laitinen*	6

Part I: Conceptual and Ontological Questions

Persons and Other Things, *Lynne Rudder Baker*	17
What Are We? *Eric Olson*	37
The Social Nature of Personal Identity, *Michael Quante*	56

Part II: Self-relationality of Persons

Person as Subject, *Dieter Sturma*	77
Arrogance, Self-Respect and Personhood, *Robin S. Dillon*	101
Unconscious Knowledge of One's Own Mind, *Andreas Wildt*	127
Non-objectal Subjectivity, *Manfred Frank*	152

Part III: Interrelationality of Persons

Persons and Practices, *Pirmin Stekeler-Weithofer*	174
Moral Agency, Self-Consciousness, and Practical Wisdom, *Shaun Gallagher*	199
Recognizing Persons, *Heikki Ikäheimo*	224
Sorting Out Aspects of Personhood, *Arto Laitinen*	248
Index	271

ABOUT AUTHORS

Lynne Rudder Baker, Distinguished Professor of Philosophy at the University of Massachusetts at Amherst, is the author of four books, most recently *The Metaphysics of Everyday Life: An Essay in Practical Realism* (CUP, in press). She has written scores of articles in journals such as *The Journal of Philosophy*, *The Philosophical Review*, *Philosophical Studies*, *Noûs*, *American Philosophical Quarterly*, *Faith and Philosophy*, and others. In 2001, Anthonie Meijers edited a volume of critical essays on her work, *Explaining Beliefs: Lynne Rudder Baker and her Critics* (Stanford: CSLI Publications).

Robin S. Dillon, Associate Professor of Philosophy at Lehigh University, has written extensively on respect and self-respect, including entries on these topics in the online *Stanford Encyclopedia of Philosophy* and the *Encyclopedia of Philosophy*, 2nd edition (Macmillan 2006). She is currently finishing a book on arrogance and self-respect.

Manfred Frank is Professor of Philosophy at the University of Tübingen. His publications include *Die Unhintergehbarkeit von Individualität — Reflexionen über Subjekt, Person und Individuum aus Anlaß ihrer 'postmodernen' Toterklärung* (Suhrkamp, 1986) *Selbstbewußtsein und Selbsterkenntnis — Essays zu analytischen Philosophie der Subjektivität* (Reclam 1991) and *Selbstgefühl — Eine historisch-systematische Erkundung* (Suhrkamp 2002).

Shaun Gallagher is Professor and Chair of Philosophy and Cognitive Sciences at the University of Central Florida. He is Visiting Professor at the Ecole Normale Supériure, Lyon (Spring 2007), and occasional Visiting Professor at the University of Copenhagen. His research interests include phenomenology and philosophy of mind, cognitive sciences, hermeneutics, theories of the self and personal identity. His books include *How the Body Shapes the Mind* (2005); a forthcoming book with Dan Zahavi, *The Phenomenological Mind* (Routledge, 2007) and a recent co-edited volume *Does Consciousness Cause Behavior?* (MIT Press, 2006). He is co-editor of the interdisciplinary journal *Phenomenology and the Cognitive Sciences*.

Heikki Ikäheimo is a Post Doctoral Research Fellow of the Academy of Finland and currently visiting scholar at the University of Frankfurt. His publications include *On the Nature of Social and Institutional Reality* (co-edited with E. Lagerspetz and J. Kotkavirta) and several articles on recognition, personhood and Hegel.

ABOUT AUTHORS

Arto Laitinen is a Research Fellow at University of Jyväskylä (from August 2007 onwards, at Helsinki Collegium for Advanced Study). His publications include *Strong Evaluation without Moral Sources* (Peter Lang, 2007), and articles on recognition, personhood and normativity. He has been a visiting scholar at Oxford, Reading, Columbia and Münster.

Eric Olson studied at Reed College and Syracuse University, and is currently Professor of Philosophy at the University of Sheffield. He is the author of *The Human Animal: Personal Identity Without Psychology* (OUP, 1997) and *What Are We? A Study in Personal Ontology* (OUP, 2007).

Michael Quante is Professor of Philosophy in University of Cologne. His publications include *Hegel's Concept of Action* (CUP, 2004) and *Personales Leben und menschlicher Tod* (Suhrkamp, 2002), *Personen* (Walter De Gruyter, forthcoming) and numerous articles on the philosophy of persons, social philosophy, ethics, German Idealism and biomedical ethics. He is Director of the Institut für Ethik in den Lebenswissenschaften (Cologne), Co-Director of the Husserl Archive (Cologne) and associate editor of the journal *Ethical Theory and Moral Practice*.

Pirmin Stekeler-Weithofer is Professor of Theoretical Philosophy at the University of Leipzig. His publications include *Hegels Analytische Philosophie – Die Wissenschaft der Logik als kritische Theorie der Bedeutung* (Sömingh 1992), *Sinn-Kriterien – Die logischen Grundlagen kritischer Philosophie von Platon bis Wittgenstein* (Schöningh 1995) and *Philosophie des Selbstbewusstseins – Hegels System als Formanalyse von Wissen und Autonomie* (Suhrkamp 2005).

Dieter Sturma has been the director of the German Reference Centre for Ethics in the life sciences and of the Institute of Science and Ethics since April 2007. He also holds a chair of philosophy at the University of Bonn. From 1998 to 2007 he was professor at the University of Essen. His main areas of research are Philosophy of Mind and Ethics.

Andreas Wildt is Docent in philosophy at the Free University of Berlin and works at the moment as analytically oriented somatic psychotherapist. His publications include *Autonomie und Anerkennung – Hegels Moralitätskritik in Lichte seiner Fichte-Rezeption* (Klett-Cotta, 1982) and numerous articles. His main areas of interest are in ethics, political philosophy, philosophical anthropology and psychology.

Heikki Ikäheimo & Arto Laitinen

Dimensions of Personhood
Editors' Introduction

This collection includes original papers on central philosophical questions concerning *personhood*. Before introducing the individual contributions, or the specific issues they tackle with, we would like to preliminarily clarify what this collection, as a whole, is about. Saying that the articles focus on personhood is not yet very informative since 'person' and 'personhood' are words with multiple and often quite unclear meanings. With these introductory remarks we wish to show that behind the multiplicity, there is a unified, even if complex phenomenon, and that it is useful to grasp it synoptically as a whole.

Consider the following question. What is the most important thing that you, me, and everyone like us, share and that distinguishes us from everything else? You and I are bound to be similar in many ways; but we are also bound to be different in many ways. Furthermore, you will most certainly consider some of our mutual similarities and differences more important than others, and so will I — and most certainly we will partly agree and partly disagree on what is more and what is less important in our similarities and differences. But is there any chance that we could *agree upon* a meaningful answer to the posed question: what is *the most important* thing that you, me, and everyone like us, have in common, and that distinguishes us from everything else?

There are two prominent candidates for an answer upon which, initial scepticism settled, we might well end up agreeing on. The first candidate is that despite all our mutual differences, and abstracting from all of our less important similarities, we are *humans*. The second candidate is that despite all our mutual differences, and abstracting from all of our less important similarities, we are *persons*.

Were we to agree that *being human* is the most important thing that you, I and others like us share we would be in an influential company.

Much of our history of ideas supports the thought that being human is something very special indeed: for the Ancients, humans were the only rational animals, for the Mediaevals only humans had immortal souls, and according to the Moderns humans are distinct from all other species as bearers of 'human rights'. Assuming that we would subscribe to one or more of these beliefs about humans, it would certainly be hard for us to see what other similarity between us could be more important than the fact that we are humans (assuming that we are).

Suppose, then, that we would want to look at this question more closely and to make it explicit to ourselves *why* we, and so many others, find being human so immensely important. Suppose that we would conclude that we find being human the most important characteristic that unites us and distinguishes us from everything else, *because* humans (in contrast to everything else) are rational beings, and/or *because* humans (in contrast to all other beings) have immortal souls, and/or *because* humans (in contrast to everything else) have some basic rights. Thus, in brief, we would conclude that the fact that we are humans is of major importance to us because of the uniqueness of the ontological, theological and/or moral position of humans in the universe.

Should we accept these views, it would of course be appropriate to evaluate their credibility. Obviously, each one of these thoughts is quite forcefully challenged today. First of all, after Darwin, we understand that the human species is one biological species among others, so that if something is a 'rational animal' it need not be, by definition, a *human* animal. It is by no means conceptually impossible that we might meet rational creatures that are not humans. (Many primatologists, we hear, actually say that the so called great apes are not that far from humans in this sense.)[1] Secondly, even if the belief in immortal souls is far from uncommon even today, it hardly is unchallenged. Perhaps there are no immortal souls (most philosophers, if that matters, do not seem to think there are). Or even if there were, is it really in our power to know that humans are *the only* mortals who have them? Finally, the claim that there are rights called 'the human rights' that all and only humans have, is despite its undeniable popularity not particularly uncontroversial, either. We do not have to go all the way to saying, like Jeremy Bentham did that human rights are nothing else but 'rhetorical nonsense upon stilts', to admit that it would be morally dubious to deny these rights from otherwise similar

---

[1] See Hurley & Nudds (2006) on debates concerning the rationality of non–human animals.

creatures (say, rational beings and/or ones with immortal souls), who just do not happen to be humans.

All in all, after such reflection, we would come to notice that much of the apparent obviousness of the central importance of being human rests on ideas that are far from unchallenged. If these ideas cannot withstand scrutiny — that is, if there at least seems to be no *necessary* connection between having rational capacities, immortal soul, rights, etc., on the one hand, and being human, on the other — then the odds are that we would conclude that being human may not, after all, be so hugely important as we first thought it to be. It may not be *the most important thing* that we and others like us share, and that distinguishes us from all other kinds of beings.

What about the other candidate for an answer to the question: despite all our mutual differences, and abstracting from all of our less important similarities, we are *persons*? Even if 'being human' is not as credible an answer as it was taken to be for a long time, central elements of this answer have not become obsolete. In fact, it is quite accurate to say that together they form the second answer. That is, leaving aside the controversial question of immortal souls, it is certainly a very significant feature you and I share, that both of us are rational beings in some relevant sense; similarly, it is certainly very important that despite our differences, and independent of our less important similarities, we are both holders of some basic rights or other moral (or normative) statuses. The notion of personhood, as it is nowadays mostly used in philosophy, combines these two ideas, but leaves out the problematic reference to a biological species.[2]

But if the idea of human being no longer unproblematically keeps together the two attributes of rationality and moral status, by attributing both of them to humans, what is the point of keeping them together by packing them somehow into one notion? Are they simply not two different attributes that we should analyse separately instead of prejudging, by terminological choice that they go together? In other words, what is the point of the notion of personhood which simply seems to be a mix of two different ideas?

---

[2] Different, more exact concepts of personhood emphasize the two attributes of 'rationality' and 'moral or normative statuses' differently, but in most philosophical discussions on personhood both elements are present in one way or another. 'Rationality' can here be understood as a general title for a number of more particular 'rational capacities' that have been proposed as characteristic of or defining personhood. Typical lists of such capacities include things like self-consciousness, capacity for moral agency, free will, capacity to think, responsiveness to normative demands, fitness to be held responsible, mastery of language, capacity to communicate, capacity to participate in norm-governed practices etc. Here it is not necessary to go into details about any of these.

The answer, which the articles in this collection support, is that it is not a matter of mere stipulation that rational capacities and moral statuses go together. Rather than being an artificial mixture, or a simple confusion, of two distinct phenomena, the composite notion of personhood grasps a real life intertwinement. The ontological and moral facts that intuitively make 'us' special form a holistic unity which it is indeed useful to try to conceive as a whole. To make this claim preliminarily plausible let us make a short excursion to the world of science (or rather moral) fiction.

Some philosophers have argued that in the imaginary situation where you and I were to meet previously unknown, intelligent-looking creatures — say, in another solar system — the most fundamental question in our minds would not be whether they are humans (obviously, they are not), but, rather, whether they are persons. But what exactly does this question mean? Wilfrid Sellars thinks that it basically means asking whether they belong to '*us*' in the sense of a *moral community*, whose members have a moral standing — rights, duties etc. — with regard to each other. Thus, for you and I to ask whether the aliens are persons is to ask whether we ought to relate to them in some fundamentally similar way we relate to each other.

John Harris looks at a similar situation from a slightly different angle and formulates it somewhat humorously: were you and I to meet intelligent, and very hungry members of an extraterrestrial species looking for food on Earth, it might be wise to think of a way to convince the visitors of the appropriateness of 'having us for dinner' in the one sense rather than the other.[3] Humans are fleshy beings full of protein and other vital nutrients, thus the right point to make would not necessarily be the argument that we are humans. Rather, it would be in our interest to convince the aliens of a morally important similarity between us and them: that despite our differences, and abstracting from our less important similarities (say that that they too have four limbs), we all — both the visitors and the earthlings — belong to an overarching 'we' of a moral community whose members have moral claims and status with regard to each other. In Sellars' terms, this would merely mean saying that we are all persons. Persons have other persons for dinner as guests, not as the meal.[4]

---

[3] See Sellars 1963, chapter VII, and Harris 1999, p. 302.

[4] Perhaps it is best to note here that of course there may be good considerations against eating *any* animals. In general, what kind of moral implications something's not being a person has, is a large topic and it is not necessary to take any particular philosophical stance on the relevant debates here.

Is 'being a person' in the sense implied by the above imaginary examples nothing else then than 'having some basic moral status'? That is certainly one possible way of *defining* what being a person is: having a moral status such as a right to life.[5] But moral statuses obviously rest on ontological features in at least two senses. First, it is more or less unanimously accepted by philosophers, and supported by common sense, that our being rational creatures gives us, or makes us deserving of, a special moral status or statuses with regard to each other. Secondly, it is clearly only rational creatures that are capable of claiming for and acknowledging or respecting, moral statuses. Therefore, having special moral statuses and having rational capacities (or moral and ontological uniqueness) are, as it were, two dimensions of the Sellarsian 'we' or moral community of persons. There is no definite answer to the question which one of these dimensions is more important, and no intuitively or philosophically obvious need to answer it, since they intimately go together. It is exactly this intimate intertwinement of the ontological and the moral dimension of what we think is important in us, that arguably makes the composite notion of personhood important and philosophically useful. The collection, as a whole, illuminates this intertwinement from different, mutually complementary points of views.

The examples above also illustrate another guiding idea of this collection: personhood, as a complex or composite topic, can be helpfully approached by focusing on the special kinds of *relations* persons have to each other, as well as to themselves. As we saw, persons, thought of as members of the Sellarsian moral community stand, or are capable of standing, in particular kinds of relations with regard to each other. This is not merely a matter of conceptual relationships, but of concrete interpersonal relationships involving special kinds of attitudes, emotions and actions (which, roughly, establish and/or respond to the relevant statuses). That persons, characteristically or perhaps by definition, stand in such relationships to each other, is related to the fact that persons also have special kinds of relationships to themselves, 'self-relations'. In philosophy, persons are typically thought of as being self-conscious, as having self-concern, second-order desires, moral conscience, first-person perspective or other epistemic and practical, conscious or unconscious ways of relating to their attitudes, emotions and actions, and to themselves as their subjects. Indeed, being self-related in such ways is widely thought of in modern

---

[5] For instance, according to Michael Tooley's definition, being a person is (nothing else than) having 'a serious right to life' (Tooley, 1972, p. 40).

philosophy as a general structural feature of what it is to be rational in the ways specific to persons in distinction to less complex beings. If a being does not have various epistemic, evaluative and conative relationships to its inner life which make it capable of controlling and being responsible for itself, then it is not a rational agent in the sense that we think is distinctive of persons.

The interpersonal relationality and the self-relationality of persons are intertwined in at least two ways. Clearly, only beings that have some such self-relations can stand as moral subjects or agents in interpersonal relations to others: you cannot establish a mutual moral relationship with a creature that has no reflexive relationship to its desires or intentions but, as it were, acts on them automatically. From another point of view, at least empirically speaking, it seems to be impossible for such 'person-making' self-relations constitutive of the way persons are rational, to develop or actualize fully, if the individual is left outside of the realm of interpersonal relationships.[6]

This collection is organized in three parts, with thematically different focuses, but also significant overlap due to the interconnectedness of the discussed issues. The first part discusses and distinguishes specific ontological and conceptual questions concerning personhood and our fundamental nature; the second part focuses on some of the most fundamental kinds of self-relations of persons, as well as their preconditions; finally, the third part focuses on interpersonal or social relations characteristic or constitutive of personhood. The collection includes both synoptic articles outlining holistic ways of conceiving a multiplicity of features or dimensions associated with personhood, and articles concentrating on specific sub-questions.

The first part opens with an article by *Lynne Rudder Baker*, introducing several themes discussed throughout the collection. In her earlier work Baker has defended a view according to which persons are beings with a 'first person perspective'. Persons, as subjects of a first person perspective, are ontologically related to their bodies through a relation that Baker calls 'constitution'. In this paper Baker elaborates on some of the details of her 'constitution view' of persons, and widens the perspective of her approach by discussing intentional relationships that persons have to things other than themselves. These relationships — which first person perspective makes possible — include moral relationships (which Baker conceives in terms of duties

---

[6] The dependence of different kinds of self-relations on interpersonal relations is widely discussed in developmental psychology. For a philosophical work systematically utilizing this general idea, see Honneth (1995).

towards other persons as well as to non-persons), interpretive relationships (in which we redescribe things in different creative ways), and productive relationships (in which persons bring about ontologically novel kinds of things).

In the next paper, *Eric Olson* introduces and clarifies the question 'what are we?' — what are we metaphysically speaking, or what is our fundamental ontological nature? He distinguishes this question from the more widely discussed questions concerning the conditions of personhood and persistence of persons. Having introduced the question, Olson points out that every account of what we are (including Baker's constitution view, and a view Olson has previously defended, according to which we are animal organisms) appears to face grave objections. One difficult problem is how to rule out, in some principled way, the threat that there are *two* things (say, an animal and a person constituted by it; or an animal and a part of an animal) thinking your thoughts. The possible solutions come in metaphysical, psychological and epistemic varieties, but none of them are likely to be very appealing.

Michael Quante distinguishes, in turn, between four different questions that get easily confused in the discussions on personhood. These are the questions concerning (a) the conditions of personhood, (b) the unity of personhood, (c) the persistence of human persons and (d) the structure of biographical or narrative 'personality' or 'selfhood'. (These all differ from Olson's question of what we are). Quante analyses closely these questions and their interrelations, and suggests that while personhood and personality are irreducibly socially constituted, our unity and conditions of persistence are not. Quante also argues that while the concept of a person is not logically tied to the concept of human being, our experiences and intuitions about what it is to be a person are inevitably intertwined with those about what it is to be human.

In the second part, focussing on the self-relations of persons, *Dieter Sturma* starts by outlining a comprehensive theory of 'persons as subjects'. His central thought is that personhood consists of a system of self-referential activities, or of dynamic self-relations which reveal themselves in expressions like: 'I think, I feel, I notice, I want, I act, I wish, I suffer, I care etc.' In Sturma's account, a systematically clarified concept of self-reference, purged of all reifying or 'egological' readings of the 'self' is a tool with which to construe a de-transcendentalized and holistic conception of personhood uniting both its ontological and moral dimensions. Such a conception takes seriously the irreducibility and ineliminability of the subjective first person perspective, and yet, does not lead to a problematic ontological dualism involving dubious non-worldly mental entities.

The next article by *Robin S. Dillon* focuses on a particularly important self-relation, namely self-respect which she, following Kant, takes to be essential to personhood. There are many varieties of self-respect, but the so called 'recognition respect' for oneself as a person involves appreciation of oneself as someone with dignity and moral status just by virtue of being a rational agent. Such recognition self-respect comes in two forms: the first is a view of oneself as someone entitled to being regarded and treated *by others* with respect, and the second concerns one's own regard and treatment of oneself as a moral and rational agent. Dillon argues that there are correspondingly two forms of arrogance, violations of these forms of self-respect, which as such corrupt our personhood. In her view, understanding the connections between different kinds of arrogance, self-respect, respect for others and personhood is the key to understanding the subtle, but profound ways in which arrogance corrupts the very qualities that make persons persons.

Whereas Dillon's focus is on self-respect, the article by *Andreas Wildt* focuses on theoretical or epistemic self-relations, and more exactly, on the unconscious ones. Wildt argues that there is a meaningful concept of unconscious knowledge of one's mental states, and shows that this concept plays a number of roles in the writings of Sigmund Freud. Freud is often seen as one of the thinkers who 'dethroned' man by depriving him of the illusion of the full mastery of himself, and this has been interpreted as a sign of the general 'death of the subject (or man)'. Yet, there is nothing particularly threatening in Freud for the theory of personhood. Unconscious self-relations are part of the complexity of what makes us persons, and therefore Freud, as the master thinker of the unconscious, is someone who cannot be ignored in attempts to come up with a synoptic conception of personhood.

Manfred Frank concludes the second part by arguing that it is necessary to presuppose, 'behind' the reflective self-relations constitutive of personhood, a non-reflective or non-relational core of personhood without which no genuinely self-reflective relations would be possible, and without which also the normative or moral status of persons would lack a *fundamentum in re*. Frank discusses a number of contemporary approaches to self-consciousness, and shows how each of them fails as a comprehensive account in that they either presuppose or leave unaccounted for this non-relational core that all genuinely first-personal consciousness or knowledge of oneself presupposes. Frank shows that Fichte, an immediate successor of Kant, was already well aware of the problems involved in the attempts to account for the core in terms of a subject-object-relation, and points out that a contemporary of Fichte, Novalis, suggested an alternative approach to the foundation of the first-person phenomena — one which conceives it in terms of the concept of feeling.

Like the second part, the third part of the book, focussing on interpersonal relations or sociality of persons, also opens with a piece outlining a broad holistic conception of what defines personhood. In it *Pirmin Stekeler-Weithofer* argues that to be a person is essentially to take part in a system of social practices. This involves not only the capacity to follow rules or norms constitutive of such practices (or *understanding*), but also the capacity to take evaluative distance from, and thus to challenge and develop further the system of practices (or *reason*). Stekeler-Weithofer criticizes reductivist programs for their incapacity to really grasp the phenomenon of personhood, and argues that a satisfactory answer to the very basic questions of philosophy point towards a comprehensive conception of personhood. According to Stekeler-Weithofer, the fundamental conviction of the German idealist philosophers from Kant to Hegel was that philosophy is ultimately philosophical anthropology. This does not mean studying man as a biological creature, but conceiving comprehensively the structures that make him, in suitable circumstances, a person with the spontaneous and critical capacities of reason — a free being.

Whereas Stekeler-Weithofer discusses *sapience in general* as what makes persons persons, *Shaun Gallagher* suggests that practical wisdom, *phronesis,* is the specific person-making feature. He illuminates the nature of practical wisdom by drawing on rival analyses of expertise. Although expertise and practical wisdom are different things, they are alike in that we can acquire them only in interaction with other persons and through habituation. In general, Gallagher argues for an embodied and intersubjective account of personhood, and supports his view with evidence from neuroscience, developmental psychology and phenomenology. According to Gallagher, such a view can account for all the items in standard lists of conditions of personhood better than views, such as Daniel Dennett's, which leave open the possibility that persons could be brains-in-a-vat.

After Gallagher, *Heikki Ikäheimo* outlines a synoptic conceptual model, in which a number philosophical and common sense candidates for features that define personhood are conceived of as interrelated, yet irreducible, 'layers' and 'dimensions' of what it is to be a person in the full-fledged sense of the word. Ikäheimo distinguishes between three layers of personhood — consisting of person-making psychological capacities, person-making interpersonal significances, and person-making institutional or deontic powers. Running through the layers there are then two dimensions — the deontic and the axiological — corresponding to the 'recognitive attitudes' of respect and love. These recognitive attitudes of 'taking something/-one as a person' are responses to the psychological layer, and directly constitutive of the interpersonal layer of the respective dimensions of personhood. Ikäheimo argues that, in a number of ways, persons bootstrap themselves into personhood collectively by taking each other as persons.

In the closing article *Arto Laitinen* asks how three aspects of personhood — capacities of individuals, normative requirements concerning the treatment of persons, and the social aspect of recognition by others — are related, and how personhood depends on them. Laitinen first defends a 'basic view' holding that while actual recognition is among the constitutive elements of full personhood, it is the individual capacities (and *not* full personhood) which ground the basic normative demands. Actual recognition in turn depends analytically on such pre-existing normative requirements: it is a matter of responsiveness to them. Anyone with the relevant capacities ought to be included into the group of persons, whether or not they actually are. Laitinen acknowledges that the basic view as such is not sufficiently refined to meet some central objections (which claim that the capacities depend on recognition; that recognition seems to have normative relevance; and that the basic view as such does not suffice to explain the equality either of persons or of humans). The basic view can, however, be refined so as to respond to these challenges, and thus to give a fuller view on how the aspects of personhood are to be sorted out.

The editors wish to thank all the authors for their contributions and co-operation, Anthony Freeman and Valerie Hardcastle for their support with editing, and the anonymous referees as well as a number of colleagues (who are too numerous to be mentioned here) for their comments on the individual texts, and Min Chen Lo for preparing the index. The book is a result of a research project, funded by the Academy of Finland, 'Limits of Personhood' (in continuation with the earlier project 'The Concept of Person'), whose members include Jari Kaukua, Jussi Kotkavirta, Pessi Lyyra, Vili Lähteenmäki, Petteri Niemi, Mimosa Pursiainen, Juhana Toivanen and Mikko Yrjönsuuri. Special thanks to the leader of these projects, Jussi Kotkavirta.

References

Harris, John (1999), 'The concept of the person and the value of life', *Kennedy Institute of Ethics Journal*, **9** (4), pp. 293–308.

Honneth, Axel (1995), *The Struggle for Recognition: The Moral and Political Grammar of Social Conflicts* (Cambridge: Polity Press).

Hurley, Susan & Nudds, Matthew (ed. 2006), *Rational Animals* (Oxford: Oxford University Press).

Lowe, Jonathan (1996), *Subjects of Experience* (Cambridge: Cambridge University Press).

Sellars, Wilfrid (1963), 'Philosophy and the scientific image of man', in *Frontiers of Science and Philosophy*, ed. Robert Colodny (Pittsburgh: University of Pittsburgh Press), pp. 35–78.

Lynne Rudder Baker

Persons and Other Things

Abstract: In the large recent literature on the nature of human persons, persons are usually studied in isolation from the world in which they live. What persons are most fundamentally, philosophers say, are human animals, or brains, or perhaps souls — without any consideration of the social and physical environments without which persons would not exist. In this article, I want to compensate for such overly narrow focus. Instead of beginning with the nature of persons cut off from any environment, I shall begin with metaphysical consideration of the world of which persons are a part. I shall then briefly describe my view of persons, according to which persons are material objects like other concrete things in the world, but are unique in their first-person perspectives. Finally, I shall consider some of the special relations that persons, and only persons, have to other things in the world.

We can understand what persons are only if we consider the world in which they live. Let us begin with that world.

The World of Encounter

First, what can we say about the world that contains persons? Persons inhabit what I'll call 'the world of encounter.' Let me specify what I mean by 'the world of encounter.' Suppose that we took a survey of everyone in the world and listed widely used common nouns for ordinary things (like chair, flower, person, cow, university, credit card, greenhouse, laboratory, and so on). Suppose that we also listed common activities (like cooking meals, going to work, meeting friends, obeying authorities, sending emails, paying taxes, and so on). Also we

Correspondence:
lrbaker@philos.umass.edu

should list social and political items (like bureaucrat, police officer, taxi driver) and institutional activities (like conferring honorary degrees, issuing search warrants, being inaugurated), and so on. Let us instruct the respondents in our survey to indicate, with respect to each kind of item that they recognize, whether or not anyone has encountered items of that kind. For any kind of item that the respondent has never heard of, let him so indicate. (Some respondents may not have heard of cell phones; some may not have heard of emails.)

The items said to exist or occur by most people in the survey provide a basis for what is included in the world of encounter.[1] We do not have to actually carry out the survey; nor must we be certain about each of the items and activities that populate it.[2] The point is that what I am calling 'the world of encounter' is common currency. The world in which we engage our friends, family and colleagues, the world that all human persons interact with — particle physicists as well as people with no formal schooling — is what I am calling 'the world of encounter'. The items that we encounter everyday are things whose existence we cannot, in good faith, deny.

One noticeable feature of the world of encounter is that it is populated by things — such as pianos, pacemakers, and paychecks — whose existence depends on there being persons with propositional attitudes. Let me introduce a term to apply to any phenomenon that either is a propositional-attitude property (like believing, desiring or intending) or is one whose existence or occurrence presupposes that there are beings with beliefs, desires and/or intentions. Call any such phenomenon an 'intention-dependent' phenomenon — or ID phenomenon for short.[3] ID objects that we are familiar with include emails, elevators, kitchen utensils, Ferris wheels, thermometers, and so on. Many ID objects depend on conventions or other forms of collective intentionality.[4] There are ID properties that stand in contrast to nonID properties — for example, being a promise as opposed to

---

[1] This is just a rough-and-ready test, not a criterion. I am simply pointing to a part of reality that we *all* take for granted. We could not survive if we didn't take medium-sized things for granted. In Baker (forthcoming), I argue for the (irreducible) reality of ordinary things.

[2] I hesitate to call the concepts used for the survey 'folk concepts', because the term 'folk' has derogatory connotations. A folk theory is just a temporary expedient of the ignorant 'folk'; it will be replaced by a true theory as soon as more sophisticated investigators get on the case. To avoid association of what 'the folk' say with false theories, I'll avoid the term.

[3] In other places, I've used the expression 'intentional object' to refer to ID objects. Although I characterized what I meant by 'intentional object' carefully, I am now resorting to the technical term 'ID object' in order to avoid confusion with uses of 'intentional object' associated with Brentano and Meinong.

[4] There are interesting comparisons and contrasts between my view of ID objects (e.g., artworks and artefacts) and Searle's notion of an institutional fact determined by the

being an audible emission, being a signature as opposed to being a mark on paper, being a dance step as opposed to being a bodily motion.

Different communities may be familiar with different kinds of ID objects; but all communities recognize many kinds of ID objects — as well as other ID phenomena like conventions, obligations, and so on. All artifacts and artworks, and most human activities (getting a job, going out to dinner, etc.), are ID phenomena: They could not exist or occur in a world in the absence of beings with beliefs, desires, and intentions. The importance of ID phenomena has been systematically overlooked by philosophers.

However, not all things in the world of encounter depend on intentionality. For example, satellites and dinosaurs could — and did — exist in a world without beliefs, desires and intentions. In the world of encounter, whether an object is an ID object or not is often insignificant: The ball is an ID object whether it is constituted by a piece of natural rubber or synthetic rubber, and, indeed, the difference between a ball constituted by a piece of natural rubber and a ball constituted by a piece of synthetic rubber is usually not a salient difference. My conception of the world of encounter allows for the distinction between ID objects and objects that are not intention-dependent, but does not take that distinction to be fundamental.

The world of encounter is, I am convinced, as real as the world of electrons and quarks is: we cannot make good sense of a supposition that the world of encounter is a vast mirage. (All of our evidence for electrons and quarks crucially depends on precision instruments, medium-sized objects in the world of encounter. So, we could not call into question the reality of the world of encounter without calling into question all the evidence that there are electrons and quarks.)[5] A complete and correct inventory of what there is, I believe, must include ordinary medium-sized objects — including persons, artifacts, artworks, economic items like bonds, legal documents like passports.

---

constitutive rule, 'X counts as Y in circumstances C.' One similarity between Searle and me is that an artwork or artefact cannot be reduced to the 'sheer physical features' of its constituter (in my vocabulary). One difference is that for Searle the 'counts as' locution 'names a feature of the imposition of a status to which a function is attached by way of collective intentionality;' whereas for me, the constituted object is metaphysically distinct from the constituting object. A statue is not just a piece of marble that has had a status imposed on it or that has been assigned a function. I heartily agree with Searle that there is much that we cannot adequately describe in physical-chemical terms. See Searle (1995).

[5] It is not novel to suppose that the knowledge gained by use of a particle-accelerator, say, depends on theories governing the particle-accelerator. If those theories were to come into question, so would the putative knowledge gained from the use of particle-accelerators.

In short: Reality includes not only nonintentional items from molecules to mountains, but also all the ID objects that I described — your credit cards, the wallet that you carry them in, the knife, fork and spoon that you eat with, and other things that could not exist in the absence of beings with beliefs, desires and intentions. Now let me sketch out a metaphysics for the world of encounter.

Constitution as a Unity-Relation

At the heart of my view is a single comprehensive metaphysical relation that unites items at different levels of reality into the objects that we experience in everyday life: the trees, the automobiles, the credit cards. I use the word 'constitution' to refer to this relation. For example, a ball may be constituted by a piece of synthetic rubber. A constituted object exists at a higher level of reality than its constituter.

Constitution, unlike identity, is a temporally limited relation: x may constitute y at one time but not at another. For example, a human body may constitute a person at one time, but not at a later time (after the person has died, say). Reality is hierarchical: Subatomic particles are on an ontologically lower level than the macroscopic objects that they make up. Ordinary material objects are constituted-at-t by other 'lower-level' things. My socks, which can survive repair of the cloth by adding new threads, are constituted by different pieces of cloth at different times. The constituting pieces of cloth in turn are constituted by molecules, and so on down to subatomic particles.

My thesis is this: All macrophysical concrete objects found in the world of encounter are constituted objects.[6] Sometimes an ordinary object is constituted by another ordinary object — as when a landscape painting is constituted by a piece of canvass with paint on it — but ultimately all ordinary material objects are constituted by aggregates of subatomic particles. As I construe it, constitution is not a part/whole relation: If x constitutes y at t, x is not part of y at t.[7] The identity of a constituted object is independent of the identity of its parts, which may change. Nor are the persistence conditions of a constituted object given by the persistence conditions of its parts. Constituted objects have different essential properties (and different persistence conditions and different causal powers) from their

---

[6] This view of reality stands in stark contrast to eliminative and reductive views. For a detailed defence of my view, see Baker (2007a). Moreover, my view is not confined to macrophysical concrete objects. To be a macrophysical concrete object is a sufficient, not a necessary, condition for falling under my view.

[7] So, 'constitutes' is not a synonym of 'composes' as mereologists use it.

lower-level constituters. E.g., my socks and the pieces of cloth that constitute them have different persistence conditions: The piece of cloth could survive being cut into a flat piece; my socks could not.

On the constitution view, reality comes in fundamentally different kinds. Each thing is of some primary kind essentially. There is no 'mere thing' behind or underlying the instance of a primary kind. Objects related by constitution are of different primary kinds. Objects of different primary kinds may have different persistence conditions. (Famously, the lump of clay has different persistence conditions from the statue.) For primary-kinds F and G — when an F (say, a lump of clay) is in certain circumstances — G-favourable circumstances (say, statue-favourable circumstances) — a new thing of a different kind, a G (say, a statue), comes into existence.[8] The distinction between ID objects and nonID objects may lie in the sort of circumstances a potential constituter must be in to constitute an object of a certain kind. For instance, statue-favourable circumstances are intentional: they include, e.g., artists with certain intentions. By contrast, satellite-favourable circumstances are not intentional: they include, e.g., a certain mass of material revolving around another celestial body. But both statues and satellites are constituted objects, and both have relational properties essentially.

Every object has its primary kind essentially, but not every kind is a primary kind. E.g., *teacher* is not a primary kind; nor is *puppy*. Teachers may cease to be teachers without ceasing to exist (e.g., they may retire); so may puppies cease to be puppies without ceasing to exist (e.g., they may grow up). A person may acquire the property of being a teacher; but a person does not constitute a teacher since *teacher* is not a primary kind. The relation between the person and the teacher cannot be constitution since constitution is a relation between things of different primary kinds, and the person and the teacher have the same primary kind: *person*.

Alas, I do not have a theory of primary kinds, nor even an exhaustive list. Indeed, there could not be a complete list of primary kinds until the end of the world. New inventions create new primary kinds. When Gutenberg invented the printing press, he created a new primary kind — a kind that changed the course of history. Even without a theory of primary kinds, however, I do have a test for a primary kind: x is of primary kind K only if: x is of kind K every moment of its

---

[8] G-favourable circumstances are external to the constituting Fs. The terms 'external' and 'relational' are themselves relative terms. Relative to an atom of sodium and an atom of chlorine, chemical bonding is an external circumstance (a salt-favourable circumstance); but relative to a salt molecule, chemical bonding is an intrinsic property.

existence and could not fail to be of kind K and continue to exist. If K is x's primary kind, then for x to lose the property of being a K is for x to go out of existence altogether. Printing presses go out of existence when barbarians smash them to bits; they do not just lose the property of being printing presses, and become something else: they go out of existence altogether.[9]

Constitution brings into being new objects of higher-level primary kinds than what was there before. To take another example, when a certain combination of chemicals is in a certain environment, a thing of a new kind comes into existence: an organism. That particular combination of chemicals constitutes (not causes) at t that particular organism. A world with the same kinds of chemicals but a different environment may lack organisms, and a world without organisms is ontologically different from a world with organisms. So, constitution makes an ontological difference (see Baker, 2000; 2002).

The combination of chemicals that in a certain environment constitutes an organism is itself constituted by a (mere) aggregate of chemicals.[10] When an aggregate of chemicals comes together in a certain way (by bonding), chemicals of new kinds come into existence. Indeed, if we descend down any chain of constitution relations, sooner or later we will come to aggregates as constituters.

For example, a river at any moment is constituted by an aggregate of water molecules. But the river is not identical to any aggregate of water molecules that constitutes it at a moment. Since that very river is constituted by different aggregates of molecules at different times, the river is not identical to any of the aggregates of water molecules that make it up. Moreover, if the water molecules in the aggregate that constitutes the river at some given time had been scattered all over the universe, the aggregate would still exist but (in the absence of another suitably located aggregate) the river would not still exist. So, although the aggregate of water molecules constitutes the river at t, constitution is not identity.[11] Another way to see that constitution is not identity is to notice that even if an aggregate of molecules, A_1, actually constitutes a river, R at t_1, R might have been constituted by a different

---

[9] I do not think that mere malfunction makes an artifact go out of existence. See Baker (2004).

[10] An aggregate of chemicals becomes a combination when there is bonding. An aggregate of H_2 and O_2 molecules is one and the same aggregate whether the H_2 and O_2 molecules are bonded or not. If they are, then the aggregate constitutes an aggregate of H_2O_2 molecules, and the H_2 and O_2 molecules then exist in combination.

[11] I am assuming here the classical conception of identity, according to which if a = b, then necessarily, a = b.

aggregate of molecules, A_2, at t_1. (For example, a dog might have removed some of the molecules in the aggregate at t_1 by drinking from the river just before t_1.) So, constitution is a unity relation that is in some ways similar to identity, but is not actually identity.

Although constitution is not identity, constitution is a unity-making relation: The one-Euro coin is constituted by a piece of metal, which in turn is constituted by an aggregate of molecules; nevertheless, it is a single coin. Things that stand in the relation of constitution have properties nonderivatively or derivatively. The coin has the property of being worth one Euro nonderivatively — i.e., what makes it worth one Euro has nothing to do with what constitutes it or what it's made of. By contrast, the constituting piece of metal has the property of being worth one Euro derivatively — in virtue of constituting something that has the property of being worth one Euro independently of what constitutes it. The one-Euro coin tapped on a glass has the property of silencing the room derivatively — in virtue of being constituted by a piece of metal. So, the unity produced by constitution allows two-way borrowing of properties — from constituted to constituter, and from constituter to constituted — and the borrowed property is had derivatively. There is a single instance of a property that is shared by both constituter and constituted. It is because constitution is a relation of unity (though not identity) that many properties are shared by both constituter and constituted.[12]

Whether we are talking about rivers, human persons, statues or other sorts of constituted things, the basic idea is this: When certain things of certain kinds (e.g., aggregates of water molecules, human organisms) are in certain circumstances (different ones for different kinds of things), then new entities of different kinds come into existence. The circumstances in which an aggregate of water molecules comes to constitute a river have to do with the relation of the water molecules to each other; they form a flowing stream. The circumstances in which a piece of paper comes to constitute a U.S. dollar bill have to do with the paper's being printed in a certain way under a certain authority. In each case, new things of new kinds — rivers, dollar bills — come into being. Rivers and dollar bills have quite different kinds of causal powers from aggregates of molecules and pieces of paper. And they have different persistence conditions from their constituters. For example, a single aggregate of molecules may persist

---

[12] Not all properties may be had derivatively. Excluded are (a) properties expressed in English by locutions using 'essentially,' 'necessarily,' 'possibly', 'primary kind' and the like; (b) identity/constitution/existence properties; (c) properties rooted outside the times at which they are had; and (d) hybrid properties. For details, Baker (2000), Ch. 2.

over a period of time during which it constitutes a river at one time and is scattered all around, constituting nothing at all, at another time. Since constitution is the vehicle, so to speak, by which new kinds of things come into existence in the natural world, it is obvious that constitution is not identity. Indeed, this conception is relentlessly anti-reductive.

To summarize this discussion of the idea of constitution: Constitution is a very general relation throughout the natural order. Although it is a relation of real unity, constitution falls short of identity. (Identity is necessary; constitution is contingent.) Constitution is a relation that accounts for the appearance of genuinely new kinds of things with new kinds of causal powers. If, say, pieces of marble constitute statues, then an inventory of the contents of the world that includes pieces of marble but leaves out statues is incomplete.[13] Statues are not reducible to pieces of marble; nor are persons reducible to human bodies. No constituted thing is reducible to what constitutes it. This is a perfectly general claim of pluralism that applies to all macrophysical objects. Constitution is not so-called 'property dualism.'

The Constitution View of Human Persons

All concrete objects in the world of encounter, I claimed, are constituted objects, and human persons are no exception. Human persons are constituted by bodies (i.e., human animals) with which they are not identical. Here is an analogy; later will come an explanation: According to the Constitution View of human persons, the relation between a human person and her body (the relation that I am calling 'constitution') is exactly the same kind of relation as the relation between a statue and the piece of marble that makes it up. When a piece of marble is suitably related to an artworld, a new thing — a statue — comes into existence. When a human body develops a first-person perspective, a new thing — a person — comes into existence. The human body does not thereby go out of existence — any more than the piece of marble goes out of existence when it comes to constitute a statue. Moreover, a human person is as material as Michelangelo's *David* is. When a human body comes to constitute a person, the human body has the property of being a person derivatively (in virtue of constituting something that is a person nonderivatively); and the person has the property of being a human body derivatively (in virtue of being constituted by something that is a human body nonderivatively).

---

[13] There is much more to be said about the idea of constitution. See Baker (2000), especially Ch. 2. I also discuss constitution in Baker (1997; 1999; 2002; forthcoming).

As I've emphasized, a person is not identical to her body. But to say that a person is not identical to her body does not mean that the person is identical to the body-plus-some-other-thing (like a soul).[14] Michelangelo's *David* is not identical to a piece-of-marble-plus-some-other-thing. If x constitutes y and x is wholly material, then y is wholly material. (Baker (2000), Ch. 2). The human body (which I take to be identical to a human organism) is wholly material and the human body constitutes the human person. Therefore, the human person is wholly material. A human person is as material as Michelangelo's *David* is.

With respect to being constituted, human persons are just like every other kind of thing in the world of encounter. If human persons are constituted by human organisms, however, then human persons are of a different primary kind from human organisms. What could make that difference? Human organisms have different persistence conditions from human persons. Human organisms have third-personal persistence conditions: whether an animal continues to exist depends on continued biological functioning. Persons have first-personal persistence conditions: whether a person continues to exist depends on its having a first-person perspective. Before explaining what a first-person perspective is, let me illustrate it with a true story:

When one of my nieces was two years old, she had a birthday party to which her many cousins were invited. One of her cousins (his name was Donald) went into her bedroom and began systematically taking toys out of my niece's toybox. When my niece saw what was happening, she was outraged. She cried out, 'Dammit, Donald, mine!' Her parents were appalled: Where, they wondered with embarrassment, had she learned the profanity 'dammit'? What interested me, however, was not her saying 'dammit,' but her competent use of the word 'mine'. She had a first-personal concept of herself: She knew that she — she herself — was the rightful owner of the toys, and that her permission was required for anyone else to play with her toys. This little story illustrates, I think, what is unique about human persons. As far as we know, of all the beings in the world, we alone have a first-personal concept of ourselves.[15] We alone understand ourselves from 'within,' so to speak; we can think of ourselves without the need to identify ourselves by means of any description, name, or other third-person referring device.

---

[14] Someone may ask: If a human person is not identical to a body or to a soul or to a body-plus-a-soul, what is she identical to? This question is a red herring. A person is identical to herself and not another thing.

[15] As I said in Baker (2000), if computers or other beings have first-personal concepts, they too are persons.

So, what is a first-person perspective? A first-person perspective is a very peculiar ability that all and only persons have. It is the ability to conceive of oneself as oneself, from the inside, as it were. Linguistic evidence of a robust first-person perspective comes from use of first-person pronouns embedded in sentences with linguistic or psychological verbs — e.g., 'I wonder how I will die,' or 'I promise that I will stay with you.'[16] If I wonder how I will die, or I promise that I'll stay with you, then I am thinking of myself as myself; I am not thinking of myself in any third-person way (e.g., not as Lynne Baker, nor as the person who is thinking a certain thought, nor as the only person in the room who is standing) at all. Anything that can wonder how it will die ipso facto has a first-person perspective and thus is a person.

What one thinks from a first-person perspective cannot be adequately translated into third-person terms.[17] To wonder how I will die is not the same as wondering how Lynne Baker will die, even though I am Lynne Baker. This is so, because I could wonder how I will die even if I had amnesia and didn't know who I was. A being with a first-person perspective not only can have thoughts about herself, but she can also conceive of herself as the subject of such thoughts. I not only wonder how I'll die, but I realize that I am having that thought. A first-person perspective cannot be duplicated. There cannot be two persons both with your first-person perspective. A molecular duplicate of me would have a qualitatively indistinguishable first-person perspective, but *not* my first-person perspective. She would not *be* me. See Baker (2000).

A being may be conscious without having a first-person perspective. Nonhuman primates and other higher animals are conscious, and they have psychological states like believing, fearing and desiring. They have points of view (e.g., 'danger in that direction'), but they cannot conceive of themselves as the subjects of such thoughts. They can not *conceive of* themselves from the first-person. (We have every reason to think that they do not wonder how they will die.) So, having psychological states like beliefs and desires, and having a point of view, are necessary but not sufficient conditions for being a person. A sufficient condition for being a person — whether human, divine, ape,

---

[16] Hector-Neri Castañeda developed this idea in several papers. See Castañeda (1966; 1967).

[17] I have defended this claim in Baker (1998; 2000; 2007b). Evidence from developmental psychology indicates that we do *not* begin from a third-person point of view, with ourselves as an indistinguishable part of a collectivity.

or silicon-based — is having a first-person perspective.[18] So, what makes something a person is not the 'stuff' that it is made of. It does not matter whether something is made of DNA or silicon or, in the case of God, no material 'stuff' at all. If a being has a first-person perspective, it is a person.

From the standpoint of evolution, first-person perspectives may have been 'selected for' by natural selection. Alternatively, first-person perspectives (like the architectural example of spandrels) may have been a by-product of some other change. My interest in the first-person perspective is not in its origin, but in its status. First-person perspectives do not appear to be biologically significant; but whether they are biologically significant or not, first-person perspectives are ontologically significant. Only beings with inner lives are persons, and a world populated with beings with inner lives is ontologically richer than a world populated with no beings with inner lives.

What I have been describing is a *robust* first-person perspective, a sophisticated in-hand capacity that can be exercised at will — the capacity to think of oneself in the peculiar first-personal way. Robust first-person perspectives are connected with use of a natural language, which is inherently social. But persons come into being before they have mastered the first-person pronoun. An organism comes to constitute a person by developing a *rudimentary* first-person perspective, which may be understood as follows:

> (Rudimentary FPP) A being has a rudimentary first-person perspective iff (i) it is conscious, a sentient being, and (ii) it has a capacity to imitate; (iii) engages in behaviour that is explainable only by attribution of beliefs, desires and intentions.[19]

A human organism is in person-favourable circumstances when it comes to have a rudimentary first-person perspective. There is a good deal of evidence from developmental psychology that at or near birth human organisms are sentient, have a capacity to imitate, and engage

---

[18] Gallup's experiments with chimpanzees suggest the possibility of a kind of intermediate stage between dogs (that have intentional states but no first-person perspectives) and human persons (that have first-person perspectives). In my opinion — for details see Baker (2000), pp. 62–4 — Gallup's chimpanzees fall short of full-blown first-person perspectives. See Gallup (1977).

[19] For details, see Baker (2005). Other primates have rudimentary first-person perspectives, but human organisms are unique in that only in human organisms are rudimentary first-person perspectives a developmental preliminary.

in behaviour explainable only by attribution of beliefs, desires and intentions.[20]

There seems to be general agreement among psychologists that developmentally there is a symmetry of self and other, that humans (as well as other higher nonhuman mammals) are social creatures. Ulric Neisser puts the 'interpersonal self' in which the 'individual engaged in social interaction with another person' at 8 weeks (Neisser, 1995). Philippe Rochat flatly asserts that the developmental origins of self-awareness are primarily social (Rochat, 1995). The idea of a first-person perspective is not Cartesian or Leibnizian: we are not monads that unfold according to an internal plan unaffected by our surroundings.

> (HP) x constitutes a human person at t if and only if x is a human organism at t and x has a rudimentary or robust first-person perspective at t,

where we take 'x constitutes a human person at t' as shorthand for 'x constitutes a person at t & x is a (nonderivative) human organism.'[21] (HP) gives only a necessary and sufficient condition for there being a *human* person.[22] There may be other kinds of persons: silicon-persons (constituted by aggregates of silicon items) and God (not constituted by anything). (HP) is silent about other kinds of persons.

In sum: There are two important aspects of the Constitution View of human persons: On the one hand, a human person has unique first-personal persistence conditions. I continue to exist as long as my first-person perspective is exemplified; if something has my first-person perspective, then that being is a person and that person is me. The conditions for the persistence of persons are absolutely unique: they are first-personal conditions that elude third-personal formulation. On the other hand, a human person is essentially embodied: I am a wholly material being, constituted by, but not identical to, my body.

So, the Constitution View of human persons satisfies two desiderata that may initially appear to conflict. First, it shows how human

---

[20] See, for example, Gopnik and Meltzoff (1994), Neisser (1995) and Kagan (1989). I do not expect the developmental psychologists to share my metaphysical view of constitution; I look to their work only to show at what stages during development certain features appear.

[21] This latter detail is a needed technicality since, on the Constitution View, *person* is a primary kind, and there may be nonhuman persons. 'Human person' refers to a person constituted by a human organism.

[22] Assuming that there is no afterlife, a person goes out of existence when she permanently ceases to have a first-person perspective. Of some patients in comas, we may not know whether the patient is still a person, or just a human organism. For details, see Baker (forthcoming).

persons are wholly part of the natural world — as much a part of the natural world as stars, trees, nonhuman animals. And yet, second, it shows how persons are ontologically unique: They alone have first-personal persistence conditions. Let us turn now to the relations that persons have to other things in the world.

Relations of Persons to Nonpersons

Some relations that persons bear to each other and to nonpersons are such that nonpersons also bear them to each other. Here are some examples of relations that are not unique to persons: (1) Constitution relations: Nonpersons, as well as persons, are constituted by other things: For example, a painting is constituted by a piece of canvass. (2) Spatiotemporal relations: A person may be three feet from the wall, and a desk also may be three feet from the wall. (3) Causal relations: A person may push, or be pushed by, an automatic door; so may a dog or a run-away golf cart. Constitution relations, spatiotemporal relations, and causal relations are ubiquitous: everything in the world — persons and nonpersons — has these relations to other things. But there are also kinds of relations that *only* persons have to other things in the world. These are relations that are made possible by first-person perspectives, and it is on these that I want to focus.[23] I want to discuss three of these kinds of relations — which I shall call 'moral relations', 'interpretive relations', and 'productive relations', respectively.

A. Moral Relations. One kind of relation that persons have to each other and to nonpersons comprises moral relations. Having first-person perspectives allows persons to be, among other things, moral agents — to acknowledge themselves as causing things to happen and to take responsibility for what they do.[24] Only persons have moral responsibilities. And they have moral responsibilities toward nonpersons as well as toward persons. For instance, persons have moral duties with respect to animals — e.g., the duty not to cause gratuitous suffering. (Cats do not have moral duties toward the mice that they play with before killing.) And persons have moral duties with respect to the biological environment — e.g., the duty not to make the Earth uninhabitable. Volcanoes do not have moral duties

---

[23] Having a first-person perspective is *sine qua non* for being a person; the three kinds of relations that I shall discuss depend on first-person perspectives but are not themselves necessary conditions for being a person.

[24] Although I do think that there is agent causality, I differ from the standard views in two ways: (i) Agent causality is not sui generis: an agent causes A in virtue of certain mental and physical events. (ii) My agent causality is compatible with whatever laws govern the world, whether deterministic or indeterministic.

toward the land that their lava covers. But we may have certain moral duties both to mice and to land. Persons are uniquely related to each other and to certain nonpersons by having moral duties toward them.

B. *Interpretive Relations.* Persons are interpreters of reality. Let me say what I mean by 'interpretation.' Interpretation is a linguistic affair. Nonverbal interpretations — such as a cellist's interpretation of a Bach cello suite or a student's interpretation of a professor's raised eyebrow — are, I think, parasitic on natural language. In the first instance, an interpretation is of something that has an already-accepted description in a context. The context is crucial. A single description may be an interpretation in one context and not in another. Think of two contexts in which aspects of Picasso's painting *Guernica* is interpreted. In the first context, an art teacher points out features of the painting to young schoolchildren, showing them how to interpret a region of line and colour as a bull. In the second context, a modern history teacher points out to high-school students that the bull represents the forces of brutality. In the first context, the description 'the bull' is an interpretation (of a region of line and colour); in the second context, the description 'the bull' is not an interpretation at all, but rather is what gets interpreted (as representing brutality).

Relative to a context, an interpretation is a redescription of something with the aim of showing it in a certain light. There is no redescription without a prior description. An interpretation, then, has three features: a context, a prior description, and a redescription. The context, which contains the relevant parties and their beliefs and interests, is the source of the prior description. An interpreter must intend the redescription to denote the same thing as the prior description. What an interpretation is an interpretation *of* is what is denoted by a description (the prior description) in a context.[25] For a redescription to be an interpretation, it must cast new light on what was denoted by the prior description (as in the case of a Freudian interpretation of someone's dream). So, interpretation does not bring in a new object, but a new way of looking at a given object.

Since replacement of a prior description by another description is an intentional activity, there is no interpretation in the absence of intentionality. Some philosophers, however, take intentionality itself to be a matter of interpretation (Dennett, 1987). That is, they hold that what is described literally, without interpretation, presupposes no intentionality, and that intentionality arises only by interpretation —

---

[25] Interpretation is intensional (with an 's'); that is, interpretation is a relation between the F and the G, where the descriptions are essential to the interpretive relation.

by replacing a prior literal, nonintentional description with an intentional description. This view is incorrect for two reasons: In the first place, as I just mentioned, interpretation presupposes intentionality, and hence cannot account for it. In the second place, intentional descriptions that apply to ID phenomena often are themselves literal, uninterpreted descriptions. That is, there are intentional descriptions that do not depend on interpretation. Consider the sentence, 'The check is in the mail,' used on an occasion to report that the check is in the mail. Both the descriptions 'the check' and 'the mail' are intentional descriptions that apply to ID phenomena (the check and the mail are both ID phenomena), and yet the descriptions ('the check' and 'the mail') are not interpretations of anything nonintentional. There is no prior nonintentional description to be replaced by 'the check'; the description 'the check' is as literal and as uninterpreted as any.

So, there are intentional descriptions that are not themselves products of interpretation. Moreover, intentional descriptions are themselves subject to interpretation. For example, suppose that the police interview a witness to a crime. The police want a bare-bones description of what happened without interpretation. In this context, the witness's report that, from across the room, she saw the suspect writing something on a yellow pad would count as a report of an uninterpreted fact. If the witness, who was across the room from the suspect, had said that she saw him writing a ransom note, she would be adding an interpretation. In this context, the prior description was 'writing on a yellow pad,' said of the suspect; the interpretation would be 'writing a ransom note.' Note, however, that 'writing on a yellow pad' is itself an ID phenomenon, an action. The bottom-level bare-bones description is thus intentional. Hardly ever would a witness be expected to give a nonintentional or purely 'physical' description. ('There was a long, thin rod-like thing in his hand, which was moving back and forth slightly above a flat surface.' —Really, would you say that to a police officer?) In an eye-witness account, 'just the facts' — the items to be subject to interpretation — are already ID phenomena. The witness would probably be considered uncooperative if she gave an account of the suspect's bodily motions. The lawyers will no doubt interpret the eye-witness account, but the eye-witness account that they will interpret, although literal, is by no means nonintentional.

In sum: On the one hand, ID phenomena — as reported by 'The check is in the mail' — do not themselves depend on interpretation. On the other hand, uninterpreted ID phenomena to which intentional descriptions apply (e.g., the suspect's writing something on a yellow pad) may themselves be subject to interpretation (as his writing a ransom note).

This independence of ID phenomena from interpretation points to an important fact: Constitution must be distinguished from interpretation. The existence of ID phenomena, like the existence of nonID phenomena, depends on constitution, and constitution itself is not a matter of interpretation.[26] For example, the spoon that you eat your soup with is constituted by a piece of metal, but to call something a 'spoon' is not ordinarily to interpret anything. Furthermore, ID objects (e.g., a pencil) are not just 'natural' (intention-independent) objects plus a socially conferred status. (Thus I differ from Searle (1995).) An ID object like a mammogram may receive an interpretation by a radiologist, say, but the mammogram's being a mammogram does not itself depend on interpretation, but on constitution. Constitution differs from interpretation in several ways, the most important of which is this: Constitution introduces a new object; interpretation does not.[27] Constitution adds to what exists; interpretation aims at understanding what exists apart from the interpretation.[28]

The point of this discussion of interpretation has been to show that persons are uniquely related to the world of encounter by means of interpretation. Along the way, I sketched a view of interpretation that shows how interpretation is related to (but *not* the source of) intentionality and that distinguishes interpretation from constitution. This sketch makes it easy to see how persons and *only* persons are bearers of interpretive relations — to themselves, to other persons and to nonpersons.[29] Now let's turn to a third kind of relation that persons, and only persons, have to nonpersons.

C. Productive Relations. By 'productive,' I mean *ontologically* productive. What I want to suggest is that persons make an ontological

---

[26] I am not ruling out the possibility that there may be some occasions on which an interpretation may be (or contribute to) an instance of constitution. For example, a judge's interpretation may contribute to the constitution of a new entity. Or a musical performance of a pre-existing piece of music may be an interpretation that is also a new entity. Thanks to an anonymous referee for these examples.

[27] Constitution is distinguished from interpretation in other ways as well. Interpretation as a relation is language-dependent; constitution is not. Interpretation is normative (there are better and worse interpretations); constitution is not.

[28] The suspect's writing a ransom note is constituted by the suspect's hand's moving in a certain way in certain circumstances; it is not constituted by his writing something. The suspect's writing a ransom note entails the suspect's writing something. But if x's being F constitutes x's being G, then it is not the case that x's being G logically entails x's being F.

[29] Since interpretation depends on prior description, our interpretive relations (to both persons and nonpersons) are not basic. But interpretations are significant in human life. Anything that can be described can be interpreted.

contribution to reality by creating novel kinds of things. Persons are producers of ontological novelty. One noticeable feature of the world of encounter that I mentioned is that it is populated by what I called ID objects: things — things like elevators and computers — whose existence depends on there being persons with propositional attitudes. The dependence is not just causal; it is ontological: Something is an elevator or a computer, not in virtue of the arrangement of particles that makes it up, but in virtue of its intended relations to other things in the world. No arrangement of particles that spontaneously coalesced in outer space would be an elevator. An artifact has its function essentially, and its function depends on what its designer or producer intends. An elevator is a device whose intended function is essential to its being the thing that it is; and its intended function (to transport people and things vertically through space) itself crucially depends on the intentions of its designer — intentions that only persons can have. The designer must be able to assess her design. She must be able to ask: Will a machine of this design perform the function that I intend? In order even to consider such a question, one must be a person. One must be aware that one has a certain intention. The existence of elevators and other artifacts ontologically depends on there being persons with beliefs, desires and intentions. It is a conceptual truth that something is an artifact only if it is intended to serve a certain purpose. It follows that there would be no elevators if there were no persons with beliefs, desires and intentions.

So, some things in the world are ontologically dependent on the existence of persons. ID objects, so prominent in the world of encounter, are such objects. Persons are responsible for the intentions, practices and conventions, that make many kinds of ID objects possible. Their existence depends on the intentional activity of persons — again, not just causally but ontologically. The intended functions of artifacts are essential to their being the objects that they are. For example, having the intended function of reproducing texts mechanically was essential to the object that Gutenberg famously made. Having the intended function of making distant objects appear closer was essential to the object that Galileo famously made. When Gutenberg invented the printing press with movable type, and when Galileo invented the telescope, new kinds of objects came into existence — objects with new kinds of causal powers and with new persistence conditions.

So, the productive relations of persons to artifacts and other ID objects make persons, unlike nonpersons, ontological contributors to reality. The world of encounter is filled with ID objects — objects whose very existence ontologically depends on intentional activity — and these are objects to which persons have productive relations. There are primary kinds exemplified in the world of encounter today that did not exist eons ago. The world that we encounter today — with its telecommunications satellites and electron microscopes — is ontologically richer than the world when the dinosaurs inhabited it. So, the third way that persons are uniquely related to nonpersons in the world is by means of what I've called their 'productive relations': persons in their unique relations to ID objects, are ontological contributors to what is in the world.

Several critics have objected strenuously to my claim that the existence of some material objects ontologically depends upon intentional activity. One critic went so far as to say, 'Baker thinks we sometimes bring things into existence by thinking about them' (Zimmerman, 2002). As an example, he cites a piece of driftwood that 'becomes a coffee table by being brushed off and brought into the house.' I reply that most artifacts like coffee tables require manufacture and manipulation of materials. The driftwood example is a limiting case. Even in this limiting case, however, the piece of driftwood comes to constitute a table only in table-favourable circumstances, which include more than 'being brushed off and brought into the house.' The piece of driftwood comes to constitute a table in part by coming to be used in a certain already-established way. Our practices and conventions, as well as our intentions, are what make one piece of driftwood constitute a table, and another piece of driftwood constitute nothing at all.

The world of encounter is filled with ID objects like credit cards, dishwashers, computers, automobiles, portraits — objects that could not exist in the absence of persons with intentions and other propositional attitudes. If we want to make sense of the world of encounter — our world — then we cannot ignore this huge category of material objects. The Constitution View, and only the Constitution View as far as I know, takes this category of ID objects seriously. Artifacts and artworks — which exist only because of our productive relations to the world — are paradigm cases of ID objects and are as much part of reality in their own right (*as* artifacts and artworks) as are rocks and trees. Persons play an ontological role in the existence of artifacts and artworks. Anyone who respects the world of encounter must take artifacts and artworks and other ID objects seriously; and anyone who takes such objects seriously, I believe, must recognize that persons make an ontological contribution to what there is.

In sum, there are at least three important ways in which persons are uniquely related to other things in the world: by moral relations, by interpretive relations and by productive relations. The most controversial of these are what I've called 'productive relations.' Productive relations make persons ontological contributors to reality.

Conclusion

The Constitution View provides a nonreductive account of the whole world of encounter that includes us persons. The world contains a plurality of primary kinds, and yet is an intelligible whole: All macroscopic objects — inanimate natural objects, animals, artifacts, artworks, persons — are constituted ultimately by aggregates of subatomic particles, without being reducible to the aggregates of particles that constitute them. In this unified world, however, persons have a unique role. Not only do persons have unique moral relations and interpretive relations to other things, but, most significantly, persons have productive relations to certain material objects — material objects (like artifacts and artworks) that could not exist in the absence of the intentional activity of persons.

The received view in metaphysics is that there is a sharp distinction between what is in the world independently of our concepts and practices and what depends on our concepts and practices — a distinction sometimes formulated as a distinction between what is mind-independent and what is mind-dependent. What are ontologically significant are thought to be molecules, pieces of wood, and other mind-independent items. On the received view, artifacts and artworks, and ID objects generally, are understood in terms of our applying our concepts to aggregates of molecules, pieces of wood, etc., and such application adds nothing to reality. I challenge this received view, and take the example of artifacts to show that a strict segregation of what really exists from what depends on persons is untenable.

In short, the Constitution View locates persons wholly within a unified material world, and yet accords persons a unique role in reality. I know of no other metaphysical view that makes better sense of the twin features of the unity of the natural world and the uniqueness of human persons.[30]

---

[30] I presented a version of this paper at the 'Dimensions of Personhood' Conference at the University of Jyväskylä (Finland). I also presented versions at the University of Geneva and at the University of Utrecht. I especially would like to thank Roberta de Monticelli, the organizer of the Workshop on Persons at Geneva; Ton van den Beld and Menno Lievers, my host and commentator, respectively, at Utrecht; and Heikki Ikäheimo and Arto Laitinen, the organizers of 'Dimensions of Personhood' at Jyväskylä. I also want to thank the two anonymous referees of this paper and the guest editors (Heikki Ikäheimo and Arto Laitinen) for comments.

References

Baker, L.R. (1997), 'Why constitution is not identity', *Journal of Philosophy*, **94** (12), pp. 599–621.
Baker, L.R. (1998), 'The first-person perspective: A test for naturalism', *American Philosophical Quarterly*, **35**, pp. 327–48
Baker, L.R. (1999), 'Unity without identity', *Midwest Studies in Philosophy*, **23**, *New Directions in Philosophy*, Peter A. French and Howard K. Wettstein, eds. (Boston, MA: Blackwell), pp. 144–65.
Baker, L.R. (2000), *Persons and Bodies: A Constitution View* (Cambridge: Cambridge University Press).
Baker, L.R. (2002), 'On making things up: Constitution and its critics', *Philosophical Topics*, **30** (1), pp. 31–51.
Baker, L.R. (2004), 'The ontology of artifacts,' *Philosophical Explorations*, **7**, pp. 99–111.
Baker, L.R. (2005), 'When does a person begin?', *Social Philosophy and Policy*, **22**, pp. 25–48.
Baker, L.R. (2007a), 'Everyday concepts as a guide to reality', *The Monist*, forthcoming.
Baker, L.R. (2007b), 'Naturalism and the first-person perspective', *How Successful is Naturalism?* Publications of the Austrian Ludwig Wittgenstein Society, Georg Gasser, ed. (Frankfurt: Ontos-Verlag, forthcoming).
Baker, L.R. (forthcoming), *The Metaphysics of Everyday Life: An Essay in Practical Realism* (Cambridge: Cambridge University Press).
Castañeda, H.-N. (1966), 'He: A study in the logic of self-consciousness', *Ratio*, **8**, pp. 130–57.
Castañeda, H.-N. (1967) 'Indicators and quasi-indicators', *American Philosophical Quarterly*, **4**, pp. 85–100.
Dennett, D.C. (1987), *The Intentional Stance* (Cambridge, MA: MIT).
Gallup, G., Jr. (1977), 'Self-recognition in primates: A comparative approach to bidirectional properties of consciousness,' *American Psychologist*, **32**, pp. 329–38.
Gopnik, A. and Meltzoff, A.N. (1994), 'Minds, bodies and persons: Young children's understanding of the self and others as reflected in imitation and theory-of-mind research', in Sue Taylor Parker, Robert W. Mitchell, and Marria L. Boccia, eds., *Self-Awareness in Animals and Humans* (Cambridge: Cambridge University Press, 1994), pp. 166–86.
Kagan, J. (1989), *Unstable Ideas* (Cambridge, MA: Harvard University Press).
Neisser, U. (1995), 'Criteria for an ecological self,' in Philippe Rochat, ed., *The Self in Infancy: Theory and Research* (Amsterdam: North-Holland), pp. 17–34.
Rochat, P. (1995), 'Early objectification of the self', in Philippe Rochat, ed., *The Self in Infancy: Theory and Research* (Amsterdam: North-Holland), pp. 53–72.
Searle, J.R. (1995), *The Construction of Social Reality* (New York: The Free Press).
Zimmerman, D. (2002), 'The constitution of persons by bodies: A critique of Lynne Rudder Baker's theory of material constitution', *Philosophical Topics*, **30** (1), pp. 295–338.

Eric T. Olson

What Are We?

Abstract: *This paper is about the neglected question of what sort of things we are metaphysically speaking. It is different from the mind-body problem and from familiar questions of personal identity. After explaining what the question means and how it differs from others, the paper tries to show how difficult it is to give a satisfying answer.*

1. The Question

What are we? That is, what are we metaphysically speaking? What is our basic metaphysical nature? What are our most general and fundamental properties? I claim that this is a real and important question. It is different from the traditional mind-body problem and from familiar questions of personal identity. It is frequently neglected. And it is fiendishly difficult to answer.

Let me first explain what the question means. I won't try to define the daunting phrases 'basic metaphysical nature' or 'most general and fundamental properties'. (I doubt whether that would be a worthwhile project.) I will try to explain what I mean by example. We can break the large question of what we are into a number of smaller and more specific ones.

What are we made of? I don't mean our chemical composition — what sort of physical matter makes us up. I want to know whether we are made of matter at all. Or are we made of something other than matter? Or partly of matter and partly of something else? Come to that, are we made of anything at all? Is there any sort of stuff, material or otherwise, that makes us up?

If we are indeed made of matter or of anything else, *what* matter or other stuff makes us up? Most materialists — those who think we are made up entirely of matter — say that we are made of all and only the matter that makes up our bodies: we extend all the way out to the surface of our skin (which is presumably where our bodies end) and no further. But a few take us to be considerably smaller: the size of brains, for instance. Someone could even take us to be material things larger than our bodies (Clark and Chalmers, 1998).

What parts do we have? Or do we have any parts at all? This is not the same as what we are made of. Philosophers who agree about what we are made of — not only about what sort of stuff, but what particular stuff — may still disagree about our parts. They may disagree, for instance, about whether we have temporal parts (see §8 below). They may even disagree about what ordinary spatial parts we have (see e.g. van Inwagen, 1981, and Lowe, 2000, pp. 15–20).

Are we substances? By a substance I mean a metaphysically independent being, as opposed to a state or aspect of something else. A dent in a car, for instance, is not a substance. It is not a part of the car: you can't take it away from the car, or move it to another car, as you could with a wheel. The dent seems to be a state or an aspect of the car — a way that the car is. But the car is not a way that the dent is. Nor does it appear to be a state or an aspect of anything else: there is nothing, it seems, that stands to the car as the car stands to the dent. The car is a good candidate for being a substance. The question, then, is whether you are like a car or like a dent. Are you a state of something other than yourself? Or an event or process that something else is undergoing, like the car's cooling off? Is there something — an organism or a lump of matter, perhaps — that stands to you as the car stands to its dent?

Do we persist through time? Do we literally continue existing for seventy years or more? Or is the sober truth that we exist only for a moment? Some say that you appear to persist only because you are instantly replaced by a being so much like you that no one can tell the difference — not even that being herself, for she inherits all your memories and other mental features. Could that be right?

This is the sort of thing I have in mind when I ask what we are metaphysically speaking. There are many more such questions: what our persistence conditions are, for instance, and which of our properties are essential to us and which are accidental. An answer to these questions would tell us what we are.

So much for the 'what' in my question. What about the 'we'? Which beings is it whose basic metaphysical nature I am asking about? By 'we' I mean we human people — where a human person is roughly someone with a human body. (I assume that we are people.

But this is not a substantive point. Anyone who disagrees can still ask what we are, and can explain what the question means in a different way.) I don't mean non-human people, if there are any. I am not asking about the metaphysical nature of people as such. I am asking only about ourselves.

That is because for all I know different sorts of people might have radically different metaphysical natures. Perhaps there could be angels or gods. Full-blown artificial intelligence might be possible, so that there could be inorganic artefacts with the same mental features as we have. These angels, gods, and inorganic artefacts would all count as people — assuming, anyway, that being rational, intelligent, and self-conscious suffices for being a person. But I doubt whether they would have the same basic metaphysical nature as we have, or for that matter the same as each other. For all I know, some people are composite material objects, while others are simple immaterial ones. In other words, I don't know whether there *is* any one metaphysical sort of thing that people as such necessarily are. Or if there is, we cannot know it until we have either ruled out the possibility of gods, thinking machines, and the like, or else shown that despite appearances people of all these sorts would have to have the same basic metaphysical nature. Because I would rather not try to settle these matters, I ask only about the metaphysical nature of us human people.

Here are two alternative ways of putting my question, or perhaps different versions of it. First, we can move from the material to the formal mode, and ask what sort of things we refer to when we say 'I'. More generally, what sort of things do our personal pronouns and proper names refer to? Second, we can ask about the nature of the beings who use those words — the ones holding the inquiry. What sort of beings think our thoughts and perform our actions? What sort of thing is now reading this sentence, and what sort of thing wrote it?

It is natural to suppose that these different formulations of the question all come to the same thing. I am whatever I refer to when I say 'I', just as Mars is whatever people refer to when they say 'Mars'. And I am whatever thinks my thoughts and performs my actions — what else could make them *my* thoughts and actions? But the questions are not strictly equivalent. As we shall see, some even say that they have different answers.

In any case, the question of what beings think our thoughts and speak our words is in a way more fundamental than the question of what things our personal pronouns and names refer to. We need to know what thinking, speaking beings there are before we can work out which of them are the referents of words like 'I'.

2. Some Answers

In understanding a question it often helps to see what would count as an answer to it; and often the answers are easier to grasp than the question itself. So here are some accounts of what we might be.

One view is that we are animals: biological organisms. Some philosophers hold this view, but not many. No one denies that there is something right in saying that we are animals. If nothing else, we at least have animal bodies. But to have a body that is an animal is not to be an animal yourself. Not, anyway, unless you are the same thing as your body — which many philosophers, even materialists, deny.

Could we be material things but not animals? Well, we could be parts of animals: brains, perhaps. Or we might be temporal parts of animals: you might be spatially the same size as your animal body but temporally shorter, in that the animal extends further into the past or future than you do. Many views are possible about what spatial or temporal parts of animals we might be. These two views can also be combined: we might be temporal parts of brains (Hudson, 2001, ch. 4).

Some philosophers deny that we are either animals or parts of animals, yet insist that we are nonetheless material things. They say that we are things made of the same matter as our animal bodies. The thinking behind this is that the same matter can make up two different objects at once. Specifically, the matter making up a typical human organism also makes up a certain non-organism; and these non-organisms are what we are (see §6 below).

Hume once said that we are 'bundles of perceptions' (1978: 252). Our bodies may be made of matter, but we ourselves are not. We are made up of mental states and events. Our parts are not cells or atoms, but memories and dreams. We are events rather than substances — rather like theatre productions.

An ancient view has it that we are simple (partless) immaterial substances. We are not made of matter, or perceptions, or anything else (Swinburne, 1984; Zimmerman, 2003).

There is even the seemingly paradoxical view that there is nothing that we are. We don't exist. There is nothing for our personal pronouns to refer to, and nothing thinks our thoughts. The atoms we call yours may be real enough; perhaps even the thoughts and experiences we call yours exist; but those atoms or mental states are not parts or states of any thinking being (Unger, 1979).

There are other accounts of what we are, but that will do for now. None of these views by itself purports to answer all my questions. They are at best partial accounts of what we are. The view that we are animals, for instance, does not by itself tell us whether we persist through time: for that, we should need to know whether animals persist, and here there is room for disagreement. Still, each of the views tells us a good deal about what we are.

3. How the Question Differs From Others

I take it that the question of what we are must have an answer. One of these views, or another one that I haven't mentioned, must be true. There must be some sort of thing that we are. *Some* sort of being is now reading this paper, or else nothing is. Likewise, when we use a singular personal pronoun like 'I' or 'she', we either refer to something or we don't. If we do, then that thing (or those things, if we refer to more than one thing) must have some basic metaphysical nature or other: it must be material or immaterial, simple or composite, a substance or a non-substance, momentary or persisting, and so on. If we don't refer to anything, that is presumably because there are no human people to be referred to.

The question of what we are is not one of the philosophical problems most of us learn about as students. But it probably won't seem completely new either. It sounds a bit like the traditional mind-body problem, and a bit like familiar problems of personal identity. How exactly does it relate to those problems?

The mind-body problem is usually taken to comprise questions about the nature of mental phenomena, such as belief and consciousness, and how those phenomena relate to non-mental matters, such as brain chemistry. My question, by contrast, is about the nature of the subjects of mental phenomena: the beings that believe or are conscious. The two are of course connected: some accounts of what we are may rule out some views on the mind-body problem, and vice versa. But the questions are not so closely connected as one might suppose. We could know a good deal about mental phenomena and their relation to the physical and still know little about the metaphysical nature of mental subjects. If all mental events turned out to be physical events in another guise, for instance, that might rule out our being immaterial substances (though not everyone agrees: see Chisholm, 1989). But it would not tell us whether we are organisms, brains, bundles of perceptions, or even whether we exist at all. Having a 'theory of mind' — an account of the nature of mental phenomena and their relation to the physical — would not tell us what we are. Likewise, knowing our basic metaphysical nature is likely to tell us little about the nature of the mental: knowing whether we are organisms or brains or bundles of perceptions won't tell us the nature of belief or consciousness. So the question of what we are is not the mind–body problem.

How does my question relate to problems of personal identity? The most familiar problems of personal identity are the *personhood question* and the *persistence question*. The personhood question asks what it is to be a person. What is necessary and sufficient for something to count as a person, as opposed to a non-person? What have people got that non-people haven't got? The persistence question asks what it takes for us (or for people in general) to persist through time. What sorts of adventures is it possible, in the broadest sense of the word 'possible', for you to survive? What sort of thing would necessarily bring your existence to an end? What determines which past or future being is you?

The question of what we are is more or less completely unrelated to the personhood question. What qualifications a thing needs in order to count as a person is one thing; what sort of things actually have those qualifications — organisms, bundles of perceptions, or what have you — is another.

Suppose for the sake of argument that something is a person if and only if it is, as Locke proposed, 'a thinking intelligent being, that has reason and reflection, and can consider itself as itself, the same thinking thing, in different times and places' (1975, p. 335). I take this to be a paradigmatic answer to the personhood question. Yet for all it says, 'thinking intelligent beings' might be material or immaterial, simple or composite, persisting or momentary. (How could something momentary 'consider itself as itself in different times and places'? Well, a thing might mistakenly consider itself as existing at different times, just as a poor man might consider himself rich.) Those who take us to be organisms, or bundles of perceptions, or immaterial substances, or any of the other things mentioned in the previous section all take those things to be thinking intelligent beings. Locke's definition, by itself, does nothing to help us choose among them. It fails to answer *any* of the questions that an account of what we are must answer. It doesn't even tell us whether we exist at all — that is, whether anything satisfies the conditions for being a person. One could have a view about what it is to be a person without having any idea what sort of things we are metaphysically speaking. (This is more or less Locke's own position.)

To know what it is to be a person is therefore not to know what we are. Likewise, to know what we are is not to know what it is to be a person. Suppose for the sake of argument that we are human animals.

That does not imply that to be a person *is* to be a human animal — even assuming that we ourselves are people. It is consistent with there being Martians or gods or angels who are people but not human animals. Nor does it imply that all human animals are people: it is consistent with the view that human animals in a persistent vegetative state don't count as people. The same goes for any other view of what we are. An account of our metaphysical nature implies virtually nothing about what it is to be a person.

The definition of personhood stands to the metaphysical nature of human people much as the definition of blackness stands to the chemical nature of the black objects on our planet. We could know what it is for a thing to be black (to have certain reflectance properties, say) without knowing anything about the chemistry of terrestrial black things. And we could know that all terrestrial black objects contain carbon without having a definition of blackness. The fact that all terrestrial black things contain carbon would imply nothing about what it is for a thing to be black. It is consistent with there being both carbonless black things and non-black things containing carbon.

What about the persistence question — what our identity over time consists in? It is also different from the question of what we are. What it takes for us to persist may be one aspect of our metaphysical nature. Knowing our persistence conditions would tell us *something* about what sort of things we are. But it wouldn't tell us much. An account of our persistence conditions would not by itself tell us whether we are material or immaterial, or what parts we have, or whether we are substances. What it takes for a person to persist through time is one thing; what sort of beings *have* those persistence conditions, or indeed whether any do, is something else.

Take, for instance, the popular view that our identity through time consists in some sort of psychological continuity: you are that future being that in some sense inherits its mental features — beliefs, memories, desires, and so on — from you; and you are that past being whose mental features you have thus inherited. Never mind the precise nature of this inheritance — whether your mental life has to be 'continuously physically realized', say (Unger, 1990, pp. 108f.), or whether we need a 'non-branching' clause to deal with cases where two past or future beings are psychologically continuous in the relevant way with you as you are now. Suppose for the sake of argument that our identity over time consists in non-branching, continuously physically realized psychological continuity. Would that tell us what we are?

Not by itself it wouldn't. It may have implications about what we are. It may rule out our being immaterial substances: it is hard to see how any sort of physical continuity could be necessary or sufficient for the persistence of an immaterial substance. It may also imply that we are not organisms, for it seems possible for any organism, even a human animal, to persist without any sort of psychological continuity at all (see §5 below). The information that we are neither immaterial substances nor organisms really would tell us something about what we are. But it would leave a lot open. Moreover, the psychological-continuity view does not actually *say* that we are not immaterial substances or organisms, and the implication might be disputed.

The psychological-continuity view therefore gives at best a radically incomplete picture of what we are. Even if we can derive some of our most general and fundamental properties from that view, few of those derivations will be straightforward, and even then the picture will be fragmentary. Yet that view is a paradigmatic answer to the persistence question. Saying what it takes for us to persist does not tell us what we are. The reverse also holds: we could know a great deal about what sort of things we are without knowing our persistence conditions.

So the question of what we are is different from the more familiar questions about mind, body, and personal identity. That may explain why it is often neglected. It is common practice to defend an account of our identity over time at great length without saying a word about what we are, except perhaps to rule out our being immaterial substances (Nozick, 1981, ch. 1; Parfit, 1984, part 3; and Unger, 1990 are just three notable examples of this). When the matter is addressed at all, it is frequently little more than an afterthought (e.g. Shoemaker, 1984, pp. 112–14).

4. The Thinking-Animal Problem

I have tried to explain what I mean by the question of what we are, and how it differs from other, more familiar questions. All we need now is an answer. What are we?

I wish I knew. Every account of what we are that I can think of faces grave objections. I cannot argue in detail for this claim here (see Olson, 2007 for that), but in the remainder of this paper I will give some examples of the troubles afflicting some of the most likely accounts of what we are.

Take the view that we are biological organisms: 'animalism'. It sounds reasonable enough on the face of it. The alternatives — that we are brains, or temporal parts of animals, or immaterial substances, or what have you — sound farfetched by comparison. There is even what looks like a powerful argument for animalism: the 'thinking-animal problem' (Carter, 1989; Olson, 2003).

Nearly everyone agrees that there *are* human animals. Better, there are around six billion human animals walking the earth — the same as the number of human people. For each of us there is a human animal, and for every human animal (barring perhaps a few pathological cases) there is one of us. Those animals are very like ourselves. They sit in our chairs and sleep in our beds; they do our work and read books and think about the future. They seem to be so like us, both physically and mentally, that it is hard to tell the difference. That makes it hard to maintain that we are anything other than animals.

Consider the animal you would be if you were any animal — 'your body', if you like. That organism would seem to be conscious and intelligent. It has just the sort of brain and nervous system that ought to enable it to think — the same one as you have. It has the same surroundings as you, and the same history. It shows all the same behavioural evidence of intelligence and conscious awareness as you do. How could something have all that, and yet fail to be conscious or intelligent? In fact the animal appears to be mentally just like you. Every thought or experience of yours would seem to be a thought or experience of the animal. What could account for any mental difference between you? That makes it look as if the animal *is* you. How could you be anything other than the being that thinks your thoughts?

Consider what it would mean if you were something other than the animal. The animal thinks. And you think. So there would be *two* beings thinking your thoughts: the thinking animal, and you, a thinking non-animal. More generally, every human person would share her thoughts with an animal numerically different from her. Every thought would have two thinkers. There would be twice as many rational, intelligent, self-conscious beings as we thought. If being rational, intelligent, and self-conscious suffices for being a person, there would be twice as many *people* as we thought. And how could you ever know which thinker or person *you* are — the animal or the non-animal? You may think you're the non-animal. But wouldn't the animal have the same grounds for believing that it was the non-animal? It would of course be mistaken. How would you know that you are not making this mistake? Even if you're not the animal, it is hard to see how you could have any grounds for believing that you're not.

Those who think that we are something other than animals — and who claim to have grounds for their view — have three possible responses to this reasoning.

First, they can say that there is really no animal that you could be. Despite appearances, there is no such thing as your animal body. Perhaps the only material things are simple particles, or masses of matter that never change their parts; or maybe the entire material world is unreal. If there are no such things as animals (and if we can know this), then there is no problem about knowing that you are not an animal. This would be a *metaphysical solution* to the thinking-animal problem.

A second response is to accept that there is an animal located where you are, but deny that it thinks as you do. It will not be easy to explain why a human organism with a healthy nervous system in normal circumstances should be unable to think. And surely there would have to be such an explanation; it couldn't just be a fundamental, 'brute' fact about human animals that they cannot think, in the way that it might be a brute, unexplainable fact about electrons that they are negatively charged. In any event, if human animals don't think, there is again no problem about knowing that we are not human animals. This would be a *psychological solution* to the problem (Shoemaker, 1999; 2004; Baker, 2000; see also Olson, 2002a).

Third, non-animalists can accept that there are human organisms, and that they think as we do, but argue that it is nonetheless possible for us to know that we — the referents of our personal pronouns and proper names — are not those animals. This would still leave us with the repugnant view that every human thought has at least two thinkers — thinkers of different metaphysical kinds, no less — but it would at least solve the epistemic problem of how we know what sort of things we are. Accordingly, we might call it an *epistemic solution* to the problem (Noonan, 1998; forthcoming; see also Olson, 2002b). (According to this view the question of what we are, or what our personal pronouns refer to, has a different answer from the question of what beings think our thoughts. It implies that I am not the being that thinks my thoughts, but rather one of several such beings.)

There is no other way of solving the thinking-animal problem — apart from accepting animalism, that is. I suspect that most of us will find these three lines of thought — the metaphysical, psychological, and epistemic solutions — unattractive. That looks like a good reason to suppose that we are animals, and a serious problem for any alternative to animalism.

5. Familiar Objections

So what's wrong with saying that we're animals? Well, it is widely held that we have properties incompatible with those of animals: different persistence conditions, for instance. Many philosophers believe that some sort of psychological continuity is both necessary and sufficient for us to persist through time. Your cerebrum might be transplanted into another head, so that the one who ended up with that organ had your memories and was psychologically continuous with you as you were before the operation. The orthodox view is that she would therefore be you: you would go along with your transplanted cerebrum. But no sort of psychological continuity is either necessary or sufficient for a human organism to persist. No human animal would go along with its transplanted cerebrum: the animal we call your body would stay behind with an empty head if its cerebrum were removed (Olson, 1997, pp. 114–19). So this popular view of personal identity over time implies that you are not an animal. Not only are you not essentially an animal; nothing that is even accidentally or contingently an animal would go along with its transplanted cerebrum.

Others say that we have different essential properties from those of human animals (Baker, 2000, p. 59). Each of us has certain mental properties, such as the capacity for first-person thought, essentially. (If having those mental properties is what it is to be a person, this amounts to saying that we are essentially people.) The claim is not merely that we could not exist *as people* if we lacked those mental properties, but that we could not possibly exist at all without them. But no biological organism has any mental properties essentially. Every human animal starts out as an embryo with no mental properties, and may end up in a persistent vegetative state in which it lacks even the capacity to acquire any. The claim that we have certain mental properties essentially is therefore incompatible with our being animals. Animalism entails that all our mental properties are merely accidental and temporary features of us.

Many philosophers take considerations like these to be a conclusive refutation of animalism. But they are not the 'grave objections' I alluded to earlier. Every interesting metaphysical claim has unwelcome consequences, and as unwelcome consequences go, these seem to me pretty mild. Couldn't we just be wrong about who would be who in imaginary brain-transplant cases, just as we can be wrong about who would be who in other bizarre cases (amnesia, brainwashing, duplication) where the usual patterns of evidence break down? And how can we be so confident that we have mental properties essentially? Compared with the thinking-animal problem, these objections sound like quibbles.

6. Constitution

To my mind, the most serious objections to animalism have nothing to do with brain transplants or essential properties. The real worry is that there might be non-animals thinking our thoughts. That would make it hard to see how we could ever know that we are animals. In other words, animalism itself may face its own analogue of the thinking-animal problem. That would leave animalists no better off than their opponents. I will discuss two possible sources of this trouble.

In §2 I mentioned the view that we are not animals, but rather non-animals sharing their matter with animals. This means that it is possible in general for the same matter to make up two or more objects (substances) at the same time. This general view is sometimes called *constitutionalism*, because most of those who hold it say that whenever two things are made of the same matter, one of them 'constitutes' the other.

A number of metaphysical puzzles about material objects support constitutionalism (Thomson, 1983; 1998; Baker, 2000). Suppose we take a lump of clay and model it into a statue of Boris Yeltsin. The lump and the statue don't seem to be the same thing. The statue seems to come into being when we make the lump Yeltsin-shaped, but the lump seems to exist before then. And even if the lump and the statue have precisely the same career, it seems that either *could* outlive the other. The lump would outlive the statue if we squashed it: that would destroy the statue but merely change the lump's shape. And if we broke an arm off the statue and burnt it to ashes, then replaced it with a new arm made of different clay, the statue would outlive the lump. But a thing cannot outlive itself. If this is right, no lump is identical with any statue. Yet the statue and the lump in our story are made of the same matter at the same time. The lump, as the jargon has it, would constitute the statue. Constitutionalism would be true.

Although constitutionalism is formally consistent with animalism, the two views sit uneasily together. Constitutionalism leads us to expect every human animal to stand to something as a clay statue stands to a lump of clay: something that would outlive the animal if it were squashed, and which the animal would outlive if one of its hands were cut off and burnt to ashes. It would be surprising, anyway, if there were a lump of clay constituting the clay statue of Yeltsin but no lump of flesh (or mass of matter, or aggregate of atoms, or some such thing) constituting Yeltsin himself. Such a combination of views would seem unprincipled, like holding that statues of men are constituted by lumps but not statues of women (but see Hoffman and Rosenkrantz, 1997, pp. 87–8, 99–100).

Now suppose you are an animal. And suppose you stand to a lump of flesh, or some such thing, as a clay statue stands to a lump of clay. This lump of flesh would be physically indistinguishable from you for as long as it constitutes you. It would have the same brain and nervous system as you have, and the same surroundings. It would show the same behavioural evidence of intelligence and conscious awareness as you do. That suggests that, while it constitutes you, the lump would *be* conscious and intelligent — indeed, it would be mentally just like you. Every current thought or experience of yours would be a thought or experience on the part of the lump now constituting you.

This would be a serious problem for those who believe that we are animals. For how could you ever know that you are the animal, and not the lump that shares your every thought? Even if you were the animal and not the lump, it seems that you could never have any reason to believe that you are. For that matter, it is a problem for anyone who takes us to be anything other than lumps of flesh. And although philosophers have held many strange views about what we are, I have yet to meet one who thought that we are lumps of flesh.

Animalists — and others — are committed to there being a solution to this problem: a way of knowing that we are not lumps of flesh. There would seem to be just three possible solutions, analogous to the three solutions to the thinking-animal problem.

One is to deny that there are any lumps of flesh, or masses of matter, or anything else made of the same matter as we are. That would be a metaphysical solution to the problem. Given that lumps of flesh or masses of matter constitute animals if anything constitutes anything, this would mean rejecting constitutionalism altogether, thus giving up an attractive account of the lump-and-statue story and many similar cases.

The second possible solution is to accept that lumps of flesh constitute us, but deny that they think in the way that we do: a psychological solution. But it is not obvious what could prevent a lump of flesh physically indistinguishable from one of us from thinking. And if there were an explanation of why no lump of flesh can think, anti-animalists — in particular those who say that we are material things constituted by animals — might be able to use it to explain why animals cannot think, thus depriving animalism of its principal support.

Finally, one might accept that there are lumps of flesh, and that they think as we do, but argue that we can still somehow know that we not those lumps: an epistemic solution. But it is hard to see how this would go. Nor is it clear that it would benefit animalists in the end: if they can argue that we could know we are not the lumps sharing our thoughts, anti-animalists might be able to argue in a similar way that we can know we are not the animals that think our thoughts, once more undermining animalism.

The problem for animalism may be even worse than this suggests. If human animals are constituted by lumps of flesh, we might expect the animals themselves to constitute thinking beings that persist by virtue of psychological continuity, or beings that have certain mental properties essentially. Although no one has ever proposed an acceptable general account of when one material object constitutes another (apart from never, that is), most constitutionalists find it obvious — so obvious as to require no further argument — that normal human organisms constitute beings that persist by virtue of psychological continuity, or that have certain mental properties essentially. If they are right, the only way to defend animalism would be to argue for an epistemic solution. But that looks hopeless. Even if we could know that we are not the thinking lumps of flesh that constitute us, I cannot imagine what grounds we could have for supposing that we are not the essentially mental beings we constitute, if there are such things.

7. Thinking Heads

Here is another example of the same trouble. Consider your head. It has a brain and sense organs, just as you have. It shows the same behavioural evidence of intelligence and conscious awareness as you do. That suggests that your head *is* conscious and intelligent, indeed that it is mentally just like you. Your head is not physically identical with you, as a lump of flesh constituting you would be. But it is hard to see why that should stop your head from being conscious and intelligent. Presumably it *would* be conscious and intelligent if the rest of you were cut away and replaced with appropriate life-support machinery. How could its being attached to the rest of you, by itself, prevent it from thinking?

If your head were able to think just as you do, this too would be a serious problem for those who think that we are animals. More generally, it would be a problem for anyone who takes us to be anything other than undetached heads — and no one thinks that we are heads. For how could you ever know that you are the animal (or whatever), and not the head that shares your every thought? Even if you were the animal and not the head, it seems that you could never have any reason to believe that you are. And if your head thinks your thoughts, it is likely that many other parts of your animal body do as well: your brain, for instance, and your upper half. Every part of the animal that includes your brain would be a candidate for being you.

Once again, animalists (and more generally those who deny that we are heads) are committed to there being a solution to this problem: a way of knowing that we are not thinking heads. Again there appear to be just three possibilities. One is to deny that there are any undetached heads — or brains, or upper halves, or any other proper parts of us that include our brains. We may accept that some of your particles are 'arranged capitally', but we must deny that they make up a head, or anything else. That would mean abandoning beliefs that we learned at mother's knee — a drastic measure (van Inwagen 1981, 1990). Second, we might accept that there are such things as heads, but deny that they think as we do (Burke 2003). But again, there is no obvious explanation of why this should be so. Finally, we might accept that our heads think as we do and argue that we can still somehow know that we are animals (or whatever) and not heads.

As before, the second and third strategies threaten to play into the hands of the anti-animalists: if our heads cannot think, or if we can somehow know that we are not our thinking heads, then anti-animalists may be able to argue in the same way that human animals cannot think, or that we can know that we are not the animals that think our thoughts.

8. The Messy View

I have tried to articulate a general metaphysical objection to animalism. There is reason to believe that there are non-animals thinking our thoughts, and it is hard to see what grounds we could ever have for taking ourselves to be animals rather than these thinking non-animals. Human animals may be excellent candidates for being us — the referents of our personal pronouns and the subjects of our thoughts and actions — but they may not be the only candidates: lumps of flesh constituting us, and our heads or brains, may be candidates too. And analogous problems arise on any sensible account of what we are.

Nor are lumps of flesh and undetached heads the only entities that animalists (and others) need to worry about. We might have temporal parts. It may be, for instance, that for each day of your life there is a part of you that is just like you are during that day, but exists at no other time. This is a consequence of the ontology of temporal parts, or 'four-dimensionalism', currently much in vogue. (Most of those who reject the constitutionalist's account of lumps and statues take this line, saying that every persisting object is composed of temporal parts, and that the statue of Yeltsin in our story is a temporal part of the lump: see e.g. Sider, 2001, pp. 154–61.) If there is a temporal part of you that extends from midnight last night until midnight tonight, this would be just as troublesome for animalists and others as undetached heads and lumps of flesh would be.

Animalists and others will hope to give metaphysical, psychological, or epistemic answers to these objections: they will hope that the troublesome entities are unreal, or that they exist but cannot think as we do, or that they think as we do but we are nonetheless able to know that we are the animals and not any of the troublesome entities. (They might say different things in different cases: that there are no lumps of flesh constituting us, that undetached heads and brains exist but cannot think, and that day-long temporal parts of human animals think as we do, but we can nonetheless know that we are not such things, for instance.)

But suppose these hopes are in vain: suppose there really are non-animals as well as animals thinking our thoughts, and that we can never know that we are the animals rather than the non-animals. In that case we could not say that we are animals. What then? Ought we to conclude that we are not animals, but rather thinking lumps of flesh, or essential thinkers constituted by animals, or heads, or temporal parts of animals? Well, no. Those views face an analogous problem: if for all we know we might be thinking lumps of flesh or heads or day-long animal segments, then for all we know we might be thinking animals. If we can't know that we're animals, we can't know that we're not animals either.

That would be a mess. We couldn't say that we are animals, because all sorts of non-animals think our thoughts too. Neither could we say that we are non-animals, because animals also think our thoughts. But if we are neither animals nor non-animals, what are we? (It's no good saying that we don't exist, if all sorts of beings think our thoughts. Clearly if anything thinks my thoughts, I do; and if I think, I exist.)

In that case, the question of what we are would have no straightforward answer. There would be no one sort of being that thinks my thoughts: many beings of different sorts would think them. And there would presumably be no one sort of being that our personal pronouns and proper names refer to, either: human animals, lumps of flesh, undetached heads, and what not would be equally good candidates for being the referent of the name 'Olson'. Perhaps that name would not refer at all. Or maybe someone who said something like 'Olson is hungry' would say many different things at once, one for each candidate for being me. Or maybe the term would have indeterminate reference: it would definitely refer to something, but it would not definitely refer to an animal, or to a lump of flesh, or to a head, or to any other particular thing.

Should I be an animal, then, or not? We could not answer either yes or no. Perhaps the best answer would be that, while it is not definitely true that I am an animal, it is not definitely true that I am not an animal, either. Likewise, if there is a lump of flesh now constituting this animal, it is not definitely true either that I am a lump of flesh or that I am not a lump of flesh. And so on, for all the other beings that think our thoughts. It is indeterminate whether we are animals, lumps of flesh, undetached heads, or any of the other thinking beings we have been considering. We might call this the *messy view* of our metaphysical nature.

How bad would the messy view be? Well, suppose it were indeterminate whether we are animals or heads. Then it would be radically indeterminate how big we are: whether we are the size of animals or the size of heads. It would be just as true to say or believe that I weigh five pounds and would fit into a hatbox as it would be to say that I weigh 150 pounds and am nearly six feet tall. Or if it were indeterminate whether we are animals or day-long temporal parts of animals, it would be indeterminate whether we persist for seventy-odd years or for only a day. It would be just as true to say that I am less than a day old as it is to say that I am forty-something. Or if it were indeterminate whether we are animals or lumps of flesh, it would be indeterminate whether we could survive being squashed, or losing a hand. It would be just as correct to say that losing a hand would kill me instantly as it would be to say that it would only make me smaller.

Of course, it may still be *customary* to say such things as 'Olson weighs 150 pounds', 'Buggins is older than he looks', and 'Bloggs has been more cautious since she lost her hand', and not customary to say 'Olson weighs five pounds', 'Buggins may look 40, but he's less than a day old', or 'Bloggs is more cautious than her predecessor — you know, the one who died when she lost her hand in the mincer'. (Nor would it be customary to say such things as 'it is indeterminate whether Olson weighs 150 pounds or five pounds'.) But although it may be customary to say the things we ordinarily say and not customary to say the outrageous things we might say instead, on the messy view the customary sayings are no more *true* than the outrageous ones.

Few of us will find the messy view appealing. But we can avoid it only if all the problems about different sorts of beings thinking our thoughts have a metaphysical or psychological or epistemic solution. And the prospects for such a solution do not look bright. Many of the candidate solutions are hardly more appealing than the messy view itself. At any rate, *I* am not confident that the problems can be solved in a satisfactory way that leaves an unambiguous answer to the question of what we are. That is why I said I don't know what we are.

In any case, the matter turns on large and difficult questions of ontology, the philosophy of mind, and epistemology: Are constitutionalism or four-dimensionalism true? What are the parts of a living organism? What does it take for a thing to have mental properties? What is the nature of self-knowledge and self-reference? Only when we have answered these questions can we know what we are.[1]

References

Baker, L.R. (2000), *Persons and Bodies* (Cambridge: Cambridge University Press).
Burke, M. (2003), 'Is my head a person?', in K. Petrus, ed., *On Human Persons* (Frankfurt: Ontos), pp. 107–26.
Chisholm, R. (1989), 'Is there a mind-body problem?', in *On Metaphysics* (Minneapolis: University of Minnesota Press), and partly reprinted in P. van Inwagen and D. Zimmerman, eds., *Metaphysics: The Big Questions* (Malden, MA: Blackwell, 1998).
Carter, W. R. (1989), 'How to change your mind', *Canadian Journal of Philosophy*, **19**, pp. 1–14.
Clark, A. and Chalmers, D. (1998), 'The extended mind', *Analysis*, **58**, pp. 10–23.
Hoffman, J. and Rosenkrantz, G. (1997), *Substance: Its Nature and Existence* (London: Routledge).
Hudson, H. (2001), *A Materialist Metaphysics of the Human Person* (Ithaca, NY: Cornell University Press).
Hume, D. (1978), *A Treatise of Human Nature* (Oxford: Oxford University Press; original work 1739).
Locke, J. (1975), *An Essay Concerning Human Understanding*, ed. P. Nidditch (Oxford: Clarendon Press; original work 1694).
Lowe, E.J. (2000), *An Introduction to the Philosophy of Mind* (Cambridge: Cambridge University Press).
Noonan, H. (1998), 'Animalism *versus* Lockeanism: A current controversy', *Philosophical Quarterly*, **48**, pp. 302–18.
Noonan, H. (forthcoming), 'Persons, animals and human beings', in J. Campbell and M. O'Rourke, eds., *Topics in Contemporary Philosophy, vol. 6: Time and Identity* (Cambridge, MA: MIT Press).

---

[1] I thank Stephan Blatti, Arto Laitinen, and Arto Repo for comments on an earlier version.

Nozick, R. (1981), *Philosophical Explanations* (Cambridge, MA: Harvard University Press).
Olson, E. (1997), *The Human Animal: Personal Identity Without Psychology* (New York: Oxford University Press).
Olson, E. (2002a), 'What does functionalism tell us about personal identity?', *Noûs*, **36**, pp. 682–98.
Olson, E. (2002b), 'Thinking animals and the reference of "I"', *Philosophical Topics*, **30**, pp. 189–208.
Olson, E. (2003), 'An argument for animalism', in J. Barresi and R. Martin, eds., *Personal Identity* (Oxford: Blackwell).
Olson, E. (2007), *What Are We? A Study in Personal Ontology* (New York: Oxford University Press).
Parfit, D. (1984), *Reasons and Persons* (Oxford: Oxford University Press).
Shoemaker, S. (1984), 'Personal identity: A materialist's account', in Shoemaker and Swinburne, *Personal Identity* (Oxford: Blackwell).
Shoemaker, S. (1999), 'Self, body, and coincidence', *Proceedings of the Aristotelian Society, Supplementary Volume*, **73**, pp. 287–306.
Shoemaker, S. (2004), 'Functionalism and personal identity: A reply', *Noûs*, **38**, pp. 525–33.
Swinburne, R. (1984), 'Personal identity: The dualist theory', in Shoemaker and Swinburne, *Personal Identity* (Oxford: Blackwell).
Thomson, J.J. (1983), 'Parthood and identity across time', *Journal of Philosophy* **80**, pp. 201–20.
Thomson, J.J. (1998), 'The statue and the clay', *Noûs*, **32**, pp. 149–73.
Sider, T. (2001), *Four-Dimensionalism* (Oxford: Clarendon Press).
Unger, P. (1979), 'I do not exist', in G. F. MacDonald, ed., *Perception and Identity* (London: Macmillan), and reprinted in M. Rea, ed., *Material Constitution* (Lanham, MD: Rowman and Littlefield).
Unger, P. (1990), *Identity, Consciousness, and Value* (New York: Oxford University Press).
van Inwagen, P. (1981), 'The doctrine of arbitrary undetached parts', *Pacific Philosophical Quarterly*, **62**, pp. 123–37, and reprinted in M. Rea, ed., *Material Constitution* (Lanham, MD: Rowman and Littlefield).
van Inwagen, P. (1990) *Material Beings* (Ithaca, NY: Cornell University Press).
Zimmerman, D. (2003), 'Material people', in M. Loux and Zimmerman, eds., *The Oxford Handbook of Metaphysics* (Oxford: Oxford University Press).

Michael Quante

The Social Nature of Personal Identity

Abstract: *In this paper the thesis that personal identity is essentially constituted by social relations is defended. To make this plausible the problem of personal identity is broken down into four interrelated sets of problems. Of these, the unity — and the persistence — problems cannot be resolved using the notion of a person and therefore personal identity in this sense is not socially constituted. But this paper argues that the conditions of personhood, and the structure of a human being's personality — which are the other two sets into which the problem of personal identity is dissolved — are best understood as being constituted by social relations, especially relations of mutual recognition.*

> Das Selbstbewußtsein ist *an* und *für sich*, indem und dadurch, daß es für ein anderes an und für sich ist; d.h. es ist nur als ein Anerkanntes.
>
> [Self-consciousness exists in and for itself when, and by the fact that, it exists for another; that is, it exists only in being acknowledged.]
>
> (G.W.F. Hegel)

My aim in this paper is to bring to light the essentially social character of the personal identity of human beings. This is a vast topic. Here I can do no more than explain my thesis that the identity of human persons is essentially constituted by social relations. In the title of the paper you find the common phrase 'personal identity'.[1] In fact I prefer

Correspondence:
Michael Quante, Philosophisches Seminar, Universität zu Köln, Albertus-Magnus-Platz, 50923 Köln, Germany. mquante@uni-koeln.de

---

[1] The literature devoted to this topic is vast. For a good overview, compare the anthologies Martin & Barresi (2003), Noonan (1993), Oksenberg Rorty (1976), Perry (1976), Quante (1999), Siep (1983) and Sturma (2001). Helpful introductions to the topic are Baillie (1993), Glover (1988), Noonan (1989), Perielhum (1970) and Vesey (1974).

more complicated phrases like 'the personal identity of human beings' or 'the identity of human persons'. Such phrases are not very elegant, perhaps, but it is necessary to speak in this way if we want to find a way out of the many dead ends and stalemates that philosophical debate about personal identity has run into.

Indeed I think the question of personal identity is often posed in a misleading way.[2] This is so for three reasons. *Firstly* the notions of 'person' and 'identity' are complicated and have different meanings in different contexts. Distinguishing these comes down to making several questions out of one and allows us to put the many intuitions surrounding personal identity in the right place.[3] *Secondly* speaking of personal identity suggests that we can give answers to the several identity-questions using no other concept than 'person'. But since all persons we know (or at least all I know) are human persons, we should take into account the possibility that not all of our identity-questions can be answered by using the notion of a person, but may depend on what human beings actually are.[4] *Thirdly*, the notion of 'identity' is used ambiguously in the philosophical analyses of personal identity. This causes extra trouble since intuitions related to numerical identity are thereby transferred into different areas, which leads the discussions astray.[5]

Therefore I want to state explicitly two premises which underlie the arguments I will present in the following:

(P1) The philosophical problem of personal identity must be broken down into at least four problems (each the subject of a set of interrelated questions).[6]

---

[2] I have defended this thesis for the first time in Quante (1995a,b); in these papers I suggested that the four questions be distinguished (and I develop that view further in this paper).

[3] I have elaborated this in Quante (2002; forthcoming).

[4] One important lesson we might learn from this is that many of the famous thought experiments so prominent in the context of analyses of personal identity are meaningless or misleading since they do not take into account the constraints stemming from what human beings are actually like; cf. Wilkes (1988).

[5] I analyse this in more detail in Quante (2001a; 2002; forthcoming); a similar point has been made by Perry (2002).

[6] Although I know of no position in which the four questions are distinguished in the way I suggest here, many philosophers have made suggestions for dividing the field in some way; cf. Korsgaard (1989) or Schechtman (1996), who distinguish between the metaphysical and the practical aspect of personal 'identity'. Dennett (1978) deals with the problems of 'conditions of personhood' and 'conditions for transtemporal identity of persons' in separate chapters, but makes no attempt to analyse the connections; the insight that

Although these four problems have to be distinguished, they are not completely independent of each other: Decisions regarding one problem can (and normally will) have consequences for solutions of the other problems. Thus answers given to the different problems have to be taken together to get the whole picture. In many places more than one solution of special problems related to personal identity are open to us. In such cases we have to have a look at the overall picture and to make explicit which demands our overall theory has to fulfil. Without this, our answers will be arbitrary — or rather, they will be more arbitrary than they need be.

(P2) It is impossible to solve or dissolve all problems related to personal identity within one single[7] approach without illegitimately reducing the complexity of the phenomena.

Having said this I want to state the thesis, which will be explained and defended in the following pages:

(THESIS) The personal identity of human beings is essentially constituted by social relations.

Since speaking of personal identity, at least in philosophical contexts, is liable to give rise to misunderstandings, or to activate the wrong sets of philosophical and pre-philosophical intuitions, I have to begin with some clarifications: Without doubt numerical identity is a relation of philosophical interest in its own right. But in dealing with the concept of personal 'identity', numerical identity is not what we are looking for.[8] To be sure, when it comes to the science fiction fantasies of fission and fusion, of the transfer of mental states from one brain to another (or to tapes or halves of brains or what have you), the formal aspects of identity become relevant. But what we are interested in here are primarily other questions, which hint at other relations and properties than numerical identity.[9]

---

questions concerning unity and persistence have to be treated separately is developed in Brooks (1994).

[7] By 'single' I mean here an approach relying either on the observer perspective or the participant perspective exclusively.

[8] To avoid confusion, 'identity' is used in this paper only in the sense of numerical identity, when I speak for myself.

[9] These are primarily practical questions concerning autonomy, moral responsibility, self-interest or personal survival; cf. Korsgaard (1989), Martin (1998), Rovane (1998) or Schechtman (1996 and 2002).

1. The Four Dimensions of 'Personal Identity'

Instead of trying to answer the question of what *THE* identity of persons might consist of, I think it helpful to distinguish four problems:

(A) *The Conditions-of-Personhood-Problem (CPP)*: Which properties or capacities must an entity have in order to belong to the class of persons?

Giving an answer to the CPP comes down to making a list of person-making characteristics. To do this is beyond the scope of this paper, but I would like to emphasize that the person-making characteristics on this list are understood here as constitutive, and not only as epistemic, criteria. The status of personhood is an important element of our social practices (think of the right one has, that one's actions or decisions are respected; of the right to sign contracts; or even the right not to be killed). Ascribing this status makes use (implicitly or explicitly) of person-making characteristics. Therefore we as philosophers shouldn't claim that the criteria guiding our social practices have to be taken as epistemic only, leaving open what the 'real' (or constitutive) criteria for being a person might be. Although such a conceptual move is possible in principle, it would impose an enormous burden of proof (how should we as philosophers defend our list of constitutive criteria which are not connected to our practices?). Furthermore, basing our practices on criteria we don't have empirical access to, would weaken the possibility of justifying our ascriptions in an unacceptable manner.

(B) *The Unity-of-Person-Problem (UPP)*: What are the conditions that must hold so that it is the case that an entity A is exactly one person at one point in time?

For example, what determines whether there are several persons per one human being, or perhaps one group person per several human beings, at one point in time? This question, although only seldom discussed in the literature dealing with personal identity, is sometimes framed in the language of 'synchronic identity'.[10] But since the relation of identity as such is not connected to time at all, this is misleading. If we ask what must be the case so that an entity A has to be counted as exactly one person at one given point in time, we try to determine the truth conditions for statements of this kind: A is one and

---

[10] In the philosophy of mind, unity-of-consciousness is discussed as a topic in its own right. In the literature dealing with personal identity this problem comes to the surface if we abandon the rule 'one human being — one person' (for example if we discuss group persons or multiple personality disorder).

only one person at t. It is evident that identity as such is of no (or only limited) help here. We have to consider what kind of entity A is. Since we are discussing persons it seems that CPP and UPP are directly connected. But things are more complicated, as the following three options show:

First, if we have characterized A as essentially a person, then we have settled that A is essentially *one* person. This is at least true if we accept the more general ontological claim that anything that is essentially an X, is precisely one X. If A were to turn into some other thing, or several things, *it* would cease to exist, and cease to be the thing it now is. (If it did *not* cease to exist, when ceasing to be an X, it could not have been *essentially* an X).What makes A a person, makes ipso facto A precisely one person, and neither more nor less. In this case the conditions of personhood entail criteria for answering the unity-of-person-problem (CPP settles UPP directly).

Second, if A is only accidentally a person, and essentially a member of some other kind X (a human being, or a Martian), then A might in principle be (in the predicative sense of 'is') one or more persons. Conditions of personhood might of course be such that there can be only one person per human being (say, 'a person is an organism with capacities F, G, H'). But conditions of personhood might also be such that there can be more persons per human being (say, one person per a stream of consciousness, or per a personality – and cases of brain bisection and multiple personality disorder might display such cases), or also just one group person per group of humans, or Martians.

Thus a more complicated variant of how CPP entails UPP is this: In the first step we have characterised A using some other sortal[11] term X (e.g. human being or Martian) which entails criteria for answering the Unity-of X-Problem for things of this kind X (the answer to the Conditions-of-X-Problem settles the Unity-of-X-Problem directly). In the second step we have answered CPP in such a way that an entity of the kind X is *exactly one person* at one point in time only if it is *exactly one* entity of kind X at this point in time. In this case the answer to CPP and the answer to the Unity-of-X-Problem deliver an answer to UPP if and only if all the conditions that make an entity of kind X at one point in time a person at that point in time, are given.

A third option is that the answer to CPP doesn't entail the provision that entities of a given kind X (say, Martians, human beings) have to

---

[11] The term 'sortal term' is used in different ways in the literature. In this paper it is used in the sense of 'general term'. This means that there are sortal terms which do provide criteria for unity and persistence ('substance sortals') and that there are sortals which do not ('phase sortals').

be exactly one person at one point in time to count as a person at this point in time. In this case we can ask whether A is a person at t at all and, additionally, we can ask whether A is exactly one person at t. In this case we can try to settle the UPP using one or another characterisation of A, in terms of some non–substance sortal Z (for example 'personality', 'stream of consciousness'). Thus we could claim that in cases of brain bisection or multiple personality, there are several persons per one human animal. If we hold this position we give up a principle normally taken for granted in accounts of human persons. This principle says that one human being is related to exactly one person (at least at any one point in time) if it qualifies as a human person at all.

(C) *The Persistence-of-Person-Problem (PPP)*: What are the conditions that must hold so that it is the case that A at t_1 is the same person as B at t_2?[12]

This is the main sense in which the problem of personal identity is posed — as the question of persistence, survival, diachronic identity or identity over time. As in the cases already discussed, using the term 'identity' here is misleading, since we are looking for relations which must (non-trivially) hold so that the identity-statement is true. (Of course, the identity-relation itself must hold for identity-statements to be true, but saying this is not informative). Our persistence-question: 'Is A at t_1 the same person as B at t_2' takes for granted that A at t_1 and B at t_2 are persons. All we want to know is whether they are the same person or not.

The first question to be asked now is whether 'being a person' entails criteria determining which relations between A at t_1 and B at t_2 must hold so that it is the case that A at t_1 and B at t_2 are one and the same person. If we answer this first question in the affirmative, CPP will settle PPP, and it only remains to determine *which* of these criteria and relations are crucial in determining the sameness of A and B at these two times.

But if we answer the first question in the negative, with a strict 'No!', then CPP cannot settle PPP and the question now is which characterisation of A at t_1 and B at t_2 can deliver criteria for persistence. Which sortal term X can answer the persistence problem regarding the entity A under consideration? Furthermore, a more general problem lurks here. Since every entity A has many qualities, we have to ask whether every sortal term can deliver criteria to answer the

---

[12] Framing the problem in this way presupposes that persistence is sortal-dependent; cf. Wiggins (2001).

persistence problem or not. Since we have committed ourselves to a negative answer (having excluded 'being a person' from the list already), we have to say which features of sortal terms make it the case that they can deliver criteria for persistence (or make it the case that they cannot).[13]

(D) *The Structure-of-Personality-Problem (SPP)*: What is the basic structure of leading the life of a person?

Persons are entities capable of standing in self-relations of various sorts. Among them are relations of self-evaluation, self-identification, and self-criticism. Persons can, in a sense to be analysed further, bring about an evaluative conception of who they are and who they want to be. In the tradition of Erik Erikson this kind of self-relationship has been called 'identity' in the sense in which we speak about a person's 'identity crisis' if, for example, she loses confidence in the values with regard to which she has oriented her life up to now; I will call this complex structure a person's personality (this is meant to cover what many philosophers have come to name narrative or biographical identity).

Distinguishing SPP from UPP and PPP does not commit me to the claim that an answer to the first is completely independent from answers to the other two. But we should not expect that answers to UPP or PPP will imply an answer to SPP, and we should give up the idea that we can solve the four problems by means of one single approach. A fortiori, we should not try to solve the UPP or PPP by analysing the structure of a human being's personality. There are many different relations between personhood, unity, persistence and personality — at least in the case of human beings — but they are more indirect and more complicated than most of the approaches I know suggest.

As I will explain below in the third section, a human person's personality is essentially constituted by social relations, i.e. my THESIS deals mainly with SPP. In defending the thesis, I will have to say something about CPP, too, since it is related to SPP. I will claim that personhood and personality are socially dependent. To pre-empt any worries that this may lead to unacceptable views concerning persistence, in part two I will point out that even if personhood is socially

---

[13] In the end, the work is done by the laws covering the natural kinds themselves, so the limitations of our linguistic practice will lead to epistemological problems only; not to ontological indetermination.

determined, the persistence of human persons is *not* socially determined, because personhood does not provide persistence conditions.[14]

Before I do this, a short terminological remark. Although speaking about 'persons' is unexceptional and without problems in everyday speech, and even in many philosophical contexts, there are certain dangers lurking in the special context of personal 'identity'. If I characterize someone as a person I describe him in a special way (attributing to him the person-making characteristics) and ascribe to him a special ethical status. Although the descriptive and the ascriptive aspects can be separated in principle, normally they go hand in hand. I will use the notion 'person' as a way of describing an entity A which qualifies as a person on the basis of the list of person-making characteristics. I will deal with human persons only, so that the notions 'person' and 'human person' are used interchangeably from now on. One consequence of this is that my arguments might not be extensible to all kinds of persons without further qualifications. But it should be clear that being a human animal is neither a necessary nor a sufficient condition for being a person.

2. The Non-Social Nature of Persistence

The relation between CPP, UPP and PPP depends on one's view on whether 'person' is a sortal term which can deliver conditions for the unity or the persistence of persons (a substance sortal).

We can ask whether 'person' delivers criteria for answering PPP, and my answer is: it depends! It depends on what we think conditions of persistence are and on the conditions of adequacy we demand for a theory of the persistence of human persons. There are several features we normally think the persistence conditions of human persons should have. They should not be arbitrary or depend on social practices and shared values, should not make the persistence of a human person depend on social or linguistic conventions, should back our modal intuitions, should respect the so-called 'only-x-and-y-principle' and, additionally, should keep in touch with our normal conception of a human person.[15] And, I would like to add, it should allow us to deliver criteria for the beginning and the end of the existence of human persons which are in touch with the criteria offered by biology and medicine. Furthermore the persistence conditions should be such that we can have epistemic access to them intersubjectively.

---

[14] Cf. Quante (2002) for a full treatment of these issues.

[15] The 'only x–and–y principle' claims that the question of whether x is identical with y depends only on x and y, and not on any third candidate, z. See e.g. Noonan (1989), p. 16.

As John Locke made clear long ago, it may be impossible to fulfil all these demands; since our commonsense idea of personal 'identity' combines the ideas of a human being and a person in a complicated and probably ultimately inconsistent manner. This tension in our ordinary understanding stems from the fact that in the normal course of things, personal 'identity' and the 'identity' of human beings are related in such a way that we do not have to distinguish clearly between our being human beings and our being persons.

But as Locke, and many of the thought experiments which followed later have shown, situations are possible in which our intuitions concerning personhood and animal- or bodily-'identity' come apart (I leave out the Cartesian alternative which Locke himself primarily had in mind as the position against which he tried to establish his own solution, since today the main frontline is between neo-Lockean approaches and animalist- or bodily-based conceptions of personal 'identity'). Locke's answer is well known: he suggests that 'person' delivers criteria which can settle PPP. Thereby the persistence conditions of human beings and persons diverge (at least in principle).[16]

Pace Locke, I do not think that 'person' can deliver criteria for persistence if we take seriously our demands for such conditions. The main reason for this is that 'person' is a complex and socially constituted property, dependent on values and cultural practices (see below). This is even the case for the first-person-perspective; so that one cannot argue that personal identity is based on first-personal-facts which are not arbitrary, contingent, or socially constituted. This is so, since either these purported facts cannot be used within a social context at all (violating this constraint) or they are dependent on the way we use first-person-statements within our social reality. Furthermore it seems clear to me that a human being can both become a person, and then subsequently lose this complex property without thereby ceasing to exist. As long as we do not claim that persons are substances which are essential bearers of the property of being a person, we can say that 'being a person' designates a complex property of entities but is not one of those sortal terms which deliver criteria for persistence.

So this is my positive answer to PPP, which will make clear why I prefer to speak about the persistence of human persons: We are

---

[16] Reading Locke in this way contradicts those who deny that Locke wanted to answer PPP at all, and who claim that he was interested in SPP only; c.f. Rovane (1998). Indeed, I think that Locke mixed up the four problems which I try to distinguish in this paper. As a result, traces of all of them can be found in his arguments; and for this reason we cannot simply claim that his theory is an answer only to one of the four problems I attempt to distinguish here.

looking for a sortal term X which provides us with criteria for determining whether an entity of the kind X at one moment in time is the same as an entity of the kind X at another moment in time. As I have argued elsewhere at length,[17] there is a special class of sortal terms delivering such criteria of persistence which fulfil most of the conditions we expect the persistence-relation for human persons to have: natural-kind terms, especially those designating biological species. These sortal terms refer indexically to actual features of the species. What these features are, is to be discovered by biology. Biological laws specify what kind of development a member of the species under consideration will normally take, which changes it can survive, and what the conditions of the beginning and the end of its existence are. Since such biological laws, although not of the *strict* kind, are neither arbitrary nor constituted by social conventions or values, they can deliver us a notion of persistence as a law-governed series of events constituting the life of an organism, so that most of our intuitions are met. And since such laws can support at least those counterfactuals wherein these laws are held constant, many of our modal intuitions are saved, too. To be sure, many of the fanciful thought experiments, stretching our concepts to merely logically possible worlds, will fall outside the scope of this account. But since I don't believe that our intuitions concerning the persistence of human beings either stem from identity or are free from the real contexts in which they normally operate, this doesn't bother me: we simply don't have clear intuitions in those cases invented in these science fiction fantasies. As Locke saw, too, we even have conflicting intuitions in some real cases, such as multiple personality disorder; since sometimes the *contingent* harmony between having a personality and being a human being breaks down.

To sum up: For all these reasons my answer to the PPP is the following: 'Being a person' does not deliver persistence conditions.[18] There are no special persistence conditions for persons. But there are special sortal terms delivering criteria for persistence which are good enough to fulfil most of what we expect. In the case of human persons the biological notion of 'being a human being' will deliver the needed criteria. If evolution were to bring into being amoeba persons, the biological notion of 'amoeba' would have to do the job. This means that there is no unique persistence-relation for all persons (unless only

---

[17] See Quante 2001a, 2002 and forthcoming.

[18] I deal with the ethical problems this might cause in biomedical ethics in Quante (2002, chapter 3 and 4) and Quante (2003).

human beings can be persons; but this is not guaranteed by the conditions of personhood, since here no reference to human beings is made). But it might be the case that we cannot find a species-neutral sense of 'being a person', since we have not excluded the possibility that the existential conditions of our being human somehow influence our understanding of what is involved in being a person in such a deep way that we cannot have a full grasp of what a nonhuman person might be.[19] I will come back to this in the concluding section of this paper.[20]

3. The Social Nature of Personhood and Personality

It is now time to take a look at the sense in which personal identity has a social nature. This is related to the first and fourth sets of questions (conditions of personhood, structure of personality).

3.1 The Social Nature of Personhood and Personality

If A and B are both persons the property of 'being a person' is instantiated twice. We do not only want to say that A and B are both persons; we also want to say that they are *different* persons. Furthermore, we do not only want to say that A and B are two different persons because they are for example two different human beings, but we also want to say that they each have their own way of being a person. 'Being a person' — so we can make this point — is exemplified by A and B individually. In the case of the property 'being blue' we can speak of two instances which exemplify different shades of blue. Or we can even restrict the criterion of individuation to the fact that the two instances of blue take place at different points in space–time.

In the case of human persons we think that this individual exemplification, which I call a human being's personality, is the result of the complex self-relations and social relations human beings can enter into. A personality is something which is brought about by human

---

[19] This problem is analogous to the question of human pain and Martian pain; another case is the possibility that our mental vocabulary cannot be used univocally for sentient beings capable of first-person-thoughts and for those sentient beings which cannot.

[20] As I understand it, my account concerning UPP and PPP is compatible with the view Eric Olson (1997) has defended — at least in the overall conclusions and in the main lines of argument. Whether what I have to say concerning CPP and SPP will cause disagreement, is not clear to me. As I understand Olson's approach, he distinguishes the value-questions related to personal identity from those related to PPP. Therefore he is not committed to the claim that only human beings can be persons. Furthermore, he is not committed to the claim that 'being a human being' and 'being a person' have the same meaning. So he might accept that there is more to say about human persons and their 'identities' than that which appears if we are in search of persistence-conditions for human persons.

beings — it is a manifestation of the active and practical character of our human mind. It is due to this fact that we take persons to be morally responsible, to be autonomous and to have a concern for themselves. Therefore neither the 'shades of ...' strategy nor the space-time criterion will suffice to make intelligible what the personality of a single human being consists in.

The complicated internal structure of a human being's personality could not be brought about if human beings did not have those features Locke mentioned in his famous answer to CPP: To be a person, he says, is to be

> a thinking intelligent Being, that has reason and reflection, and can consider it self as it self, the same thinking thing in different times and places (Essay, II, XXVII, § 9).

Without being able to think first-person-thoughts, without having consciousness of the flow of time, without having access to past actions and experiences in memory; and without having, through anticipation, a sense of one's own future to be designed in the light of one's own actions, plans and projects, human beings would neither be able to lead their lives as persons, nor would they be able to take and ascribe responsibility for their actions, or claim respect for their autonomy, as resulting in a personality of their own making.[21] Herein we find the answer to the question of why and how CPP and SPP are deeply connected: Among the conditions of personhood there must be all those features and capacities which *enable* an entity to develop a personality of its own, in this way expressing its own perspective and its own individuality. Having a personality is a necessary and sufficient condition for being a person, and vice versa.[22]

---

[21] Reading Locke's famous definition as an answer to CPP shows that a lot of what Locke has to say about the essentially first-personal-structure of personhood can be understood as an indirect contribution to SPP and is not to be taken as an answer to PPP (as the defenders of the memory-criterion in contemporary debates suggest). This explains the strand of his arguments dealing with 'person as a forensic term', and questions of responsibility and punishment. But Locke himself tried to give an answer to both SPP and PPP at once. In recent years some authors have defended theses similar to mine. E.g. Schechtman (1996) proposes a twofold distinction of issues ('reidentification' and 'characterization'–issues), in contrast to my fourfold scheme. Schechtman's twofold distinction is not fine-grained enough to enable the formulation of the thesis, that in answering CPP and SPP, sociality is important, but in answering UPP and PPP, it is not. In these terms, Schechtman's view amounts roughly to the claim that SPP is social, but PPP not. Cf. also Rovane (1998) and Velleman (1996). Space does not allow a longer discussion of these accounts here.

[22] Two clarifications are in order: Firstly, this claim commits me to the thesis that being a subject of first-person-thoughts (or experiences) does not suffice to qualify the entity in question as a person. Secondly, the claim stated above is too crude if we want to discuss

In which sense, then, is being a person a socially mediated affair? I will have to restrict myself here to some brief remarks. First of all, we have to distinguish between the status of being a person and the person-making characteristics we rely on (implicitly or explicitly) in ascribing this status. Although the person-making characteristics can come in degrees and although there are different ways of fulfilling this list sufficiently so that the status of personhood can be ascribed, we should not think of the status of being a person as coming in degrees or having different meanings (related to the concrete way an entity fulfils the list of person-making characteristics). Since in our social practices the status of being a person entails a special moral significance, we should take personhood (in the status-sense) as a threshold[23] concept.[24] It is clear that being a person in this status-sense is by definition a socially mediated affair. But is it plausible to claim that being a person in the sense of being an entity that fulfils the list of person-making characteristics is a social fact, too?

The list of person-making characteristics we find in our social practices is complex, and varies between cultures and historical epochs and, at least in our society, between different contexts. As I see it, it would be idle for philosophers to try to define the essence of personhood; reducing the complexity and flexibility we actually find in our daily practice of attributing personhood. Personhood is not a scientific kind, but saying this does not exclude the possibility that some of the person-making characteristics might be describable in scientific terms. But the fact that an item is counted as a person-making characteristic cannot be explained without reference to social practices. Nor can the comparative weight that the various criteria will have, when we ask whether an entity has fulfilled the list of person-making characteristics, be explained without reference to our social practices and the aims and senses related to them. Furthermore, most

---

the context of personality disorders. But as it stands, it suffices for the purposes of the present paper.

[23] There is a threshold that every entity has to pass to count as a person. Every entity which has passed it counts as a person in the full sense, independently of how far beyond the threshold it has passed.

[24] We should bear in mind two things. On the one hand 'being a person' is not the only aspect of moral value. It might be that some single items on the list of person-making characteristics are of moral value on their own. If this is the case it might be plausible to claim that this moral value comes in degrees, just as the person-making characteristic itself does (this is important in bioethics when we discuss the ethical status of human non-personal life). On the other hand it seems plausible to me that some of the person-making characteristics are also relevant for ascribing responsibility and personal autonomy. And it might be an attractive option not to understand responsibility and personal autonomy as threshold concepts. But that is another story.

of the items on every plausible list of person-making characteristics will come in degrees, so that another dimension for social interpretation comes into play. To be sure, this argument cannot show, in principle, that the list of person-making characteristics cannot be explicated by philosophers without relying on those social practices in which these criteria are embedded. But I think it sufficient to put the burden of proof on those who claim that our list of person-making characteristics can be made intelligible without taking social practices as constitutive for the list and its internal structure.[25]

So let me come finally to the claim that the personality of a human person is essentially constituted by social relations. The claim that being a person is *essentially* constituted by social relations stands for the thesis that we cannot reduce the intersubjective dimension of personhood to the causal role of socialisation or a triggering event. Personhood is *essentially* constituted by social relations if it is possible to be a person only within such relations. Just as the rules of chess constitute the fact that a move is a castling, these social relations constitute the fact that someone is a person. This is not a matter of actualising a potential alone (although this must be part of the story). Being a person, taking responsibility, or demanding respect for one's personality are possible only in a social world constituted by social rules. They are not something purely natural, understandable from the 'sideways-on view' of science, or from a detached 'view from nowhere'. All this comes into view only from within our life-form, within which we take ourselves and others as moral agents, as persons and as individuals, each trying to develop her own personality, expressing who she is and who she wants to be. If one accepts that being a person, and the structure of the list of person-making characteristics are socially mediated, it is easy to accept that the structure of a human being's personality is socially mediated, too. As was stated above, it is a result of the complex self-relations and social relations human beings can enter into.

3.2 Indirect defence of the THESIS

If it is understood that the THESIS deals with CPP and SPP but not with UPP or PPP there are no good reasons to deny the THESIS. So I would like to defend the THESIS indirectly: There are some objections and worries which make philosophers hesitate to accept the

---

[25] Taking the criteria embedded in our social practices as only epistemic criteria would be a necessary move in denying that being a person is a social fact. As noted above, this move would give rise to sceptical worries concerning our ethical practice, which should be avoided. My thanks to Tim Henning, who prompted these clarifications.

THESIS. Showing that these objections can be refuted and that the worries are not necessary is sufficient for establishing the THESIS (if it is understood that we are not dealing with UPP or PPP).

(i) The first objection

The first objection claims that being a person is not *socially* constituted in the sense the THESIS maintains.[26] The suggestion is that we have to distinguish two different roles social norms can have: In the *constitutive* sense, social norms are necessary and sufficient for having a property (or having a special status, e.g. being a piece in a chess game). If something is used as a chess piece it has this status (and it makes no sense to ask whether it really has this status or not). In the *regulative* sense the social norms used to ascribe a property (or a special status) to an entity, can be criticized if we ask whether the entity in question really has this property (Schmid gives the following example: Some substance X is regarded as a remedy but — due to scientific discovery — we can argue that X is not a remedy at all, since it does not have those features, Y, necessary for being a remedy, i.e. supporting our health, curing illnesses etc.). Now the objection is that being a person is not dependent on social norms in the constitutive sense, but these norms are to be understood in the regulative sense: If X has all the person-making characteristics it is simply wrong not to ascribe being a person to X.

As a reply I firstly want to say that the distinction between the constitutive and regulative use of social norms is not as clear as it might seem to be. In the case of a chess piece there are some features, Y, which are necessary for attributing the status of 'chess piece'. Therefore we can criticize someone taking an entity X as a chess piece, if X does not have the features Y. Secondly, I think it is more important to ask what the relation is between these features Y and the status ascribed. As I understand it, taking social norms only in the regulative sense presupposes that the relation can be reduced to the person-making characteristics, and that this list can be analysed without social relations being part of the analysis.

As I explained above (section 3.1), it is important to distinguish between the status of personhood, the individual way an entity fulfils the list of person-making characteristics, and these characteristics themselves. Ascribing personhood and understanding someone's

---

[26] Hans Bernard Schmid has raised this objection in personal correspondence. As I understand him, he equates the THESIS with conventionalism, taking the latter to be something which implies arbitrariness. I don't accept equating my account with conventionalism if this is taken to imply a commitment to constructivism or antirealism; cf. Quante 2001b.

personality relies on these person-making characteristics; and a particular ascription to a single entity relies on the concrete list (this is a default-and-challenge-structure). Therefore the status is constituted by the ascription, but we can challenge such an ascription by showing that in a particular case the default basis is not given. Thus the possibility of excuses and corrections is no argument against the social character of being a person, and the burden of proof remains with opponents of the THESIS.

There is one further premise the first objection has to rely on: It has to take for granted, that taking others and oneself as persons *and* being treated as a person by others (let's call this the R-condition)[27] are not essential elements in our list of person-making characteristics. If this R-condition is on the list, not even the suggested regulative reading will help, since concerning this item the constitutive reading comes into play again, and the social nature of personhood and personality directly results from this person-making characteristic. But if the R-condition is not on the list, I claim that the person-making characteristics should be regarded as insufficient conditions only so that the status of being a person cannot be reduced to having the features on the list. Certainly, we can criticize someone for treating an entity X as a person even though X does not have the necessary features. And without doubt we can (and should) criticize someone for not treating as a person an entity X, which has the person-making characteristics. But engaging in such criticism *is* a way of regarding X as a person, and admitting that such criticism is adequate does not commit me to the thesis, that being a person can be reduced to having the person-making characteristics.[28]

(ii) The second objection

The THESIS claims that being a person is *essentially* constituted by social relations, which is to say that social relations not only are necessary to develop and actualise the person-making characteristics (minus the R-condition), but are also actually constitutive, in the sense that being a person demands being treated as a person by others and

---

[27] Like Hegel (R, § 36) or Dennett (1976, pp. 177 f.) I am inclined to put these two conditions on the list of person-making characteristics; an analysis of Hegel's concept of a person is given in Quante (2004a).

[28] In personal correspondence Schmid claims that it is neither necessary for being a person that I regard myself as a person, nor that somebody else does. I deny this premise, but I agree that most of the person-making characteristics can be described without referring to the property of 'being a person'. It is just that 'being a person' is simply not reducible to these enabling conditions (minus the R-condition). I thank him for prompting these clarifications.

regarding oneself and others as persons, too. One can be an actual person only within actual social relations.[29] This claim has been challenged by the following counter-example.[30]

Is Robinson Crusoe (while living alone on the island) a counter-example to the THESIS? We can describe his case in such a way that his being a person is constituted by social relations in the causal sense, but not in the sense I call essential. But what is at stake here? Surely we can agree that Robinson still has the person-making characteristics, and we can even accept that he treats himself as a person. So it seems that he is a person.

Well, since this is an extraordinary case I *could* accept this exception to the THESIS, but I think I do not have to: *Either* we who ask ourselves whether Robinson Crusoe is a person in these circumstances thereby provide an instance of the necessary social relation (this means that our consideration of the case is not irrelevant, but counts as one of the constitutive factors). *Or* else our question has changed, since we now want to know whether Robinson Crusoe can take himself to be a person in isolation. Since Robinson Crusoe can remember having been treated as a person and having treated himself and others as persons before, I see no reason to deny this.[31] But accepting this does not commit me to the thesis that being able to do this is sufficient for having the status of being a person. The reason is that Robinson Crusoe's capacity has been constituted by social relations in the past. And although now (when we are debating this question) this is social constitution only in the generic sense, there has been essential constitution in the past.[32]

(iii) The third objection
The worry that the THESIS can give rise to stems from the fact that being a person is an ethically important status — at least in our culture. Is it not a consequence of the THESIS that you cannot mistreat someone in not recognizing him as a person since recognizing him in

---

[29] To be sure, a lot of work has to be done to make explicit the different ways in which social rules and persons are constitutive.

[30] To be sure, arguing in this way is begging the question; but the same holds for the other conclusion. Therefore all I can do here is to show that I can accept everything plausible concerning Robinson Crusoe without being committed to giving up the THESIS. These worries have been raised by Arto Laitinen and Heikki Ikäheimo; my thanks to them for their comments and for prompting me to clarify my position.

[31] Cf. my analysis of Hegel's position concerning 'being a person' and 'being an agent', where I admit this possibility, in Quante (2004b), pp. 73–91.

[32] Someone might want to object that this reply is question-begging. It is so indeed, but the purpose of my argument here is to show that I can give a plausible interpretation of the case compatible with the THESIS.

THE SOCIAL NATURE OF PERSONAL IDENTITY 73

such a way is a necessary condition for his being a person at all? This is a serious challenge, but things are more complicated. Firstly, we have to say that the THESIS does not demand that *everybody* has to treat X as a person to make it the case that X is a person. Secondly: If I consider a scenario in which X has all the features on our list of person-making characteristics except being recognized in his community, I *counterfactually* treat him as a person if I claim that the members of that community have done something wrong. If I *actually* treat X as a person, while other members of my community do not, we can ask (in the default-and-challenge-way) who has made a mistake here regarding the person-making characteristics.[33] Or we can ask who is making a moral mistake. In cases like these it is an open question whether X is a person or not, although it might not be an open question whether X is the bearer of some of the person-making characteristics.[34] Like many other ethical questions, settling this issue is a complicated social affair. As in all these cases, there are facts beyond the ethical or social realm we can refer to if we want to decide whether X is a person. But these facts alone cannot settle the issue since *we* have to decide in the end.

To sum up so far: Personal identity in the sense in which this is the topic of CPP and SPP is *essentially* constituted by social relations, since this dimension of our existence is part of evaluations and meaning, not only function and cause. If we avoid committing ourselves to the existence of Cartesian Egos, souls, or something of that kind, there must be a causal and functional basis describable in impersonal terms or from the sideways-on-view. But this basis can be taken only as the set of enabling conditions since the entities which come into view from within our personal stance are neither reducible to nor identical with those entities which come into view from within the impersonal stance. Since these former entities are not only initiated causally but are what they are only within a social world of shared meanings they are essentially constituted by these social relations.

3.3. Some tentative conclusions

Does the position defended in this paper not commit me to the thesis, well known in the philosophy of mind, that there are no single notions

---

[33] This might be the case when we debate whether human embryos are persons or not.

[34] Another case is that X calls on me to treat her as a person. If I understand this challenge properly, this is sufficient for me to be obliged to treat X as a person. Therefore we have to distinguish carefully between cases of not treating X as a person (maybe mistakenly) and mistreating X as a non-person (knowing that she has called on me to be treated as a person).

of personal 'identity', personhood or person? If 'identity' is taken as unity and as persistence, I have indeed committed myself to this thesis. Indeed I am deeply sceptical about all philosophical attempts to define a notion of person or personhood in which no traces of our being *human* persons are retained. Our concepts are deeply influenced by how things really are, and many philosophical attempts to define purified notions for all logically possible worlds seem to me idle talk. Our intuitions show that we simply do not have clear intuitions in all these science–fiction fantasies that many philosophers dealing with personal 'identity' take at face value. The concept of a person we use and understand is not free from our experiences of being *human* persons.

But there is no conceptual link between 'being a person' and 'being a human being' such that only human beings can be persons. If it is the case that only human beings are capable of being persons this is no conceptually necessary connection. But we do not have a clear opinion about what it is to be a person who is not of the human kind. If one day we meet entities which we cannot but understand as non-human persons, maybe we will learn how to modify our present concept. But we will still have to take *our* understanding as the starting point. Probably we will then learn to use these notions as we have learned to use mental predicates in the case of animals not capable of first-personal mental episodes — in an *analogical* way. As in the case of human pain and Martian pain or the pain of non-human animals: a difference in the essence of pain must not and should not lead to a difference in ethical value.

Sometimes I think coming into contact with non-human persons would prompt the same process of learning we have had, and have to go through when coming into contact with human persons in other cultures. In such — much more familiar — cases the *social* facts are different. And since social facts also frame our self-understanding and our interpretation of what it is to be a person, the situation might be similar. As I do not believe that the discovery of cultural pluralism has led to the discovery of a trans-cultural ethics I do not believe that we will discover a trans-species concept of personhood we can use intelligibly. At other times I am not sure that this line of argument gets things right. But I am sure that we will not get an answer by means of conceptual analysis, or the method of thought experiments.[35]

---

[35] Thanks to Heikki Ikäheimo, Arto Laitinen, Eric Olson, David Schweikard and an anonymous reviewer for many helpful suggestions to improve this paper.

References

Baillie, J. (1993), *Problems in Personal Identity* (New York: Paragon).
Baker, L.R. (2000), *Persons and Bodies* (Cambridge: Cambridge University Press).
Brooks, D.H.M. (1994), *The Unity of the Mind* (New York, St. Martin's Press).
Dennett, D.C. (1976), 'Conditions of personhood', in A. Oksenberg Rorty (ed.), *The Identities of Persons* (Berkeley: University of California Press), pp. 175–96.
Dennett, D.C. (1978), *Brainstorms* (Sussex: Harvester).
Glover, J. (1988), *I: The Philosophy and Psychology of Personal Identity* (London: Penguin).
Hegel, G.W.F. (R), *Grundlinien der Philosophie des Rechts*. Edited by J. Hoffmeister, Hamburg: Felix Meiner Verlag 1955.
Korsgaard, C.M. (1989), 'Personal identity and the unity of agency', *Philosophy & Public Affairs*, **18**, pp. 101–32.
Locke, J. (E), *An Essay Concerning Human Understanding*, edited with an introduction by P.H. Nidditch (Oxford: Clarendon Press, 1975).
Martin, R. (1998), *Self-Concern* (Cambridge: Cambridge University Press).
Martin, R. & Barresi, J. (ed. 2003), *Personal Identity* (Oxford: Blackwell).
Noonan, H. (1989), *Personal Identity* (London: Routledge).
Noonan, H.W. (ed. 1993), *Personal Identity* (Aldershot: Dartmouth).
Oksenberg Rorty (ed. 1976), *The Identities of Persons* (Berkeley: University of California Press).
Olson, E.T. (1997), *The Human Animal* (Oxford: Oxford University Press).
Penelhum, T. (1970), *Survival and Disembodied Existence* (London: Routledge & Kegan Paul).
Perry, J. (ed. 1975), *Personal Identity* (Berkeley: University of California Press).
Perry, J. (2002), *Identity, Personal Identity, and the Self* (Indianapolis: Hackett).
Quante, M. (1995a), 'Die Identität der Person: Facetten eines Problems', *Philosophische Rundschau*, **42**, pp. 35–59.
Quante, M. (1995b), 'Wann ist ein Mensch tot?', *Zeitschrift für philosophische Forschung*, **49**, pp. 167–93.
Quante, M. (1997), 'Ist die diachrone Identität der Person infallible?', in M. Willaschek (ed.), *Feld-Zeit-Kritik* (Münster: LIT), pp. 124-133.
Quante, M. (Ed.) (1999), *Personale Identität* (Paderborn: UTB).
Quante, M. (2001a), 'Menschliche Persistenz', in D. Sturma (ed.), *Person* (Paderborn: Mentis), pp. 223–57.
Quante, M. (2001b), 'On the limits of construction and individualism in social ontology', in: E. Lagerspetz, H. Ikäheimo & J. Kotkavirta (Eds.), *On the Nature of Social and Institutional Reality* (Jyväskylä), pp. 136–64.
Quante, M. (2002), *Personales Leben und menschlicher Tod* (Frankfurt am Main: Suhrkamp Verlag).
Quante, M. (2003), 'Wessen Würde? Welche Diagnose?', in: L. Siep & M. Quante (Hrsg.): *Der Umgang mit dem beginnenden menschlichen Leben* (Münster: LIT), pp. 133–52.
Quante, M. (2004a), '"The personality of the will" as the Principle of Abstract Right', in R.B. Pippin & O. Höffe (ed.), *Hegel on Ethics and Politics* (Cambridge: Cambridge University Press), pp. 81–100.
Quante, M. (2004b), *Hegel's Concept of Action* (Cambridge: Cambridge University Press).
Quante, M. (forthcoming), *Person* (Berlin: DeGruyter).
Rovane, C. (1998), *The Bounds of Agency* (Princeton: Princeton University Press).

Schechtman, M. (1996), *The Constitution of Selves* (Ithaca, NY: Cornell University Press).
Schechtman, M. (2002), 'Self and self-interest', in: A. Musschenga, W. van Haaften, B. Spiecker & M. Slors (Eds.), *Personal and Moral Identity* (Dordrecht: Kluwer Academic Publishers), pp. 25–49.
Siep, L. (ed. 1983), *Identität der Person* (Basel, Schwabe).
Strawson, G. (1997), 'The Self', *Journal of Consciousness Studies*, **4** (5–6), pp. 405–28.
Sturma, D. (ed. 2001), *Person* (Paderborn: Mentis).
Velleman, J.D. (1996), 'Self to Self', *Philosophical Review*, **105**, pp. 39–76.
Vesey, G. (1974), *Personal Identity* (Ithaca, NY: Cornell University Press).
Wiggins, D. (2001), *Sameness and Substance Renewed* (Cambridge: Cambridge University Press).
Wilkes, K. (1988), *Real People* (Oxford: Clarendon Press).

Dieter Sturma

Person as Subject

Abstract: *Persons are present in the social realm of reasons and make active use of their ability to express themselves. They have a sense of self-reference and lead their lives in the perspective of possible self-consciousness and possible autonomy. For understanding what it means for a person to be a subject one must avoid egological reifications. Expressions like 'self' or 'self-reference' do not refer to entities. They can only be introduced in a way that meets standards of semantic control. Self-reference proves to be an inner-worldly phenomenon that expresses itself indirectly in reflexive attitudes and activities over time.*

1. Introduction

Egological expressions like 'I' or 'self' have been introduced by philosophy in the course of its exploration into the realm of human consciousness. In particular, the epistemology and philosophy of mind in the 17th century pioneers in answering the traditional question 'what is man?' with the help of an egological vocabulary that consists mainly of linguistic reifications of personal pronouns and a corresponding system of indicators, quasi-indicators and reflexives. The egological vocabulary has to be considered as a semantic and systematic innovation. It was not used in ancient philosophy. We can find first traces of this innovation in Augustine. He brings the principle of inwardness into philosophy. According to this principle, reflecting persons have a particular epistemic attitude to their own mental states. Descartes uses this principle in developing his famous *existo*-argument — but without using the expressions 'I' (*Ego, moi*) in a specific philosophical sense. He still works with the old concept of a *substantia cogitans*. It was Locke and Leibniz who developed the specific

Correspondence:
dieter.sturma@uni-bonn.de

philosophical sense of reified personal pronouns. With the expressions 'self' or '*moi*' they refer to a subject in the dimension of human consciousness that is characterized by self-awareness, inwardness and reflection. Yet, we can find no extensive analysis of the meaning of 'self' and related concepts in their works or in other classical works of epistemology and philosophy of mind. They presuppose a general meaning of egological concepts, but never spell it out.

Looking back on the conceptual politics of the classical philosophy of mind since the 17th century, one can identify in a first semantic approximation a general function of the egological expressions. Although the expression 'self' has sometimes been used as a synonym for 'person' or even 'soul', it mostly designates the internal subject of the identity of self-consciousness over time, or the subjective perspective of consciousness and self-consciousness that is persistent over time. Because of this persistence many philosophers have been tempted to treat 'self' as an expression for an object or at least for a quasi-object. Despite the early criticisms of Hume and Kant egological reifications secured their place in the philosophy of mind and related disciplines in the humanities and social sciences, which they still have not completely lost. Correspondingly, self-consciousness or self-awareness has been understood as a specific epistemic attitude of a reflecting person toward herself.

The last two centuries witnessed the decline and fall of classical egological vocabulary. This process started already in classical German philosophy with the criticism of narrow egological conceptions of subjectivity, and was pushed forward by thinkers like Schopenhauer, Nietzsche, Darwin, and Freud who raised fundamental doubts on the alleged sovereignty of the self. In contemporary philosophy the egological vocabulary was attacked from two sides: from the neostructuralist movement, with its proclamation of the death of the subject (see Foucault, 1966, pp. 333 ff.; 1994), and from the linguistically orientated analytic philosophy (see Ryle, 1949). Although the neostructuralist line of criticism received a great deal of attention, its arguments never reached a sufficient degree of systematic clarity.[1] On the other hand, the criticism coming from analytic philosophy touched the core of traditional philosophy of mind. These criticisms purported to show that the traditional concepts of the 'I' and the 'self' have no

---

[1] Neostructuralism simply declared the 'death of the subject' but never referred to specific arguments of the classical philosophy of mind. The neostructuralist criticism does not take into account that prominent classical positions of German Idealism — like the ones of Fichte, Schelling and Hegel — show no inclination to presuppose a sovereignty of a self or subject in the sense of an individual person.

referent. Conceptual analysis merely left space for weak conceptions of subjectivity that focus on 'qualia', 'higher-order states' or 'meta-representation' — in other words, for conceptions of subjectivity that eschew any genuine reference to the self.

The expression 'person' has remained largely unaffected by the severe criticisms that have been directed against traditional accounts of the mind, and it has survived the huge wave of linguistic criticism that has been directed against egological vocabulary. This immunity of the concept in question may be due to its social significance and its apparent lack of explicit reference to a self. The concept of the person generally refers to someone who can act and react in the social space of reasons. As an actor in the social space of reason, a person is both a subject and object of self-ascription, and ascriptions of specific self-relations and practical attitudes. For example, in talking about the recognition and rights of a person, one does not necessarily refer to any strong conception of the self, and one can avoid any explicit use of other egological terms. Additionally, much attention has been paid to the importance of the concept of the 'person' in recent bioethical controversies. Yet, in the field of bioethics, the meaning of the concept often remains vague or ideologically laden. Bracketing the question of self-reference, the concept of personhood nonetheless presents us with a broad, and sometimes blurred, semantic field that stretches from early 20th century debates in philosophical anthropology to specific areas in contemporary analytic philosophy, from controversial deployment in bioethics to uncontroversial use in ordinary language.

Nevertheless, the concept of person is one of the last concepts from the philosophical tradition that is still allowed in contemporary discussions. Although the absence of any explicit reference to the 'self' has definitely contributed to the survival of the concept person, it is not ultimately wholly independent of egological vocabulary. Given neostructuralist and analytic criticisms, it may be dangerous to unveil this dependence, but one should not seek the uneasy peace that results from superficial misunderstanding. In the following, therefore, the framework of the philosophy of person is reconstructed in relation to its egological commitments and, more specifically, in relation to the concept of the self. The analysis of the self-referential features in the life of a person will be restricted to a conception of the self as the perspective of an individual being.[2] Thus an abstract conception of the subject, like that presented in Spinoza or Hegel, will be excluded. This discussion prepares the ground for a constructive and methodo-

---

[2] In the narrow sense, the term 'subject' designates a self-referential perspective — not a self.

logically clarified account of the semantics of 'person', an account that includes the concept of the self, and yet avoids the standard criticisms of conceptual analysis. This conception of the person will be in the position to carry much of the burden of self-reference in philosophy of mind *and* ethics.

As pointed out, the concept of the self has been developed in philosophical theories and has later found its way into everyday language. At least metaphorically one can thus speak of the term 'self' (or 'I') as a philosophical invention. Despite its seemingly unproblematic use in everyday language, however, the concept of the self presents a number of peculiarities that are connected with the somewhat atypical phenomenon of self-consciousness. Considering this complicated development, it should come as no surprise that the meaning of the term 'self' remains controversial. In the aftermath of the linguistic turn, a straightforward definition cannot be expected. One has to follow a more complicated strategy: because of the constructive origins of the egological vocabulary, one has to reconstruct the rise and fall of the concept of the self in modern philosophy since Descartes. Only after a systematic evaluation of the classical theories of subjectivity will it be possible to secure a place for the concept of the self in contemporary philosophy. One should also be aware that these classical theories have been distorted by a number of simplistic and polemical interpretations. This is especially true for Descartes' approach, an approach that many contemporary thinkers hold responsible for the pitfalls of the philosophy of mind.[3] Therefore, the contemporary philosophy of personhood must first revise a number of popular misconceptions about traditional positions on the self and subjectivity.

The expression 'person as subject' can only be analysed in relation to a semantically controlled concept of the self, that is, one that avoids Cartesian reifications and starts with a non-reifying account of an inner-wordly self-awareness. This does not mean that nothing can be gained from Cartesian insights. It will turn out that the systematic fate of the concepts 'person' and 'self' are, in fact, intertwined. An analysis of 'person as subject' requires a broad theoretical perspective on subjectivity, one that includes both the insights of traditional and contemporary philosophy — with special emphasis on Descartes, Kant, Heidegger, Wittgenstein and Sellars.

---

[3] See, for example, Kenny (1989) and Dennett (1991).

2. The Philosophical Discovery of Self-consciousness

Descartes' epistemology lays the systematic ground for the concepts of the 'self' and 'self-consciousness'. Through his method of radical doubt, Descartes undermines the certainty of our experience and questions the referential relationship between mental states and the world of objects and events. He discovers that with the exception of immediate self-awareness and expressions of analytical truth, all propositional attitudes are in principle open to error. Neither tradition, nor sense perception, nor linguistic reference is immune to doubt. But in a situation in which I express or mentally conceive the sentence, 'I exist,' it is impossible for me to be wrong. The linguistic expression of my existence cannot be doubted at the moment of its utterance. The sentence, 'I do not exist,' is self-defeating, since it already presupposes the very existence that it denies.[4]

Descartes views this kind of self-evidence as the paradigm of a clear and distinct idea, one that remains untouched by sceptical considerations. However, he also believes that we can deduce, 'from this self-evident awareness of our own existence, the sentence 'sum res cogitans'. He argues that all propositions about myself apart from those asserting my existence and the presence of my consciousness, can be called into question. Accordingly, the only certain truth about my existence is that I am a thinking thing — 'sum tantum res cogitans' (see Descartes, 1964, VI. 9). This claim first introduces the philosophy of the self, even though the formula, 'sum res cogitans,' does not contain the term 'self'. The pivotal role of this claim is surprising, since there is no obvious sense in which this formula adds anything new to more traditional conceptions of the substance. Descartes' innovation is indeed obscured by his use of the concept of substance, for the innovative elements of his approach actually stem from his discovery of the principle of inwardness. According to this principle, consciousness and reflection form the basis of knowledge. Thus Hegel rightly pointed out that Descartes' principle of inwardness presented a turning point in modern philosophy (cf. Hegel, 1971, p. 120). Descartes' systematic introduction of consciousness retained its foundational significance throughout the history of modern philosophy, and in more recent times its importance has only been somewhat reduced by the linguistic turn.

---

[4] See Descartes (1964), II. 3; cf. Ayer (1956), pp. 44-52. Descartes operates in this passage with the formula 'I exist', but the certainty of self-consciousness expresses itself also in the formula 'I think'. The formula 'I think' (*cogito*) covers all forms of mental activities (*cogitationes*). That is why a sentence like 'I *believe* there is a unicorn' is undubitable as long as it is used authentically.

Descartes' principle of inwardness stands in sharp contrast to the traditional assumption that there is a symmetric relation between the *modus essendi*, the way of being, and the *modus intelligendi*, the way of knowing. Earlier periods in philosophy were aware of subjectivity and consciousness, but with the possible exception of Augustine, they did not assign systematic significance to these phenomena. From the perspective of everyday experience, it is not necessary to learn the physiology of the eye in order to see, and in a similar sense, for a long time there was no epistemological interest in consciousness or self-consciousness — despite the important role of self-reference in propositional attitudes. Admittedly, there were approaches like nominalism, which early on presented challenges to this traditional understanding, but this exception does not alter the general picture.

The title of Descartes' Second Meditation expresses the essence of the principle of inwardness: the nature of the human mind is better known than the body. Regardless of its dualist implications, this title indicates that the thinking person should provide the decisive starting point for every epistemological investigation. Neither tradition nor external authority provides us with epistemological guarantees; instead, the subject must find such guarantees within the realm of the mind. This is Descartes' version of Augustine's formula, '*in interiore homine habitat veritas*' (Augustine, 2006, XII.1).

The core of the principle of inwardness is the *existo*-argument of the Second Meditation. We should note that this argument does not contain the famous phrase, 'cogito ergo sum'. The truth of the *existo*-argument is already accessible from the perspective of everyday experience. The reasons for this, however, can only be revealed in epistemological reflection, and it is likely that Descartes himself was unaware of these reasons. He asserts that a dubitable sentence, like 'S sees x,' becomes certain if it can be transformed into a sentence like 'I am aware that I see x'. In this respect, there is a difference between 'cogito' and 'existo,' because the expression 'existo' already presupposes the activity of thinking. Every state of certainty of my existence is already a state of consciousness. Therefore the *cogito*-argument is more comprehensive and includes the *existo*-argument. This can be interpreted as the priority of the 'I think' over the 'I exist'. That is why, the 'ergo' in Descartes' 'cogito ergo sum' is by no means redundant, contrary to what Alfred Ayer claimed in his famous criticism of Descartes (cf. Ayer, 1956, pp. 44–52).

The certainty of the *cogito*-argument as well as of the *existo*-argument depends on the semantic context of the self-referential assertion of existence: in grammatical terms, the assertion must be made in the first-person singular, present tense, indicative, active. The self-referential expression of existence must be specified by the pronoun 'I'. But the indicating function of the pronoun 'I' should not be confused with the 'I' as a metaphysical concept. In other words, the indicator 'I' should not be transformed into a term that stands for a substance.

With the principle of inwardness, Descartes has left us a complex heritage since an essential part of this heritage does consist in the reification of the self — i. e. in the assumption that the term 'I' refers to a thing. This assumption makes traditional philosophy of mind seem unacceptable to many contemporary philosophers. Yet, the reification of the self is only one part of the Cartesian heritage. Descartes' legacy also includes his discovery of the systematic function of the 'cogito' and the irreducibility of self-consciousness. The Cartesian heritage is thus a complex matter, and one should shy away from hasty rejections *in toto*.

3. The Rejection of Reification and Self-Identification

Empiricist theories have criticized the semantic reification of the term 'self' harshly. Hume's epistemology represents this type of criticism. He conceives a mental geography that limits the realm of experience to the intentional contents of consciousness. According to Hume (1978), 'we can never conceive any thing but perceptions' (p. 216). For Hume, self-consciousness is the awareness of conscious states as conscious: he says, 'consciousness is nothing, but a reflected thought or perception' (p. 635). Introspection can show merely the contents of mental states, and does not reveal a subject of consciousness:

> When I turn my reflection on *myself*, I never can perceive this *self* without some one or more perceptions; nor can I ever perceive any thing but the perceptions. 'Tis the composition of these, therefore, which forms the self (p. 634).

This criticism is later taken up by Husserl,[5] who identifies the subject of thought with the unity of mental contents (*Verknüpfungseinheit*) (Husserl, 1975, p. 10). This approach to consciousness, however, provides no explanation as to how the mental data, which appear successively at different points in time, can be understood as elements of *one* or unified experience of distinct objects. Hume explicitly admits this to be a problem for his theory, since the propositional content of experience cannot be explained by the linear succession of mental data:

---

[5] Cf. Husserl (1975), Chap. 1. Husserl later changed his theory with regard to this point.

> But all my hopes vanish, when I come to explain the principles that unite our successive perceptions in our thought or consciousness. I cannot discover any theory, which gives me satisfaction on this head (Hume, 1978, pp. 635f.).

Kant's famous criticism of the empiricist conception of the subject is that a merely functional connection of mental events would add up to a 'multicoloured self', which would be as manifold and disconnected as the events (cf. Kant, 1968a, p. 134). He argues that mental data cannot set themselves in relation to each other by their content alone. Solely on their own, such data 'know' nothing about each other. This, however, does not mean that one is allowed to return to Cartesian reifications. According to Kant, the subject of consciousness can only be known indirectly through the structuring of mental contents. His critical concept of a subject designates only an instance of self-reference and does not contain any predicates of a *substantia cogitans*.

In his influential criticism of Descartes' philosophy of mind, Gilbert Ryle denies any special status for the phenomenon of self-consciousness. He interprets self-consciousness as simply a higher order state of consciousness.

> To concern oneself about oneself in any way, theoretical or practical, is to perform a higher order act, just as it is to concern oneself about anybody else (Ryle, 1949, p. 195).

According to Ryle, higher order states of consciousness are non-reflexive: they do not contain themselves, and they cannot report anything about themselves. Ryle states that self-commentary is logically condemned to eternal penultimacy.[6] He claims that there is nothing out of the ordinary about the phenomenon of self-consciousness. He argues that any attempt to attach other properties to self-referential mental acts falls prey to the 'systematic elusiveness of the self':

> The only anomaly of the 'I' consists in its systematic elusiveness: 'I' is like my own shadow; I can never get away from it, as I can get away from your shadow. There is no mystery about this constancy, but I mention it, because it seems to endow 'I' with a mystifying uniqueness and adhesiveness (Ryle, 1949, p. 198).

Although Ryle's criticism of self-reference might appear somewhat superficial, his basic point, that the concept of the 'I' or 'self' does not identify an object, is generally accepted. It is almost a commonplace in contemporary philosophy that self-consciousness is not identical

---

[6] See Ryle (1949), p. 195. Cf. also James (1967), p. 6: 'To say that I am self-conscious, or conscious of putting forth volition, means only that certain contents, for which self and "effort of will" are the names, are not without witness as they occur.'

with self-identification — i.e. with picking oneself out as a particular object. But here one has to keep in mind that the illusions of Cartesian philosophy are related to self-identification only, and not to self-awareness or self-reference in general.

The difference between self-*identification* and self-*reference* is clarified by Wittgenstein. He reveals the linguistic reason behind Descartes' fallacy:

> We feel then that in the cases in which 'I' is used as subject, we don't use it because we recognize a particular person by his bodily characteristics; and this creates the illusion that we use this word to refer to something bodiless, which, however, has its seat in our body. In fact this seems to be the real ego, the one of which it was said, 'Cogito, ergo sum' (Wittgenstein, 1964, p. 69).

Wittgenstein shows that the expression 'I' is an important semantic element of self-referential attitudes but it does not identify a self or something with bodily characteristics. However, Wittgenstein does not deny 'the peculiar grammar of the word 'I'':

> The word 'I' does not mean the same as 'L.W.' even if I am L.W., nor does it mean the same as the expression 'the person who is now speaking'. But that doesn't mean: that 'L. W.' and 'I' mean different things. All it means is that these words are different instruments in our language.[7]

Wittgenstein's analysis of the peculiar grammar of 'I' confirms the special status of self-consciousness. He works out the complicated linguistic system of self-referential expressions and does not adopt an eliminativist position. Nevertheless, some successors of Wittgenstein turned his reflections on self-referential terms into an expression theory. According to the expression theory, a referential term consists in general of two elements: use and reference. The concept 'I' is, however, on this view, defined solely by its use: the term 'I' — unlike other singular terms such as names, indexicals, and definite descriptions – has no referential function.[8] This approach obviously follows the strategy of elimination by mere definition, yet it has significantly contributed to Anti-Cartesian tendencies in recent philosophy of mind.

Recent evaluations of the concept of self-reference in analytic philosophy reveal a difference between self-identification and self-reference, even though they do not identify objects in the same

---

[7] Wittgenstein (1964), p. 67. Cf. Ryle (1949), p. 197: 'An "I" sentence indicates whom in particular it is about by being itself uttered or written by someone in particular. "I" indicates the person who utters it.' Wittgenstein has pointed out that this not the meaning of 'I'.

[8] Cf. Anscombe (1975); Malcolm (1979); Kenny (1979).

manner as other singular terms. The absence of an identifiable object of reference in self-consciousness does not imply the absence of any referential structure in self-consciousness. On the contrary, states of consciousness must involve some kind of reference to a subject of consciousness that can interpret itself in time. This hints at a unique form of reference that has no direct analogue in the realm of spatio-temporal objects. An account of such unique states of self-reference can already be found in Kant's epistemology.[9]

4. The Systematic Function of 'I think'

Kant agrees with Hume and contemporary analytic philosophy that the concepts 'I' and 'self' do not designate an object or fulfil the function of a proper name. But the systematic elusiveness of the egological vocabulary never led Kant to doubt that the 'I that thinks' is, nevertheless, a subject. He is the first to recognize that self-consciousness is not a cognitive attitude in the traditional sense. His theory of self-consciousness unfolds as a reconstruction of the epistemological function of the 'I think'. This theory is constituted by transcendental concepts, which are supposed to determine the conditions of possible experience in general. Within Kant's systematic evaluation of experience, the expression 'I think' is a constitutive function of all propositional attitudes without itself being a datum or object of thought. It stands for the structure of consciousness in the sense of possible self-consciousness. The 'I think' thus stands not for actual self-awareness, but for the specific form of consciousness. This form is the reason for the capability of persons to have self-consciousness with regards to all their tokens of consciousness.

While self-ascriptions refer to properties and dispositions of persons in space and time, and therefore, belong within the context of propositional attitudes, the 'I think' forms the base of all mental acts, and under no circumstances can it be turned into an intentional object of consciousness. Since self-consciousness only reveals itself *within* a process of thinking *something*, it would be senseless to look for an invariant 'I' that stands for an inner object. This peculiar feature of the 'I' explains its systematic elusiveness. Kant's 'I think' thus implicitly or explicitly denotes self-reference, and there can be no knowledge of an I or a self beyond the relations of the subject of consciousness. For

---

[9] See Sturma (1997), pp. 129–46.

this reason, Kant holds that the principle of the identity of self-consciousness is an analytic sentence.[10]

The conceptual difference, between the identity of self-consciousness over time and the identity that exists in all my self-ascriptions, corresponds to the difference between the concept of the self and the concept of the person. It also indicates the difference between the epistemology and the ontology of persons. The identity of self-consciousness over time presents itself in the self-referential structures of mental acts, while the subsistence of persons rests upon the conditions of existence in space and time. Therefore, the expression 'I exist thinking' is expressed in synthetic judgements that depend on given intuitions (cf. Kant, 1968a, B 409).

Kant coins the formula, 'I exist thinking' to express the unity of self-consciousness and existence (cf. Kant, 1968a, B 420). In this formula the expression, 'I exist,' takes on the shape of an empirical sentence: 'I exist thinking'.[11] In the sentence, 'I exist thinking,' Kant has found a precise formula for the complicated relation between the concepts of existence, self and self-consciousness. His embedded 'I think' does not reject the Cartesian starting point, but places it in an empirically meaningful context. In doing this, Kant demonstrates the connection between the semantics of self in the sense of a subjective perspective and person as a subject in space and time. In the expression 'I exist thinking' he merges the *existo*-argument and the *cogito*-argument. For a person, existing means existing *as* thinking. Her self-consciousness turns out to be a self-referential process in time wherein 'I exist' and 'I think' are inseparable for the person who lives her life in space and time. This is the reason why Kant takes the sentence 'I exist thinking' to be an empirical sentence. Self-consciousness does not set the person apart from the world – as Descartes' *existo*-argument suggests, but places her in the world and unveils her being *in* the world.

5. The Irreducibility of Subjectivity

In addition to the difficulties involved in clarifying the concept of self-consciousness, a contemporary philosophy of person must face the challenge of eliminative naturalism. The natural sciences supply

---

[10] See Kant (1998), B 408: 'The proposition of the identity of myself in everything manifold of which I am conscious is equally one lying in the concepts themselves, and hence an analytic proposition.'

[11] See Kant (1998), B 428: 'The proposition 'I think' or 'I exist thinking,' is an empirical proposition.'

an abundance of theories and models that reveal the physical and biological dependent conditions of the human life-form. Many naturalist approaches interpret this dependence as a proof of the eliminativist claim that the life of a person, like the existence of all other spatio-temporal objects, can be reduced to a network of chance and necessity. Although this interpretation does not follow from the physical and biological dependence of the human life-form, it has not left philosophical discussions unaffected. In particular, many contemporary philosophers of mind take the methodology of the eliminativistic version of naturalism for granted, and focus exclusively on the objective perspective of the third-person, completely ignoring the first person perspective (cf. Churchland, 1986).

Scientific eliminativism manifests itself as a radicalization of naturalism — but is not identical with naturalism in general. While naturalistic approaches assume that the world of nature, including the human life-form, constitutes a closed system, scientific eliminativism takes the language of the natural sciences as the indisputable authority on what there is.[12] The approach of scientific eliminativism excludes on metaphysical grounds the most important realm of the philosophy of mind: the epistemic, emotive and moral states of self-conscious persons. Mental states and acts have a number of properties that can be addressed in a narrow physicalist theory, but they all require the first-person perspective — otherwise, one could not speak of experience at all.

Narrative theories of the self, which are held by Derek Parfit, Daniel Dennett, and Richard Rorty, present another approach that is antagonistic to traditional approaches. These narrative theories present a subtle form of eliminativism. They assume that there are only self-representations without a centre, and they envisage the experience of a person in terms of a weak form of continuity. They compare the identity of self-consciousness with the identity of associations like clubs, nations, and information networks. Accordingly, they construe the self as an illusion of a narrative centre of gravity.[13]

---

[12] There are a number of problems with scientific eliminativism. These problems include: (a) ontological generalization, (b) the one-sided use of nomological and deductive methods of explanation, and (c) the lack of sound epistemological justification. The internal difficulties of the physicalist approach cannot be further pursued here. For a critique of eliminativism in the philosophy of mind, see Sturma (1997), pp. 58–96, Sturma (2005), pp. 26–44.

[13] See Dennett (1991), p. 425 f.: 'A self, according to my theory, is not any old mathematical point, but an abstraction defined by the myriads of attributions and interpretations (including self-attributions and self-interpretations) that have composed the biography of the living body whose Center of Narrative Gravity it is. As such, it plays a singularly important

Dennett and Rorty's narrative theory of self-consciousness presents a good example of the multi-coloured self — i.e. of a self that merely consists in the succession of mental events. Kant exerted the entire weight of his epistemology against this conception of the multicoloured self. A multi-coloured self would be a self without identity of self-consciousness over time, and thus it could not know anything about itself.[14] But Parfit, Dennett, and Rorty do not draw these inevitable conclusions. They remain in an inconsistent twilight zone, exploiting features of self-consciousness and the narrative sense of self, without acknowledging the epistemological necessity of justifying the concept of the identity of self-consciousness over time. Nonetheless, a contemporary philosophy of the person must learn from these various eliminativist strategies. Specifically, it must provide an inner-worldly account of self-awareness as a cornerstone for the analysis of self-reference and the mind.

The strategy of eliminativism assumes on the whole a very simple understanding of the world. We should question the adequacy of this account in the light of the complex reality in which we live. For instance, it is not clear that an acceptance of naturalistic assumptions automatically precludes the epistemic and moral perspective of a person. In this regard, the history of philosophy provides some important alternatives. We find examples of non-eliminativist naturalism in almost every period of the history of philosophy; these examples include Aristotle, the Stoics, Leibniz, Spinoza, Rousseau, Kant, Schelling, and Hegel. One might also mention Wittgenstein, Feigl, Sellars, Strawson, McGinn and McDowell.[15] None of these thinkers succumb to the temptation of premature elimination, and they work with a complex model of reality, a model that includes monistic features in its ontology and dualistic features in its epistemology. They follow a method that avoids the extremes of scientific eliminativism without falling back on the dogmatic dualism of mind and body. A good example of this approach can be found in Herbert Feigl's philosophy of mind. As one of the founders of the Vienna Circle, Feigl never seriously questioned the methodical paradigm of Logical Empiricism. Still, he remained unconvinced that the problem of the relation

---

role in the ongoing cognitive economy of that living body, because, of all things in the environment an active body must make mental models of, none is more crucial than the model the agent has of itself.'

[14] Kant distinguishes between the identity of self-consciousness over time and the identity of a person, see Kant (1968 a), A 361-A 366, A 381-A 405.

[15] Cf. MacArthur, De Caro (2004).

between mind and body constitutes a mere pseudo-problem.[16] His philosophy of mind is characterized by the approach to intergrate an adequate phenomenology of human consciousness into a monist ontology.

Non-eliminativist approaches to mind in general and self-consciousness in particular have gained ground in recent philosophy.[17] These positions take up arguments for the irreducibility of subjectivity, and they try to overcome the established opposition between traditional and analytical philosophy of mind. In Kant's epistemology we already find the outlines of an approach that combines a weak form of naturalism with a non-eliminativist account of the mind.

According to Kant's original insight, philosophy of mind must treat the first- and the third-person perspectives as equally irreducible. This sets Kant apart from the post-Kantian constructions of German Idealism, in which an anonymous third-person perspective, in the guise of a first-person perspective, is dominant.[18] It also sets him apart from the main stream of contemporary philosophy of mind, which is dominated by behaviouristic, functionalistic and materialistic accounts that rely exclusively upon the third-person perspective.

There are a number of important approaches in contemporary philosophy of mind that develop non-eliminativistic perspectives. Colin McGinn has developed an argument for the irreducibility of a dual aspect approach. He argues for the doctrine of *perceptual closure*, for the claim that we can never become directly aware of the connections between our conscious states and their underlying physical conditions. Donald Davidson proposes a different method. He points out that we must expect anomalies when determining the connection between mental states and events. His concept of 'anomalous monism'[19] accepts the validity of monism without thereby supposing that subjective experiences can be eliminated. Davidson explicitly

---

[16] See Feigl (1967), pp. 4 and 6: 'Positivism, more distinctly than any other point of view, with its notorious phobia of metaphysical problems and its marked tendency toward reductionism, was always ready to diagnose the mind-body puzzle as a *Scheinproblem*. [...] I am convinced, along with many contemporary philosophical analysts and logicians of science that *all* of these problems have been unnecessarily complicated by conceptual confusion, and to that extent are gratuitous puzzles and pseudoproblems. But I feel that we have not yet done *full* justice to any of them.' Cf. Sturma (1998).

[17] Such positions are held among others by Chisholm, Castañeda, Perry, Nagel, McGinn, and McDowell.

[18] In German Idealism concepts like 'I' (*Ich*) or 'subject' do not refer to a subjective view, but to general features of human consciousness.

[19] Davidson (1980), p. 214. The notion is indebted to Feigl's concept of nomological danglers, see Feigl (1967), p. 61; cf. Sturma, (1998), pp. 80–3.

refers to Kant, who first made the paradigmatic attempt to combine naturalism and epistemological dualism.

6. Semantic Descent

Traditional philosophy of mind has left an ambivalent legacy. While both the discovery of the systematic function of the expression 'I think,' and the proof of the irreducibility of subjectivity proved invaluable, the reification of the concepts 'I' and 'self' should be rejected. The move from '*sum tantum res cogitans*' to 'I exist thinking', as paradigmatically performed by Kant, cannot be reversed. The same applies to the semantic transformation from a conception of the 'I' as a noun to an account of the 'I' as a self-referential indicator. The implicit reifications of the egological vocabulary in traditional philosophy of mind should remind us of the importance of semantic sensitivity: sentences like 'I have a self', and 'I am a self' should be understood metaphorically rather than literally.

It seems to be the fate of the traditional heritage that it is only viewed in the light of its obvious weaknesses. If the contributions of the classical philosophy of mind were properly understood in all of their complexities, contemporary approaches would benefit greatly. The alternative between traditional dogmatism and contemporary eliminativism can be avoided when the presupposition that the concept of the self refers to something directly is abandoned. Semantically, this concept cannot stand alone: it must refer to a subject in space and time. Nonetheless the concept fulfils an explanatory function with regard to the deep structure of human consciousness, as Kant showed in his systematic interpretation of the expression 'I think'. Therefore, the self must be conceived in the sense of a self-referential perspective as an inner-worldly phenomenon. If we want to secure a place for the concept of the self in contemporary philosophy, we must support the concept with empirical content and self-referential structures. These criteria are fulfilled by the concept of a person, a concept that stands for a subject located in space and time. Accordingly, a contemporary philosophy of person, which addresses the linguistic means of self-understanding, leads beyond dogmatic dualism, on the one hand, and linguistic or scientific eliminativism, on the other hand.

The interpretative function of the egological vocabulary is paradigmatically reconstructed in the semantic constructivism of Wilfrid Sellars (1956), though he focuses more on mentalistic vocabulary in general, and does not pay specific attention to egological vocabulary. Sellars' analysis is nonetheless helpful for the semantic clarification of self-referential expressions. According to his approach, mentalistic vocabulary should be treated in the same manner as other theoretical concepts. This account provides an answer to the question, 'what is the thinker doing?' (Ryle, 1971). Mentalistic expressions describe or explain the observable behaviour of a person. They designate the self-understanding that constitutes the form of a human life, and do not literally depict an object. The cultural development of expressions like 'person', 'self-consciousness' and 'self', both in philosophy and in ordinary language, provides strong evidence for this approach.

7. Self and Person

The concepts of 'person' and 'self' have different histories; these histories do not converge until the late 17th century. The philosophical term 'person' goes back to Middle Stoicism, and throughout history its meaning has undergone several expansions and retractions. The semantics of this concept were connected with metaphysics, theology, ethics, philosophy of mind, and everyday psychology. In Antiquity and the Middle Ages, the concept of the person does not presuppose or include the notion of the self. Although the concept of the person received a metaphysical and moral status, it lacked any explicit conception of self-consciousness. As we have seen, the semantic outlines of the concept of the self first – and only implicitly – emerge in the philosophy of Descartes.

Locke is the first to establish a connection between the person and the self. His account fuses the semantics of the concept of the self with the semantics of the concept of the person. For Locke a person is a thinking, intelligent being that has reason and reflection, a being that can consider itself as itself. It is a being that can recognize itself as the same thinking thing in different times and places.[20] With the notion of concern, Locke introduces practical and moral components into his conception of the person.[21] In Locke, 'self', 'reflection', 'reason', and 'morality' constitute essential elements in the concept of the person. However, it is not always clear whether the terms 'self' and 'person'

---

[20] Cf. Locke (1975), p. 335 [II. 27 § 9] 'This being premised to find wherein *personal Identity* consists, we must consider what *Person* stands for; which, I think, is a thinking intelligent Being, that has reason and reflection, and can consider it self as it self, the same thinking thing in different times and places [...].'

[21] Cf. Locke (1975), pp. 345 f. [II. 27 § 25]: 'This every intelligent Being, sensible of Happiness or Misery, must grant, that there is something that is *himself*, that he is concerned for, and would have happy; that this *self* has existed in a continued Duration more than one instant, and therefore 'tis possible may exist, as it has done [...].'

have the same meaning for him. While he often uses both terms interchangeably, he sometimes uses the term 'self' in the narrow sense to designate the subject of self-consciousness, without being aware that he is thereby deviating from the established synonymy of the concepts 'self' and 'person'.

Looking back on Locke's approach, and bearing in mind the systematic problems in recent philosophical positions, it should be clear that his thesis about the synonymy of the concepts 'person' and 'self' cannot be justified. In particular, Kant has shown that the concepts 'self' and 'person' belong to different semantic fields.[22] It is obvious that Locke did not notice the difference between the identity of self-consciousness and identity of a person through time, and this disregard leads to a number of flaws in his theory.

Despite its apparent weakness, Locke's position had a great deal of influence on the course of the modern philosophy of person. The methodical gains in his arguments can be seen by means of a rough comparison with Descartes. According to Locke, the 'soul' and the 'unity of consciousness' are not coextensive concepts. Locke replaces metaphysical speculations with a new set of considerations regarding the facts of consciousness. The subject of consciousness is no longer analysed with regard to properties of a soul or *res cogitans*, but rather, it is analysed in terms of identifiable connections in consciousness, such as those formed by memory and concern. This empirical approach allows for an incorporation of the concept of the self into the philosophy of the person, even after the linguistic turn. The concept of the person plays a role in theoretical language games, as well as in the language games of everyday life. It can be approached in terms of a number of related notions, including 'self-reference', 'intentionality', ' the space of reasons', 'reasons for action', 'life-plan', 'recognition', and 'respect'. The semantic core of the concept of a person can be summarized by saying that the term 'person' refers to a being that lives in a social space and possesses the capacity for self-consciousness, deliberation, and action.

Within the main stream of contemporary philosophy, the concept of the person signifies the more or less uncontroversial subject of epistemic and moral attitudes. In fields of applied ethics, such as bioethics, however, the semantics have not yet been sufficiently clarified. Particularly, the temporal extension of the concept 'person' is contested. The debate unfolds between two extremes, the first of which equates personal and biological life, and the second of which

---

[22] See section 4.

limits the notion of a person to temporal periods of self-conscious activity.

Recent approaches in the philosophy of person modify the classical problems of the philosophy of the self in accordance with new methodological considerations. The controversy between the simple view and the complex view of a person is an example of the continuation of classical theoretical options. The simple view construes self-consciousness and personal identity as facts that are not open to empirical verification.[23] This theoretical perspective even considers the possibility that personal existence persists after the disintegration of the body. In contrast, the complex view maintains that self-consciousness and personal identity can only be understood on the basis of material and psychological relations or continuities.[24]

Another discussion regarding the concept of the person focuses on practical attitudes and self-referential evaluation over time.[25] John Rawls, Thomas Nagel, Harry Frankfurt, and Charles Taylor have emphasized the relationship between the standpoint of a person and her normative perspectives over time. They differentiate between a person that remains on the surface of behaviour within the social realm, and a person that makes value judgements and secures by this her identity over time. In this context, it becomes apparent that time consciousness is a constitutive element of personal existence. Leading the life of a person depends upon an epistemic and practical understanding of one's position in time. To summarize, one can say that contemporary philosophical accounts of the person deal with epistemic and moral attitudes that constitute the centre of the human life-form.

8. Space of Reasons and Sense of Self-reference

The expression of the personal standpoint is deeply rooted in the syntax of human language. Sellars describes this as our presence in the logical space of reasons. He gives the example of the use of predicates. The term 'red' would not be a predicate if it did not possess the syntactic characteristics that are common to all predicates.[26] These characteristics go hand in hand with propositional attitudes, which are

---

[23] Cf. Chisholm (1976; 1981) and Swinburne (1986).
[24] Cf. Williams (1973); Wiggins (1967; 1980); Parfit (1984).
[25] Cf. Rawls (1971); Parfit (1984); Taylor (1985); Wollheim (1984); Nagel (1986); Frankfurt (1988).
[26] See Sellars (1956), pp.75 f.: 'The essential point is that in characterizing an episode or a state as that of *knowing*, we are not giving an empirical description of that episode or state;

the adequate reactions to situations in which red properties are identified. According to Sellars, the actions and behaviour of a person could not be made intelligible without appeal to the space of reasons.[27]

However, the space of reason is not the only essential feature of the human life-form. Persons are not merely present in the space of reasons; they also make active use of their ability to express themselves — i.e. they have a linguistic *sense of self-reference*. With good reason, persons ascribe attitudes and actions to other persons, which they would also ascribe to themselves. In particular, they assume that other persons have similar sensitivities and self-referential attitudes, and they assume that other persons acknowledge specific values and follow similar life-plans. Persons mutually ascribe — metaphorically speaking — a self to each other as the center of epistemic and moral activity.

Human attitudes and emotions cannot develop without language. Subjectivity and inwardness are not passive states: they must be expressed. Thus, the development of human emotions depends upon linguistic differentiation. States like love, grief, hate, resentment, self-respect, and remorse all rest upon a complicated system of distinct concepts and terms, and they can only take on a structured form and semantic consistency in the space of reasons. In this sense, language is the dimension of self-expression.

Persons have a sense of self with regard to themselves and other persons. The self consists in a person's self-referential perspective in the space of epistemic, moral and aesthetic reasons. The sense of self provides a person with certain independence within the context of the social realm. A person's sense of self is the source by which the person determines and comprehends the continuities that persist through time.[28]

---

we are placing it in the logical space of reasons, of justifying and being able to justify what one says.'

[27] See Sellars (1956), p. 76. Cf. McDowell (1994), p. 125: 'In being initiated into a language, a human being is introduced into something that already embodies putatively rational linkages between concepts, putatively constitutive of the layout of the space of reasons, before she comes on the scene. [...] Human beings mature into being home in the space of reasons or, what comes to the same thing, living their lives in the world; we can make sense of that by noting that the language into which a human being is first initiated stands over against her as a prior embodiment of mindedness, of the possibility of an orientation to the world.'

[28] See Taylor (1985), p. 97: 'A person is a being who has a sense of self, has a notion of the future and the past, can hold values, make choices; in short, can adopt life-plans. At least, a person must be the kind of being who is in principle capable of all this, however damaged these capacities may be in practice. Running through all this we can identify a necessary (but not sufficient) condition. A person must be a being with his own point of view on

The internal connection between a sense of self-reference and the capacity for a life-plan presents a manifestation of self-determination, a manifestation that exhibits itself in the social realm. In the social realm, persons discover a variety of models for orienting the contingent circumstances and psychological complexities of their individual lives. A rational life-plan cannot preclude contingency and variety; on the contrary, it must acknowledge the constitutive role that such elements play in self-determination, especially, when attitudes towards certain options may vary greatly over time. Therefore, the sense of self-reference must be realized *within* the linguistically mediated complexities of social life, not outside of it.

In everyday life, the sense of self-reference unfolds as a normative concept that points to an ethics of earnestness (*Ernsthaftigkeit*). According to the ethical ideal of earnestness, a person who takes herself seriously will perform or not perform certain actions, and will accept or not accept certain situations in her life. In practice, this ethical ideal employs moral self-criticism as means of autonomy. This criticism rests upon the notion that there is a strong distinction between the better and the worse ways of leading one's life. As long as a person chooses her reasons for actions in seriousness, her life acquires a distinctive contour, regardless of her success or failure in pursuing this life-plan.

The practice of self-criticism provides a means to avoid self-alienation. In a self-alienated life, the person acts like a quasi-object, like a being without any normative sense of self-reference (cf. Sartre, 1943, I, 2). Heidegger addresses this problem in his accounts of authenticity (*Eigentlichkeit*) and resoluteness (*Entschlossenheit*).[29] His deployment of these concepts establishes the difference between authentic and inauthentic existence.[30] However, Heidegger's theory of authenticity develops an existential perspective that lacks a strong moral or normative component. He speaks of an existential projection, which embraces the entire range of potentiality-for-being. This projection

---

things. The life-plan, the choices, the sense of self must be attributable to him as in some sense their point of origin.' In this passage Taylor speaks of a sense of self, not of a sense of self-reference. But his explanation avoids clearly the fallacies of semantic reification that is normally connected with the non-metaphorical use of the expression 'self'.

[29] For the social and cultural philosophical background of the concept of authenticity cf. Taylor (1991). Taylor's reconstructions refer to theoretical connection, which far surpass the narrow existential approaches and start with Rousseau's conception of self-determination.

[30] Cf. Heidegger (1962), p. 312: 'Authentic Being-one's-Self takes the definite form of an existential modification of the 'they'; and this modification must be defined existentially.'

should not be understood as a life-plan, in the moral sense of that term.[31]

Contrary to Heidegger's existential analysis, earnestness cannot be treated as morally indifferent. Earnest existence implies a determination to develop the moral dimensions of one's life. Therefore, from the standpoint of earnestness, questions about the meaning of life do not merely consist in the demarcation of a range of potentiality-for-being: earnestness also requires a reflective expansion of our values, goals, and ethical ideals. The decisive factor in moral self-criticism is self-respect.[32] Kant understands self-respect as the awareness of one's own moral personality, where this feature is understood to be distinct from intellect and character. In his approach, self-respect turns out to be the decisive condition for earnestness. According to this understanding, persons can only join in relations of moral recognition if they have self-respect. Only somebody who respects himself can respect others.[33] In this sense, earnestness binds self-consciousness to morality.

9. The Person as Subject: A Summary

The general framework for the notion of a person as subject is determined by (1) the criticism of self-identification (Kant, Wittgenstein, Ryle), (2) the irreducibility thesis (Descartes, Kant, Wittgenstein, Nagel, McGinn), (3) the distinction between self and person (Kant), (4) the integration of self and person (Locke, Kant), (5) the expression of a sense of self-reference in the space of reasons (Sellars, Taylor), and (6) the normative importance of authenticity and self-respect (Kant, Heidegger, Sartre, Rawls). In all of these determinations, the relation between self and person remains somewhat mysterious. We cannot conceive a person without a self-referential perspective; likewise we cannot conceive a self-referential perspective without the notion of person. Yet, 'person' seems to be the wider concept, and

---

[31] Cf. Heidegger (1962), p. 145: 'The character of understanding as projection is constitutive for Being-in-the-world with regard to the disclosedness of its existentially constitutive state-of-Being, by which the factical potentiality-for-Being gets its leeway [Spielraum]. And as thrown, Dasein is thrown into the kind of Being, which we call 'projecting'. Projecting has nothing to do with comporting oneself towards a plan that has been thought out, and in accordance with which Dasein arranges its Being. On the contrary, any Dasein has, as Dasein, already projected itself; and as long as it is, it is projecting. As long as it is, Dasein always has understood itself and always will understand itself in terms of possibilities.'

[32] Kant speaks of respect for oneself ('Achtung für sich selbst') or self-esteem ('Selbstschätzung'); see Kant [1968d], p. 399, cf. Kant (1968c), pp. 36 f., Kant (1968d), pp. 434 f.

[33] Cf. Rawls (1963; 1971, pp. 440–6).

'self' the narrower concept. But the problem remains — in other words we cannot clearly define the relations between these two concepts. At most, one can state some kind of mutual entailment. This complicated situation explains the common, but false philosophical assumption that 'self' and 'person' are synonymous concepts.

The complicated semantic relation between 'self' and 'person' can be taken as a sign of the peculiar grammar of self-reference. At first glance, the expression 'self' appears to be an incoherent concept. It is composed of elements that depend upon first-, second-, and third- person perspectives. In addition to this, the concept of the self contains descriptive elements, insofar as it refers to the core of the person, and normative elements, insofar as it involves authenticity and autonomy.

The semantic and epistemic problems in identifying self-reference should not lead us to the hypothesis that the self is an object, which future generations will discover more about. Wittgenstein rightly warned that this hypothesis would lead to a new form of reification – a reification in which we tacitly assume that there is at least a thing that we can take as a self. Instead, the concept of the self should be taken to describe metaphorically a system of self-referential activities. It should be understood as a term that expresses the self-relation, or self-referential activities, of a person. In this respect, it indicates the perspective of the human life-form. The self cannot be identified, but it expresses itself indirectly. It reveals itself in the activities we refer to when we say: I think, I feel, I notice, I want, I act, I wish, I suffer, I care etc. The systematic structure of these self-referential activities is summarized in Kant's formula 'I exist thinking'. All these activities leave traces in the social realm, and in relation to personal identity, life-plan, concern, autonomy, and earnestness, these activities of the person take on the form of self-referential continuities that persist through time. In this respect, the metaphorical expression 'self' grasps an essential feature of being a person. This systematically and semantically clarified concept of self-reference allows us to speak of the person as a subject.[34]

References

Ameriks, K. (2000), *Kant's Theory of Mind. An Analysis of the Paralogisms of Pure Reason* (Oxford: Oxford University Press).

Ameriks, K., Sturma, D. (eds.) (1995), *The Modern Subject: Conceptions of the 'Self'' in Classical German Philosophy* (Albany: State University of New York Press).

Anscombe, G. E. M. (1975), 'The First Person', in S. Guttenplan (ed.), *Mind and Language* (Oxford: Clarendon Press), pp. 45-65.

---

[34] For helpful comments I thank Lynne Rudder Baker, Heikki Ikäheimo and an anonymous reviewer of the *Journal of Consciousness Studies*.

Augustine (2006), *On the Trinity, Books 8-15* (Cambridge Texts in the History of Philosophy) (Cambridge: Cambridge University Press).
Ayer, A. J. (1956), *The Problem of Knowledge* (Harmondsworth: Penguin).
Bermúdez, J.L. (1998), *The Paradox of Self-consciousness* (Cambridge, MA: MIT).
Cassam, Q. (ed.) (1994), *Self-Knowledge* (Oxford: Oxford University Press).
Cassam, Q. (1997), *Self and World* (Oxford: Clarendon Press).
Chisholm, R. M. (1976), *Person and Object* (London: Allen and Unwin).
Chisholm, R. M. (1981), *The First Person* (Brighton: Harvester Press).
Churchland, P. S. (1986), *Neurophilosophy: Toward a Unified Science of the Mind-Brain* (Cambridge, MA: MIT Press).
Davidson, D. (1980), *Essays on Actions and Events* (Oxford: Clarendon Press).
Dennett, D. C. (1981), *Brainstorms. Philosophical Essays on Mind and Psychology* (Brighton: Harvester Press).
Dennett, D. C. (1991), *Consciousness Explained* (Boston: Little, Brown).
Descartes, R. (1964), *Œuvres de Descartes, Volume VII: Meditationes de Prima Philosophia* (ed. Ch. Adam and P. Tannery) (Paris: Vrin).
Feigl, H. (1967), The 'Mental' and the 'Physical'. *The Essay and a Postscript* (Minneapolis: University of Minnesota Press).
Foucault, M. (1966), *Les mots et les choses. Une archéologie des sciences humaines* (Paris: Gallimard).
Foucault, M. (1994), 'La pensée du dehors', in *Dits et écrits*, Volume I: 1954-1969 (Paris: Gallimard), pp. 518-539.
Frankfurt, H. G. (1988), *The Importance of What We Care About: Philosophical Essays* (Cambridge: Cambridge University Press).
Hegel, G. W. F. (1970), *Grundlinien der Philosophie des Rechts*, Werke, Volume 7 (Frankfurt am Main: Suhrkamp).
Hegel, G. W. F. (1971), *Vorlesungen über die Geschichte der Philosophie III*, Werke, Volume 20 (Frankfurt am Main: Suhrkamp).
Heidegger, M. (1962), *Being and Time*, trans. by J. Macquarrie and E. Robinson (Oxford: Blackwell).
Heidegger, M. (1979), *Sein und Zeit* (Tübingen: Niemeyer).
Hume, D. (1978), *A Treatise of Human Nature* (ed. L. A. Selby-Bigge and P. H. Nidditch) (Oxford: Clarendon Press).
Husserl, E. (1975), *Fünfte Logische Untersuchung* (from the text of the first edition from 1901) (Hamburg: Meiner).
James, W. (1967), 'Does Consciousness exist?', in *Essays in Radical Empiricism* (Gloucester, Mass.: Smith).
Kant, I. (1968a), *Kritik der reinen Vernunft*, in Werke, Volume III. Akademie-Textausgabe (Berlin: de Gruyter).
Kant, I. (1968b), *Grundlegung zur Metaphysik der Sitten*, in Werke, Volume IV. Akademie-Textausgabe (Berlin: de Gruyter).
Kant, I. (1968c), *Kritik der praktischen Vernunft*, in Werke, Volume V. Akademie-Textausgabe (Berlin: de Gruyter).
Kant, I. (1968d), *Die Metaphysik der Sitten*, in Werke, Volume VI. Akademie-Textausgabe (Berlin: de Gruyter).
Kant, I. (1998), *Critique of Pure Reason*, trans. by P. Guyer and A. W. Wood (Cambridge: Cambridge University Press).
Kenny, A. (1979), 'The First Person', in C. Diamond and J. Teichman (eds.), *Intention and Intentionality* (Brighton: Harvester Press), 3-13.
Kenny, A. (1989), *The Metaphysics of the Mind* (New York: Oxford University Press).
Leibniz, G. W. (1986), *Nouveaux Essais sur l'Entendement humain – Neue Abhandlungen über den menschlichen Verstand*. Philosophische Schriften, Volume III (Frankfurt am Main: Suhrkamp).

Lewis, D. (1979), 'Attitudes De Dicto and De Se,' *Philosophical Review* 88, pp. 513-543.
Locke, J. (1975), *An Essay Concerning Human Understanding* (Oxford: Clarendon).
MacAthur, D., De Caro, M. (2004), *Naturalism in Question* (Cambridge, Mass.: Harvard University Press).
Malcolm, N. (1979), 'Whether 'I' is a Referring Expression', in *Intention and Intentionality*, ed. C. Diamond, J. Teichman (Brighton: Harvester Press), pp. 15-25.
McDowell, J. (1994), *Mind and World* (Cambridge, MA: Harvard University Press).
McGinn, C. (1991), *The Problem of Consciousness* (Oxford: Blackwell).
Nagel, Th. (1970), *The Possibility of Altruism* (Oxford: Clarendon Press).
Nagel, Th. (1986), *The View from Nowhere* (Oxford: Oxford University Press).
Nagel, Th. (1997), *The Last Word* (Oxford: Oxford University Press).
Parfit, D. (1984), *Reasons and Persons* (Oxford: Clarendon Press).
Perry, J. (ed.) (1975), *Personal Identity* (Berkeley: University of California Press).
Quante, M. (2002), *Personales Leben und menschlicher Tod. Personale Identität als Prinzip der biomedizinischen Ethik* (Frankfurt am Main: Suhrkamp).
Rawls, J. (1963), 'The Sense of Justice', *Philosophical Review* 72, pp. 281-305.
Rawls, J. (1971), *A Theory of Justice* (Cambridge, Mass.: Belknap Press).
Ryle, G. (1949), *The Concept of Mind* (London: Hutchinson).
Ryle, G. (1971), 'The Thinking of Thoughts. What is 'le Penseur' doing?', in *Collected Papers, Volume II* (London: Hutchinson), pp. 480-496.
Sartre, J.-P. (1943), *L'être et le néant. Essai d'ontologie phénoménologique* (Paris: Gallimard).
Sellars, W. (1956), *Empiricism and the Philosophy of Mind* (Cambridge, Mass.: Harvard University Press 1997).
Shoemaker, S., Swinburne, R. (1984), *Personal Identity* (Oxford: Blackwell).
Strawson, P. F. (1959), *Individuals. An Essay in Descriptive Metaphysics* (London: Methuen).
Sturma, D. (1997), *Philosophie der Person. Die Selbstverhältnisse von Subjektivität und Moralität* (Paderborn: Schöningh).
Sturma, D. (1998), 'Reductionism in Exile? Herbert Feigl's Identity Theory and the Mind-Body Problem', *Grazer Philosophische Studien* 54, pp. 71-87.
Sturma, D. (2005), *Philosophie des Geistes* (Leipzig: Reclam).
Sturma, D. (Hg.) (2001), *Person. Philosophiegeschichte – Theoretische Philosophie – Praktische Philosophie* (Paderborn: Mentis).
Swinburne, R. (1986), *The Evolution of the Soul* (Oxford: Clarendon Press).
Taylor, Ch. (1985), *Human Agency and Language. Philosophical Papers 1* (Cambridge: Cambridge University Press).
Taylor, Ch. (1989), *Sources of the Self. The Making of the Modern Identity* (Cambridge, Mass.: Harvard University Press).
Taylor, Ch. (1991), *The Ethics of Authenticity* (Cambridge, MA: Harvard UP).
Wiggins, D. (1967), *Identity and Spatio-Temporal Continuity* (Oxford: Blackwell).
Wiggins, D. (1980), *Sameness and Substance* (Oxford: Blackwell).
Wilkes, K. V. (1988), *Real People* (Oxford: Clarendon Press).
Williams, B. (1973), *Problems of the Self. Philosophical Papers 1956-1972* (London: Cambridge University Press).
Williams, B. (1981), *Moral Luck. Philosophical Papers 1973-1980* (London: CUP).
Wittgenstein, L. (1964), *The Blue and Brown Books: Preliminary Studies for the 'Philosophical Investigations'* (Oxford: Blackwell).
Wollheim, R. (1984), *The Thread of Life* (Cambridge: Cambridge University Press).
Wright, C. (1998), 'Self-Knowledge: The Wittgensteinian Legacy,' in C. Wright, B. C. Smith, C. Macdonald (eds.), *Knowing Our Own Minds* (Oxford: Clarendon Press), pp. 13-47.

Robin S. Dillon

Arrogance, Self-Respect and Personhood

Abstract: *This essay aims to show that arrogance corrupts the very qualities that make persons persons. The corruption is subtle but profound, and the key to understanding it lies in understanding the connections between different kinds of arrogance, self-respect, respect for others and personhood. Making these connections clear is the second aim of this essay. It will build on Kant's claim that self-respect is central to living our human lives as persons and that arrogance is, at its core, the failure to respect oneself as a person.*

The arrogance of other people can be laughable, irritating, insulting, enraging, even dangerous — their arrogance can make our lives worse to lesser and greater degrees. But arrogance can also diminish the life of the arrogant. Under the name of 'pride,'[1] arrogance has long been decried as the deadliest of the 'deadly sins:' a vice that is 'death to the soul.' Gabriele Taylor (1994, p. 145) helpfully glosses this as 'corruption of the soul,' taking 'corruption' in the literal sense of 'destruction or dissolution of the constitution of a thing which makes that thing what it is' (*OED*). One of the aims of this essay is to show that arrogance is corruptive in just this way: it subverts the very qualities that make persons persons. The corruption is subtle but profound, and the key to understanding it lies in understanding the connections among

Correspondence:
rsd2@lehigh.edu

---

[1] Although nowadays we tend to think of pride as a wonderful emotion that should be celebrated and fostered as widely as possible, the sin of pride is something rather different. As the *O.E.D.* makes clear, from their entry into the English language in the high Middle Ages the words 'pride' and 'proud' have referred to something bad: an overweening opinion of oneself which gives rise to an attitude of superiority and contempt for others, i.e., arrogance. *Oxford English Dictionary,* s.v. 'pride,' 'proud.'

arrogance, self-respect, and personhood. Making these connections clear is a second aim of this essay.

In making these connections I draw on Kant, who argued that self-respect is central to living our human lives as persons and that arrogance is, at its core, the failure to respect oneself as a person. This may seem surprising, for if we think of arrogance in connection with respect, we are more likely to think of it as disrespectful of other people. To be sure, much arrogance is disrespectful of others. But for Kant, the viciousness of arrogance does not lie solely in the fact that it disrespects others. Arrogance is at bottom a pernicious moral perspective that misvalues and so disrespects the self. This failure of self-respect involves the corruption of rational judgment and the distortion of moral agency, and it gives rise to attitudes and conduct that misvalue and disrespect other people and things. Arrogance perverts our abilities to value, to make rational judgments, and to act autonomously, abilities that are, on the Kantian view, constitutive of personhood. Arrogance, that is, corrupts the person-defining powers of rational moral agency. Self-respect, which I hold to be the virtue opposing the vice of arrogance, involves the proper valuing of self that makes moral agency, fully rational judgment, and proper valuing of other people and things possible.

Understanding the connections among arrogance, self-respect, and personhood is complicated, however, by the fact that none of these three concepts is univocal. There are, I maintain, different kinds of arrogance, different kinds of respect and self-respect, and different senses in which a human being is a person. In this essay different kinds of arrogance are distinguished and are mapped with different kinds of self-respect and respect for others and different senses of personhood, in order to explain how arrogance corrupts personhood.

1. Arrogance

1.1. Interpersonal arrogance

Let me begin by distinguishing two kinds of arrogance, which I'll call 'interpersonal arrogance' and 'unwarranted claims arrogance.'[2] Consider the former first. I expect that most of us think first of arrogance

---

[2] Interpersonal arrogance is one form of what I elsewhere call 'status arrogance:' an arrogance that is essentially a matter of regarding oneself as having a higher normative status than other things. Arrogance toward nature is a non-interpersonal form of status arrogance. I have elsewhere used the term 'primary arrogance' to refer to what I am here calling 'unwarranted claims arrogance.' The latter term, though uglier, better captures what is distinctive to it.

as essentially interpersonal, a matter of how someone treats other people.[3] The arrogant individual is generally thought to be someone who thinks he is better than other people, who looks down on others and treats them contemptuously, disdainfully, peremptorily, or without consideration, making it clear that he views them as less important, less worthy than his very important, very great self. This view of arrogance is expressed in the definition given in the *American Heritage* dictionary: 'a sense of overbearing self-worth or self-importance, marked by or arising from an assumption of one's superiority towards others.' Like its synonyms 'proud,' 'haughty,' 'disdainful,' and 'supercilious,' being arrogant is said to involve 'an inflated ego and disdain for what one considers inferior.' We can distinguish two important aspects of arrogance in this definition: (1) having a high opinion of one's worth or importance and (2) regarding oneself as superior to inferior others. Arrogance can begin in the belief that one's merits — one's talents, abilities, or accomplishments — are greater than those of others or that one has a high social status. But its hallmark is regarding oneself as superior in the sense of having a higher normative status than others, by virtue of which one is entitled to treat them as inferiors, to make demands on them and expect their deference, to insist that one's needs and wants take precedence over their, or to dismiss or ignore them.[4]

Although disdain is identified as the typical expression of arrogance, there is, in fact, a wide range of types of arrogant interpersonal engagement. You can see it in the driver who refuses to wait his turn at the merge point, the 'expert' who writes off your views without considering them or treats your ignorance with contempt, the student who demands that you drop what you are doing and attend to his needs *now*, the co-worker who regards her project as so much more important than yours that it deserves a greater share of the department's resources, the relative who insists he knows what's best for you and acts for you without your knowledge or consent. We call arrogant those who aggressively disparage the defective human specimens that

---

[3] Such a view of arrogance is explicated by Tiberius and Walker (1998), who argue that arrogance is essentially 'an interpersonal matter. It consists in a particular way of regarding and engaging in relations with others' (p. 381).

[4] Arrogance thus differs from conceit in three ways. To be conceited is to have an unduly high opinion of one's merits, to think one has greater worth than one in fact has. But an arrogant individual, first, need not be conceited: someone who is very talented and accomplished can have a well-founded high opinion of his merits and yet be arrogant. This is because, second, the arrogant individual, unlike the merely conceited one, takes his worth to be greater than that of others, and, third, he takes his greater worth to ground a superior normative status.

surround them, those who are laughingly or haughtily insolence, those who hold themselves disdainfully aloof from others, those who are bountifully but domineeringly condescending, those with self-important expectations of deference from others, those whose self-absorption renders them oblivious to the effects of their activities on others, those who self-centredly presume that their desires take precedence over the well-being of others, those who treat others with kindly and well-meant but high-handed paternalism, those who are manifestly unconcerned with the well-being and rights of others and consider only how they can manipulate them, those who disregard others deemed too insignificant to notice.

Interpersonal arrogance has four broad dimensions. The first is a settled conception of the self as having a distinguished worth or significance and a valued position that others do not share — superiority, intrinsically greater importance, objective priority, centrality. One regards oneself as special in some important way; one matters, in one's view, a great deal and in a way that others do not, and certain things — rights, privileges, esteem, deference, precedence, respect — are taken to be one's due to which others cannot make a similar claim. Other people are excluded from the level of significance and worth on which one dwells; they are conceived as occupying a different and lower plane of existence and so as not warranting on their own account the kind of consideration, rights, privileges, and respect that a higher-level being is due, although one may generously grant these undeserved things to them. Essential to interpersonal arrogance, then, is a conception of one's worth and status in relation to others.

The second dimension is the attitude the arrogant person takes toward this first set of 'facts'. The arrogant person not only values the self highly but highly values having a worth and status that is both great and greater than others': when one thinks about it, however frequently or infrequently, it is a pleasurable thought and satisfying in its rightness. The significance of one's worth and status, of the distinction between self and other, between superior and inferior, important and irrelevant, governs perception, thought, expectation, judgment, attitude, emotion, desire, will, and conduct in one's encounters with others. The valuing of self-valuing is an essential part of the mindset of interpersonal arrogance.

The third dimension is the inordinance of the valuing of self in relation to others. By 'inordinate' I do not mean simply excessive, in the way conceit is an unduly high opinion of one's abilities and accomplishments; I mean disordered, in the sense of unreasonable and defective in some morally significant way. Valuing oneself excessively in comparison to others is one form of inordinate valuing, but self-valuing and the valuing of self-value can also be distorted in respect to their grounds, their justification, the kind of valuing they involved, the implications one draws from them, the weight they have in one's cognitions, attitudes, desires, and will, and their manifestation in attitude and behaviour. Arrogance is a matter of what one values and does not value and of how one values or doesn't value it, and of how one's valuing, not valuing, and devaluing of certain things affect whether and how one values or disvalues other things; it is a matter as well of the strength and of the connection or separation of one's valuing of these things with regard to one's valuing of other things and to one's other motives and drives, and of the effect of one's valuing and disvaluing on one's attention, perception, thought, and judgment. Arrogance is marked by a systemic perversion of valuing: inordinance in the valuing of self, self-worth, and others produces inordinance in these other dimensions. The mindset that characterizes arrogance is thoroughly disordered, inordinate throughout.

The fourth dimension of interpersonal arrogance is the manifestation of this mindset in one's attitudes towards and, typically, treatment of other people. There is no particular mode of treatment of others that is uniquely arrogant. How it is manifest can vary widely, and not just from one individual to another but also for an individual from one kind of situation to another: an arrogant person can be aloof with the neighbours, insulting with one individual, and presumptuous with another, and all without having the least mind to hurt anyone; another might be cruel and disparaging to his wife, intending to hurt her, but condescending to his patients and ostensibly aiming to benefit them. The inordinate valuing of self and self-worth in relation to others generates a framework for one's engagements or refusals to engage with others, within which the particular details of interactions can take a variety of shapes. But what is common to all the modes of attitude and interaction — whether they are openly contemptuous or courteous, disregarding or interfering — is that they deny others some acknowledgement, consideration, honour, concern, credit, some proper valuing that is their due. The attitudes and treatment, that is, involve disrespect of others. They reinforce the false valuation scheme in which one is superior, more important, or central in relation to others who are inferior, secondary, or inconsequential.

While the conception of one's more worthy self can be distinctively individuating ('I am uniquely special; my needs and wants are objectively more important than those of others'), it can instead be part of one's identity as a member of a certain group, class, or people — 'our kind' as opposed to 'those others', the arrogant heart of racism, sexism, religious animosity, and others forms of bigotry and oppression. The character trait of arrogance pervades the whole of one's psyche, but it can be quite selective in its targets: the arrogant needn't think of themselves as having a greater worth and status than all other humans or groups of humans. Moreover, arrogance with respect to some people is compatible with acknowledged inferiority of self to other people, indeed can be compensation for, protection against, and expression of a sense of inferiority. But interpersonal arrogance can also be just what it appears: the expression of absolute confidence in what one takes to be one's objectively greater worth and higher normative status.

The heart of interpersonal arrogance, then, is the inordinate valuing of oneself vis-à-vis others. One issue not addressed thus far is motivation: why do arrogant people have this view of the worth or self and others? We'll return to this issue in section 3.

1.2. Unwarrantable claims arrogance

Interpersonal arrogance is essentially a matter of how one regards and interacts with others in light of how one values oneself. But not all forms of arrogance involve relations to other people. Consider the following three examples. (1) A beginner investor bought stock only to watch the price fall. Reflecting on lessons learned, he says 'I did kind of have this arrogance that because I owned it, it was going to go up' (Rosen, 2001). (2) Soon after John F. Kennedy, Jr., his wife Carolyn Bessette Kennedy and her sister Lauren Bessette were killed in July, 1999, when the private plane he was piloting crashed, I read, on the one hand, numerous eulogies of Kennedy that spoke of his humility and modesty in his relations with other people, surprising in one so iconically famous and privileged, and, on the other, several criticisms blaming his arrogance for the crash. The arrogance lay, it was said, in his trying to fly a too-powerful plane in bad visibility conditions when he was not trained to fly using instruments and with a recently-broken ankle that was too weak to work the pedals that controlled the plane. The arrogance lay, that is, in the apparent assumption that he was capable of transcending constraints and risks that might hamper or cow others, that he was somehow immune to the laws of physics and the realities of nature that evening.[5] (3) Young wizard-in-training

---

[5] Alas, while I kept copies of several eulogies extolling the humility, I've lost the references for the criticisms of arrogance. However, a similar pairing of judgments can be found in Horowitz (1999).

Harry Potter, who had had been forbidden to leave Hogwarts School for his own protection, was caught sneaking out by Professor Snape, who snarled, 'Famous Harry Potter is a law unto himself. ... Famous Harry Potter goes where he wants to, with no thought for the consequences. ... How extraordinarily like your father you are, Potter. ... He too was exceedingly arrogant. ... Your father didn't set much store by rules either ... Rules were for lesser mortals' (Rowlings, 1999, p. 284). Later, thinking he had saved Harry from being murdered by someone whom Harry then defends, Snape repeated the charge: 'You would have been well-served if he'd killed you. You'd have died like your father, too arrogant to believe you might be mistaken' (Rowlings, 1999, p. 361).

Snape thinks that Potter assumes he has a right to act however he wants, never mind the rules, and that he claims knowledge that he doesn't have; to label him arrogant is to say both that he has no such right and no such knowledge and that he ought to know that doesn't. Kennedy and the investor claim both a certain ability or power and an immunity from foreseeable harms — to call them arrogant is to say that the abilities they do have give them no reason to think that they are able to do what they claim to be able to do, and that any reasonable person would know that. These cases remind us that the adjective 'arrogant' derives from the verb 'to arrogate,' which the *OED* defines thus: 'to assume as a right that to which one is not entitled; to lay claim to and appropriate (a privilege, advantage, etc.,) without just reason or through self-conceit, insolence, or haughtiness (from L., to ask or claim for oneself).' Arrogance is 'the taking of too much upon oneself as one's right; the assertion of unwarrantable claims in respect of one's own importance; undue assumption of dignity, authority, or knowledge; aggressive conceit, presumption, or haughtiness.' This form of arrogance is essentially a matter of making unwarrantable claims, so I call it 'unwarrantable claims arrogance.'

Three dimensions of unwarrantable claims arrogance are worth noting. First, its core is the disposition to arrogate, to lay claim to or appropriate things of significance, such as rights and other entitlements, status, authority, knowledge, or ability, without warrant and despite good reasons not to. The arrogant act, think, feel, and desire as if they were entitled to do so, although they aren't and they should know it, or as if they had certain qualities or abilities or held certain positions or had a certain importance that they don't and they should know it. It is of the essence of arrogation that the claims, assumptions, and takings are not just unwarranted but unwarrantable, and that the individual is in a position to know this but does not acknowledge it: one arrogates in the face of, in contempt of countering evidence or reasons. Arrogance is not, however, a matter of mistake, stupidity, or irrationality. The arrogant person always has subjectively the strongest reason for claiming and assuming what he does: he wants it. What distinguishes the arrogant person from the merely desirous person is that the former presumes entitlement or truth: that he wants it gives him a right to it and so he shall have it, that he wants it to be true makes it true.

Second, the things towards which the disposition to arrogate is directed are all things that are connected in some way to high status and great worth. They are what would be due a person of higher rank or greater importance, what would be warranted if one were more than one is, what would befit or be a proper expression of a superior or more significant being. Appropriating them can thus be a means of elevating self and self-worth, or it can be a mark of antecedent inordinate valuing of oneself.

Third, unwarrantable claims arrogance can operate in a variety of ways and on different levels. It is sometimes expressed openly, in explicit assertions, claims, and demands, but it is typically more subtle and stealthy than that: a matter of inexplicit assumption, unarticulated taking for granted, implicit expectation, a matter of presumption, of taking something as fact before the fact without questions of reasons, evidence, warrant, or justification ever even arising. That is, unwarrantable claims arrogance is much more a matter of what goes without saying and without thinking, more a matter of understanding, interpretation, construal, and perception than of inference, explicit belief, and declaration. It tends to operate stealthily, without thought, and unconcerned about, inattentive to, or contemptuous of truth and reality. Rather than being the product of rational consideration, one's views and choices are governed by impulse—by desire, fear, hope, loathing—but they exude an absolute confidence in their rightness which puts them beyond the need for justification, examination, reflection. Unwarrantable claims arrogance thus involves a pattern of cognitive distortion that is marked by a failure to engage in critical reflection and thus to engage rationally with oneself as a rational being.

As with interpersonal arrogance, one issue which this description of unwarrantable claims arrogance does not address is that of motivation: why do presumably rational people make unwarrantable claims? I return to motivational issues in section 3.

Interpersonal arrogance and unwarrantable claims arrogance are different kinds of arrogance: they comprise different beliefs, attitudes, objects, and desires. But they are connected in one important way: interpersonal arrogance always involves unwarrantable claims arrogance. (The reverse is not true: latter is broader in application.) The attitudes about the worth of self in relation to others that characterize interpersonal arrogance involve the arrogation of worth, status, importance, and the arrogation of entitlements that non-reciprocally expand one's own action options while constraining the actions of others.[6]

2. Self-Respect, Personhood and Dignity

2.1. Self-Respect

Interpersonal arrogance and unwarrantable claims arrogance express a self-valuing or seek a value for the self that is inordinate. By contrast, self-respect involves appropriate self-valuing; it is '*due* respect for oneself' (*OED*). At the core of each kind of arrogance is a conception of the self and an orientation to the existentially vital issues of self-worth and to the implications of self-worth that is fundamentally flawed, and the badness of each traces to failures of self-respect.

Those who have self-respect understand themselves to have a worth or importance that is morally significant, they value themselves as beings of morally significant worth, and they value valuing themselves appropriately. They thus have a sense not only of their worth but also of how they should value themselves and how appropriate self-valuing should be made manifest in their actions, attitudes, purposes, and pursuits. To respect oneself is to be practically engaged with one's self and the world in way that is structured by a conception of oneself as valuable and properly self-valuing. Self-respect, then, is not a simple psychological state, but is, rather, a complex of multilayered and interpenetrating phenomena — it comprises all those aspects of cognition, valuation, affect, expectation, motivation, action, and

---

[6] Interpersonal arrogance can both develop out of and in turn give rise to further unwarrantable claims arrogance. For example, the unwarrantable assumption that one is unusually intelligent might lead one to suppose that one is intellectually superior to others; the presumption that intellectual superiority is what really matters might give rise to an assumption that one occupies a loftier position overall. The appropriation of superior status might in turn engender contempt for others that one deems inferior in intellect and status and the assumption that one is entitled to their deference. It might also engender claims to knowledge that one doesn't have or to superiority along some other dimension. The sphere of arrogation expands through a series of steps, each step being a matter not of explicit reflection on the reasonableness of such a move but, rather, of taking-more-for-granted, each implicit taking motivated by a desire for what the next step provides. And what it provides is a kind of self-value that such a self values, a self-value that is morally problematic.

interaction that compose a mode of being in the world whose heart is a proper appreciation of oneself as having morally significant worth.

Because the notion of morally significant self-worth is the organizing motif for self-respect, and because in the dominant Western tradition two kinds of morally significant worth are ascribed to persons, two kinds of self-respect can be distinguished. The first is *recognition self-respect*,[7] which centres on what we can call 'status worth,' which is intrinsic worth that is grounded in such things as one's essential nature as a person, membership in a certain class, group, or people, social role, or place in a social hierarchy. The individual with recognition self-respect recognizes certain norms as entailed by the worth she has as what she is, and she values herself appropriately by living in accord with them. The second kind is *evaluative self-respect*,[8] which has to do with an acquired moral worth which we can call 'moral merit.' Moral merit denotes a superior or excellent quality or worth that is based on the extent to which one's character and conduct accord with and honour what one is. Individuals earn or lose moral merit and so deserve or don't deserve more or less evaluative self-respect through what they do or become.

Although both kinds of arrogance are connected in morally problematic ways to evaluative self-respect, I focus in this paper on their connections with recognition self-respect. Further, while different modes of status worth yield different configurations of recognition self-respect, I will focus on dignity, the absolute and intrinsic worth that, on the Kantian view, all persons have simply in virtue of their moral status as persons. So I will be concerned in the rest of this essay with dignity-based recognition self-respect, which is to say, with respect for oneself as a person. Recognition respect for oneself as a person involves recognizing that one is a person, valuing oneself as a person ought to be valued, and living in light of this understanding and appreciation of oneself as having dignity just in virtue of being a person and of the moral constraints that arise from that dignity.

I'll return to the questions of what dignity is and what it is to be a person shortly. I want first to explain further what it means to live in light of the appreciation of oneself as a person, and to do so I need to draw one more distinction. I have argued elsewhere that there are different forms of dignity-based recognition self-respect (Dillon, 2003; 1997; 1992), but I will focus in this paper on just two of them, which I

---

[7] I take the term 'recognition respect' from Darwall (1977).

[8] I derive the term 'evaluative self-respect' from Hudson (1988). Darwall calls this 'appraisal self-respect.'

call 'interpersonal recognition self-respect' and 'agentic recognition self-respect.' Interpersonal recognition self-respect involves a view of oneself as entitled to be regarded and treated by others with respect for one's dignity as a person. Every person, just as a person, has a fundamental worth by which, as Kant says 'he *exacts* respect for himself from all other rational beings ... and (can) value himself on a footing of equality with them' (Kant, MM 6:435).[9] To have recognition respect for oneself as a moral equal involves living in light of an understanding of oneself as a person among persons, as a member of the moral community with a status and dignity equal to every other person and thus as morally owed respect, that is, interpersonal recognition respect, from all other persons. Interpersonal recognition self-respect thus involves having some conception the kinds of treatment from others that would count as one's due as a person and treatment that would be degrading or beneath one's dignity, desiring to be regarded and treated appropriately, and judging disregard and disrespectful treatment by others to be morally objectionable and so being disposed to refuse to acquiesce in it.

Agentic recognition self-respect involves an appreciation of oneself as a moral agent, a being with the ability and responsibility to act autonomously and value appropriately. A self-respecting person regards the dignity she has as a person as both demanding and constraining the exercise of her agency in living her life, as giving rise to a responsibility to shape herself and direct her living so that they are congruent with and honour her dignity as a person. Someone who respects herself as a moral agent takes her responsibilities seriously, especially her responsibilities to live up to her dignity as a person, to govern herself fittingly, and to make of herself and her life something she believes to be good and worthy of herself. So, a self-respecting person regards certain forms of acting, thinking, desiring, and feeling as befitting her as a person and other forms as self-debasing or shameful, and she expects herself to adhere to the former and avoid the latter. Indeed, she understands the latter as what she must not and cannot do or be, no matter what she might gain from it, and she restrains herself from what she regards as unworthy of herself as a person.

---

[9] References to and citations of Kant's works in the text are given parenthetically to the appropriate volume of *Kant's gesammelte Schriften* (published by the *Preussische Akademie der Wissenschaften*, Berlin: Georg Reimer, 1907) and to the translation used, the abbreviation for which is noted in the References.

2.2. Personhood and dignity

Central to Kant's moral theory is the claim that all persons are unconditionally owed respect simply because of the dignity they possess as persons. It is important, therefore, to be clear about these two concepts.

Three senses of personhood. In the Kantian framework, we can understand what it is to be a person in three related ways. First, to be a person is to be a rational being (G 4:428), which is to say, a being with two ordered capacities which distinguish rational beings from all other beings; Kant calls these rational capacities 'humanity' and 'personality' (R 6:7). Humanity is 'the capacity to set ends' (G 4:437; MM 6:392), which is, as Korsgaard (1996, 114) puts it, 'the capacity to decide, under the influence of reason, that something is desirable, that it is worthy of pursuit or realization, that it is to be deemed important or valuable...as an end...' That is to say, humanity is the rational capacity to value: to recognize or to accord objective value to things, value that is distinct from their being merely what one happens to desire. This capacity to value also includes capacities to evaluate things comparatively, to organize values into a system and so to form an idea of one's own happiness, to figure out and manipulate means to ends, and to determine oneself to action based on one's valuings and evaluations (Wood, 1999, pp. 118–22). And it is, very importantly, the capacity to value oneself, to regard oneself as having objective value. Humanity is the rational capacity that makes it possible for humans to be agents: beings capable of acting independently of the natural forces of animal instinct and impulse. Personality is the rational capacity that makes it possible for humans to be moral agents. Whereas humanity is the capacity to value, personality is the higher-order capacity to value morally and to be motivated to act solely by one's recognition of moral value, that is, solely on the basis of one's rational conception of the moral law and rational beings as having supreme worth and by one's respect for them as supremely worthy (G 4:435, 439–440; R 6:27). The capacity of personality is identical with autonomy, the rational capacity to legislate the moral law for oneself and freely to bind oneself to obey it. These two capacities, humanity and personality, then, are the ground of our personhood; to be a person in the first sense is to be capable through rationality of valuing and of valuing morally appropriately.

Beings who possess these two capacities, Kant holds, thereby have a certain moral worth and moral status; and to be a person is, in the second place, to have this worth and status. In virtue of their humanity, rational beings are ends in themselves, which is to say that they have a value that is objective and unconditional and that they are therefore always to be valued and treated as ends and never to be valued and treated merely as means, as things whose worth is conditional and subjective, i.e., depends on their being desired (G 4: 427–430). Rational beings 'are called persons because their nature already marks them out as ends in themselves...and imposes...a limit on all arbitrary treatment of them.' (G 4: 428). Now, all ends in themselves are equally ends; that is, in virtue of their humanity, rational beings all have equal absolute worth, and so the status of each in the moral community is that of an equal among equal, each of whom is morally constrained to treat every person always as an end in themselves. In virtue of their personality, their higher moral capacity of autonomy, rational beings have a yet higher worth, dignity, which is an objective worth that is absolute and supreme. Dignity is absolute worth in the sense that it is a value that has no equivalent: it cannot be compared with, replaced by, or exchanged for any other value (G 4:434–436). It is also absolute in the sense that a rational being has dignity unconditionally, solely in virtue of being a person in the first sense. Dignity is thus a worth that is independent of personal qualities, social status, and accomplishments and failures: it is not worth that one has to earn or that can be bestowed on one by others or that one could lose or be stripped of. Dignity is supreme in the sense that it is a value that is higher than and therefore trumps all other values. Respect is the appropriate acknowledgment of dignity (G 4:436); hence, in virtue of their higher order capacity for moral agency, rational beings are unconditionally owed respect (G 4:429, MM 6:435). All rational beings have equal dignity and thus the status of each in the moral community is that of an equal among equal, each of whom is unconditionally owed the unconditional respect of all. Persons are thus, in a second sense, beings with the objective and unconditional worth of ends in themselves and the absolute and supreme worth of dignity who thus have the moral status of equals who owe and are owed respect and treatment as ends in themselves.

There is a third sense in which we can understand personhood, as an identity. For to be a person is also to have a conception of oneself as a person in the first two senses: to understand oneself to be not merely another animal but a rational being with these two capacities, to have a conception of oneself as able to value objectively and morally and as having objective value and moral worth, and to identify oneself to oneself as standing in a certain relation to other persons (MM 6:435). To be a person is also to have a certain identity to others: to be recognized by other persons as likewise a person. This is how it makes sense to say that slaves are nonpersons: although they are persons in the first sense in virtue of their rational capacities and persons in the second sense in virtue of their inherent and ineradicable dignity, they are (in violation of the moral law) not identified by other persons as persons. Although the recognition by others as a person is extremely important, I set it aside for the purposes of this paper to attend to personhood as, in the third sense, self-identity.

Dignity and comparative worth. The dignity that all persons possess and that grounds respect is a matter not of degree but of categorical distinction — a being either has dignity or it doesn't — and it is absolute and incomparable moral worth. Dignity thus contrasts with the kind of worth with which interpersonal arrogance is concerned, which is comparative social worth: it essentially involves comparison among persons and it is a matter of degree, of higher and lower, superior and inferior. Interestingly, humanity, the capacity to value rationally, which in the *Groundwork* is the ground of the fundamental equal moral status of persons (G 4:428–429) and in the *Critique of Practical Reason* and the *Metaphysics of Morals* is usually effectively identified with personality as the ground of incomparable dignity (C 5:87, MM 6:418, 420, 436),[10] is identified in the *Religion* as the capacity to value persons comparatively (R 6:27). Comparative valuation of persons is said to be the natural propensity to seek to gain worth in the opinion of others and to acquire superiority and ascendancy over others. Now, comparison of one's own character and conduct against the standards of virtue set by the moral law determines another kind of moral worth, a moral merit which Kant calls 'inner worth' (G 4:397-399, MM 6:435, 441), a worth grounded in the extent to which one realizes (or not) the capacity of personality through goodness of will; such comparison is a moral duty that expresses and upholds one's dignity (MM 6:393, 438–442). But the self-worth that is sought through comparison with others is not grounded in humanity and personality nor in morally worthy qualities of character and conduct, and it is a self-worth in virtue of which humans are decidedly unequal. Comparison among persons by any social measure of status worth or merit — position, relationship, wealth, power, abilities, conduct, accomplishments, beauty, honour, and so on — pits each individual against every other in zero-sum competitions to gain more self-worth

---

[10] However, in the *Metaphysic of Morals* (6:434), humanity is identified as the capacity to set ends and is said to give a rational being a mere price as one useful thing among others; it is explicitly contrasted with personality and with having dignity, being worthy or respect, and equality.

by gaining a higher worth that is a reflection how one is valued by others.

3. How Arrogance Forsakes Self-Respect and Corrupts Personhood

Arrogance is a vice principally because its failure to respect the self subverts the very qualities that make persons persons. Let me approach the explanation of this by first explaining how, on Kant's view, arrogance is a violation of the categorical moral requirement to respect other persons as persons (3.1). After that I will discuss two forms of arrogance and self-respect (3.2, 3.4), and corresponding forms of corruption of personhood (3.3, 3.5).

3.1. Interpersonal arrogance and interpersonal recognition respect for others.

In the *Metaphysics of Morals* Kant writes, 'Arrogance [*Hochmut*] (*superbia* and, as the word expresses it, the inclination to be always *on top*) is a kind of ambition [*Ehrbegierde*] (*ambitio*) in which we demand that others think little of themselves in comparison with us ... arrogance demands from others a respect it denies them' (M 6: 465).[11] This presumptuous 'lack of modesty in one's claims to be *respected* by others,' which Kant also calls 'self-conceit [*Eigendünkel*] (*arrogantia*)' (MM 6:462), is 'a vice opposed to the respect that every human being can lawfully claim' (MM 6:465).

The respect arrogance denies others is interpersonal recognition respect. This is the practical acknowledgement of the dignity of persons; it is both the only fitting response to a being with dignity and a categorical moral duty: one formulation of the Categorical Imperative, the supreme principle of morality, declares that our fundamental moral obligation is to respect persons.[12] Interpersonal recognition respect for someone as a person among persons involves, at least implicitly, recognizing that she is a being with dignity, valuing her as a being with dignity, understanding the moral constraints on moral agents to which the dignity of persons give rise, having the attitudes that such appreciation involves, and acting in regard to her only in

---

[11] Kant often inserts Latin terms in parentheses after various German words and sometimes gives synonyms in German. In the text I have inserted the German terms in italics in square brackets. The italicized Latin terms in parentheses are Kant's.

[12] I follow Wood (1999) in reading the second formulation of the Categorical Imperative—'Act in such a way that you treat humanity, whether in your own person or the person of any other, never simply as a means but always at the same time as an end'—as saying that our fundamental moral obligation is to respect persons.

morally appropriate ways out of this appreciation of her as a person. As Kant puts it, respect for others is 'to be understood as the *maxim* of limiting our self-esteem by the dignity of humanity in another person, and so as respect in the practical sense (*observantia aliis praestanda*)' (MM 6:449). The duty of respect is a negative one 'of not exalting oneself above others,' which is 'contained in the maxim not to degrade any other to a mere means to my end (not to demand that another throw himself away in order to slave for my end)' (MM 6:450). In fulfilling this duty I 'keep myself within my own bounds so as not to detract anything from the worth that the other, as a human being, is authorized to put upon himself' (MM 6:450). What this last point makes clear is that what is at stake in the duty to respect others is their self-respect, that is, their interpersonal recognition self-respect. All persons have a moral right to posit an absolute inner worth in themselves; but more than this, they have a moral duty to value themselves as ends in themselves, beings with dignity, and equal persons among equal persons. The duty to respect others thus includes the duty to refrain from anything that would threaten another person's right and duty to respect themselves, and to do this out of modesty, i.e., by willingly restricting our claims to be valued by others (MM 6:462).

Interpersonal arrogance involves disrespect of other persons in at least two ways. First, it denies the intrinsic dignity of others. The arrogant person does not regard others as his equals in moral importance whose rights, projects, views, or feelings he has to take into consideration when deciding how to act. Rather, he regards them as annoying obstacles he has to deal with, or as incompetent or dim-witted idiots that he has to take in hand, or as things he might use to further his desires, or simply as morally irrelevant. Importantly, though, he does not see them as sources of moral constraints on getting what he wants. Second, interpersonal arrogance strikes at the self-respect of others. For the arrogant individual demands not only that others value him more highly than he deserves but also that they value themselves much less than they deserve. Specifically, he demands not just that they think of themselves as, for example, less intelligent or their projects as less worthwhile, but that they think of themselves as having a fundamentally lower status than he does, as deserving less in the way of basic respect and common courtesy than he does.

The motivation for interpersonal arrogance — the 'ambition' with which Kant identifies arrogance, the desire 'always to be on top' — is the desire to heighten self-esteem, an attitude of self-approval that is different from interpersonal recognition self-respect.[13] The difference lies in the kind of self-worth which each is grounded in and expresses. Interpersonal recognition self-respect is grounded in dignity and expresses one's understanding of oneself as a being of absolute and supreme worth who is therefore the moral equal of every other person; it rests on a moral conception of self-worth. Self-esteem expresses and is grounded in the comparative/competitive social conception of self-worth. In the *Lectures*, Kant makes it clear that the kind of self-worth the arrogant person cares about is essentially comparative and competitive. Arrogance is an inclination to think highly of oneself, but it asks 'not what one is worth, but how much more one is worth than another'; the arrogant person 'already believes in his own worth, but he esteems it solely by the lesser status of other people' (L 27:241). The arrogant person can't have the worth he values unless others manifestly have little worth in comparison to him and his superiority is confirmed by how others value him and themselves; hence he is disposed to demand esteem from others, to make it clear to everyone how little he values them, and to demand that they acknowledge their inferior worth and status.

3.2. Interpersonal arrogance and interpersonal recognition self-respect

It is important to note that while interpersonal arrogance might seem to be the excess of interpersonal recognition self-respect, it isn't. For while the arrogant individual makes an unwarrantable claim to superior worth, because dignity is a non-comparative, non-scalar form of worth, the arrogant person can't claim more dignity than his due. Rather, what he claims isn't dignity at all but competitive comparative status worth. And because this self-valuing necessarily and

---

[13] I use the term here as it is used in contemporary American psychology. See, e.g., Coopersmith (1967), Rosenberg (1979), Baumeister (1994), Mruk (1999), where self-esteem is defined as 'a positive attitude toward the self', 'feeling good about oneself,' or 'self-approval,' which may or may not (depending on the theorist) be based on one's assessment of one's abilities and achievements but is always socially comparative in that it (a) partially consists in reflected appraisals of others or involves one's view of one's acceptability to others, (b) involves self-assessment by social standards, and/or (c) is typically caused and sustained by acceptance and praise from significant others. Mruk (1999) contains a comprehensive review of the relevant psychological literature. Let me note that Kant uses the terms 'self-esteem' [*Selbstschätzung*], 'self-respect' [*Achtung für sich selbst*] and '*reverentia*' interchangeably to refer to interpersonal recognition self-respect (consciousness of one's dignity as a person); indeed, he uses the first far more often than the second term in this connection. But he also uses the term 'self-esteem' [*Selbstschätzung*] to refer to what I have called 'evaluative self-respect' (appreciation of one's moral merit or 'inner moral worth') and to refer to self-valuation that is morally ungrounded. I use the term exclusively for the latter.

incoherently denies or subordinates the supreme and equal dignity of all, it is antithetical to interpersonal recognition self-respect. Thus, the valuation of self at the heart of interpersonal arrogance manifests an utterly false view of the worth of persons (G 4:436, 439; C 5:73). The problem is not just that arrogant individual does not regard others as ends in themselves, or is motivated by considerations of self-esteem to deny that others are his equals in fundamental worth and status, which makes him liable to treat them disrespectfully. The deeper problem is that he does not and, within the value framework under which he operates, cannot regard any being, himself included, as a being with dignity unconditionally deserving of respect. The valuing he demands from others is extrinsic, a 'price,' to use Kant's terms, that constitutes an exchange value (G 4:434). Thus, Kant says, the arrogant person is always '*mean [niederträchtig]* in the depths of his soul. For he would not demand that others think little of themselves in comparison with him unless he knew that, were his fortune suddenly to change, he himself would not find it hard to grovel and to waive any claim to respect from others' (MM 6:466). And 'meanness' or self-abasement [*Niederträchtigkeit*], as Kant say in the *Lectures*, is the opposite of self-respect (L 27:349).

The close connection between self-abasement and arrogance is also highlighted in Kant's discussion of the latter in connection with servility, one of the vices opposed to our duty to respect ourselves, i.e., to have interpersonal recognition self-respect (MM6:434–437). Servility, which Kant also calls false or lying humility, is deliberate self-abasement: 'the disavowal of all claim to any moral worth in oneself' (MM 6:435–436). This, he says, 'is contrary to one's duty to oneself since it degrades one's personality' (MM6:436). That is, in conveying to others a sense of himself as something less than a being with dignity, the servile person violates the duty of interpersonal recognition self-respect.[14]

As Kant makes clear, however, servility is not simply a matter of misunderstanding human worth; it is motivated self-abasement, and it is motivated, as lies typically are, by a desire for something else. The servile person disavows his true moral worth because he wants to be valued in some other way, 'to acquire' as Kant says 'borrowed worth' (MM, 6:435). Servility is a ploy in the competition for comparative

---

[14] Interpersonal recognition self-respect corresponds to what Kant calls 'proper pride (*animus elatus*) (*Stolz*)' or 'love of honor [*Ehrliebe*]' which is 'a concern to yield nothing of one's human dignity in comparison with others' (MM 6:465). But this is precisely what the servile individual does yield as he invites others to regard him as a being of a lesser kind.

self-worth: if gaining greater worth in the eyes of others is unsuccessful, an individual can 'borrow worth' from others in other ways, for example, be valued by them for his humbleness or usefulness. Whatever the specifics, the servile person, in trading his dignity for something else he wants, makes himself 'a plaything of the mere inclinations and hence a thing' (MM 6:420). Two sets of inclinations dominate here: the servile person's own desire for self-esteem that requires being valued by others, and the feelings and desires of those whose favor he seeks, especially their desire for a self-esteem that feeds on the deference of others. What, at bottom, makes servility wrong, Kant explains, is that it is a violation of the 'prohibition against depriving [oneself] of the *prerogative* of a moral being, that of acting in accordance with principles, that is, inner freedom' through the willingness to let one's choices be determined by the inclinations rather than by reason (MM 6:420). Thus, as Kant describes it here, servility is not the possibly blameless misunderstanding of one's basic rights and status as a person that might, for example, characterize someone who was raised to believe she was a lesser sort of being than others. It is rather the deliberate and so culpable devaluing of oneself, and it is self-devaluation twice over. Servility is the devaluation of one's moral worth and status vis-à-vis others. And insofar as it involves the subjection of one's power of rational choice to inclinations, servility devalues that which, on Kant's view, is most truly one's self: the rationality that makes one a person. (We'll return to this point in section 3.4.) As a doubly false valuation of the self, then, servility is the failure to have interpersonal recognition self-respect.

Interpersonal arrogance, in which the arrogant person inflates his worth vis-à-vis others in order to heighten his self-esteem, involves precisely the same false valuing and failure to respect the self as servility. For the servile and the arrogant share a view of the moral community as not a relation of equals but a settled hierarchy of two moral castes, the servile taking himself to belong to the lower order of beings with lower status worth who deserve less in the way of consideration and respect from others, and the arrogant taking it for granted that he is of the morally superior caste (perhaps its only member), entitled by virtue of his greater worth and higher status to respect from others that they do not deserve from him. In valuing himself inordinately, the arrogant person values himself just as falsely as does the servile person. As with servility, arrogance also involves the subjection of the will to the inclinations; the arrogant person makes himself a 'plaything of the mere inclinations and hence a thing' and so fails to respect himself as an end in himself. The servile person sets his value in relation to others too low, the arrogant person sets it too high, and each does this because he wants to esteem himself and thinks, wrongly, that this self-valuation is more important. Interpersonal arrogance involves a failure of interpersonal recognition self-respect: not valuing an absolutely valuable being — himself — as he morally ought to be valued.

3.3. Interpersonal arrogance and the corruption of personhood

Personhood is corrupted in three ways by interpersonal arrogance. First, the self-valuing that interpersonal arrogance involves is self-destroying. What the arrogant individual wants is to be securely and objectively more worthy, securely and objectively superior to others. But the demand that others respect him makes their 'respect' worthless because it must be insincere, and his demanding makes it more than likely that he won't even get insincere respect, 'for the more he shows that that he is trying to obtain respect, the more everyone denies it to him' (M 6:465). Moreover, the value he is accorded by others and so by himself is not in the least objective: the valuing of others is subjective, arbitrary, and highly variable, and the 'self-worth' he derives is not really *self*-worth at all. The ground of self-worth is thus pulled out from under him.

Second, to value oneself so inordinately is, Kant says, to make oneself a thing. That is, it is to make oneself something other than and less than a person. Making oneself a thing does not, however, involve failing to be a person in the sense of lacking or losing the rational capacities of humanity and personality, nor in the sense of losing the dignity and moral status of persons, for it is impossible to lack or lose these; it involves not identifying oneself to oneself or to others as a person in the first two senses. The failure to be a person is not a matter of metaphysics or status but of valuing. But so long as the arrogant individual makes himself a thing to himself and to others, he makes himself unable to exercise the capacity to value morally that makes him a person in the first two senses; and so he might just as well be a thing metaphysically and in status: he has made his personhood irrelevant to himself and he invites others to disregard it as well.

Third, Kant's analysis reveals that the rational capacities themselves are led by arrogance into self-destruction. For the perversion of humanity, the rational capacity to value, in its propensity for competitive comparative valuing of self and others and hence for interpersonal arrogance, thwarts personality, the rational capacity to value persons, including oneself, morally correctly.

Kant holds that the propensity to value oneself as higher than others is 'rooted in a reason which is practical but only as subservient to other incentives' (R 6:28). That is, the perversion of humanity and thwarting of personality that interpersonal arrogance involves traces to a deeper arrogance, an unwarrantable claims arrogance, that even more directly subverts moral agency and corrupts personhood. I take this up in the next section.

3.4. Unwarrantable claims arrogance and agentic recognition self-respect

In contrasting arrogance with servility, Kant identifies 'moral arrogance [*Tugendstolz*] (*arrogantia moralis*)' as 'a conviction of the greatness of one's moral worth [*moralischen Werth*], *but only from failure to compare it with the law*' (MM 6:435, emphasis mine). The emphasized clause suggests that arrogance is not only a matter of unjustifiable claims to superiority over others but also of ascribing worth to oneself independently of the moral law. That is, moral arrogance is the arrogation by one's desires for self-esteem of the authority to determine self-worth through the refusal to acknowledge the moral law as the supreme condition of all worth of persons. This is unwarrantable claims arrogance, and it involves a failure of agentic recognition self-respect.

Whereas interpersonal recognition self-respect is the practical appreciation of oneself as a person among persons, agentic recognition self-respect is properly acknowledging and valuing oneself as a moral agent, which involves, among other things, taking seriously the responsibilities of moral agency. For Kant, the most central of these is the responsibility to realize one's personality, one's capacity for moral valuing and autonomous agency, by choosing to act through rational motives, i.e., from respect for the moral law, submitting oneself to the absolute authority of the moral law, which is to say, to the dictates of one's own rationality unimpeded by the importuning of the inclinations. One claims too much moral worth out of the arrogantly unwarrantable claim of moral authority for one's inclinations and so the subordination of one's capacity for rational judgment. This is a debasement of one's dignity as a rational being, and a failure of agentic recognition self-respect, for no self-respecting moral agent would subordinate their rational autonomy to their desire for self-esteem.[15]

The arrogant person, out of the desire to heighten or maintain self-esteem, adjusts the law and its standards to his actions, by representing as law something that encourages him to do what he wants and then calls it right, so that he can think well of himself for doing his moral duty, no matter what in fact he does. And he does this by casting the merely contingent features of his personal psychology as objectively justified principles with unconditional authority over all agents. His desire for self-esteem thus claims the kind of authority that is possessed only by the moral law generated by pure practical reason.

Arrogance is thus the chief obstacle to morality and must therefore be struck down to make possible the practical acknowledgment of the true authority of the moral law. This striking down of arrogance is experienced first as humiliation and then as respect both for the moral law and for ourselves as authors of the law (C 5:74). And respect for the moral law and for our own dignity as autonomous law-givers, are, Kant maintains, among the subjective grounds of the possibility of morality — did we not experience them, morality would be impossible (MM 6:399-403).

How unchecked arrogance poses such a threat to morality becomes clear when we understand its mode of operation.[16] An agent can't think well of himself morally without acknowledging moral standards and taking his conduct, motives, attitudes, or character to conform to them. Someone of modest merit, great demerit, and a compelling desire to think well of himself arrives at a high opinion of himself not by ignoring the moral law or thumbing his nose at it — which Kant

---

[15] Kant treats arrogance in a similar way in his explanation in the *Critique of Practical Reason* of how the moral law becomes an incentive, that is, how it can directly determine our choice of action independently of our inclinations. There Kant contrasts self-love [*Selbstliebe, Eigenliebe*] with what he calls self-conceit [*Eigendünkel*] or arrogance (*Arrogantia*) (C 5:73). Consciousness of the moral law affects self-love and self-conceit differently, and through these effects the law becomes an incentive. Whereas self-love is 'checked' by pure practical reason so that self-benevolent actions are restricted to agreement with the law, pure practical reason *'strikes down'* self-conceit altogether, since all claims to esteem for oneself [*Selbstschätzung*] that precede accord with the moral law are null and quite unwarranted...' (C 5:73). Arrogance has to be struck down and not just constrained because it poses a insidious threat: '[The] propensity to make the subjective determining grounds of one's choice into an objective determining ground of the will in general is called self-love; when it makes itself legislative and an unconditional practical principle, it can be called self-conceit...[S]elf-conceit...decrees the subjective conditions of self-love as laws' (CB 5:74). As Beck (1960, 291) puts it, arrogance is 'the inclination to take one's own subjective maxims and interests as having the authority of law.'

[16] I am indebted to Bernard Reginster for calling my attention to and helping me to understand this process.

regards as impossible for a rational being (R 6:35) — but rather by taking himself to meet the demands of the law which he 'flatters himself that he inwardly reveres' (MM 6:430). Though he does not meet the law's standards, his inclinations 'secretly work against' the law (C 5:86) in at least three ways to produce a judgment of high merit. First, the arrogant person deceives himself about the standards for moral conduct, pretending that the law only advises rather than commands inescapably and unconditionally the strict performance of all duties (L 27:623). Judging himself by such lax standards, he can't but look good. Second, he deceives himself about himself, both about the moral quality of his actions and, very importantly, about his motives for acting; he pretends to himself (as he has to) that his motive for acting is the motive of duty, which is the only motive that gives actions moral worth, when his real motive is his desire to think well of himself. Through this self-corrupting double self-deception, the arrogant person's conduct and motives can appear morally worthy to him. Third, he 'tinkers with the moral law' (L 27:465), adjusting the law and its standards to his actions so that he can think well of himself as doing his moral duty, no matter what in fact he does.

This last move is the most seriously wrong one; indeed, Kant identifies it as the deepest source of evil in human nature, in which 'the mind's attitude is ... corrupted at its root' (R 6:30). For it involves not merely the frailty of wanting to do right but being too weak to resist temptations, nor the impurity of needing to be pushed by our inclinations to do what we know we ought to do, but the 'depravity' or 'perversity' of subordinating the incentives of the moral law to those of the inclinations (R 6:29–30). The most fundamental way in which humans go wrong lies not in the fact that one pays attention to one's inclinations in deciding what to do, but in their insubordination. It lies, that is, in 'revers[ing] the moral order of his incentives in incorporating them into his maxim,' making 'the incentives of self-love and their inclinations the condition of the compliance with the moral law' (R 6:36). In this way the arrogant person is able to pass off what he wants to do for what he ought to do, representing as law something that encourages him to do what he wants and calls it right. The desire for self-esteem thus makes self-love a 'legislative and an unconditional practical principle' (CB 5:74), usurping for itself the kind of authority that is possessed only by the moral law generated by pure practical reason.

3.5. Unwarrantable claims arrogance and the corruption of personhood

Unwarrantable claims arrogance might have seemed to be one moral flaw among many others to which imperfect humans are inevitably liable. But understood as claiming for one's inclinations the authority of objective moral law, it is the most serious of vices: the failure to value one's capacity for autonomous rational agency which stands as the chief obstacle to the moral agency and rational judgment. It is not an excess of which agentic recognition self-respect is the mean; rather, it is a radically deformed value system altogether different from self-respect. As the contrary of this form of arrogance, agentic recognition self-respect is the first condition of the possibility of moral agency and judgment. The person with agentic recognition self-respect values unconditionally the autonomous exercise of rational judgment and will, takes seriously the responsibilities that lie on moral agents in virtue of their capacity for rational autonomy, and regards morally worthy conduct as the only fitting expression of the consciousness of one's dignity as a moral agent. The arrogant person values self-esteem above all; consequently, his judgment is perverted, his agency corrupted, his autonomy undermined, and his dignity degraded.

The arrogant individual gives absolute priority to his inclinations over reason 'just as if (inclination) constituted our entire self' (C 5:74). In such a case, Kant says, the individual 'throws (himself) away', 'abandons', 'surrenders', or 'abdicates' his personality (MM 420, 425, 429; L 27:341–348). That is not to say that the rational capacities or the dignity and status of equality have been annihilated; they are still there, irrevocably part of his nature. So, in one sense, his arrogance doesn't matter morally: it doesn't change him metaphysically into a lower order of being, it does not alter his moral worth or status. But in another sense, the way in which it doesn't matter matters morally. For the arrogant person's personhood does not matter to him; as far as he is concerned, his rational capacities for morality might just as well be annihilated: in abandoning them, throwing them away, he has eradicated them from his view of himself. He does not identify himself to himself as a being with the capacity for rationally autonomous moral agency and judgment. And, in acting as if these capacities had been really eradicated, he has made the realization of both his personality and his humanity impracticable. For not only is his capacity for moral valuing thwarted, but his capacity to set ends, to make rational judgments of the value of ends and so of himself, is subverted:

when inclinations rule, there is no objective valuing, there is only desire, and so the ground of self-worth has been pulled out from under him; his humanity might just as well have 'dissolve(d) ... into mere animality' (MM 6:400).

Aristotle tells us that we become what we practice being. Kant tells us that when we practice not respecting ourselves, arrogantly denying personhood, we make ourselves something less than a person.[17]

References

Baumeister, R.F. (1994), 'Self-esteem', *Encyclopedia of Human Behavior,* Vol. 4., ed. V.S. Ramachandran (San Diego, CA: Academic Press).
Beck, L.W. (1960), *A Commentary on Kant's Critique of Practical Reason* (Chicago, IL: University of Chicago Press).
Coopersmith, S. (1967), *The Antecedents of Self-Esteem* (San Francisco, CA: Freeman).
Darwall, S. (1977), 'Two kinds of respect', *Ethics,* **88** (1977), pp. 36–49, reprinted in Dillon (1995).
Dillon. R. (2003), 'Respect', *The Stanford Encyclopedia of Philosophy* (Fall 2003 Edition), ed. Edward N. Zalta, URL = <http://plato.stanford.edu/archives/fall2003/entries/respect/>.
Dillon. R. (1997), 'Self-respect: moral, emotional, political,' *Ethics,* **107**, pp. 226–49.
Dillon. R. (ed. 1995), *Dignity, Character, and Self-Respect* (New York: Routledge).
Dillon. R. (1992), 'How to lose your self-respect', *American Philosophical Quarterly,* **29**, pp. 125–39.
Horowitz, D. (1999), 'The Last Kennedy', *FrontPageMagazine.com*, July 18; available < http://frontpagemag.com/Articles/ReadArticle.asp?ID=1182>
Hudson, S. (1988), 'The nature of respect', *Social Theory and Practice,* **6**, pp. 69–90.
Kant, I. (1785/1996), *Groundwork of the Metaphysics of Morals,* in *Practical Philosophy,* ed. and trans. M. J. Gregor (Cambridge: Cambridge University Press). Cited as G.
Kant, I. (1788/1956), *Critique of Practical Reason,* trans. Lewis White Beck (Indianapolis: Bobbs-Merrill Company). Cited as *CB*.
Kant, I. (1788/1996), *Critique of Practical Reason,* in *Practical Philosophy,* ed. and trans. M. J. Gregor (Cambridge: Cambridge University Press). Cited as C.
Kant, I. (1793/1996), *Religion Within the Boundaries of Mere Reason,* trans. by G. di Giovanni, in *Religion and Rational Theology,* ed. A. Wood and G. di Giovanni (Cambridge: Cambridge University Press). Cited as R.
Kant, I. (1797/1996), *The Metaphysics of Morals,* in *Practical Philosophy,* trans. and ed. by M. J. Gregor (Cambridge: Cambridge University Press). Cited as MM.
Kant, I. (1997), *Lectures on Ethics,* ed. P. Heath and J.B. Schneewind, trans. P. Heath (Cambridge: Cambridge University Press). Cited as L.
Korsgaard, C. (1996), *Creating the Kingdom of Ends* (Cambridge: Cambridge University Press).

---

[17] I am deeply indebted to Arto Laitinen, Heikki Ikäheimo, and Joel Anderson for their generous comments on an earlier version of this paper.

Mruk, C. (2006), *Self-Esteem Research, Theory, and Practice: Toward a Positive Psychology of Self-Esteem*, 3rd ed. (New York: Springer).

Rosen, S. (2001), 'Invest when you're young and get lifelong dividends in knowledge', *The (Allentown, PA) Morning Call*, March 4.

Rosenberg, M. (1979), *Conceiving the Self* (New York: Basic Books).

Rowlings, J.K. (1999), *Harry Potter and the Prisoner of Azkaban* (New York: Scholastic Press).

Taylor, G. (1994), 'Vices and the self', *Philosophy, Psychology and Psychiatry*, Royal Institute of Philosophy Supplement 37, ed. A. Phillips Griffiths (Cambridge University Press), pp. 145–57.

Tiberius, V. and Walker, J. (1998), 'Arrogance,' *American Philosophical Quarterly*, **35**, pp. 379–90.

Wood, A. (1999), *Kant's Ethical Thought* (Cambridge: Cambridge University Press).

Andreas Wildt

Unconscious Knowledge of One's Own Mind
A Neglected Element in Freud's Theory of the Unconscious

Abstract: Freud's principal contribution to clarifying persons' relations to themselves lies in his exploration of the dynamic relations between conscious and unconscious processes. This paper addresses another aspect of Freud's ideas, one to which he himself and his followers accorded insufficient attention, namely, unconscious knowledge, in particular, unconscious knowledge of one's own mind and hence of one's own unconscious.

First I show that Freud's idea of unconscious knowledge of one's own mind is epistemologically coherent and that it can be understood in different ways within the framework of his basic concepts. I then discuss select examples of such knowledge from his clinical and theoretical writings. In conclusion, I pose the question of the scope of these ideas for depth psychology.

Without doubt, Freud enriched our knowledge of the relation of persons to themselves more than any other thinker. Yet it is not obvious what his specific contribution to this topic was. Since Romanticism, the idea of an unconscious part of the mind has played a central role in philosophy and medicine. The concept of a motivated unconscious, i.e. of repression or defense [*Abwehr*], was developed by Schopenhauer and Nietzsche. Then Josef Breuer invented a procedure in cooperation with his patient Anna O. to make this dynamic unconscious conscious, the 'cathartic' method. Freud drew on this in developing

Correspondence:
awildt@zedat.fu-berlin.de

his psychoanalytical method and theory. In the latter, the self-relation of persons is thematized in two ways, first as regards how a person relates to her unconscious as such and, second, with regard to how she achieves and integrates an awareness of her unconscious.

In what follows, I am concerned with a particular aspect of the first kind of relation of a person to her unconscious, namely, with unconscious *knowledge* of the latter. This cognitive aspect is by no means central to Freud's self-understanding. Rather he is primarily interested in the dynamic interrelations between conscious and unconscious processes. His basic idea is that defence is never completely successful but is always reflected in changes in consciousness that provide clues for bringing it to consciousness. The idea of an unconscious knowledge of one's own mind goes further and is important for correctly understanding what is involved in becoming aware of one's own unconscious. For, insofar as an unconscious knowledge of one's own unconscious already exists, its coming to awareness and its integration need not be understood exclusively, or even primarily, as a cognitive process but also, above all, as a volitional and emotional one. I cannot discuss this point in more detail here.

In what follows, I will show that the idea of an *unconscious knowledge* of one's own mind, and hence of one's own unconscious, can be found in Freud's writings, that it is coherent, and that it leads to interesting hypotheses. However, the idea of unconscious knowledge — and in particular of unconscious knowledge of one's own unconscious — did not find expression in Freud's explicit self-understanding, but only in the form of metaphorical images. Freud dethroned consciousness by stripping it – or, to be more precise, by stripping the *ability* to become conscious – of its status as the criterion of the mental. Yet, at the same time, he did not challenge the privilege of consciousness as a necessary condition of all knowledge. Even in Freud's writings in which the idea of unconscious knowledge is important, it could never quite overcome the customary connection between knowledge and consciousness. Thus the textual evidence is contradictory. Freud did not accord his idea the sustained attention it deserves and the Freud literature has, to my knowledge,[1] almost entirely ignored it. This in no way alters the fact that it is an important element in Freud's theory of the unconscious.

My reflections fall into three parts. In the first I will show that the idea of unconscious knowledge and its specific forms is already

---

[1] I know only a modest portion of the Freud literature, though considerably more than I quote here. However, I do not claim to understand French psychoanalysis.

present in Freud's terminology for the unconscious, that it is conceptually coherent, that nevertheless it is not taken into account in Freud's explicit uses of the term 'knowledge', and that it can be understood in different ways within the context of Freud's basic conceptual apparatus. In the second part I will cite and discuss select instances of such knowledge to be found in all periods and all parts of Freud's psychoanalytic theory construction. In the brief final section I inquire how deeply the said idea in question could extend into depth psychology.

1. On the Idea of 'Unconscious Knowledge' in the Context of Freud's Terminology and Theory

Freud does not speak of an 'unconscious knowledge of the mind.' To my knowledge, Freud never speaks of 'unconscious knowledge' at all, and certainly not of 'unconscious knowledge of the unconscious'[2]; however, this does not mean very much because it remains a quite unusual way of speaking that initially sounds decidedly paradoxical or confused. However, there are precisely or largely equivalent expressions for both in Freud. Thus he speaks in several places of 'knowledge in the unconscious,'[3] of a perception of unconscious contents by the unconscious[4], of unconscious understanding and interpretation of the unconscious[5], and of 'unconscious knowledge' [*Kenntnis*][6] of the unconscious. How should 'unconscious knowledge' be understood more precisely in the present essay and what meaning can it have in the context of Freud's theory?

---

[2] I am not conversant with all of Freud's psychoanalytical writings, though I do know most of them. I have not taken Freud's correspondence into account. Freud's writings are quoted from the *Standard Edition* (Roman numbers refer to volumes, Arabic to page numbers). There is no entry for 'knowledge, unconscious' in the Index to the *Standard Edition*, though there is one for 'knowledge, conscious, and not knowing'. The passage in question (XII, 142) can be understood in such a way that Freud implicitly differentiates between conscious und unconscious knowledge [*Wissen*]. Occasionally Freud speaks of 'unconscious recollection' [*unbewusster Erinnerung*] and of 'unconscious memory' [*unbewusstem Gedächtnis*]. I have found no reference to '*unbewusstes Wissen*' in Freud though he does speak of '*unbewusste Kenntnis*,' which the *Standard Edition* translates as 'unconscious knowledge' (see n. 6 below).

[3] VII, 49; X, 129.

[4] XII, 115f.; XII, 320; XIII, 159; XIV, 194.

[5] VI, 42.

[6] VI, 254, 256, 258. Freud speaks of '*unbewusste Kenntnis*' rather than of '*unbewusstes Wissen*.'

1.1 On the concept of 'unconscious knowledge' and its specifications

Even today talk of 'unconscious knowledge' is quite unusual and, for that reason alone, at first unclear and perhaps puzzling. According to the standard definition in contemporary 'analytic' philosophy, 'knowledge' means at a minimum 'true and justified (or grounded) belief'. Thus the concept 'knowledge' has at least three components: truth, belief, and justification or grounding. The philosophical debate is mainly concerned with the more precise meaning of 'justification' or 'grounding' and whether 'knowledge' has additional semantic components.[7] I need not address these issues here. All that is important in the present context is that, in speaking of 'unconscious knowledge', I use the term 'knowledge' in the full sense that satisfies at least the three standard conditions of the concept of knowledge. What, then, does 'unconscious knowledge' mean more precisely?

First, 'unconscious' knowledge means more than 'intuitive' knowledge. We can call knowledge merely 'intuitive' when its possessor is not able to justify his true and well-founded belief himself. Hence intuitive knowledge is associated with a cognitive deficiency, though this does not usually consist in being unaware that one has the *belief* in question. However, that is the case with unconscious knowledge. All unconscious knowledge is intuitive knowledge because it cannot be associated with the ability on the part of its possessor to justify his true and well-founded belief. Conversely, however, intuitive knowledge is by no means always unconscious.

Second, 'unconscious' knowledge in this context does not mean merely 'implicit' knowledge. 'Implicit knowledge' is a central concept in contemporary epistemology, linguistics, cognitive science, and psychology, and it is sometimes glossed (in German) as 'unconscious knowledge'.[8] However, the concept of 'implicit knowledge' is much broader and more vague than my concept of 'unconscious knowledge'. If I am correct, the former is a successor concept of 'tacit knowledge', which originated in linguistics and epistemology[9] and whose primary meaning, as suggested by the word 'tacit', is an unarticulated, or even inarticulable, knowledge. Insofar as the lack of articulation here only relates to the justification of the knowledge, it is simply a matter of intuitive knowledge. But insofar as it refers to the

---

[7] See Bieri (ed.) 1987, Part 1.

[8] E.g. in Dornes, 292, 308ff.

[9] Michael Polanyi's book *The Tacit Dimension* (1966) appeared in German translation in 1985 under the title 'Implizites Wissen.'

correct belief, it could also be a case of unconscious knowledge, especially when it is a matter of *inarticulable* knowledge.

Many things are subsumed under 'tacit' or 'implicit knowledge' that cannot be called 'knowledge' in a sense relevant here. First, the kind of 'knowledge' that underlies complex activities serves as an orienting model in this regard. This so-called 'procedural knowledge,' however, is less a matter of knowledge of states of affairs or 'knowing that ...' than of 'knowing how ...,' thus an ability[10] that can also be described as at once practical and intuitive knowledge. Second, 'implicit knowledge' is used in part to refer to information processing in the brain or its results. Already in the nineteenth century scientists commonly spoke of 'unconscious inferences' that are constitutive features of perception. However, to use the term 'unconscious' in connection with this kind of information processing is in a certain sense misleading because it does not concern psychic processes at all but physiological processes in the brain that could also be performed by artifacts. This also holds for so-called 'learning processes' based on conditioning and habituation that are also often meant in contemporary uses of the concepts 'implicit knowledge' and 'implicit memory'.

Thus the concept of 'implicit knowledge' as it is now generally used is not suitable as an explication or replacement of the concept of 'unconscious knowledge' for a number of reasons. In the first place, it often does not refer to mental phenomena at all. In addition, it often does not refer to knowledge in the full sense of propositional truth, but merely to an ability. And, finally, it often refers to a form of knowledge that is not articulated, though it is normally articulable. Only when it concerns the mental and (under normal conditions) inarticulable knowledge of states of affairs can it be 'unconscious' in a sense proper to depth psychology.

Third, 'unconscious' knowledge means more than knowledge that the subject does not know about. As we shall see in the second part of this essay, in two of his most important writings Freud expressly assumed 'that there is knowledge of which the person concerned nevertheless knows nothing' (XV, 102). This is in the first instance merely a knowledge that the subject does not know about. But here Freud means, in addition, a knowledge that is marked by the conscious conviction that one has no knowledge of its object; and Freud evidently

---

[10] On this distinction, see Bieri (1987), pp. 13f. Instead of speaking of 'propositional knowledge,' as is customary in analytic philosophy, I prefer to speak of 'knowledge of states of affairs' because I want to avoid the assumption that 'knowing that...' must be linguistically structured.

believes that such a knowledge must be unconscious. This may be an overhasty inference.

The possibility of knowledge that the subject does not know about is also recognized to some extent by contemporary epistemology,[11] though the latter focuses exclusively on conscious knowledge and belief. For, whereas epistemology is mainly interested in the question of whether 'knowledge' always implies 'knowledge (and hence belief) that one knows,' or whether it may not be connected with doubt or epistemic indecision concerning this knowledge, Freud is interested in a knowledge that involves in addition a pronounced disbelief, and hence the certainty and assurance on the part of the individual that he does not know. It is by no means contingent, but rather constitutive, for the epistemic states of which Freud speaks that knowledge of them is unconscious.[12] Since the belief-condition for the concept of knowledge is fulfilled here, it is a genuine instance of knowledge, but it must be a case of unconscious belief and hence of unconscious knowledge.

The concept of 'unconscious' knowledge has now acquired sharper contours through the differentiation between 'intuitive', 'implicit', and 'unknown' knowledge. Nevertheless the impression may persist that we are dealing with a contradictory concept. This impression rests no doubt in part on the fact that the concept of 'knowledge' is for the most part understood in such a strong sense that it cannot designate something that is simultaneously intuitive, implicit, and 'unknown'; however, there may be a deeper reason for this impression. This reservation could be finally dispelled only by providing explicit definitions of the concepts 'unconscious' and 'knowledge', something I cannot attempt here. Nevertheless I can draw on the fact that the concept of 'implicit knowledge', in the sense of inarticulable knowledge, is already current and offers at least a plausible explication of 'unconscious knowledge'. As regards the main topic, I rely on the fact that the examples that I present in the second part of the essay drawing on texts of Freud render the intelligibility and indispensability of the concept of 'unconscious knowledge' sufficiently plausible.

---

[11] E.g. Dretske (1971).

[12] In the 'Introduction' to the Lectures, there is a passage where Freud differentiates between 'unconscious' [*unbewusst*] and 'unapprehended' [*ungewusst*]: psychoanalysis is 'obliged to maintain that there is unconscious thinking and unapprehended willing' (XV, 22; German: *unbewusstes Denken und ungewusstes Wollen*). Unfortunately, Freud does not give any indication concerning what he meant by this distinction. In light of my reflections in the present text, 'unapprehended' could point to a weaker form of non-knowing than 'unconscious.' Could it be that here Freud wanted to imply that willing, in contrast with having an belief, is already unconscious when it is not known?

However, to want to justify the concept of 'unconscious knowledge' simply by appealing to elementary facts of 'unconscious perception' (in the subliminal sense) seems questionable to me. First, 'perception' normally refers to a phenomenal consciousness that is clearly specific to higher animals. Subliminal 'perception,' by contrast, is a 'cognitive' process that may merely involve discriminating sensory stimuli and 'knowing' and 'cognizing' patterns, an ability shared by higher and lower animals and by the sensors of plants and artifacts, and hence clearly does not justify speaking of 'knowledge.' Second, 'knowledge' always refers to states of affairs.[13] Even phenomenal perception refers not only to qualities but also to facts. Hence, we can already acquire knowledge through phenomenal perception before we understand language. This is not true without qualification of subliminal perception.

Complex forms of subliminal perception evidently give rise to knowledge that as a consequence must be unconscious knowledge. Thus our intuitive knowledge of the feelings of others rests not only on conscious perception, but also in large part on subliminal perception of their facial expressions and gestures. Freud assumed, at any rate, that we have unconscious perception and unconscious understanding not only of the conscious mental life of others but also of their unconscious (see section 2.3 below). If anything is paradoxical concerning talk of 'unconscious knowledge,' then it is not that it refers to knowledge of the unconscious of others. At most, the concept of an 'unconscious knowledge of the unconscious' that refers exclusively to one's own mind could be paradoxical.

This suspicion certainly cannot be confirmed by reference to Freud's writings. Freud describes affective self-experience quite naturally as 'internal perception' (XIX, 21) and thereby assumes 'that internal objects are less unknowable than the external world' (XIV, 171). Even if one is unwilling to accept both of these ideas, nevertheless knowledge based on affective self-experience is a non-inferential, hence direct or immediate, form of knowledge, though it is not for this reason incorrigible.[14] And this surely also holds for all knowledge of one's own unconscious, including knowledge of unconscious thoughts.[15] It is also clear that it is easier for knowledge to be

---

[13] Cf. Bieri (1987), pp. 11ff.

[14] See Rorty (1970).

[15] To my knowledge, Freud nowhere speaks of 'immediate knowledge,' only of 'immediate consciousness' (XX, 32) and 'direct experience'(XIV, 167; German: *unmittelbare Erfahrung*). This always means an experience 'through consciousness' (*ibid.*), hence

unconscious if it is immediate. Hence much can be said for the possibility of an unconscious knowledge of one's own unconscious, provided that there is such a thing as unconscious knowledge. Even though self-knowledge is normally supposed to be more difficult than knowledge of others, it does not follow that this also holds for immediate knowledge of the unconscious.

1.2 *Freud's various uses of 'knowledge'*

It is perhaps time that we acknowledged that these conceptual subtleties are quite foreign to Freud. Freud was not a philosopher. For the most part, he quite naturally assumed — in complete agreement with the philosophy of his time, as it happens — an opposition between the unconscious and knowledge: 'Now all our knowledge is invariably bound up with consciousness. We can come to know even the unconscious only by making it conscious' (XIX, 19). Since Freud wanted to develop a science of the unconscious, he naturally does not intend this opposition in an absolute sense, but primarily in the sense that knowledge of the unconscious must be a form of *inferred* knowledge.[16] Sometimes Freud even says of unconscious processes: 'In themselves they cannot be cognized' (XIV, 187). This statement obviously rests on a sceptical interpretation, vaguely indebted to Kant, of a physiological theory of perception (*ibid.*). However, Freud is not serious about his epistemological scepticism.[17] If he excludes the possibility of a knowledge of the unconscious, then he clearly intends a non-inferential, immediate knowledge, specifically an immediate knowledge of one's own unconscious.[18]

To the extent that, in direct contradiction with this, Freud nevertheless repeatedly assumes an immediate knowledge of one's own unconscious,[19] as I will show in detail in the second part, this could be because, first, he wants to describe special, particularly complex phenomena that seem to justify such a concept. This is certainly often the

---

conscious experience. Thus speaking of an 'immediate' or 'direct' and 'unconscious experience' would be incompatible with Freud's terminology.

[16] XV, 65; XIV, 166.

[17] Compare XIV, 171 with XIX, 23.

[18] XVI, 277; XXII, 69f.; XII, 263; XIX, 16 n., 24; VIII, 162; X, 12 n. 3; cf. n. 15 above. Sometimes one encounters in the literature the view that knowledge of the unconscious is impossible for conceptual reasons, for instance because such knowledge would have to be 'given in a consciousness' (as in Knapp [1984], p. 264). This is, of course, nonsense.

[19] To my knowledge, Friebe (2005) first drew attention to these contradictions in the texts (see especially pp. 79 ff., 91 ff.). Friebe's book provided me with important confirmation and encouragement, even though I do not subscribe to his Kantian epistemology.

case, especially with forms of (more or less conscious) insincerity or disingenuousness (toward oneself)[20] and of splitting just below the level of consciousness,[21] especially in compulsion neuroses, phobias,[22] and in special psychoses.[23] I will discuss such phenomena in part in the second part.

Second, Freud's often disconcertingly cognitive way of speaking could be an artifact of specific features of his theory-construction, in particular his 'meta-psychological' distinctions between different psychic 'rooms' [*Räumlichkeiten*], 'organizations,' 'systems,' 'structures,' 'instances,' etc., above all between 'id,' 'ego,' and 'superego.' In fact, Freud unhesitatingly says that 'the superego knew more than the ego about the unconscious id' (XIX, 51; cf. XX, 117). And in the *Interpretation of Dreams* he introduces a 'censorship' or 'censor,' which he also describes in the *Lectures* as a 'watchman,' who 'examines' [*mustert*] and 'recognizes' the mental impulses of the unconscious (XVI, 295).

Now Freud immediately concedes that these ideas are 'crude,' 'fantastic,' and 'incorrect' (XVI, 296). They are, of course, incorrect in that here mental functions and contents are personified and something like thoughts and wishes attributed to them. But Freud insists that these are 'preliminary working hypotheses' that are 'not to be despised insofar as they are of service in making our observations intelligible' (*ibid.*). In my view, this must be understood in such a way that each individual person does indeed recognize her (own) unconscious through her unconscious functions or instances of the superego, the censor or the watchman, and acquires knowledge of her unconscious; however, this must be a matter of an *unconscious* cognition and knowledge.[24] Freud's figurative language does not merely create an

---

[20] III, 117.

[21] XII, 148; XIII, 207; VI, 266.

[22] X, 196 n. 1, 223, 228f., 248f.; X, 124; XVII, 85, 104f., 120.

[23] XXIII, 201f.; cf. Breuer in: I, 46.

[24] A further merit of Friebe (2005, pp. 91 ff.) is to have taken Freud's figurative representation here seriously. However, I do not find Friebe's conceptual articulation of Freud's metaphors convincing. The same holds for the earlier work of Bartels (1976, pp. 44 ff.). Of course, the difficulty has been remarked and discussed not only by philosophers such as Bartels and Friebe, but also by psychoanalysts. An authoritative textbook says the following on this topic: '*This censoring takes place completely outside consciousness*. The scanning and scrutiny of instinctual wishes and their derivatives involved in the censorship necessarily presumes the existence of a form of 'unconscious awareness' in the Preconscious' (Sandler *et al.* 1997, pp. 68 at.). The German translation at this point (Sandler *et al.* 2003, p. 80) even speaks of 'unconscious consciousness' [*unbewusstes Bewusstsein*].

appearance of an unconscious knowledge of the unconscious but is, on the contrary, a legitimate and plausible illustration of the latter.

Third, it could be that Freud, in this and in related contexts, intends talk of 'knowledge' and 'cognition' in a weaker sense than the customary one, perhaps so weak that it can be described as 'invalid' or 'merely metaphorical.' Freud's talk of 'examining' and 'cognizing' may also be more appropriate than that of 'recognizing' and 'knowing.'

There is at least one place where Freud clearly speaks of 'knowledge' in a loose sense, but he makes this explicit by writing 'as though'.[25] Sometimes Freud places the word 'to know' [*wissen*] in quotation marks[26] or indicates through his formulation that the word is intended in a weaker sense,[27] while only vaguely hinting in what sense. Thus there are clear indications that, even when Freud is speaking of the unconscious, he uses 'cognition' and 'knowledge' in the strict, stronger, and non-metaphorical sense.

In some places Freud distinguishes between different forms of knowledge. But these differentiations are epistemologically innocuous. Thus Freud distinguishes between 'two kinds of knowledge' [*zweierlei Wissen und Kennen*] in the case of compulsion neuroses.[28] However, he only means that the compulsive neurotic, in contrast to the hysteric, has not forgotten his (recent) traumata but does not know their meaning because he isolates the associated emotions and suppresses them.

Even Freud's more fundamental distinction between two 'different sorts of knowledge'[29] in the therapeutic situation does not point to an epistemologically relevant differentiation within the concept of knowledge. As long as the patient has not grasped the truth of what is communicated by the therapist, far from having (conscious) knowledge, he does not even have the (conscious) *belief* it presupposes, nor *a fortiori* the ability to ground the latter. However, as Freud observed, it frequently occurs that the patient acquires this belief, though often in a way that cannot support knowledge but instead through the suggestive effect of positive transference.

Unfortunately, the authors do not offer a theoretically cogent clarification of this, at least *prima facie*, contradictory description.

[25] XIV, 170.

[26] XX, 28; but cf. section 2.1 below.

[27] XVII, 120; further XXIII, 94, 101.

[28] X, 196 n. 1.

[29] XVI, 281.

1.3 What meaning can 'unconscious knowledge of one's own unconscious' have in the context of Freud's basic conceptual apparatus?

Freud famously distinguished between different meanings of 'unconscious' and 'the unconscious', in particular between the 'preconscious' and the 'dynamic unconscious.' This raises the question of how these concepts can or should be understood within the framework of Freud's other basic concepts when speaking of 'unconscious knowledge of the unconscious'. I would like to address this question here only to the extent that it is useful for the discussion of the material in the second part of the essay. I will discuss some wider implications of Freud's concepts of the unconscious briefly in the third part.

Analytic philosophers of language have focused their criticism on the nominalization of the adjective 'unconscious' into 'the unconscious', a move that Freud himself does not even problematise. I do not wish to address this here. At any rate, when I speak of 'the unconscious', I am not assuming that this is some kind of psychic region, instance, or system in Freud's sense.[30] Here I understand the term 'the unconscious' simply as a totality of unconscious mental processes, states, characteristics, etc.

Freud's fundamental distinction within the quality 'unconscious' is between 'preconscious' and 'unconscious' in a somehow 'dynamic' sense. In logical terms, talk of 'unconscious knowledge of the unconscious' can accordingly mean four things: 'preconscious knowledge of the preconscious', 'preconscious knowledge of the unconscious', 'unconscious knowledge of the preconscious', and 'unconscious knowledge of the unconscious'. Are these merely logical or are they also real possibilities, at least within the context of Freud's basic assumptions?

Even without a more detailed explication of the concepts 'preconscious' and 'unconscious', one can state with certainty that there cannot be 'unconscious knowledge of one's own preconscious' because the 'unconscious' is clearly 'unconscious' in a stronger or deeper sense than the 'preconscious'. It is also questionable whether talk of an 'unconscious' knowledge — where 'unconscious' is understood in the full Freudian sense — is even meaningful.

---

[30] Freud expressly abandoned talk of a 'system' of the unconscious with his emphasis on the unconscious parts of the 'ego' and 'superego' in his so-called 'structure theory' (XXII, 71f.; cf. XIX, 18). The conceptual scope of this self-criticism is generally underestimated, for example in the now common description of the structure theory in terms of 'second topography.'

It would indeed be problematic if this 'unconscious' could consist only of *figurative* 'representations,' hence of drive-representations, wishes, fantasies, and memories. But it also clearly includes (non-figurative) 'thoughts' and beliefs, hence possibly also true and justified beliefs, hence knowledge. However, it could be that beliefs can be 'unconscious' only when they are false or falsely grounded, irrational beliefs. In order to answer this question, we must clarify in greater detail what 'unconscious' (in the somehow 'dynamic' sense) is supposed to mean in this context.

At first sight, it seems clear that by 'dynamic unconscious' Freud always means something like 'repressed' or, more generally, 'repelled' [*abgewehrt*]. Yet this is by no means the case. Freud introduces the concept of the dynamic unconscious in such a way that he first distinguishes thoughts into 'conscious' and 'unconscious' in a purely 'descriptive' sense, and then thematizes ideas 'with a certain dynamic character, ideas keeping apart from consciousness in spite of their intensity and activity' (XII, 262). Thus here a 'dynamic unconscious' merely refers to an unconscious that is causally effective *as such*. 'Dynamic' accordingly means something like 'explanatory' in contrast to 'descriptive.' Freud duly also calls this explanatory unconscious simply 'unconscious' in contrast to the 'preconscious.' 'Preconscious' in this context means the descriptive unconscious[31] that, once it has achieved a certain level of intensity, gains access to consciousness 'with no difficulty' (XII, 263) or, to be more precise, 'without any special resistance' (XIV, 173).

In Freud, 'unconscious' in this dynamic or explanatory sense extends beyond the repressed or repelled in two respects. First, it also includes the agency of repression or repulsion, hence the Freudian 'censor' and 'watchman,' and consequently parts of the 'ego' and the 'superego.' Unfortunately Freud recognized this fact only later and in part when he ceased to speak of the repressed/repulsed unconscious as 'the unconscious' or 'the dynamic unconscious' and spoke instead of 'the id' (or of a part of it). Above all, however, Freud and his followers never concluded that they should now reproblematize the concept of the 'dynamic unconscious' and then either restrict it to what is repelled or use it as a higher-level concept covering both what is

---

[31] A hopeless confusion prevails in some texts of Freud and his followers over whether the concept 'descriptive unconscious' is supposed to be a generic term for 'preconscious' and (dynamic) 'unconscious' or a synonym for 'preconscious' (compare XIX, 15 with XXII, 71f.). In my view, this confusion can be cleared up only by abandoning the concept 'descriptive unconscious' and replacing it simply by 'non-conscious.' The latter then functions as an unambiguous generic term for 'preconscious' and 'dynamic unconscious.'

repelled and the agency of repulsion. However, since Freud's — and even Breuer's — original criterion for the dynamic unconscious was the *inability* to become conscious (II, 222ff.; XIV, 173), it strikes me as appropriate to treat the concept as a generic term.[32] Regrettably there are as yet no terms for the two subspecies of the dynamic unconscious. I call them simply the 'repelled unconscious' and the 'repelling unconscious.'

Second, in Freud the unconscious-mental also belongs to the 'unconscious' that has not even become an object of censorship, and hence has not even confronted the alternative between being repelled or not (see XII, 264). Although this unconscious is completely incapable of becoming conscious, it strikes me as misleading to speak here in terms of a 'dynamic unconscious' because as yet no defence mechanism is at work. One could perhaps speak here of a 'primary unconscious'. But this dimension of the unconscious postulated by Freud is not relevant for the idea of unconscious knowledge of the unconscious in Freud, since clearly he does not assume that knowledge of any kind is involved here. Nevertheless, we must ask whether such an 'unconscious' can be something mental at all.

In light of these preliminary conceptual remarks, we can answer the question in what more precise sense there can be 'unconscious' knowledge of (one's own) 'unconscious' in Freud. If 'unconscious' here means 'dynamic unconscious', then the knowledge in question can be either 'repelling unconscious' or 'repelled unconscious'. Freud obviously assumes a repelling-unconscious knowledge when he assigns the ego a watchman function. The hypothesis that the knowledge can be repelled unconscious, hence an object of repulsion, is also at least plausible. It seems to me, at any rate, that with every repeated act of repelling, a knowledge of what is repelled must also be repelled. This is particularly true of 'repression proper' as opposed to 'primal repression' (XIV, 148).

Assuming that it is a matter of the person's preconscious knowledge of himself, the object of the knowledge in question can certainly be preconscious and, assuming it is a matter of unconscious knowledge, it can certainly be repelled unconscious. It remains open whether one's own dynamic unconscious can also be an object of *pre*conscious knowledge and whether one's own repelling unconscious can also be an object of *un*conscious knowledge. The answers to these questions are clearly connected with further questions that

---

[32] Freud himself does this explicitly in a later passage (XXII, 71), though without acknowledging the contradiction with his frequent usage elsewhere.

remain in part unresolved in Freud's theory. For Freud wavers between describing the repelling function as dynamic unconscious and as preconscious[33] and hesitates to assume a 'second censorship' on the threshold between the preconscious and the conscious.[34]

Freud's idea of an unconscious knowledge of (one's own) unconscious has been largely ignored by the Freud literature (for exceptions, see fns. 19 and 24 above). However, one occasionally encounters assertions to the contrary.[35] In the textbook of Sandler *et al.*, the discussion of Freud's theory of 'second censorship' leads the authors to represent much of the preconscious as simultaneously dynamic unconscious, and even to conclude that 'we can see the division between what is conscious and what is unconscious as being a matter of degree' (Sander *et al.*, pp. 100, 154f.). Of course, this would also legitimize talk of 'unconscious knowledge (of one's own unconscious)' (cf. n. 24 above).

2. Examples of Unconscious Knowledge of One's Own Mind in Different Areas of Freud's Theory

Now that we have shown that the idea of an unconscious knowledge of one's own unconscious is at least implicitly present in Freud's terminology and theory of the unconscious, that it is conceptually coherent, and how it can be understood in the context of Freud's theory of the unconscious, the way is open to discuss Freud's thematization of this knowledge in different areas of his theory. Due to limitations of space, I can do this here only by way of examples and in an abbreviated form. The sections on hypnosis, the psychopathology of everyday life, on compulsion neuroses, and on childhood must be reserved for later publications.

2.1 Hysteria

In the *Studies on Hysteria*, Freud describes witnessing demonstrations conducted by Bernheim that his experimental subjects following hypnosis were able to remember their experiences while under hypnosis in spite of vehement assurances to the contrary, provided only that Bernheim insisted upon this with sufficient emphasis. Freud continues as follows:

---

[33] Contrast XIV, 192f. and XIX, 18 with XXIII, 162ff.
[34] On the assumption of a 'second censorship,' see XIV, 193.
[35] See Cavell (1993), pp. 183, 194f.

This astonishing and instructive experiment served as my model. I decided to start from the assumption that my patients knew everything that was of any pathogenic significance and that it was only a question of obliging them to communicate it. Thus when I reached a point at which, after asking a patient some question such as: 'How long have you had this symptom?' or: 'What was its origin?,' I was met with the answer: 'I really don't know,' I proceeded as follows. I placed my hand on the patient's forehead or took her head between my hands and said: 'You will think of it under the pressure of my hand. At the moment at which I relax my pressure you will see something in the front of you or something will come into your head. Catch hold of it. It will be what we are looking for. — Well, what have you seen or what occurred to you?'

On the first occasions on which I made use of this procedure (it was not with Lucy R.) I myself was surprised to find that it yielded me the precise results that I needed. And I can safely say that it has scarcely ever left me in the lurch since then. It has always pointed the way which the analysis should take and has enabled me to carry through every such analysis to an end without the use of somnambulism ...

This business of enlarging what was supposed to be a restricted consciousness was laborious – far more so, at least, than an investigation during somnambulism. But it nevertheless made me independent of somnambulism, and gave me insight into the motives which often determine the 'forgetting' of memories. I can affirm that this forgetting is often intentional and desired; and its success is never more than *apparent*. (II, 110 f.)

This striking and fascinating passage shows like few others Freud as a discoverer of genius. Since reading it I have been struck by the fact that I have never to my knowledge encountered it — nor the corresponding passage from the *Lectures* that I will cite in the next section — in the literature on the unconscious. This striking neglect cannot be justified by fact that, in the *Studies*, Freud himself points out the limits of this method of suggestion and pressure, and begins the process of replacing it by the method of free association. For if the 'model' of Bernheim's experiments had lost its validity not only for Freud's therapeutic procedure but also for proving the existence of unconscious knowledge of oneself, then Freud could not have cited this evidence at the beginning of his presentation of the theory of dream interpretation in the *Lectures*, and indeed with such emphasis. Evidently the transition to the method of free association not only marks a fundamental turning point in Freud's development but also signals a discrepancy between different levels of his theoretical self-understanding. Whereas in the clinical writings and the writings on the theory of dreams mentioned hypnotic experiments served Freud as evidence for *unconscious knowledge of oneself* in particular, in his metapsychological writings they serve only as an initial proof that there is an unconscious in the 'dynamic' sense *at all*.

Not only was the therapeutic method described in the quotation from the *Studies* in need of revision, however, but also Freud's theoretical comments on it. Here Freud states that the success of forgetting 'is never more than *apparent*' (*ibid.*). This strikes me as not altogether appropriate, or at any rate as ambiguous. As long as patients are incapable of remembering, notwithstanding sincere self-examination, then their *forgetting* is really, not merely apparently, successful. The subsequent recollection only indicates that their *non-knowledge* is 'apparent' in the sense that they have an unconscious knowledge of what they remember. The *forgetting* is 'apparent' in the strict sense only when the patients — more or less consciously — mislead or deceive themselves[36] concerning the fact that they do not know and have forgotten.

In fact, a closer examination of the case study of Lucy R. shows that here Freud does not demonstrate repression in the strict, dynamic unconscious sense, but only forms of more or less conscious self-delusion. Admittedly, Freud speaks repeatedly of '(deliberate) repression' of events, ideas, inclinations, etc., but here this concept does not refer to an unconscious process, or at any rate not unequivocally. This is shown by Freud's more detailed descriptions of this 'deliberate repression' (II, 113 n.) and of the resulting non-knowing (II, 117). Freud does go on to describe how he succeeded in bringing to light 'a still earlier scene' behind the initially remembered scene 'which was the really operative trauma' (II, 120); but even this 'trauma' does not make the erotic desires and hopes of the patient and the experiences that frustrate them fully unconscious.

Hence Freud's striking talk of 'the peculiar situation of knowing and at the same time not knowing' (II, 165; II, 117 n. 1) remains ambiguous. Evidently, Freud also wants to *describe* a state of *unconscious* knowledge and of simultaneously conscious non-knowledge, but here he can

---

[36] In contemporary analytic philosophy, there is a controversy over whether 'self-deception' can exist at all or whether the concept is contradictory. This is due in part to the ambiguity of the relevant words. 'Self-deception' certainly exists in the sense that one can be mistaken about oneself or that one's self-perception can be erroneous. This is a problem, if at all, concerning the possibility of actively and intentionally deceiving oneself or lying to oneself about oneself. In my opinion, lying and deception are always intentional, and hence more or less conscious, acts or 'acts of volition' [*Willkürakt*], as Freud sometimes says (II, 123). Hence 'self-deception' and 'existential lies' [*Lebenlügen*] can only be partially successful. Active self-delusion [*Selbsttäuschung*], by contrast, can be completely successful, but only as long as its intention remains unconscious. For a discussion of the philosophical debates over 'self-delusion,' also from a psychoanalytic perspective, see Löw-Beer (1990).

only *explain* a state of more or less successful self-delusion. Freud finds an explanation for fully successful, hence *unconscious*, self-delusion only in his later theory of early childhood trauma and the 'belatedness' of its pathogenic effects and in his theory of childhood sexuality and two-stage sexual development.

Freud's commentary on the later case history of 'Dora' show that he clung to the idea of the hysteric's unconscious knowledge of what he has forgotten and repressed even after the development of a specifically analytic form of therapy. There Freud explicates 'the patient's inability to give an ordered history of their life' (VII,16) as follows:

> In the first place, patients consciously and intentionally keep back part of what they ought to tell — things that are perfectly well known to them — because they have not got over their feelings of timidity and shame (or discretion, where what they say concerns other people); this is the share taken by *conscious* disingenuousness. In the second place, part of the anamnestic knowledge, which the patients have at their disposal at other times, disappears while they are actually telling their story, but without their making any deliberate reservations: the share taken by *unconscious* disingenuousness. In the third place, there are invariably true amnesias — gaps in the memory into which not only old recollections but even quite recent ones have fallen — and paramnesias, formed secondarily so as to fill in those gaps... In the further course of the treatment the patient supplies the facts which, though he had known them all along, had been kept back by him or had not occurred to his mind. (VII, 17 f.).

This knowledge is, of course, likewise conscious, as far as 'conscious disingenuousness' goes. As far as both the 'true amnesias' and 'unconscious disingenuousness' go, however, this knowledge must be unconscious. In distinguishing between 'true amnesias' and 'unconscious disingenuousness,' Freud does not mean that there is no genuine forgetting in the case of 'unconscious disingenuousness,' but only that it is a case of — more or less conscious — self-deception. In fact, in this case the patient in the therapeutic situation does not have at her disposal a (conscious) knowledge 'which the patients have at their disposal at other times' (*ibid.*). In the former cases, her self-delusion is strictly *unconscious* and free of 'resolution,' if also not devoid of (unconscious) intent[37], and hence may imply strictly *unconscious knowledge*.

---

[37] Freud makes interpretation of the quoted passage difficult by speaking of 'unconscious dishonesty' and by failing to distinguish explicitly between 'intention' [*Absicht*] and 'resolution' [*Vorsatz*] – the English translation of '*Vorsatz*' by 'deliberate' even obscures the difference. An intention may be unconscious, as Freud states in earlier works, but a

Freud explicitly assumes two further kinds of unconscious knowledge of oneself in 'Dora,' namely, knowledge of sexual procedures and practices (such as oral sex) 'in the unconscious' on the part of 'inexperienced girls' (VII, 49) and children's knowledge of the connection between bedwetting and masturbation which is later retained in the unconscious (VII, 74). On the other hand, I wonder whether this knowledge should not be more correctly described as 'half-conscious' or 'more or less conscious' or 'more or less unconscious.' It is clearly 'unconscious,' if at all, only in the sense that it is not verbalizable.

2.2 Dreaming

In presenting his theory of dreams in the *Lectures*, Freud assumes that dreaming is a psychic phenomenon and that the dreamer, when asked about the meaning of his dream, generally responds, in contrast with many cases of mistakes or parapraxes, that he knows nothing about it. Then Freud surprises his audience by asserting 'that it is quite possible, and highly probable indeed, that the dreamer *does* know what his dream means: *only he does not know that he knows it and for that reason thinks he does not know it*' (XV, 101). Concerning the assumed fact 'that there is knowledge of which the person concerned nevertheless knows nothing' (XV, 102), however, Freud qualifies it as 'a fact, incidentally, which cancels itself in its very naming and which nevertheless claims to be something real — a contradiction in terms' (XV, 102 f.). But evidently Freud does not take this logical reservation altogether seriously, for otherwise he could not continue his enquiries in a field in which it had already been shown that such knowledge exists.

Freud finds this proof in demonstrations by Bernheim of the kind which we already discussed in the previous section. From the possibility of posthypnotic memory, Freud also infers in the *Lectures* that the patient who has awoken from hypnosis 'had known it earlier as well. It was merely inaccessible to him; he did not know that he knew it and thought he did not know it' (XV, 103).

That even the dreamer should have such an (unconscious) knowledge of his dream is probable, according to Freud, for the simple reason that dreaming and hypnosis are related states.

---

resolution cannot be so in my opinion – any more than an act of will can be unconscious. 'Disingenuousness' or insincerity can assume different forms – in particular, one must distinguish between being insincere toward others and toward oneself; but in my view, at any rate, it always involves a deliberate and hence (more or less) conscious form of conduct, as do lying and deception. Instead of speaking of 'unconscious disingenuousness,' therefore, Freud should have spoken more correctly of 'unconscious self-delusion' (cf. previous fn.).

Freud concludes that: 'It is very possible, then, that the dreamer knows about his dream; the only question is how to make it possible for him to discover his *knowledge* and communicate it to us' (XV, 104). This leads him to the following procedure:

> We do not require him to tell us straight away the sense of his dream, but he will be able to find its origin, the circle of thoughts and interests from which it sprang. You will recall that in the case of the parapraxis the man was asked how he had arrived at the wrong word '*Vorschwein*' and the first thing that occurred to him gave us the explanation. Our technique with dreams, then, is a very simple one, copied from this example. We shall once more ask the dreamer how he arrived at the dream, and once more his first remark is to be looked on as an explanation. Thus we disregard the distinction between his thinking or not thinking that he knows something, and we treat both cases as one and the same. (XV, 104 f.)

In this way Freud introduces his method of dream interpretation based on free associations on the dream in the *Lectures* quite differently from his approach in the *Interpretation of Dreams*. At the latest by the quoted passage, however, the reader might begin to have doubts whether the chosen route really leads to the goal of proving that the dreamer already had prior knowledge of the meaning of his dream. The example of a mistake presented here is not pertinent because the motivation was (more or less) conscious from the outset. Bernheim's demonstrations, which Freud no longer draws upon in the last passage, would serve as a suitable model here only if the dream interpretation, similar to the analysis of hysterical symptoms, hinged on uncovering memories. Although Freud duly states in the quoted passage that he will 'once more ask the dreamer how he arrived at the dream' (*ibid.*), this can be understood in the first instance only as a question concerning the 'day's residues,' which, according to Freud, trigger the dream but are not its cause. Moreover, Freud's question does not cohere fully with the analytical method of free association on the dream because it focuses on the *genesis* of the dream.

Freud goes on to prove that the method of free association on the dream does in fact lead as a general rule to the discovery of the meaning of the dream. This certainly constitutes a strong argument for the determination of mental life by the unconscious, as Freud emphasizes, but it by no means shows that an unconscious knowledge of the unconscious exists and that the associations are steered by this. The assumption of this unconscious knowledge does provide a plausible justification for the fact that the method of free association leads to a meaning that was previously unconscious; however, it by no means follows that the converse inference is also justified.

The fact of unconscious knowledge of the meaning of the dream reappears at the very point where, according to Freud, the method of association breaks down, namely, in understanding the symbolism of dreams. The symbolic form of expression of dreams gives rise to the following problems for Freud:

> It is not easy to account for this fact by the help of our psychological views. We can only say that the knowledge of symbolism is unconscious to the dreamer, that it belongs to his unconscious mental life. But even with this assumption we do not meet the point. Hitherto it has only been necessary for us to assume the existence of unconscious endeavors — endeavors, that is, of which, temporarily or permanently, we know nothing. Now, however, it is a question of more than this, of unconscious pieces of knowledge [*unbewusste Kenntnisse*], of connections of thought, of comparisons between different objects which result in its being possible for one of them to be regularly put in place of the other. These comparisons are not freshly made on each occasion; they lie ready to hand and are complete, once and for all. This is implied by the fact of their agreeing in the case of different individuals — possibly, indeed, agreeing in spite of differences of language. (XV, 165)

Freud is, of course, correct that the correspondences in dream symbolism among individuals, and in particular among different languages, cultures, and eras, poses a major problem that may be solvable only by a psychoanalytic theory of cultural tradition. But the fact of 'unconscious pieces of knowledge' should pose no problems for Freud, for this is what he has just assumed.

2.3 Psychoanalytic Therapy

In section 2.1 we saw that the *Studies* were based on the programmatic assumption that the patients have an unconscious knowledge of the causes of their symptoms and that the therapist's task is to force them to articulate this knowledge (and in the process facilitate a cathartic release of the associated emotions). Once Freud had registered the force of the countervailing resistances and had interpreted them as an expression of the unconscious repelling of unbearable emotions, he abandoned the method of suggestion and pressure in favor of that of free association by the patients. He developed on this basis the specifically psychoanalytic procedure involving the 'oscillating attention' of the therapist, dream interpretation and the analysis of resistances, transference, and countertransference. Freud never explicitly returned to the basic commitment of the *Studies* that patients have unconscious knowledge of the genesis of their symptoms.

Thus it seems plausible to interpret Freud's turn to the specifically psychoanalytic procedure in such a way that he abandoned this commitment. However, we have already seen that he based his presentation of the theory of dreams in the *Lectures* once again on his old conviction that unconscious knowledge exists. However, the same does not hold for Freud's presentation of his theory of the neuroses and of treatment, even in the *Lectures*. Nevertheless, I see no reason to assume that Freud abandoned his old conviction — on the contrary. However, Freud no longer needed simply to postulate the truth of this conviction in order to be able to ground an effective therapeutic procedure upon it. But now he explicitly assumes that an unconscious knowledge of the unconscious on the part of the therapist makes therapeutic access possible and he can cite patients' oral testimony to prove that they always had an unconscious knowledge of the context of their illness.

As regards the unconscious knowledge of the therapist, Freud, in a frequently quoted passage from the 'Recommendations to Physicians Practicing Psychoanalysis,' requires that the therapist 'must turn his own unconscious like a receptive organ towards the transmitting unconscious of the patient' (XII, 115). Now it is hardly surprising that the therapist should acquire an unconscious knowledge of the patient's unconscious based on his subliminal perception of his patient's expressive behavior. This rests on a general human capacity that Freud repeatedly emphasized (XII, 320; XIII, 159). But the requirement concerning the appropriate relation of the therapist to himself that Freud derives from this is striking: 'that he should have undergone a psycho-analytic purification and have become aware of those complexes of his own which would be apt to interfere with his grasp of what the patient tells him' (XII, 116). By 'becoming aware' [*Kenntnis*] is certainly meant in the first instance explicit knowledge. But it can also be understood as a heightened responsiveness to the contents of the unconscious, or any rate intuitive, knowledge of the unconscious concerning its own resistances.

As regards the patient's unconscious knowledge of his own unconscious, Freud recalls in 'Remembering, Repeating, and Working-Through' the 'old hypnotic technique' and the subsequent evolution of his psychoanalytic procedure, without mentioning his former suggestion-technique of exploration and its basic presupposition that the patient has unconscious knowledge, and then continues:

> At this point I will interpolate a few remarks which every analyst has found confirmed in his observations. Forgetting impressions, scenes or experiences nearly always reduces itself to shutting them off [*Absperrung*]. When the patient talks about these 'forgotten' things he seldom fails to add: 'As a matter of fact I've always known it; only I've never thought of it.' He often expresses disappointment at the fact that not enough things come into his head that he can call 'forgotten' — that he has never thought of since they happened. Nevertheless, even this desire is fulfilled, especially in the case of conversion hysterias. (XII, 148).

Accordingly, the confession: 'As a matter of fact I've always known it, only I've never thought of it' concerns not just cases of the 'shutting off' or splitting off of what was experienced, but presumably also genuine amnesias.[38] A further argument can be adduced for this. In the course of his increasing recognition that mental illnesses refer back to early stages of childhood that are subject to ever more thorough amnesia, Freud increasingly emphasized that analytic reconstructions often remain constructs that cannot be directly confirmed by memories. On this topic, he says in his later work 'Constructions in Analysis,' among other things:

> It is of all the greater interest that there are indirect forms of confirmation which are in every respect trustworthy. One of them is a form of words that is used (as though by general agreement) with very little variation by the most different people: 'I didn't ever think' (or 'I shouldn't ever have thought') 'that' (or 'of that'). This can be translated without any hesitation into: 'Yes, you're right this time — about my *unconscious*.' (XXIII, 263)

Taking our orientation from the earlier quotation, it seems plausible to supplement the reaction of the patient 'I didn't ever think of that' with: 'but as a matter of fact I've always known it.' In the cases Freud has in mind, such a confession could not rest on a conscious recollection, but that is not really necessary either because there are sufficient analogous cases in which the subject becomes aware that the knowledge was previously unconscious. That such an unconscious knowledge of what has been reconstructed, though it cannot be remembered, exists, also provides a good explanation for the fact that the analysand often responds to the communication of the construction 'with an

---

[38] However, in the *Rat Man* Freud says with reference to compulsion neuroses and hysteria: 'In order to differentiate between the two kinds of repression we have on the surface nothing to rely upon but the patient's assurance that he has a feeling in the one case of having always known the thing and in the other of having long ago forgotten it' (X, 196). This could support the view that the confession of the patient in 'Remembering, Repeating, and Working-Through' does not hold for cases of genuine amnesia.

association which contains something similar or analogous to the content of the construction' (*ibid.*).

In one place, however, Freud seems to regard the alleged original and unconscious knowledge as an illusion, indeed as a false memory, namely, in the work 'Fausse Reconnaissance (Déja Raconté) in Psycho-Analytic Treatment':

> There is another kind of *fausse reconnaissance* which not infrequently makes its appearance at the close of a treatment, much to the physician's satisfaction. After he has succeeded in forcing the repressed event (whether it was of a real or of a psychical nature) upon the patient's acceptance in the teeth of all resistances, and has succeeded, as it were, in rehabilitating it — the patient may say: '*Now I feel as though I had known it all the time.*' With this the work of the analysis has been completed. (XIII, 207)

But could this task be fulfilled if this were a case of an illusory sensation? Perhaps here Freud sees the admission of the patient as a matter of an illusory memory (also) because he has temporarily[39] forgotten his idea of unconscious knowledge.

3. On the Scope of Freud's Idea of Unconscious Knowledge of One's Own Mind

Having demonstrated in the second part that the thesis of an unconscious knowledge of one's own mind, and of one's own unconscious, is not just a daring idea of the early Freud but is to be found in several periods and areas of his psychoanalytic theory, we must now examine the scope of this idea within his theory of the unconscious. This question arises both at the level of clinical theory and at that of a general depth psychology and 'metapsychology.' But since this idea is not part of Freud's declared self-understanding, such questions admit only tentative answers by appeal to Freud's writings. Here I must set questions of clinical theory to one side due to restrictions of space.

At the level of a general depth psychology, we must ask, first, whether an unconscious knowledge of oneself is characteristic of all memories. Must we say: 'If I can remember something, then it is only because I have unconscious knowledge of what I remember and of myself as the subject of the past experience'? And is this a claim about the meaning of concepts or an empirical claim? Second, one must ask whether unconscious knowledge of oneself exists only with regard to

---

[39] The work quoted was published in 1914, hence before the *Lectures* and approximately contemporaneous with 'Remembering, Repeating, and Working-Through.'

memories or also with regard to other mental phenomena, such as dreams, present desires, convictions, etc.

At the level of 'metapsychology,' which I understand here as a general depth psychology under specifically Freudian premises, one must ask whether, first, whether there is unconscious knowledge of everything that is unconscious in the dynamic sense and whether, second, this also holds for the domain of the non-conscious for which I have proposed the concept of a 'primary unconscious.' For although this is 'unconscious' in the strict sense, and hence is not preconscious for example, nevertheless it is not unconscious in the dynamic sense.

As to the first question, I refer to how pathogenic forms of (unconscious) defence [*Abwehr*] relate to non-pathogenic forms in this regard. Presumably, a non-pathogenic form of defence is more compatible with knowledge of the repelled than a pathogenic one. Hence, if unconscious knowledge of the pathogenically repelled exists, then unconscious knowledge of the non-pathogenically repelled also exists. The main question is whether unconscious knowledge refers to that what is repelled [*das Abgewehrte*] or more to the repelling agency [*das Abwehrende*]. Insofar as repulsion (or the repelling agency) is more accessible to consciousness than what is repelled, it is also a more likely object of unconscious knowledge.

The second question is more difficult to answer. Freud assumes that every psychic process is initially unconscious (XII, 264). Since the primary unconscious concerns in any case mental life that has not yet been confronted with the possibility of defence at all, or at any rate not yet with the possibility of repression (see section 1.3 above), the argument for unconscious knowledge based on the censor or watchman function loses its force here. By primary unconscious, Freud presumably means — mainly or exclusively — the constitution of the individual (and of the species) that is temporally prior to defence or repression. But it remains open which early period in particular Freud has in mind here.

Finally, I would like to mention the theoretical possibility of generalizing the idea of unconscious knowledge of the unconscious to such an extent that it can serve to *define* the concept of the 'unconscious mind' as such. But here I can't address the more fundamental philosophical question of the definition of the concept of the 'mental-unconscious'. I must also leave unanswered the question of the extent to which unconscious knowledge shapes the self-relation of persons. However, Freud provided good reasons for assuming that it is important for this relation.

References

Bartels, Martin (1976), *Selbstbewusstsein und Unbewusstes. Studien zu Freud und Heidegger* (Berlin: De Gruyter).
Bieri, Peter (1987), 'Generelle Einführung.' In Bieri (ed.), *Analytische Philosophie der Erkenntnis* (Bodenheim: Athenaeum), pp. 9-72.
Cavell, Marcia (1993), *The Psychoanalytic Mind. From Freud to Philosophy* (Cambridge, MA: Harvard University Press).
Dornes, Martin (2000), *Die frühe Kindheit. Entwicklungspsychologie der ersten Lebensjahre* (Frankfurt am Main: Fischer).
Dretske, Fred I. (1971), 'Conclusive reasons', *Australasian Journal of Philosophy*, **49**, pp. 1–22.
Freud, Sigmund (1953ff.), *The Standard Edition of the Complete Works of Sigmund Freud* (London: Hogarth Press).
Friebe, Cord (2005), *Theorie des Unbewussten. Eine Deutung der Metapsychologie Freuds aus transzendentalphilosophischer Perspektive* (Würzburg: Königshausen & Neumann).
Knapp, G. (1982), 'Begriff und Bedeutung des Unbewussten bei Freud.' In Dieter Eicke (ed.), *Tiefenpsychologie, Band 1: Sigmund Freud – Leben und Werk* (Weinheim: Beltz), pp. 261–83.
Löw-Beer, Martin (1990), *Selbsttäuschung. Philosophische Analyse eines psychischen Phänomens* (Freiburg: Alber).
Polanyi, Michael (1966), *The Tacit Dimension* (Garden City, NJ: Doubleday).
Rorty, Richard (1970), 'Incorrigibility as the mark of the mental.' *Journal of Philosophy*, **67**, pp. 399–424.
Sandler, Joseph *et al.* (1997), *Freud's Models of the Mind: An Introduction* (Madison, CT: International Universities Press).
Sandler, Joseph *et al.* (2003), *Freuds Modelle der Seele. Eine Einführung* (Gießen: Psychosozial-Verlag).

Manfred Frank

Non-objectal Subjectivity

Abstract: *The immediate successors of Kant in classical German philosophy considered a subjectivity irreducible to objecthood as the core of personhood. The thesis of an irreducible subjectivity has, after the German idealists, been advocated by the phenomenological movement, as well as by analytical philosophers of self-consciousness such as Hector-Neri Castañeda and Sydney Shoemaker. Their arguments together show that self-consciousness cannot be reduced to a relation whereby a subject grasps itself as an object, but that there must be a core of subjectivity always already familiar with itself before reflection. A number of contemporary accounts of self-consciousness are unaware of these old and new arguments, and flawed in that they do not account for the core 'non-objectal subjectivity' necessary for self-consciousness and personhood.*

An old idealistic intuition whispers to us that there is an innermost, inalienable kernel of subjectivity, and that this kernel forms the essence of what we call 'personhood'. There are further essential properties that also belong to personhood: in Kant's tradition, moral accountability or imputability, which is in turn based upon our freedom or autonomy, and in Strawson's understanding embodiment, which makes us spatio-temporally identifiable by other people (Strawson, 1963). But the core of personhood seems to be what the later Schelling referred to as 'original' (*urständlich*) and the later Schleiermacher as 'non-objectal' (*ungegenständlich*)[1] subjectivity (Schelling, 1856–64, I/10, p. 133; Schelling, 1992, pp. 29, 31, 35ff., 53, 96, 118ff., 408; Schleiermacher, 1960, § 3; 2001, Vol. II, p. 288). Only if we acknowledge this core, can we make the formulation of the

Correspondence:
manfred.frank@uni-tuebingen.de

---

[1] Throughout the text 'gegenständlich' will be translated as 'objectal' [transl.].

categorical imperative understandable, according to which I should never treat people (only) as means (i.e. as objects), but always (also) as ends (Kant, 1900ff., IV, 428 ff.). That is, were there no such thing as non-objectal subjectivity, the implementation of the imperative would have no *fundamentum in re*: personhood must have a subject-characteristic which is irreducible to objectness.

This idealistic intuition typically finds expression in phrases such as: I want to grasp the subject that I am in its pure subjectivity. Yet when I define this subject (through reflection), it becomes an object to me and ceases to be pure subject. 'It is only there insofar as I do not grasp it, and insofar as I grasp it, it is no more' (Schelling, 1856–64 I/4, p. 357, note 2; cf. I/10, pp. 99ff.). An old model for this formulation is what the Neo-Platonists say of pure matter: 'If you don't look for it, it shows itself, but reach for it, or try to know it, and it will escape' (Schelling, 1856–64, II/1, p. 13). Schelling's immediate model however is Kant who in the *Critique of Pure Reason* wrote: 'Now it is, indeed, very evident that what I must presuppose in order to cognize an object at all, cannot itself be cognized as an object ...' (Kant, 1996, A, p. 402). In the paralogism chapter of the *Critique* Kant had repeatedly described the difficulty of apperception, of grasping oneself not via objectal representation, but *as such*, roughly as follows: In trying to say who I am I must attribute to myself some, for example perceivable, qualities. As soon as I put to myself the question of the legitimacy of these attributions, however, it becomes clear to me that I could only make them if I was previously already familiar with the meanings of 'I' or 'my'. So I feel compelled to choose myself (or the concept 'I')[2] as the 'correlate of my comparisons', which should resolve for me which property defines me. Yet, in this way I presuppose exactly that which I had laid claim to bring to knowledge. (A, pp. 366, 345ff.)

The self-assured tone of naturalism pervading the newer subject-theories has obscured the general philosophical understanding for Kant's problem. For naturalism it is settled that if there is such a thing as subjectivity at all, it is to be found among the natural entities. Natural entities are however — ontologically — objects (*res*); and discourse about anything objectal is a discourse *de re*. It thus seems self-evident that subjects form a particular class of objects.

I leave open here whether the naturalistic option or attitude really forces this conclusion. It suffices for me that naturalists mostly draw

---

[2] Elsewhere Kant stresses that 'I' is in fact not a concept but rather a perception or even a feeling, e.g. Kant 1900ff., XXVIII/1, 206, Z. pp. 3ff.; § 46 of the *Prolegomena* in ibid., IV, p. 334. Further references and an interpretation of this conflict in Frank (2002, pp. 41ff.).

this conclusion without questioning. This is accompanied by a lamentable tendency to banalize the specificity of the first-person phenomenon or to replace it through models of third person access. The 'reflection-model' and the 'model of inner perception' which turn an outward look into an inward one belong here (cf. Moran, 2001, pp. xxxiii, 1–5). Yet, analytical theory of the subject has shown since as early the mid-1950s (Geach, 1957), that epistemic self-attributions in the sense of what David Lewis (1983) terms '*attitudes de se*' cannot be traced back to knowledge *de re*. The precise spelling-out of this intuition must be credited to the unforgettable pioneering achievement of Hector-Neri Castañeda 'without whom nothing'. In '"He" — A study in the logic of self-consciousness' (Castañeda, 1966) he argued for the first time in detail that knowledge about ourselves is in principle different from knowledge about objects.[3]

I. Castañeda's Argument

Castañeda's argument requires prior understanding of the semantics of 'self-consciousness'. 'Self-consciousness' — a 'mongrel concept' as Ned Block calls it (Block, 1995, pp. 227ff.) — can mean either (A) consciousness of the owner of the consciousness (the *subject* or *I*), or (B) consciousness of *mental states*.[4] Let us call the first type 'egological' and the second type non-egological' self-consciousness. It is also important to note here that non-egological self-consciousness can further be understood in two senses: Either as (B.a) consciousness of the *mental states, acts or experiences themselves*, or as (B.b) consciousness of the *contents* of these mental states, acts or experiences. (See Frank, 1991.)

Only the second aspect of self-consciousness (B) is thematized by the Castañeda of the 1960s. His aim is to expose the linguistic mechanism by which we attribute self-consciousness to other subjects. This happens through the so-called 'he himself'-locution,[5] which Castañeda designated graphically by means of an asterisk after the (apparent) personal pronouns of the third person singular (*he*/she**, or *he** for short). According to this rule of speech *he** stands for the *'he' of self-consciousness*. Castañeda's thesis now reads that the 'I' of self-knowledge is not reducible to what we refer to with name-words,

---

[3] At the same time he showed that knowledge *de se* is also different in kind from knowledge of facts (propositional knowledge, knowledge of states of affairs) or knowledge *de dicto*. For the purposes of my argument I need not develop this aspect.

[4] In both sentences 'of' is to be read in the sense of 'directed at' (eds.).

[5] The expression comes from Chisholm (1981, p. 17).

with substitutes for name-words (indexical expressions of all kinds) or with descriptions. It follows from this that *he** — contrary to appearances — is not a pronoun or other indexical expression: Castañeda calls '*he**', as well as 'here' and 'now' *quasi-indicators* (Castañeda, 1999, pp. 61ff.).

Sentences which formulate intentional statements are exemplary for this thesis. These are sentences with a main clause in which an intentional verb is attributed to a person, e.g.: 'Paul believes (thinks, knows, hopes, wishes etc.)'. The dependent sub-clause then expresses the 'propositional content' of what is intended, as in: 'Paul believes, that Marie will be the next Harvest Queen.' Here we have what is known as a belief *de dicto*. Namely, Paul believes the *dictum* (what is said, the proposition), 'that Marie will be the next Harvest Queen'. But Paul can also have what the Scholastics termed a belief *de re*. This means simply that he has a conviction about something (or someone), as for example in the sentence: 'Paul believes *of Marie*, that she will be the next Harvest Queen.' Finally, Marie can also have a belief about herself and also know that it is about herself. In this case she has a belief *de se* or self-consciousness: 'Marie believes, that *she** (*herself*) will be the next Harvest Queen.' Yet, not all beliefs about oneself are beliefs *de se*. Let us consider the following formulations:

(a) Marie, the youngest graduate from Schriesheim, believes that the youngest graduate from Schriesheim will be the next Schriesheim Harvest Queen (*de dicto*);
(b) There is an x such that x is identical with the youngest graduate from Schriesheim, and x is believed by x to be the next Harvest Queen (*de re*);
(c) The youngest graduate from Schriesheim believes that she* herself will be the next Harvest Queen (*de se*).

The following implication-relationships exist between these formulations (cf. Chisholm, 1981, pp. 18–20, who explicitly follows Castañeda).

First, (a) implies (b) (*de dicto* implies *de re*): If a person, who is the youngest graduate from Schriesheim believes the *dictum*, that the youngest graduate from Schriesheim will be the next Harvest Queen, there is someone who is identical with the youngest graduate from Schriesheim and who is believed by exactly this person to be the next Harvest Queen. One might suspect that this move from an indirect (intensional) context into a direct (extensional) one is unauthorized. That is however not the case, since (a) identifies 'the youngest graduate' outside the intensional context. In other words: the existence of the youngest graduate is established independently of the content of the belief.

Secondly, (b) does not imply (a) (*de re* does not imply *de dicto*): That x is believed by x to be the next Harvest Queen and x is identical with the youngest graduate from Schriesheim, does not imply that x believes that the youngest graduate in the place (who she is) will be the next Harvest Queen.

Thirdly, (c) does not imply (a) (*de se* does not imply *de dicto*): That the youngest graduate believes of herself that she will be chosen as Harvest Queen does not imply that she necessarily believes that the youngest graduate will become the Harvest Queen, (that is, if she does not identify herself in the *de se* version as Marie, the youngest graduate).

Fourthly, (a) does not imply (c) (*de dicto* does not imply *de se*): If the youngest graduate believes that the youngest graduate will be the next Harvest Queen, she does not need to know that with the label 'the youngest graduate from Schriesheim' she makes reference to herself.

Fifthly, (c) implies (b) (or, *de se* implies *de re*): If somebody believes something about herself, she believes it about somebody.

Sixthly, (b) does not imply (c) (or, *de re* does not imply *de se*): If x is regarded by x as the next Harvest Queen (and is in addition the youngest graduate from Schriesheim), neither of these things need to be among the contents of her self-belief (x may be identical with the youngest graduate without knowing it; and she may identify x who will become the Harvest Queen, without knowing that she herself is x).

There will be no dispute concerning most of these theses. At most, the sixth proposition may encounter objections. Since – one could object – if someone is x and this same someone is regarded by herself as x, then she has a belief about herself.

This is true. However, it does not ensure what is clearly the case in (c), that the subject of the belief already also has a belief about herself *as* about herself. In other words: Not all self-*consciousness* is necessarily already *self*-consciousness, or self-consciousness *de se*. If I regard the man shown in the mirror over there as x, and if I am this man without knowing it (since I have not noticed the mirror), then I really do regard myself as x, but I have thereby no self-consciousness *de se*. This was the well-known experience of Ernst Mach: as he boarded a Viennese bus he observed a man boarding in the same rhythm on the other side, at the sight of whom the thought flashed through his head: 'What a shabby pedagogue is boarding the bus!' (Mach, 1886, p. 34). Mach did not realize that he was referring to himself, having not noticed the mirror on the opposite side. (Note that

Ernst Mach did, however, attribute to himself the fact of having had a perception.)

It might finally still be objected that Marie's belief *de se* nonetheless retains the form of a belief in a proposition ('that she will be the next Harvest Queen'). But Chisholm thinks he has shown precisely through the elucidation of the implication-relationships between the three example sentences that this is a mere appearance. In fact there can be no such thing as a first-person proposition because of the logical special status of the subject of epistemological self-attributions (Chisholm, 1981, p. 20).

In the present context only the sixth proposition is important: the irreducibility of *de se* to *de re* attitudes. What this proves is that self-consciousness is not a special instance of object-consciousness. But what then is it? This has not been shown by Castañeda and Chisholm. They have confined themselves to the negative proof of the irreducibility of non-objectal consciousness to object-consciousness without asking how the structure of non-objectal consciousness might be understood more precisely. The weight of this negative proof must nonetheless not be underrated. We need to pursue its consequences a step further. What the failure of the attempt to reduce knowledge *de se* to knowledge *de re* shows is that with self-consciousness we have to do with a fundamentally different kind of consciousness than object-consciousness. As Dieter Henrich showed in 1966, this point was already clearly seen by Johann Gottlieb Fichte (Henrich, 1982).

II. A Fundamental Insight of Johann Gottlieb Fichte

Fichte's insight consisted in the discovery of the failure of what Henrich calls the reflection-model of self-consciousness. This model implies that self-consciousness comes about either through a consciousness of the I as an object (egological version), or through a kind of higher-order consciousness which is directed towards a first order consciousness (non-egological version). In this way consciousness discovers itself in the position of an object. And since, according to this model, all knowledge consists of knowledge of objects (whether of individuals, universals or facts), self-knowledge too is explained as knowledge of a particular type of object.

The circularity of this attempt at an explanation is glaring and yet as far as we know, it went undetected in the classical attempts to explain self-consciousness before Fichte.[6] But self-consciousness *exists*, says

---

[6] With the possible exception of Johann Bernhard Merian, as Udo Thiel (1996) has shown.

Fichte. There can be nothing false in the phenomenon, only in its (viciously circular or regressive) theoretical elucidation. Indeed, the reflection-model of self-consciousness does not stand up to the scrutiny which follows. I will depict the Fichtean argument here only in broad outline, having discussed it more fully and in detail elsewhere (see e.g. Frank, 1991; 2002).

Let us first consider the egological version of the false reflection-theory. According to it the I obtains knowledge of itself through reflection — through entering into a reflective relation with itself, and thereby, as it were, setting its eyes on itself. However, if it holds that there is knowledge only of phenomena which occupy an object-position in relation to a knower, and if what we are after is the I as a subject, not as an object, then there seems to be no way for the I to have knowledge of itself. In fact, the reflection-theory, as Kant takes it over from Descartes and Leibniz (but also from numerous thinkers of British empiricism, see Frank, 2002), must then presuppose the phenomenon whose structure it assumes to explain. It was for this reason that Fichte accused it of 'sophistry' in his lectures on the *Wissenschaftslehre nova methodo* (Fichte, 1992).

What about the non-egological version of the reflection theory? If self-consciousness only came about through a 'piling up' of consciousnesses, where a lower-order consciousness was attested to by a higher-order consciousness, then there would be no self-consciousness at all. This is because for each last consciousness the same condition would once again apply whereby in order for it to become conscious of itself, it would have to be made into an object by a successive consciousness, which again would be non-self-conscious, and so on *ad infinitum* (see also Sartre, 1991). But since there is self-consciousness, the model is false.

That the model is false means that consciousness must be acquainted with itself *immediately*, independently of objectification by a successive consciousness. Fichte expresses this by talking of the complete non-differentiability of subject and object in self-consciousness (compare Sartre, 1991, p. 382). In Kantian terminology an immediate consciousness is an intuition (*Anschauung*). Since, in contrast to sensory intuition, it has no object in space and time, but rather intuits the being of the pure spontaneity of apperception, it has to be thought of as 'intellectual intuition' according to Fichte.

III. The Objection Against the Inward Glance — or Perception Model of Self-Knowledge

Fichte's argument was scarcely acknowledged either by his contemporaries or by later theorists of consciousness and was met largely by silence. Had he been familiar with the writings of British empiricism and the post-Cartesian and post-Leibnizian German Enlightenment, he would have had a much richer frame of reference for his arguments (Frank, 2002), as well as possibly a wider reception. The phenomenological movement (Franz Brentano, Hermann Schmalenbrach, Jean-Paul Sartre; see Frank, 1991) later rediscovered the substance of Fichte's insight without being directly influenced by him.

Contemporary philosophy of mind has mostly ignored these forerunners — with occasional exceptions such as Chisholm (1981), Castañeda (1999) or Nozick (1981). Yet the argument itself is known today, even if little heeded. The most impressive exception is Sydney Shoemaker. Shoemaker speaks in this connection of the *inner sense* or *inward glance* model,[7] but since Shoemaker also speaks expressly of 'inner perception,' his target can as informatively be called the *perception-model* of self knowledge or self-consciousness. Shoemaker is also one of the few to make the distinction between egological and non-egological conceptions of self-consciousness. We clearly possess both consciousness of I and consciousness of mental states. In both cases there is knowledge, but its object is different.

In what follows I do not want to comment on the ontology of these two object areas, and hence will not address myself to questions of the type 'is the I a mental or a physical entity (or both)?'; or 'do states of consciousness consist in stimulations of the nerve fibres, or are they separate mental events (or both)?' My attention is rather directed towards the nature of the first-person knowledge that we have of these two object-areas. In other words, I am enquiring into the structure of both types of self-consciousness. Let us take a look at what Shoemaker says.

In the first of his three Royce lectures on *Self-knowledge and 'inner sense'* (in Shoemaker 1996) Shoemaker distinguishes explicitly, in three separate sections (IV–VI), knowledge directed to the owner of consciousness from knowledge directed to consciousness.[8] 'Consciousness' is then divided into intentional and non-intentional states.

---

[7] Many — such as Richard Moran (2001) — have partly or completely aligned themselves with Shoemaker.

[8] '... it is useful to separate the questions whether the *self* is the object of quasi-perceptual introspective awareness, and the question of whether mental entities of various kinds are' (Shoemaker, 1996, p. 208).

Shoemaker terms both types of knowledge 'introspective' in the broadest sense of the word. He casts doubt on whether either of these types could be understood analogously to the types of knowledge that we have of (natural) objects.

The perception model of self-consciousness accepts, notoriously in Locke's version, that all consciousness is essentially consciousness of something which exists independently of the consciousness of it. This something can be a worldly object ('external perception') or an object of our spiritual life ('inner perception'). In this view knowledge of the self and knowledge of mental states are 'quasi-perceptions'.[9]

This view is untenable — and indeed independently of the (additional) question of whether the evidential status of both sorts of knowledge differs, that is, whether self-perceptions enjoy an epistemic priority over knowledge of the so-called external world (as for instance Brentano, Meinong and Chisholm think). Shoemaker has attempted to show the untenability of the view by refuting a number of assumptions connected with the perception model of self-consciousness. What these assumptions have in common is that they interpret the object of self-consciousness as an independently existing object.

In what follows I will make selective use of Shoemaker's arguments against the perception-model. If self-consciousness is to be understood in terms of the perception model, the following four assumptions — generally applicable to object-perception — should apply to it:

(1) Consciousness of perceivable facts (or, consciousness that a perceivable object is thus and so) proceeds via the *consciousness of that object*, that is, via demonstrative reference to the individual contained in the propositional content of my conviction (e.g. 'that tree there is an ash', 'that man there in the mirror is me').

(2) Sensory perception provides me with *information supported by identification*; it 'individuates' the object from the mass of other objects.

(3) At least a few *intrinsic qualities* of the perceived object can be determined; otherwise its relational qualities would be left 'hanging in the air'.

(4) I can direct my concentration towards objects of perception; I can pick them out through efforts of *attention* (Shoemaker, 1996, pp. 205ff.).

---

[9] I discount the trivial objection that we have no special organ for 'inner perceptions' in the way that we have ears or eyes for external ones (see Tugendhat, 1979, pp. 16 ff.; Shoemaker, 1996, p. 207).

As to self-consciousness as consciousness of the I, or egological self-consciousness, at least conditions (1), (2) and (4) do not apply to it. As opposed to sensory perception, I cannot enter into a standpoint-dependent observer-relation with myself as an I. Neither can I individuate myself in self-knowledge as an I from a mass of other objects. And finally, neither can I nor need I bring myself into an informative identificatory relationship with myself through attention, since — before every object-presentation — I always already know that I am I (Shoemaker, 1984a, pp. 8ff. and 1984b, pp. 102–5).

The last point is particularly important. It shows most convincingly that the perception model of self-knowledge is untenable. As Shoemaker puts it: 'Perceptual self-knowledge presupposes non-perceptual self-knowledge, so not all self-knowledge can be perceptual' (Shoemaker, 1984b, p. 105). For Ernst Mach to be able to attain a form of self-knowledge through a mirror-image, he must already possess a first-person knowledge of himself *as* of himself, which cannot — at the expense of an infinite regress — be based on identification (contrary to the second assumption) (Shoemaker, 1996, p. 211).

But how do things stand with the non-egological sense of 'self-consciousness', according to which the objects of self-knowledge are intentional or phenomenal states? Let us begin with propositional attitudes (i.e. intentional states). They cannot be individuated through perceptions because conditions (1), (3) and therefore also (4) are clearly not fulfilled here.

According to condition (3) perceptual information must be based upon intrinsic qualities. Assuming that that the content of our attitudes is largely determined by the world (the premise of externalism), then relational properties come into play. 'Inner perception' cannot authoritatively grasp these, since what should be 'perceived' according to the perception model are inner qualities of the attitude (Boghossian, 1989, p. 11). Yet, contents of attitudes are not straightforwardly 'in the head' (Putnam, 1975 and 1981; for the contrary view see Burge, 1979) to be 'perceived'. Shoemaker in fact thinks that intentions have *no* non-intentional characteristics and therefore no phenomenal characteristics which might be discovered quasi-perceptively 'in the head'.[10]

---

[10] This thesis has been debated since Husserl. Attitude-modes can be thought of as quasi-phenomenal, as in Husserl's discussion of act-characters: we somehow 'experience a feeling' when we make judgements about the Berlin Castle, for example, that we like it, or entertain a wish in relation to it (Husserl, 1980, II/1, p. 374; cf. also the distinction between act-quality and act-matter in § 20, pp. 411ff.). Also Meinong talks of '*zumutsein*': 'the qualitatively unique that we experience when we see red or think of red belongs […] not to the objects, but to the content. And that we experience (*zu Mute ist*) a different feeling

The object-perception model thus founders on the introspectively inaccessible properties of intentional content.

Self-knowledge is different from perception also because perceptual individuation of objects can be mistaken, whereas we cannot mis-identify or mistake attitude-modes such as wishes or convictions for other attitude-modes (against this cf. Bernecker, 1996). Our epistemological access to convictions, hopes, etc., is not mediated by judgements which include anything like demonstrative reference (compare conditions (1) and (2)).[11]

Let us turn finally to the way in which the mind has knowledge of non-intentional experiences and sensations (*Erlebnissen und Empfindungen*). These were the preferred example in the empiricist theories of 'internal sense', which in these theories could reckon with a certain intuitive plausibility, connected with the surface-grammar of statements such as 'I feel hunger', 'I feel pain', or 'I feel a sharp pain in my right knee joint'. Such statements suggest that there are two different things: the pain, and the sensation of it. This is nonsense of course: pain simply hurts *per se*. It does not additionally need (in an act of 'higher order' grasping) to be quasi-perceived or represented in order to reveal its unwanted quality. This points to a property of phenomenal states, which the phenomenological tradition from Brentano to Sartre has described as the unity of the existence and the self-givenness of consciousness (Sartre, 1991, pp. 379ff.).

The unity-thought has more recently received new impetus from Kripke's proof of the dissimilarity of the relationships between, on the one hand, intermediate molecular movement, warmth and the feeling of being warm, or between H_2O, water and the feeling of being watery, and, on the other hand, C-fibre stimulation, pain and the feeling of being in pain. Kripke's well-known argument runs as follows: something can be warm, without the feeling of warmth (or I can experience a watery sensation, without there being water). But something cannot be pain without feeling painful. Since identity is a necessary relation, the being and self-givenness of pain necessarily coincide, but that of pain and C-fibre stimulation do not (Kripke, 1980, pp. 152 and 154).[12]

---

when we see first red and then green is also down to content rather than objects' (Meinong, 1975, p. 59).

[11] Admittedly, Shoemaker does not answer the question of *how* one should then conceive of this form of knowledge.

[12] See also Chalmers: '... *all it is* for something to be in pain is for it to feel like pain. There is no distinction between pain and painy stuff, in the way there is a distinction between water and watery stuff. One could have something that felt like water without it being water, but

This necessary relation may be aptly expressed thus: being necessarily brings with it self-givenness.

In short, objections against the perception model of sensations can be summarised as follows.

First of all, the model fails because of lack of demonstrative reference (1). It is not the case that we have sensory data before our mind's eye and identify them. We do indeed represent objects, but we do not also represent our representations of objects to this end, and we certainly do not represent our sensations as separate objects.

Secondly, for the same reason, and equally contrary to appearances, the model of inner perception founders on criterion (2). That is to say, we do not experience experiences by means of individuating and distinguishing them from one another like natural objects.

Thirdly, as to presentations of hallucinations or afterimages, it is indeed tempting to compare these with presentations of perceptual objects (so that at one time we see the sun, and another time an *image* of the sun). However, while we learn something from natural objects and never have an exhaustive view of all their nuances, imaginations are essentially poor: they only make sensuous or schematise the concept that interprets them. Sartre spoke about this with reference to afterimages or imagined objects as 'quasi-observation' (Sartre, 1940, pp. 18ff.) — meaning that we do not really have perceptions, let alone observations of them.[13] Sartre interprets afterimages in the same way as Shoemaker: they themselves are not represented, and their veridical nature consists only in that that they represent worldly objects afterwards, as it were.

Yet we should not draw the wrong conclusions from the externalist critique of the perception model of self-consciousness. That is, the intuitive plausibility of the sensory data theory calls for — as regards criterion (3) — a certain qualification of content-externalism, at least in the extreme variations of Harman and Tye (Harman, 1990; Tye, 2002). The position that contents are not intrinsic features of consciousness, but rather representatives of publicly accessible surfaces of natural objects, would indeed provide an additional argument against the inner perceptibility of states of consciousness. But this position goes too far in two respects: (a) it does not account for the what-is-it-likeness or qualitative character of experiences; and (b) it makes it incomprehensible why we keep on talking about a

---

one could not have something that felt like pain without it being pain. Pain's feel is *essential* to it' (Chalmers, 1996, p. 147; cf. pp. 133 and 146).

[13] The difference between observations and perceptions is that the former involve attention.

representational *consciousness* at all. If the metaphor of 'mental glass' is overstretched, consciousness dissolves into nothingness and disappears into the surfaces of objects which it then also no longer brings into consciousness and thus to knowledge.

I find the latest development within the philosophy of mind, of replacing the expression 'inner perception' with that of 'introspection', to be unfortunate. The source of the metaphors remains ultimately the same. Perceptions and introspections have in common that both are non-inferential and that there is epistemic certainty 'beyond reasonable doubt' concerning both. They differ, however, in that the objects of perception exist independently of consciousness of them, while — as we have seen above — it makes no sense to separate, or to make independent, the being of consciousness from its self-givenness.

Yet, for example David Armstrong does exactly that with his Humean thesis that the process which leads from mental states into knowledge of these states should be causally interpreted. Armstrong regards the components of the causal relation as contingently connected *distinct existences*, so that the first can appear without making the break-through to knowledge (Armstrong, 1968). Shoemaker, on the other hand, sees the *distinct existence argument* as nonsensical (Shoemaker, 1996, pp. 224ff.).[14] But did not Shoemaker himself claim something quite similar when, in 'Functionalism and qualia', he talked of a reliable mechanism, which converts qualitative states into qualitative beliefs? The difference lies in the fact that Shoemaker characterised the primary experiences that are converted into veridical judgements as *already introspectively given*. According to him 'it is of the[ir] essence ... to reveal themselves to introspection' (Shoemaker, 1996, p. 242).

IV. The Second-Order Model of Self-Knowledge

The so called *second order* model of self-knowledge is a variation of the reflection-model. It in fact comes even nearer to the reflection model attacked by Fichte because it leaves the mode of consciousness which is responsible for the becoming conscious of the first order consciousness undefined, whereas the inner perception theory conceives of it in terms of perception. One advocate of this model is D.H. Mellor

---

[14] Without reference to Armstrong, Tugendhat is interesting here, drawing on Husserl's theory of inner perception: 'The weakness of this conception is obvious: according to it, an experience [simultaneously] represents another experience b; how can this amount to self-consciousness at all?' (Tugendhat, 1979, p. 53)

(1977 / 1978). According to Mellor *beliefs* are dispositions which are, in mostly non-conscious ways, inferentially interconnected with other beliefs and are conscious (= reflected, explicitly recognized, bathed in the light of attentiveness)[15] only in very few cases. They become conscious via 'a new mental state' which grants a type of assent to the prior unconscious one. One now *believes, that one believes*.

Richard Moran describes the idea in the following way: mental states only become cognitively interesting in their becoming *conscious*, not beforehand (2001, p. 28). Tacit convictions are not knowledge (let alone self-knowledge) for as long as 'they are not explicitly reflected upon' (p. 27). However, false or misleading beliefs will receive not assent but dissent on reflection (p. 28). Moran's decisive objection against this is that if beliefs are in principle unconscious, so too are *second-order* beliefs (the *reflections* on the first-order beliefs). No consciousness can arise from the piling up of unconscious mental states over one another (pp. 29ff.). In the end, talking of a second-order belief does not in any way contribute to the elucidation of the specific difference between *first-person* and *third-person* consciousness of one's own beliefs. Any elucidation of this would have to make clear how an 'unmediated' consciousness of one's own attitudes is possible and why it is that *only one's own* attitudes are knowable in this way. Consciousness of one's own mental states *modifies* these states — although not by 'standing outside them, but finding its way into them' so that they thereby not only exist, but concern *me* — while the observation of a tree or of someone else's behaviour does not change it qualitatively (pp. 30ff., xiii, a point on which Moran, on p. 36, agrees with Sartre). Moran talks here of the 'adverbial function' of consciousness.

The best known living advocate of the *second-order* model is however not Mellor, but, again, David Rosenthal (see Rosenthal, 1991). His theory of higher order thought explains the advent of consciousness out of conscious-less states via an iteration of non-conscious mental states. 'Non-conscious' because each last higher level (second-order) consciousness in the chain is itself a first order consciousness, as long as it does not turn out to be within reach of a reflecting (higher level, second-order) consciousness, which again is non-conscious. According to Rosenthal S's mental state M becomes conscious when S has a second order thought that she is in the state M. And it

---

[15] There is widespread unclarity concerning the capacities of so-called attentiveness or attention (*Aufmerksamkeit*), which many philosophers of mind confuse with consciousness as such, without explaining how attention relates to the findings of the elementary (inattentive) experience.

becomes 'introspectively' conscious when S has a third order thought that she has the (second order) thought that she is in state M. So subject S is at time t_1 in the mental state M. At time t_2 S has the thought that S is in the mental state M. And at time t_3 he thinks that S thinks that S is in the mental state M.

Lynne R. Baker (1998) has shown that there are two possible interpretations of this suggested theory. According to the first interpretation, none of the thoughts in the iteration are first-person (or *de se*) thoughts about oneself (as being in the mental state of the lower degree). According to the second reading, the higher order thoughts of S have to be *de se* thoughts about herself. The problem, according to Baker, is that on the first reading Rosenthal's model leaves *de se* thoughts about oneself as oneself unaccounted for, and on the second reading it presupposes them. The first account fails, since having thoughts concerning one's mental states does not necessarily mean that one knows that they are one's own thoughts. In Baker's example S reads a PET scan of her brain and has thoughts concerning the states that the scan scans — without knowing that it is her brain that is being scanned and thus that it is her own thoughts that she is thinking about. On the second account S's thought about her being in state M is a thought she has concerning herself as herself*, and thus the model does not explain genuine *de se*-states or first-person thoughts but includes them in the explanation.[16] Yet how exactly a thinker might successfully come to a self-conscious mental state irreducible to *de re* is something that Baker herself does not explain any more than the authors whom she criticizes.

V. The Comparator Model

The so-called *comparator model* was developed in the 1950s by neuro-physiologists, in order to explain how a person's intentions or wants are translated into embodied action, as well as to understand how in schizophrenic states patients sometimes identify their actions as not their own. To understand these schizophrenic phenomena it was considered necessary to explain how the consciousness of the identity of the deliberating (mental) and the acting (physical) subject — and with it the consciousness of self-authorship of action — comes about. Even animals can distinguish between changes in their behaviour brought about internally (through their own will) and externally

---

[16] See Baker (1998), pp. 338–9.

(through the environment) (see e.g. von Holst & Mittelstaedt, 1950; Sperry, 1950; Frith, 1992; 2004; Gallagher, 2000; 2004).

In reference to Shoemaker's classic essay 'Embodiment and Behavior' (1976, reprinted in Shoemaker, 1984a, pp. 113–18), Campbell (2004) has recently taken up the model again, in order to explain schizophrenia through malfunctions of the so-called comparator. Again, the model should explain how people calibrate their movements in order to achieve a desired result. According to it, a motor instruction for body movement is sent to the 'motor system', and a so called 'efferent-copy' of this instruction is sent to a further centre — the comparator. The efferent-copy is stored in the comparator and is 'compared' (hence the name) with proprioceptive, visual or other perceptual information relating to the movement which was actually carried out. According to whether or not a copy of an instruction for the action actually taking place is present in the comparator, a change is registered as being caused by the self or by something else. It is important to note that the founders of this model understand it as a subpersonal cognitive mechanism, which typically does not step over the threshold of consciousness — we are not usually conscious of the mechanism through which a plan of action is associated ('compared') with the sensory (bodily) feedback of the relevant bodily movement.

In order to make disturbances in this mechanism understandable, Campbell must first take issue with the Cartesian intuition of the immunity to error of conscious self-reference. He does this by differentiating between two levels, following the famous Reichenbach-rule according to which a sign H refers to anyone who uses it competently (Reichenbach, 1947).[17] In other words H (which of course is a stand-in for the real life word 'I') is 'token-reflexive'. This is then a simple logical rule in whose application I cannot make a mistake, but through which neither do I acquire any substantial knowledge about myself. Who the concrete person is who uses the sign H to stand for himself is not established on this elementary level. That only happens on a second level. It is not infallibly settled whether H is really predicatively F (or identical with F) (Campbell, 2004, pp. 480ff.). This, according to Campbell, is why referential error is fully consistent with Cartesian self-evidence (pp. 485ff.).

Campbell's idea is to use the *comparator model* to explain the possibility of passing over from the first level of the (vague, implicit or simply abstract, namely attained through the use of the 'I'-rule)

---

[17] It has been shown many times that this rule does not apply unconditionally. Cf. Castañeda's proof of the unanalysability of quasi-indicators (Castañeda, 1999, pp. 64, 80ff.; Kaplan, 1989, pp. 519 ff.; also Frank, 1991, pp. 367ff.).

self-knowledge to the second of (explicit, content-rich or embodied) self-identification, and of 'trading' identity from the first to the second level. In order to do that we merely have to understand acts of thinking and speaking as real mental or physical events — as *actions* (pp. 484ff.). According to Campbell, whereas the thoughts 'I am tired' and 'I am thirsty' can be grasped by everyone for themselves on the first level (in the first person), the inference of 'I am tired' and 'I am thirsty' to 'So I am both: tired and thirsty' can only be guaranteed through the recognition of the identity of the concrete person in both thoughts (idem). The *comparator model* can explain this: if I formulate a thought, an instruction for forming the thought will first be formed and its copy then compared in the comparator with the thoughts that were really formed (p. 485). In case the comparator malfunctions, one or both of these thoughts may be left without the certainty that they are my thoughts. In such a case I do not have the right to draw the conclusion that there is someone who is both tired and hungry. A breakdown of the comparator explains then the coexistence, characteristic of schizophrenia of the first-person perspective and the experience that some of the thoughts that I have are being formed by someone else, or that they are being stolen (pp. 486ff.; Frith, 1992).

The phenomenological plausibility of what Campbell wants to explain is obvious to the extent that no-one — besides stubborn substance-dualists — deny the transition from the mental to the bodily. But the *comparator model* devised to support this explanation does not withstand closer examination. For one thing, the comparator model is concerned with purely mechanical-motor processes which operate on the sub-personal level and are not conscious. Shaun Gallagher (2000, 2005) has shown that the breakdown of the 'comparator' cannot explain I-disturbances of the type of schizophrenic symptoms (non-self-agentive thoughts), since a failure of the comparator would apparently lead also to a feeling of non-authorship or alienness of the higher order thought according to which the lower order thoughts are alien or authored by someone else. Yet schizophrenics normally experience as their own their (higher order) thoughts that some of their (lower order) thoughts are not their own. Gallagher writes „[the comparator model] would need to explain why a higher-order cognition that fails to generate a sense of agency for a particular thought or experience is itself experienced as self-agentive' (Gallagher, 2005, p. 14). Thus, in order to explain what Campbell wants it to explain the comparator would at least have to malfunction in a curiously selective way.

There is, however, another objection. The comparator compares the copy of a sub-personal intention (is there such a thing?) with information about realized action (such as a thought) and mediates the results back to the sub-personal body. But how can the copy of a *de re* self-referring loop which involves no consciousness, not to mention self-consciousness, generate self-consciousness without changing or falsifying the thing that is copied? The copied thing contains no self-consciousness *de se*, and therefore it cannot be expected that the copy contains it either. In other words, that which, according to the model, should function as the criterion for whether an action is one's own, has no ownness to it and therefore, in fact, cannot function as the criterion. Here we have one more consideration suggesting that 'reflective self-understanding of [one's] own engagement with the world' (Campbell, 2004, p. 487) presupposes a non-reflective consciousness of the subject as well as of its mental states. This necessary pre-condition is something that the comparator-model does not account for.

VI. Conclusion

I began with an excursion into the German Idealists Kant, Fichte, Schelling and Schleiermacher in order to remind us of a problem. These thinkers namely knew something which, with a few important exceptions, has been forgotten by today's philosophy of mind: self-consciousness and self-awareness cannot be the results of an inwardly-turned look, of a higher-level reflection or of a comparator. All these attempts at explanation — and many similar ones which I could not discuss here — presuppose the thing that is to be explained and thus move in circles.

All of this suggests that self-consciousness must be thought of as an ontologically quite special phenomenon. We have treated it almost exclusively in negative terms, in that we have established what it *isn't* and why definitive attempts to explain its nature *fail*. But what is it positively? We only stand a chance of answering this question when we begin to distrust attempts which presuppose in self-consciousness — as indeed our word usage itself almost unavoidably suggests — a kind of duality, a reflective kind of relation. Why should we rule out that neurobiology might introduce us to a structure which resists the subject-object schema?[18]

Attempts to think of self-consciousness a-relationally were made by Fichte's early-Romantic contemporaries, above all Novalis (cf.

---

[18] Cf. the admittedly aporetic considerations in this direction in 'Reflexivity' (Nozick, 1981, pp. 71ff.).

Frank, 2002). Interestingly, Novalis called a non-self-objectivizing consciousness 'feeling' (*Gefühl*). Current research into feelings and emotions is working out attempts at integration in this area. Ned Block has, in numerous publications, discussed phenomenal consciousness which exists independently of intentional attitudes ('phenomenal consciousness without access consciousness'). Peter Goldie has emphasized in his classic work on emotions that propositional attitudes like wishes, hopes, fears, loves etc. ought not, as is customary, to be seen as free from qualia. According to him every emotion is somehow felt (Goldie, 2000, Ch. 3).

This immediate givenness through feeling must not however be understood once more in terms of intentional attitudes. Goldie says this only against the 'over-intellectualisation' of emotions and leaves pure thoughts or beliefs devoid of feelingness. The view that thoughts or beliefs have no feelingness to them is, however, not uncontroversial. For instance, it was not Husserl's view (Husserl, 1980, V), nor that of the representatives of the idea that there are concept-qualia (Horgan and Tienson, 2002; Siewert, 1998 and 2003). If every consciousness — or, as Husserl would say, every experience (*Erlebnis*) — involves in itself a feeling (Siewert 1998), be it intentionally referred to an object or state of affairs, or not (as with, according to Block (1995; 2003), pain or orgasm for example) an alternative perspective emerges, under which we have to characterise the manner in which persons are non-objectally familiar with their consciousness and its owner, that is, of themselves. I will pursue this perspective in future research.

Translated from German by Sheridan Burnside

References

Armstrong, David (1968), *A Materialist Theory of the Mind* (London: Routledge and Kegan Paul).
Armstrong, David (1984), 'In defence of inner sense', in D.M. Armstrong & Norman Malcolm, *Consciousness & Causality* (Oxford: Blackwell), pp. 108–37.
Baker, Lynne Rudder (1998), 'The first-person perspective: A test for naturalism', in: *American Philosophical Quarterly*, **35** (4), pp. 327–43.
Bernecker, Sven (1996), 'Externalism and the attitudinal component of self-knowledge', *Noûs*, **30** (2), pp. 262–75.
Block, Ned (1995), 'On a confusion about a function of consciousness', *Behavioral and Brain Sciences*, **18**, pp. 227–87.
Block, Ned (2003), 'Mental paint', in M. Hahn and B. Ramberg (ed.), *Reflections and Replies, Essays on Tyler Burge* (Cambridge, MA: MIT Press).
Boghossian, Paul (1989), 'Content and self-knowledge', *Philosophical Topics*, **17** (1), pp. 5–26.

Burge, Tyler (1979), 'Individualism and the mental', *Midwest Studies in Philosophy*, **4**, pp. 73–121.
Campbell, John (2004), 'The first person, embodiment, and the certainty that one exists', *The Monist*, **84** (4), pp. 475–88.
Castañeda, Hector-Neri (1966), '"He" – A study in the logic of self-consciousness', *Ratio*, **8**, pp. 130–57.
Castañeda, Hector-Neri (1999), *The Phenomeno-Logic of the I. Essays on Self-Consciousness*, ed. James G. Hart and Tomis Kapitan, (Bloomington and Indianapolis: Indiana University Press).
Chalmers, David J. (1996), *The Conscious Mind. In Search of a Fundamental Theory* (New York Oxford: Oxford University Press).
Chisholm, Roderick (1981), *The First Person. An Essay on Reference and Intentionality* (Brighton/Sussex: The Harvester Press).
Fichte, Johann Gottlob Friedrich (1992), *Foundations of Transcendental Philosophy (Wissenschaftslehre nova methodo)*, trans. and ed. Daniel Breazeale (Ithaca, NY: Cornell University Press).
Frank, Manfred (1991a), *Selbstbewusstseinstheorien von Fichte bis Sartre* (Frankfurt am Main.: Suhrkamp). Partial English translation by Simon Critchley, Peter Dews, Dieter Freundlieb und Wayne Hudson: 'Fragments of a History of the Theory of Self-Consciousness from Kant to Kierkegaard', *Critical Horizons. Journal of Social and Critical Theory*, vol. 5, 2004, pp. 53–136.
Frank, Manfred (2002), *Selbstgefühl. Eine historisch-systematische Erkundung* (Frankfurt am Main: Suhrkamp).
Frith, Christopher D. (1992), *The Cognitive Neuropsychology of Schizophrenia* (Hillsdale, N J: Erlbaum).
Frith, Christopher D. (2004), 'Comments on Shaun Gallagher: Neurocognitive models of schizophrenia: A neurophenomenological critique', *Psychopathology*, **37**, pp. 20–22.
Gallagher, Shaun (2000), 'Philosophical conceptions of the self: Implications for cognitive science', *Trends in Cognitive Sciences*, **4** (1), pp. 14–21.
Gallagher, Shaun (2004), 'Neurocognitive models of schizophrenia: A neurophenomenological critique', *Psychopathology*, **37**, pp. 8–19
Geach, Peter (1957), 'On beliefs about oneself', *Analysis*, **18**, pp. 23–4.
Goldie, Peter (2000), *The Emotions. A Philosophical Exploration* (Oxford: Clarendon Press).
Harman, Gilbert (1990), 'The intrinsic quality of experience', in: J. Tomberlin (ed.), *Philosophical Perspectives, 4, Action, Theory and Philosophy of Mind* (Atascadero/CA: Ridgeview Publishing Co.), pp. 31–52.
Henrich, Dieter (1982), 'Fichte's original insight'. Trans. David Lachterman. *Contemporary German Philosophy* 1. (Univ. Park, PA: Penn State University Press), pp. 15–53. Originally: 'Fichtes ursprüngliche Einsicht', *Subjektivität und Metaphysik. Festschrift für Wolfgang Cramer*. Eds. D. Henrich & H. Wagner (Frankfurt am Main: Klostermann 1966), pp. 188–232.
von Holst, Erich & Mittelstaedt, Horst (1950), 'Das Reafferenzprinzip (Wechselwirkungen zwischen Zentralnervensystem und Peripherie)'. *Naturwissenschaften*, **37**, pp. 464–76.
Horgan, Terence & Tienson, John (2002), 'The intentionality of phenomenology and the phenomenology of intentionality', in: David Chalmers (ed.), *Philosophy of Mind* (Oxford: Oxford University Press), pp. 520–31.
Husserl, Edmund (1980), *Logische Untersuchungen*, 6. Aufl., Tübingen: Max Niemeyer. In English: Logical Investigations, trans. J.N. Findlay (London: Routledge, 1973).

Kant, Immanuel (1900ff.), *Kants gesammelte Schriften*. First Berlin: Reimer, later Berlin und Leipzig: de Gruyter.
Kant, Immanuel (1996), *Critique of Pure Reason,* translated by Werner S. Pluhar (Indianapolis: Hackett Publishing Company).
Kaplan, David (1989), 'Demonstratives', in: Joseph Almog, John Perry and Howard Wettstein (eds.), *Themes from Kaplan* (New York: Oxford University Press), pp. 481–563.
Kripke, Saul (1980), *Naming and Necessity* (Oxford: Blackwell).
Lewis, David (1983), '*Attitudes De Dicto and De Se*'. In his *Philosophical Papers*. Volume I (New York & Oxford: Oxford University Press), pp. 133–59.
Mach, Ernst (1886), *Beiträge zur Analyse der Empfindungen* (Jena: Gustav Fischer).
Meinong, Alexius (1975), 'Über die Erfahrungsgrundlagen unseres Wissens'. In: R. Haller, R. Kininger und R. M. Chisholm (eds.), *Gesamtausgabe*, (Graz: Akademische Druck- und Verlagsanstalt), Bd. V, 1–113.
Mellor, David Hugh (1977–78), 'Conscious belief', *Proceedings of the Aristotelian Society*, **LXXXVIII**, pp. 87–101.
Moran, Richard (2001), *Authority and Estrangement. An Essay on Self-Knowledge* (Princeton and Oxford: University Press).
Nozick, Robert (1981), 'The identity of the self', in his *Philosophical Explanations,* (Cambridge: MA, The Belknap Press of Harvard University Press), pp. 27–114.
Putnam, Hilary (1975) 'The meaning of "meaning"', in his *Mind, Language, and Reality. Philosophical Papers, Vol. 2*, (Cambridge: Cambridge University Press), pp. 215–71.
Hans Reichenbach (1947), 'Token-reflexive words', in his: *Elements of Symbolic Logic* (New York: Free Press), pp. 284–7.
Rosenthal, David M. (1991), 'Two concepts of consciousness', in D.M. Rosenthal (ed.), *The Nature of Mind* (Oxford: Oxford University Press), pp. 462–77.
Sartre, Jean-Paul (1940*), L'Imaginaire. Psychologie Phénomenologique de L'Imaginaire* (Paris: Gallimard). In English: *The Imaginary: A Phenomenological Psychology of the Imagination.* (revised by Arlette Elkaim-Sartre, transl. Jonathan Webber (London: Routledge).
Sartre, Jean-Paul (1991), 'Conscience de soi et connaissance de soi' (A lecture for the French Philosophical Society, June 2th 1947). In: Frank (1991a), 379 ff.
Schelling, Friedrich Wilhelm Joseph (1856-64), *Sämmtliche Werke*, ed. K.F. A.Schelling (Stuttgart: Klett-Cotta).
Schelling, Friedrich Wilhelm Joseph (1992), *Urfassung der Philosophie der Offenbarung,* 2 Volumes. Edited by Walter E. Ehrhardt (Hamburg: Meiner).
Schleiermacher, Friedrich (1960), *Der christliche Glaube. Nach den Grundsätzen der Evangelischen Kirche im Zusammenhange dargestellt.* Siebente Auflage. Erster Band. Edited by Martin Redeker (Berlin: de Gruyter).
Schleiermacher, Friedrich (2001), *Dialektik*. 2 Volumes. Edited and with introduction by Manfred Frank (Frankfurt am Main: Suhrkamp).
Shoemaker, Sydney (1984a), *Identity, Cause, and Mind. Philosophical Essays* (Cambridge: Cambridge University Press).
Shoemaker, Sydney (together with Richard Swinburne) (1984b), *Personal Identity* (Oxford: Blackwell).
Shoemaker, Sydney (1996), *The First Person Perspective and Other Essays* (Cambridge: Cambridge University Press).
Siewert, Charles P. (1998), *The Significance of Consciousness* (Princeton, NJ: Princeton University Press).

Siewert, Charles P. (2003), 'Consciousness and intentionality', in: *Stanford Encyclopedia of Philosophy,* im Internet:
 http://plato.stanford.edu/entries/consciousness-intentionality
Sperry, R.W. (1950), 'Neural basis of the spontaneous optokinetic response produced by visual inversion', *Journal of Comparative and Physiological Psychology,* **43**, pp. 482–9.
Thiel, Udo (1996), 'Between Wolff and Kant: Meiner's theory of apperception', *Journal of the History of Philosophy,* **23**, pp. 213–32.
Tugendhat, Ernst (1979), *Selbstbewusstsein und Selbstbestimmung. Sprachanalytische Interpretationen,* (Frankfurt am Main: Suhrkamp). In English: *Self-Consciousness and Self-Determination.* Transl. by Paul Stern (Cambridge, MA: MIT Press).
Tye, Michael (2002), 'Representationalism and the transparency of experience', in: *Noûs,* **36** (1), pp. 137–51.

Pirmin Stekeler-Weithofer

Persons and Practices
Kant and Hegel on Human Sapience

Abstract: *Man's rational capacities rest on education and this makes the form of human sapience interpersonal. As persons, however, we do not take part in the tradition of sapience only passively. That is, mere rationality in Kant's sense, i.e. the faculty of following implicit norms or explicit rules, is not enough for personhood. It requires also reason in Hegel's sense, i.e. free active participation in developing 'the idea' (eventually of good human life), as well as 'the concept', i.e. joint generic knowledge that defines the inferential content of our words and sentences. In making reasonable proposals for developing these persons are themselves the free 'spirit' of the human world.*

Introduction

We do not become persons like apples grow on trees; nor do we jump off Jupiter's ear in the full armour of personal competence, as Minerva did in mythology. It rather seems to be a truism that education and formation (*Bildung*) are necessary preconditions for personal competences like those of thinking or judging, planning and performing actions. In his lectures on anthropology and on education, even Kant makes this point; whereas in the *Critique of Pure Reason* he had been reluctant to talk about such 'empirical' preconditions for objective knowledge or conceptually informed experience. In the *Critique of Pure Reason* Kant wanted to keep logical and transcendental (i.e. presuppositional) analysis of the general forms of judgements separate from mere stories about their origin — as they are told, for example, in the writings of Hobbes, Locke, Hume, Condillac, or Herder. In

Correspondence:
Prof. Dr. Pirmin Stekeler-Weithofer, Institut für Philosophie, Universität Leipzig, Beethovenstrasse 15, 04107 Leipzig, Germany.

his anthropology, however, Kant makes clear that being a person means that one has developed the competence of successfully taking part in a whole system of joint human practice. It is precisely this system which Hegel refers to under the title '*Geist*' or 'Spirit', and sometimes also by the words 'Knowledge' or 'Concept'; used as umbrella-titles (with capital letters, so to speak). Hence, Hegel's word 'World-Spirit' refers, in the end, to nothing else than *our development of human sapience*.

But any attempt to make human sapience in this wide sense explicit has to deal with the following problem. The very question of what sapience is presupposes that we already somehow know what we are looking for. We might think, for example, of *sentences* like the following: Sapience is a human faculty which ensures that human perception is always already informed by concepts,[1] and thereby makes objective experience possible. We can distinguish in sapience further aspects like consciousness, intelligence, rationality, or reason. But when we turn from the level of abstract reflection, expressed in such sentences, to the level of real existence, the logical order must be reversed: In reality, we always start from sapience as it is already (in a certain sense 'holistically') given in our lives, namely in the way we perform 'sapient' (intelligent) actions as consequences of (more or less accurate) perceptions of the world around us. That is, it is only our reflective analysis that splits sapience up into different moments or partial faculties such as perception and conceptual thinking, or the planning and performing of actions. The real existence of sapience as a faculty comes as a kind of unit, as a result of learning to take part in a general form of life.

There is a deep problem of articulation here. For we are inclined to say, with Hegel, that the generic form of sapience should not be conceived of simply as a more or less stable object of reflection, as a 'substance', but, also, as a kind of 'subject', which governs individual life. But then, this 'subject' cannot be different from *us*. Its existence is *our* existence. *We* are this subject. On the other hand, this *We* does not refer only to a fixed set of individual persons, as is the case when you and I say that *we* do this or that together. It refers to a *generic We*. In this difficult generic sense, Hegel's *Weltgeist* is humankind itself. The word refers *in a generic way* to us, insofar as we take part in the development of humankind according to its 'idea'.

The task of philosophy is to make this idea of humankind explicit, in some of its most relevant general aspects and in its unity. This is the

---

[1] For versions of this thought, see McDowell (1994); Pinkard (1994); Pippin (1988).

reason why Hegel demands a kind of systematic analysis and synthetic account of human life-forms (*Gestalten des Lebens*) or human practices in their relations to each other. The goal is a coherent picture of the practices that make us human. Unfortunately, this understanding of why we need a 'system' in philosophy has got lost in the meantime.[2] There are two reasons for this. The first argument understands system-building as subjective construction — as if every philosopher wanted to have his own theory, in which his private contentions were somehow made deductively or inferentially coherent, just as every poet seems to have his own style. Hegel himself ridiculed this idea. The second argument says that a 'complete' picture of all human practices is impossible anyway, or that it is not even clear what form such a 'complete' picture might take. Indeed, completeness is always relative to relevance. Hence, in any given context we must reflect on the relevant aspects in order to judge if an account of human sapience is sufficient or not, if it is too general or too specific. And we have to understand why the latter can often be worse. It is a rather misleading idea (attributed not without some grounds to the later Wittgenstein) that philosophy should *always* teach us differences.

Note also that the word 'system' has a double meaning. In one sense, it refers to the ordering of our representation; in another, to the ordering of the objects to be represented. Hence, we have to distinguish, on the one hand, between the system of human practices as it is 'for itself' (*für sich*), i.e. as it really exists in our actions, and, on the other, our (in a large part verbal) image or model of it. The double meaning at stake here is a systematic feature of our language that we can also see in the way we use the word 'history': it can stand for *stories* told ('as such' or *an sich*), for untold historic *facts* ('for themselves'), as well as for facts as they are truly represented in history ('as such and for themselves', *an-und-für-sich*). We even use words like 'number' or 'concept' or 'word' or 'proposition', sometimes for the representations or the signs we use (for example in 'the number he wrote down'), and sometimes for abstract objects. When we talk about abstract objects such as contents or concepts, we usually reflect on complex practices. (Think, for example, of a sentence like: 'the concept of number presupposes a well-ordering defined for the representations like number-terms or symbols'.) To be too 'rigorous' in separating these different usages by means of different words will just increase the number of ambiguities. We had better make the relative distinctions explicit only in contexts where this is necessary or helpful.

---

[2] See also Stekeler-Weithofer (2006).

Language itself is a social practice. Speaking a language and understanding it requires education and material knowledge. It requires, first, knowing how to do things with words. But then it requires theoretical or propositional knowledge also. Since thinking should be seen as performing silent symbolic acts, just as we learn to read silently or as we do our verbal planning, it depends heavily upon pre-given social institutions and practices.[3] The resulting problem is this. If my personal competence (of thinking) consisted only in my ability to behave in sufficient accordance with given conventions or norms in a group of humans, including the norms of using language in a 'correct' way, the difference between me and a bee taking part in bee dances that help bees in finding blossoms, sucking honey and feeding their offspring would not seem to be very big. Demonstrating personal competence would mean nothing more than behaving in accordance with certain patterns of successful co-ordination of group behaviour. The difference of this to bee dances would merely be one of the complexity of co-ordination of behaviour.

But the main task of philosophical anthropology is to make the obvious *difference* between animal behaviour and human actions explicit. Even though we should not be blind with respect to similarities, merely focussing on similarities in behaviour is not enough. So what is the difference between *sentience* and *sapience*, as Robert Brandom (1994, p. 5) has put it, or rather, between the mere *subjectivity* of (higher) animals on one hand, and the *rationality* and *reason* of humans on the other? Subjectivity consists, roughly speaking, in a kind of self-steered reaction to what the *individual animal* senses ('perceives') and 'feels'. How rationality and reason goes beyond subjectivity is our question here.

The general relevance of philosophical reflection on the relation between practice and personhood, pre-given institutions and personal competence lies in the comprehension of human autonomy, of free will and free action. Insofar as a proper understanding of autonomy is its final goal, philosophy *is* philosophical anthropology. This is the main insight, and project, of the philosophy of German Idealism in Kant, Fichte, and Hegel, who set out to defend a reasonable concept of free action against pictures of the world (*Weltanschauung*) that are the results of sweeping interpretations of empirical observations, and of causal explanations in terms of laws in the natural sciences. If we understand nature in the old, Greek and Latin, sense of the words

---

[3] That they are 'pre-given' means that they exist already before the birth of the individual and cannot be changed by his will alone.

'*physis*' and '*natura*', it is simply the realm of events that happen *all by themselves*, and this means: *without interference from human actions*. But in order to comprehend this very difference, and the relation between mere nature and the world at large, or between knowledge about nature and knowledge about ourselves, Hegel had seen that we need a *realistic* – that is, not merely formal or ideal (i.e. utopian) — account of knowledge and science which also accounts for their development. This means that we have to distinguish between *science* in the *revisionist* sense of 'natural science' (*Naturwissenschaft*), which only has nature (including our bodies as in medicine) as its topic, and *scientia*, which includes the humanities (*Geisteswissenschaft*) and especially philosophy. For philosophy has, among many other things, the logic of scientific explanation, as well as concepts like truth and reality, empirical investigation and generic justification as its themes.

As regards reflecting on sapience, Fichte, and with him Hegel and Heidegger, had seen that in any use of the word 'I' I must distinguish between the performance of the speech act by me and the reference of the word 'I', despite the fact that there is a kind of identity expressed in the utterance. The question is, what does this identity consist of? Even when I ask 'Who am I?' I already have to take into account the fact that I am such that I can ask such a question. That is to say, the question already asks for an account of the difference between ourselves as *persons*, and as objects of our possible knowledge. It is into this context that Kant's so called transcendental analysis is to be placed: Kant reflects on the logical or categorical pre-conditions for meaningful claims about empirical knowledge, but also for claims to be a person: Only a person can say 'I think …', 'I claim …', 'I believe …', 'I want …' and 'I intend …' This is so if 'saying' means more than just making noises (that also could be produced by a parrot or a computer); specifically, if it means making meaningful moves in a language game. In fact, transcendental analysis simply tries to make explicit some basic implicit structural norms that make it possible for sentences or utterances, as well as perceptions, to have 'determinate content'.

The question of what sapience is has now turned into the question of what truth, knowledge, and science are. There is an important, yet mostly unknown, thread in philosophical reflection that leads from Kant, Hegel, Nietzsche, Marx and others to Martin Heidegger or, for that matter, to William James and John Dewey. It is defined by the attempt to reconcile the idea of individual freedom and personal authenticity not only with our scientific knowledge of the natural world at large, but also with our dependence on social conventions and historical developments. According to my reading, Hegel saw long before Nietzsche that if personal competence were nothing but the result of training and the moulding of behaviour according to pre-given conventions, autonomy would virtually disappear. The defence of moral autonomy and expressive authenticity, which lies at the heart of Kant's philosophy as well as that of Fichte and of the Romantics, would fail. Hence, for Hegel the task is to reconcile the ideas of personal autonomy and authenticity with our dependence on social conventions and institutions, i.e. on pre-given forms of joint behaviour and common practices.

Today, most efforts in so called analytical philosophy seem to consist in producing theories that aim at a *reduction* of 'mental entities and processes' to material things and physical events, or rather, at a reduction of the respective vocabularies and explanations. Alternatively, we find seemingly more modest theories that talk about local or global *supervenience* of mental idioms with respect to physical explanations. The latter should tell us what 'really' happens, whereas mental talk is imprecise, even if practically helpful — be it reducible to 'physics' or not. All these theories want to make the 'subjective' way we view ourselves as persons consistent with the thesis of an 'objective' causal connectedness of the world. The corresponding principle of 'sufficient causes' says that any event is caused by other, earlier, events and any 'real' explanation has to take place, in the end, in ways explicable in terms of the natural science of physics.

In all these efforts we can see an implicit assumption. It says that the concept of nature (i.e. the object of natural sciences) coincides (in a certain way) with the 'real world' of all our experiences, including the experiences we have of our own actions and life. It is absolutely crucial to see that for Hegel this question was still open. That is, Hegel does not start with the dogmatic belief that such presumptions about causality, objective reality, nature and the world of experience are true. He rather takes the view that it is absolutely unclear what a *sufficient reason* for such a belief could be, and what the principle of *sufficient causes* really says.

On the other hand, Hegel is totally willing to accept this much: Any real intention and action must have consequences in the real world. And any act of thinking is just a silent use of language or of other symbolic devices taking place in the real world. Hence, we need a satisfying comprehension both of our dependence on our implicit cultural heritage, and of what free action involves. Moreover, we have to comprehend what it is to actively take part in the free, but joint, enterprise of improving the complex system of our institutions, if we want to comprehend what it is to be a person with self-consciousness, reason, and autonomy.

It is the practice of being human, taken as the whole system of institutions, which provides us with the possibility of understanding, *Verstand* or 'rationality'. But rationality is not a sufficient condition for leading a *full* human life as a *full person*. For this, we need to take part in a culture of reason (*Vernunft*). According to Hegel, reason means taking a practical attitude to institutions, or the idea and project of *developing* the human practice. Here the question arises, however, as to what we mean by the word 'reason', and how we should distinguish between merely 'rational' and more fully 'reasonable' *(vernünftig)* judgements, inferences, and actions.

1. The Most General Question of Philosophy

Already Kant's central, and overall, question of philosophy 'what is man' (see Kant, 1988, p. 29) seeks to know what are the 'essentials' of being a full human person. The question aims at a *concept* of being human or being a person, which should make the *implicit conditions* for *being a person* explicit.

Conceptual questions are often seen as merely linguistic, terminological or logical questions of definition, of conceptual criteria and 'analytically necessary' inferences. This is one of the reasons why the conditions for being a person are usually dealt with in an *empirical* way. This means that the question is taken as enquiring after the *empirical conditions* for developing and having the necessary competence of being a person or counting as a person. For example, our idea of personal identity seems to rest on our *memory*, as Locke and others have suggested. Without memory, it seems, our 'stream of consciousness' does not have the inner unity needed for personal identity. Only memory seems to unite the ever-changing present sensations or 'inner experiences' (*Empfindungen*) in the flux of time and turn them into 'my experience' (*meine Erfahrung*).

However, having the complex memory by which we can keep track of what we have done, thought, or experienced, and of what we intended to do, did do, or have not yet done, obviously already relies on a quite well-developed *linguistic* competence. Even if the empiricist talk about an immediate stream of consciousness is not untrue, it resembles in vagueness what Heraclitus already seems to have pointed out with respect to a real stream: The different waters are united in a stream when and only when we can (or could) track their flow from the beginning to the end. Heraclitus does not say that we cannot enter the same river twice (as Plato has it). Rather, he says that if we were to focus on the different waters, we would never be able to refer to the (same and identical) stream. In this sense, the unity of a person does indeed seem analogous to the unity of the river, and the difference between different sensory and intellectual states really does seem analogous to the difference between different waters. The local unity of the stream of a river seems to be a good metaphor for the chronological unity produced by personal memory.

Now, Hegel shares with Heraclitus the insight into the crucial (defining) role of language (logos) for determining conceptual content. And both authors seem to presume that their readers see the role of good judgment of *relevance* for any appropriate understanding of language and speech. They know that there is always an infinite possibility of all-too-fine or otherwise irrelevant distinctions and observations, as we can see from the discussion of the unity of a river. For example, the much-debated question of how many 'personalities' I might have (or our schizophrenic friend or our neighbour suffering from a rare split-brain disease, just to name a couple of examples) is not relevant to understanding what it is to be a person in the first place. We could even say that there is no genuine philosophical question about how we should count 'personalities'. Count as you wish. Only tell us what you mean by your counting and what it is good for. In other words, the question should never be what we *can* distinguish, but what we have to distinguish if we want to achieve certain ends.

Moreover, a practical 'unity' of myself is always already presupposed from the start when I talk about *my* sensations or *my* perceptions, *my* memories or *my* (self-) consciousness. Sensations, perceptions, memories etc. must already be my or your or her perceptions — or they are nothing at all. Hence, the question of what role memory plays in keeping track 'of myself', as we say, is already distinct from the question of what *it is to be a person* having such memories. If we think this through, we will understand why the question posed by the 'empiricists', as to how the unity of a plethora of memorized mental states *defines* a person is already wrongly posed from the outset.

If we now turn back to the question of what a (human) person is, we have to distinguish between different uses of the words 'man' and 'person'. Sometimes they are used in a rather low-key sense, as when we refer to a biological species, or when we say 'there are five persons allowed in the elevator', in other times in a much fuller sense as in Kant's emphatic use of 'mankind' or in an exclamation like: 'you have first to become a person!' For Hegel, at least sometimes, the use of 'man' presupposes the competence of *rationality*, whereas somebody is a *person* in a fuller sense of the word if and only if she *'has reason'*.

In the philosophical analysis of Kant and Hegel, *rational understanding* (*Verstand*) consists in the ability to *follow pre-given rules correctly*, or rather, to be able to judge and act according to certain *implicit norms, general principles and explicit rules*. Reason (*Vernunft*), on the other hand, is the competence of *explicit conceptual analysis* and *meta-level reflection*, as it is needed in *autonomous* judgements *about* the forms and norms and rules of actions. For Hegel, understanding is not enough in order to be a *person*. His rationale is this: If I speak 'as rational man' (as a *zoon logon echon* or *animal rationale*), and 'understand' what others say, and if I act or react accordingly in my further speech acts or non-linguistic acts, this shows I am able to draw correct inferences according to a pre-given system of implicit norms. These norms define what is a 'logically' or 'conceptually' correct inference. They define 'rationality' or 'understanding': these terms name the competence to act according to such a system of norms or rules of correct inference. Being rational is being able to judge and act, at least in principle, according to these norms and rules. For the individual, this ability is indeed a precondition of being human in the sense of being a *competent* member of the species man. We assume that 'normally,' more or less every member of our species is able to learn the trick, i.e. to learn to understand his language and other norms and rules of rational behaviour and rational action. It is for this reason that we say that man, as a *species*, is a rational being.

On the other hand, a certain amount of logical *reflection* is a precondition for *reason*, that is, for conceptual self-consciousness. Hegel's word for meta-level reflection is 'speculation'. Even though any logical analysis belongs to the 'speculative' level of reflective thinking, Hegel's 'speculative' logic is a kind of meta-logic. In a similar way, his philosophy of history is a kind of meta-history reflecting on the different concepts of history and the different forms in which we re-present history. (In correspondence to these different forms of representation, there are different sets of criteria we use when we judge the 'truth' of historical accounts, or rather the fulfilment of their conditions of satisfaction). Hegel's philosophy of nature is speculative in this same sense, and has nothing to do with talking nonsense about nature and natural science in the pejorative sense of 'wild speculation'. Rather, his philosophy of nature wants to be a kind of meta-science. It wants to reflect on the different concepts of nature, on the different ways nature is present to us, and on the different forms in which nature is re-presented by us in different natural sciences, in ordinary discourse and in poetic developments of new ways of dealing with nature.

Comprehending a practice fully (*Begreifen*) means *to grasp its idea* in a reflective, and therefore autonomous and explicit way. The idea in question is *the form* of the practice according to its correct understanding — or rather, since we need more than implicit understanding in the sense of mere practical know-how, according to its *sufficiently good and reasonable comprehension*.

We do not have adequate words to express certain differences. We have said, for example, that *rationality* is the competence of knowing how to use the implicit norms and explicit rules *of rationality*. We say that the *idea of practice* is what is comprehended when we make the form and norm *of a practice* explicit and when we make autonomous judgements about it. In the same way, for Hegel any *concept* is a system of norms that determines what it is to use a word or sentence properly in making distinctions that come together with corresponding inferences. We understand a concept, as the content of the corresponding words or symbolic acts, when we can follow the norms. But we *comprehend* the concept only if we are able to explicitly *talk about it* as a *form* of a practice. We do this in logical analysis, properly understood.

One of Hegel's basic insights is this: Any usage of concepts, and any practice, has already been reflected on with respect to its form and norm, its reason and justification — most often not by me (or 'us' in a narrow sense), but by others. In this sense, any generic practice is already reflected 'in itself' (*in sich*).

For Hegel, a concept is a practice. It is, as such, the very practice of using the corresponding word(s) or symbolic acts (as types), by which the concept is represented in a linguistic system or practice. Hence any conceptual knowledge already 'includes' reason. And any practice 'exists', if it exists, as an 'idea'. This simply means that it exists in the way an implicit form of practice exists, namely, as a way in which we decide if something belongs to that practice or fits in with it or adds a new but fitting feature to it. Think, for example, of the 'idea' of law as a development of practices or institutions: we use the idea of law as a system of leading principles when we make judgements about what belongs to law what does not, or what improves law and justice, and what does not.

An idea, in Hegel's sense, can now be taken to be a modern reading of Plato's concept of *eidos* as a *form in life and practice*. Such an idea or form is something entirely different from a 'mere idea' in the sense of a mere subjective proposal to act or judge according to some accidental inspiration or fantasy.

Now speculation or speculative analysis in its broadest sense in Hegel's writing is simply the enterprise of making implicit forms and norms of human practice explicit — in order to help us to become more autonomous with respect to the use of pre-given forms. The task is to stabilise or improve human sapience, not by intensified or expanded *training* in *following norms*, *conventions* or *rules blindly*, as Wittgenstein suggests, but by deepening free comprehension.[4] Speculative reflections on the forms of our practice include the 'logic' of actions and practices. They usually result in *new schemes or new articulations of explicit principles or rules*. But a merely formal use of explicit rules remains in the realm of mere rationality. Therefore, mere replacement of implicit practices of inference by new schemes of formal deductions does not as such make us more self-conscious with respect to the content of our speech, and a mere schematism of rules can as well support as inhibit reason (*Vernunft*). Schematic rules have the advantage that it is easy to see whether they are followed correctly. This is the reason why mathematics is so important. But only if we know how the formulas of formal languages relate to real sentences or propositions about the world in which we live, and how schematic deductions relate to conceptual inferences, do we really comprehend the use of mathematics and other formal languages. For this, we need to know how a pre-given practice of using language is improved by formalization. Since this is so, no 'conceptual analysis' is merely 'descriptive' or 'empirical'. It is already 'normative' in a meta-level sense: It contains judgments and proposals about how we *should* speak, judge, 'reason', 'argue', and act (from now on) — if we want to judge and act 'reasonably'. This normativity, guided by the idea of the good development of human affairs or practices, is the reason why philosophy can never be only 'empirical' (descriptive); and why merely 'empirical' studies of human life and society, which do not go into practical consequences and the normative evaluations of these, are never good and true enough.

Moreover, since questions of norms which have practical consequences are always disputed between different persons, there is no 'static' knowledge and no 'eternal truth' about human affairs. All

---

[4] Wittgenstein is the modern philosopher who has shown us the importance of the notion of a practice for philosophical analysis. But he seems to put too much emphasis on following rules in the sense of schematic norms – with the rather unhappy consequence that his philosophy is in some danger to turn into a kind of relativistic behaviourism.

judgements about implicit norms, principles, or explicit rules, including judgements as to their proper use are, in a certain way, *free*. We cannot defend such judgements by an appeal to pre-given or presupposed norms. We rather have *to ask for free acknowledgement of our free arguments*.

Therefore, Richard Rorty seems to understand the peculiar status of philosophical reflection and argumentation better than most of his critics, who do not realise that they fall into a kind of dialectical trap when they attempt to fight the alleged relativism of the idea of free acknowledgement. The trap is the unholy alternative between sheer traditionalism and mere subjective dogmatism. The problem is so dramatic because the most ardent defenders of universal rules argue in a dogmatic, i.e. a teaching and preaching way — as if the audience consisted of children.[5] But the very difference, and the relationship, between rationality and reason, corresponds, in a certain sense, to the difference, and relationship, between a youth and an adult. A youth has to learn to reproduce standards of rational understanding. But rational understanding — which includes proper dealing with all kind of norms of conceptual inference — is only *the basis* for becoming a full *autonomous person*.

In order to comprehend free argumentation and reflection properly, we must see it as an *appeal* for the free acknowledgement of certain norms or rules; which can be 'old' ones in the sense that they are now being made explicit in some way, or they can be part of a new proposal for changing an 'old' practice. When we say that we need a *reason* for any such appeal or proposal, we usually do *not* mean sentences we already have agreed upon (or 'nodded to') and deductive inferences (of an already accepted form), by which other sentences follow. We rather need a satisfying answer to the question of why it makes sense to support the proposed form or reform of a common practice, as it is made explicit by the proposed principles or rules. In this context, Hegel sees that giving 'reasons' means showing why this or that explication and comprehension of a given practice, or this or that proposal to change it in this or that aspect is better than some already established understanding of it. In the end, any such 'reason' is to be seen as involving the proposal for some reform. It has to be understood, with Hegel, as a 'moment', i.e. as a moving force, in our project of humanity and culture, of 'solidarity', as Rorty says (see Rorty, 1986). If we

---

[5] As a result, universalists argue, ironically, in an ethnocentric, if not egocentric way. They assume, implicitly, that their own, implicit, standards (norms, principles, or rules) of 'proper' judgment, 'correct' inference, 'rational' argumentation, and 'right' action must be followed by anyone who is counted (by them) as rational.

take all things together, it is the project of jointly developing the possibilities of a good life as free persons.

Strange as it sounds now, a free person is not bound to mere rationality. She is not bound in her judgments and actions to the first–order norms or rules of basic human competence, and even less, in her argumentations and inferences, by the first-order rules of formal logic. In their basic form, the latter in any case apply only in already formalized realms of discourse, as in mathematics. Not to acknowledge this (relative) autonomy in reasonable judgments and arguments means, implicitly, to hold that a limited practice and its formal schemes of behaviour are not only 'rational', but 'infallible' or 'non-revisable'. But this would be sheer dogmatism, the opposite of reason.

Now we can say that (autonomous) persons in Hegel's sense are not limited to following the implicit norms and explicit rules of rationality. In following the norms and rules of a particular limited practice, they can distinguish between good and bad experiences. And we do not just appeal to pre-given criteria, when we evaluate such a free judgement as reasonable. We rather compare it with traditional knowledge and common sense, i.e. judgments which others have already taken account of, and considered reasonable. If we can show that some new proposal for developing certain forms or norms of human practice, or some generic knowledge or conceptual inference, serves our needs better than the forms and norms that are traditionally considered as 'rational', then we can say that the new proposal is reasonable. Of course, we do not have any means of compelling anybody to accept such arguments. All we can do is ask for insight and acknowledgment — after providing a comparison between the problem-solving powers of the competing proposals.

This short sketch of Hegel's reflection on the difference between *rational* man and *reasonable* person already shows that human actions should be understood not only as the result of rational decisions, but also as the results of free judgements. In fact, having good reasons in this fuller sense of *Vernunft* is something other than referring to already well-established rules of inference and corresponding premises. Similarly, having good reasons in this sense seems to be less than having a 'convincing proof'. But it is more. It presupposes some knowledge of the limitations of the whole level of 'convincing proofs' in the context of 'merely rational reasoning'. Therefore, the usual quest for 'sufficient reasons' for a thesis or a proposition stays altogether in the realm of pre-established norms and rules, and does not leave this realm of mere rationality. This holds for judgements about individual acts as well as for judgements about joint actions, and it holds even for the historical development of whole practices and forms of social life.

2. Free Will as a Merely Intelligible Object or 'Noumenon'

Let us now come back to Kant's and Fichte's basic philosophical question, which can be seen as identical, as soon as we understand that the right form of the question 'what is man' is, in the end, *'who am I'*, i.e. *who are we — as human beings*? In the latter versions, we need the *context or background* of the situation in which such a question is asked. If we do not know this, it will be unclear what kind of answer will be appropriate, and which particular answer will be sufficient. The same holds for questions like 'Where am I' or 'Where are we?' Moreover, there is also a specific logical difficulty in articulating knowledge of oneself as a free person.

What Kant says, is that free will is the only merely intelligible 'thing' of which it can be shown that it really exists. In distinction to empirical motives such as desires that prompt certain behavioural reactions according to some pattern, free will works, according to Kant, outside the order of time. These are rather mystifying claims and we should take them rather as a formulation of the puzzle than as its solution.[6]

At least some hints of the solution can, however, already be given now. Free will is not to be understood as an entity. It is rather a kind of power (Hegel: *Kraft*) or *energeia*. As such it appears in the 'empirically real' world, like any *competence*, only in the context of actual action and practice. Kant himself suggests that freedom of the will exists only in the peculiar human way in which we orient our actual actions by actualizing pre-controlled schemes of actions at will. The peculiarity of this human way can be understood only differentially, i.e. by understanding and comprehending the difference between (free) human actions and animal behaviour, and between animal behaviour and mere physical events, as Hegel adds in his philosophy of nature.

In Hume's picture, it is *my immediate desire* and *my subjective experience* which prompts my behaviour. In this picture of 'decision by desires', no account is taken of the difference of human actions from animal behaviour. Yet reflections on possible means and possible success, i.e. 'rational beliefs' and 'rational choice', already

---

[6] See also Stekeler-Weithofer (2003).

presuppose the possibility of explicit 'instrumental reasoning'. That is, 'rational thinking' presupposes linguistic competence, knowledge of non-present possibilities, and counterfactual inferences. But as Kant points out, if we simply act according to our strongest subjective desire and our deepest individual beliefs about means and ends, our actions do not yet differ much from animal behaviour. This is the form of action, which Hegel terms *'realm of rational animals'*, as I would like to translate his somewhat strange German expression *'geistiges Tierreich'* (Hegel, 1977, chapter V, section C, paragraph a). The form of life of such a man is, I take it, that of an *animal rationale* or, what amounts to the same, a *homo oeconomicus*.

Hegel points out some 'inner contradictions' in this 'form of life': The first problem is that any *homo oeconomicus* relies for his instrumental rationality on knowledge, which he has to learn from others. Therefore this man, who wanted to be so independent and strives for certainty and security, at least in his own picture of himself, must *trust* other persons. And he must *believe* what traditional knowledge teaches him. For this, he must, for example, assume that what his teachers say is true in general — and does not only serve their own interests. That is, he must assume that *the others* are not mere rational men in the economic or instrumental sense. This means, in the end, that 'rational man' uses *and abuses* the contributions of other men.

Another problem is that our behaviour cannot be at the same time 'causally explained' by the schemes of rational choice and, if the schemes are not met, criticised by them as 'faulty'. For if the schemes 'explain' actual behaviour, how can we use them as norms in the criticism of behaviour that does not follow the scheme? This tension between a descriptive or explanatory use of the desire-belief theory of human action, and its normative use, by which we can criticise actual behaviour as irrational, is not solved in the debates about modern decision theory at all. This is astonishing, taking into account that Hume and his followers are almost overly dogmatic about the impossibility of deriving an 'ought' from an 'is'.

Explanations of actions in terms of rational choice in the framework of leading desires and beliefs are even more problematic: Not everything which seems to be rational is really reasonable. And rational grounds and good reasons do not 'force' us at all to behave in this way or another. They are objects of consideration in the making of free decisions and actions.

On the other hand, Hegel sees clearly that the very possibility of instrumental rationality already presupposes some co-operative practice of common knowledge. Without such knowledge I cannot make plans at all – because I cannot 're-present' expected outcomes of possible decisions or actions. Hence, Kant is mistaken when he declares that instrumental reasoning belongs to 'nature'. Kant thinks that if I act according to my desires and wishes, even when using common instrumental knowledge about the means that lead to ends, my actions are more or less merely natural behaviour. Hegel does not quite agree. If an action can be 'explained' by 'belief' and 'desire' (or rather, by knowledge and intention) in the framework of rational choice, it can *not* be explained by schemes of pure natural science. The reason is that human belief and knowledge about means, ends, human wishes, and intentions already belong to the sphere of 'spirit', of human sapience, and not to the sphere of animal behaviour and merely subjective 'intelligence'.

As a result, not only culture and history, but natural science and technology, too, must be seen as topics of philosophy (and of the 'moral sciences' or *Geisteswissenschaften*): We must comprehend them as special regions of human practice. Merely for the purpose of *understanding* science and technology (including mathematics and formal logic), we may *not need philosophy*. For this it may suffice to learn by taking part in the implicit practice of science, and to use normal schemes of logical or methodological inference or scientific rationality — without further reflection on the criteria of scientific investigation and articulation, or on the abstractness and formality that always is connected with merely verbal teaching and learning. But *comprehending* what we do when we use scientific procedures, and understanding the formal logical and methodological rules involved in making 'rational' (or even 'valid') judgements and inferences is more than such an understanding in the sense of mere knowing how to do things properly. Comprehending means knowing what we do and being able to talk in a reasonable way *about* the very 'concept' (idea and project) of science. And it should include knowing about the limitations of scope of different sciences, that follow from their different methods of inquiry and different forms of articulation.

For our purposes, it may be useful to list a number of central points on which Hegel, despite the idiosyncrasies of his terminology, is much clearer than Kant:

1. Instrumental planning already presupposes *jointly controlled knowledge* about what we can expect to be the results of certain actions under certain standard conditions.

2. Instrumental actions presuppose that some things can be done *at will*, i.e. that certain actions schemes can be actualized, only if the actor wants this to happen.

3. If we call actions that can be *performed immediately* (here and now) '*spontaneous*', we can say that simple speech acts in which we articulate plans or intentions (or 'decisions') are spontaneous. More complicated free actions are made possible by learning to perform the corresponding action-schemes at will, after we have performed the speech act of decision–making in a spontaneous way.

4. But then we have to exercise control, if our plans or intentions are to be realized in the proper way. We learn how to do this by taking part in a joint practice of controlling the performances of intentions (in a roughly similar way to which we control the fulfilment of promises).

5. This helps us to understand the sense in which Kant can say that the *will*, conceived of as the *morally positively evaluated generic action*, that I have to, or want to perform does not exist as such *in space and time*, not even 'in me'. This is the same sense in which the meanings of words or the contents of propositions as such, in contrast to their representations, do not exist in space and time.

6. Already, thanks to the faculty of instrumental reasoning, my actions are (at least to some degree) independent of the merely present states of immediate desire and merely instinctive dispositions that we attribute to animal behaviour.

7. The words 'free' and 'will' are nothing other than tools by which we express the difference between animal behaviour and planned human action.

8. In the first phase of education to personhood we learn to perform spontaneous acts and increasingly complex action schemes at will. But the second phase, in which we learn to make free judgements *about* the forms or schemes we have learned, and hence to participate in a joint practice or culture of reason, also starts very early; perhaps with the first why-questions, in which, so to speak, the subjectivity of the questioner and the objectivity of the expected answer meet.

This list may not be sufficient for understanding what free action is. But it is already enough to bring to light a peculiar linguistic problem. The difficulty is to articulate general forms of human life that cannot be observed directly and nevertheless exist implicitly. They 'work', so to speak, in the 'background' of any particular human action.

3. The Challenge of Cognitive Science

Almost every other day we can read in essays and journals all around the world claims like these: Central positions of Western thought have to be revised. Concepts like freedom, guilt and responsibility, just as the idea of an immortal soul, are outdated. Human behaviour is determined by processes of communications between neurons. No instance or entity that might be called 'I' or 'free will' has been found in the investigations of the behavioural and brain sciences. Authors like Wolf Singer, a leading neuro-physiologist in Germany, and others draw far-reaching consequences from these claims.[7] They say that, while these 'insights' should bring about greater indulgence towards other men, even for criminals and murderers, at present only researchers in the cognitive sciences see the 'contradictions' in our moral and legal judgments. Philosophers may be tempted to ridicule these claims, or, as they are advertized, 'insights'.[8] But even so, it is important to understand the respects in which Singer's criticism of traditional ways of speaking about mental phenomena actually has a point.

The first thing is to acknowledge that we do need a better comprehension of *our talk about free will* and *understanding*, or, more generally, of our use of words like 'I', 'my mind', 'my self', 'consciousness', 'spirit' or 'soul', not to speak of moral vocabulary like 'responsibility', 'remorse' and 'conscience'. There is also a real need to demystify 'scientific' explanations and formal theories of mental processes and mental events, intelligent behaviour and autonomous action.

---

[7] See, for instance, Singer 2003, 2004. There are hundreds, if not thousands books and articles telling the same story. For another example, see Vertosick (2002), which tells us that the essence of life and intelligence is a complicated network of interacting and communicating subunits. This, however, tells us not much more than truisms about the form we articulate complex structures and processes: We can always talk about units and subunits, or rather, systems and their parts and elements, and about relations and functions between them — simply because our language splits up in noun phrases or names and verb phrases or (relational) predicates. Yet, we should not be satisfied with such system-theoretical 'explanations' that do not tell us much more than something trivial about the linguistic form of the plan or project of explanation. Compare Thompson (1995).

[8] For instance, no serious philosophical thinker after Kant has defended the metaphysical thesis of an immortal soul.

That is, we need to combat reifying ways of conceiving mental life in terms of separate entities or realms of entities. In order to do this, it is illuminating to begin with a criticism of any 'ontic' reading of Plato's philosophy, which we can identify as the original source of the idea of an eternal human soul. This conception has become a kind of 'folk psychology', and found its way into almost all religious contexts of Christian or Muslim world-view, with their dualism of body and soul and of matter and mind. According to this dualism, we have to distinguish between sense and intellect; between bodily states, like desire, and 'spiritual' powers like intelligence and will; between sensitivity and rationality; between perception and thinking; i.e. between 'worldly' *sentience* and supposedly 'transcendent' *sapience*.

In Descartes' philosophy, we find a new foundation for this dualism, or rather, a reflection reminding us of arguments which were already more or less familiar to Plato or St. Augustine, to name only the two most important figures in the history of the idea of the soul. Descartes distinguishes between the world of the thinking subjects and the world of empirical bodies which form the objects of our thoughts. Any loud or silent act of thinking (or symbolic act), performed by me, presupposes my existence as a *res cogitans*, as the agent who is thinking (or is able to use the symbols according to some common norm of correctness). But this does not help us to understand what agency is. It was a mistake of Descartes to think that the question 'who am I?' is answered simply by the expression '*res cogitans*'. As such, the answer is empty. It only serves to introduce *the* open question of modern philosophy: the question of what it means to be able to think and to be an actor performing an act, be it a speech act or an act of some other kind.

However, Descartes' philosophy inaugurated many of the subsequent developments in ('British') Empiricism and ('German') Idealism. It reminded us again, after St. Augustine, that reference to the world of the *res extensae*, the bodily things, *presupposes* the faculty of thinking; of the use of language, symbols, and concepts. Kant turns this insight, roughly, into a distinction between two different realms and ways of scientific analysis: the first empirical and the second transcendental. In empirical, or 'natural' science we articulate 'objective experience' by means of propositions that talk about things, or physical objects. In 'transcendental', i.e. logical or conceptual science, we make the implicit forms and norms of thinking (i.e. of a meaningful use of symbols in discourse) explicit.

Kant uses the model of classical mechanics in his transcendental analysis of the basic forms and normative conditions that reference to real, physical, things and events presupposes. As a result, he does not address the differences, and the relations, between our everyday way of referring to the world in everyday language, and the ideal models employed in scientific theories. Nor did Kant, or the Newtonians for that matter, really reflect on the peculiar topics, methods and conceptual frameworks which characterized the then 'new' natural sciences such as chemistry, the physics of magnetism and electric energy, or biology, which has living processes and the various different life forms as its field of study. When it comes to our knowledge of ourselves, we find in Kant's philosophy an unorganised mixture of merely formal theories (including the reflections in Kantian 'transcendental philosophy'); subjective 'introspections' and opinions; psychological or physiological observations and 'explanations'. We can see the problem by looking at Kant's obscure term *'mundus intelligibilis'*. He introduced this in order to distinguish the empirical world, as the sensible world, (*'mundus sensibilis'*) from the abstract entities that we talk about when we focus on concepts and forms. These abstract things do not exist in the world of experience. That is, we cannot 'see' forms or other 'merely intelligible' objects of our thinking and speaking. What 'empirically' exists are only the 'embodiments' of such forms in real actions or acts, and real practice. Empirically, we only have access to overt behaviour that happens here and now, or there and then.

I have already suggested that the distinction between an actual act (as a token) and the form of an action (as a reproducible type or action scheme) corresponds to Kant's distinction between the *mundus sensibilis* and the *mundus intelligibilis*. Now, it is crucial to comprehend this as a merely conceptual distinction; not as a claim that there exists a *hinterwelt* of 'things in themselves', as many readers of Kant understand it. At least according to Hegel, the term 'in itself' should be read simply as expressing the conceptual truism that we cannot 'see' mere forms (of actions). Therefore we cannot 'see' free will either. The same holds for spirit or mind, as well as for any thought or any content of a speech act.

There is nothing more mysterious in this than in the fact that we cannot 'see' a *number* or the *meaning of a word*. In fact, it is merely an indication of a lack of elementary logical and philosophical education when someone like Singer 'disproves' the reality of any such 'thing' as free will, or mind, or 'the I' by declaring that he has not found these things in the brain. Already Frege had ridiculed the attempt to look into the brain in order to find 'numbers' or 'meanings' or 'senses'. They do not exist there, at least not *as* numbers or *as* meanings. In fact, they neither exist 'in' a mind nor 'in' a brain, regardless of the obvious fact that we would not be able to deal with representations of numbers or with words in a correct way if our brains did not work properly.

In order to see the consequences of the claim that Kant's free will, too, is a mere abstract object of reflection, which in reality does not exist 'as such', but is a way of speaking about the form of human action in contrast to animal behaviour, we can refer to what Wolf Singer says about the 'paradoxical situation' of neuroscientists. As normal people they talk *as if* freedom of the will and responsible actions existed. But in their research, they arrive at (what they call) 'knowledge' that all human decisions, even their own, are, *in reality*, 'conditioned'.

Nobody denies that our actions have necessary physical and chemical preconditions, 'without which nothing'. But the existence of necessary conditions should not be confused with causal necessitation. That my actions, of course, have conditions does not mean that *I cannot help but* behave in a certain determined (in principle predictable) way. On the contrary, the more we know about the conditions of how to bring about an effect the better we can act by using this knowledge. Things get paradoxical in the sense of Singer only if we forget how limited and parochial all the results of scientific investigations are. We forget this, if we forget their *background*.

In other words, scientists like Singer may *say* whatever they like about the alleged non-existence of responsibility and freedom, morality and guilt. Yet, as acting persons they will not give up moral judgements, or at least we hope so. Nothing more is needed for seeing the practical contradictions involved in any sweeping attack on mental vocabulary, as it is used not only in describing and explaining actions, but also in planning, intending and (at least implicitly) in performing actions.

4. Limited ('Finite') Backgrounds and Unlimited ('Infinite') Reflections

In performing a speech act, in any act of thinking or deliberating, I focus on a topic, and not on myself as the actor or speaker. Even when I reflect on myself, my very act of reflection, and the way in which I reflect, remains in the background. Reflection never thematizes the whole of its background — there is in general no 'absolutely reflective' relation of me to myself, of us to ourselves. Therefore, we will never 'fully' know who we are. This was noticed by all the major followers of Fichte, such as Hölderlin and Hegel. As Schiller says:

'When the soul *speaks*, it is unfortunately not *my authentic soul* which speaks'.[9] This is to say no more than that in any expressive performance of an act of thinking and reflection, I do something that is not totally clear to me. The reason is that speaking is not *immediate,* but always 'mediated' by pre-given forms, patterns, and schemes of how to speak properly. We rely on forms and conventions of common language, of common practice, and common sense. The same holds for thinking: thinking is making use of linguistic articulation in a 'private' context of verbal planning and individual reflection — an inner discourse of the soul, as Plato already says. We play the game of being speaker and hearer at once. We ask ourselves questions and give answers on an inner stage. Hence, this kind of private reflective thinking is systematically secondary to public discourse. Hobbes and Hume, Kant and Herder, stressed this in different ways long before Wittgenstein.

The fact that there are limits to the extent to which implicit norms, forms, and competence can be made explicit was later brought into focus once more in Wittgenstein's discussion of rule following: We cannot express everything, because at least knowledge of how to use language always remains presupposed in the background. If we propose a rule like the following: start with 0 and always add two, we understand this rule only if we understand counting and the procedure of leaving the uneven numbers out in a series of numerals. Whatever I make explicit, and however I do it, I always presuppose some pre-knowledge or competence with respect to the practice I am talking about and the form of explication I am using. From a logical point of view, Wittgenstein's insight is systematically related to what the German Romantics had already realised: No expressive act can ever be *as a whole* the topic of reflection. It follows from this that we must acknowledge certain limitations to what can be included in the focus of our talk. This holds especially for the claims of the cognitive and brain sciences. Their scope covers only a limited sphere within the unlimited totality of human life and practice, including the complex practice of a science with its divisions of topics, methods, and labour.

When we investigate the neuro-physiological preconditions for taking part in the complex social practice called 'intelligent thinking and acting', we already presuppose a background understanding of what it means to take part properly. Moreover, mere description and explanation of *average* behaviour in a group of people will never add

---

[9] 'Warun kann der lebendige Geist dem Geist nicht erscheinen? / Spricht die Seele, so spricht ach! Schon die Seele nicht mehr'. Schiller, 'Sprache', *Sämtliche Werke in zwei Bänden*, Bd 1, p. 118.

up to an understanding of the *form* of the practice in question — in the sense of knowing what is *right or proper* action in the group in question. This is simply because it is possible that many or even most persons quite often behave in a wrong way. Mere empirical description is never enough to arrive at full comprehension of a normative practice.

The normative conditions or proprieties of intelligent, rational and reasonable, right or appropriate behaviour and action, as well as the ways in which these norms and proprieties exist, are out of the scope of such investigations, belonging rather to the background which they presuppose. It is simply a logical mistake not to acknowledge this limitation. A similar point holds for technical devices such as robots and computers that model *particular forms* of rational behaviour. The methods used for, and the results obtained from such modelling are important in their own way. Yet they belong to a mere province of the whole realm of human investigation, knowledge and practical competence. In the same way, calculation and mathematics belong to a mere province of our practice of making use of symbols, even though a fairly important one. Hence, we have to comprehend the distinction between limited topics, addressed in particular sciences by already-established methods, and the unlimited realm of *what can be made the topic* of our talk and investigation by introducing new methods of investigation and, perhaps, new forms of speech.

This leads us to Hegel's distinction between the 'finite' realms of 'normal' discourse or 'normal' science on the one hand, and the 'infinite' realm of what could be made explicit or what could be articulated or made the focus of normal rational discourse on the other. This difference is certainly not easy to grasp. But the idea is this: the 'finite' realm comes with a fixed set of logical forms and rational inferences that count as formally valid, whereas the 'infinite' realm is defined only negatively as lying outside any already given and known realm of finite discourse. Yet this is only a first, as such still naïve (*schlichte*) characterisation of the infinite realm of *possible* topics. Because this characterisation is, as such, not *good enough*, Hegel calls it *simple*(-minded) infinity (*schlechte Unendlichkeit*).[10]

In fact, Hegel's deepest logical insight seems to me to be this. If we want to talk about the infinite, i.e. if we surpass or trespass the boundaries of a well-established realm of discourse, for example in the

---

[10] Hegel's differentiation between the limited or finite and the unlimited or infinite is concerned with the problem of bringing implicit forms of life and actions into the focus of explicit reflection, making them the topic of judgments. I.e. Hegel does not talk here about the infinity of time, space, numbers, or about the immortality of the soul (cf. Hegel, 1970, vol. 5, pp. 261–4, 276–7, 288f and vol. 6, pp. 385f).

direction of its implicit *background*, we have to use *another form of language*. Hegel calls this form of conceptual reflection 'speculative', and says that if we reflect on a concept in the most general way possible, i.e. including all reasonable developments of its use, we see that the concept as such is *free* — it is as free as our proposals to develop its uses are. We have seen why these are not bound to pre-given rules and criteria of propriety and correctness. Simply making explicit something that was not explicit before already brings about some change, at least in our attitude towards it. If it does not change our concepts, for example by introducing finer distinctions and revised schemes of inference, at least it changes, in some way, the way we deal with the things in question. This already happens when we shift topics and change backgrounds, or when we try to 'fuse' or 'merge' different horizons of understanding, as Gadamer calls the enterprise of enlarging our scope of limited perspectives by adding new ones.

The mistake of many cognitive scientists can be now expressed in a way that makes partial use of Hegel's terminology. Their mistake consists in the fact that they interpret their empirical and therefore limited findings in a speculative and transcendent way. They do not do this because they profess to believe in a metaphysical world behind the phenomenal world of experience and perception. Rather, they wrongly think that the metaphysical belief in a kind of *hinterwelt* is *the only way* to transcend the limits of empirical knowledge.

But there is another, more dangerous and more widespread version of transcendent belief. It is the belief that the whole phenomenon of activating personal competence can be explained in terms of the immediate 'forces' which move my body, starting from sensory input and proceeding via inner calculation according to learned schemes of rational thinking or 'understanding', to behavioural output in the form of speech acts or non-verbal action. Ironically, it is not Hegel (who *thematizes* the problem of an absolute perspective and an unlimited truth) but the empirically-working scientist, who mixes up the perspectives. In fact, it is the behavioural and brain sciences, rather than philosophy, that today put forward beliefs about the working of the human mind and its development, that are 'metaphysical' or 'speculative' in the pejorative sense. In contrast, as we have seen, a truly comprehensive philosophical account of being a person requires an extremely wide scope, and sensitivity to a multitude of perspectives: it has to deal somehow with all of the basic questions of philosophy.

References

Brandom, Robert B. (1994), *Making It Explicit. Reasoning, Representing, and Discursive Commitment* (Cambridge, MA: Harvard University Press).
Hegel, G.W.F. (1970), *Wissenschaft der Logik, Werke in 20 Bänden, Bd. 5, 6* (Frankfurt: Suhrkamp).
Hegel, G.W.F. (1977), *Phenomenology of Spirit*, translated by A.V. Miller (Oxford: Oxford University Press).
Kant, Immanuel (1988), *Logic*, translated by Robert S. Hartman and Wolfgang Schwarz (New York: Dover Publications).
Kant, Immanuel (1996), *Critique of Pure Reason*, translated by Werner S. Pluhar (Indianapolis: Hackett Publishing Company).
McDowell, John (1994), *Mind and World* (Oxford: Oxford University Press).
Pinkard, Terry (1994), *Hegel's Phenomenology, The Sociality of Reason* (Cambridge: Cambridge University Press).
Pippin, Robert B. (1989), *Hegel's Idealism: The Satisfactions of Self-Consciousness* (Cambridge: Cambridge University Press).
Rorty, Richard (1986), 'Solidarity or objectivity?', in *Post-Analytic Philosophy*, ed. John Rajchman & Cornell West (New York: Columbia University Press), pp. 3–19.
Schiller, Friedrich von (1870), *Sämtliche Werke in zwei Bänden*, Bd. 1 (Leipzig, Wien, Tefchen: Verlag von Karl Prochaska).
Singer, Wolf (2003), *Ein neues Menschenbild? Gespräche über Hirnforschung* (Frankfurt a.M.: Suhrkamp).
Singer, Wolf (2004), 'Selbsterfahrung und neurobiologische Fremdbeschreibung', in Christina Geyer (ed.), *Hirnforschung und Willensfreiheit. Zur Deutung der neuesten Experimente* (Frankfurt a.M.: Suhrkamp), pp. 30–65.
Stekeler-Weithofer, Pirmin (2003), 'Noumenal will in Kant's theory of action: Reasons and causes as intelligible forms of understanding', in *Graduate Faculty Philosophy Journal*, New School University NY, Volume 24, Number 1.
Stekeler-Weithofer, Pirmin (2006), 'The question of system. How to read the development from Kant to Hegel', *Inquiry*, **49** (1), pp. 80–102.
Thompson, Michael (1995), 'The representation of life', in *Virtues and Reason*, Rosalind Hursthouse *et al.* (Oxford: Oxford University Press).
Vertosick, Frank Jr. (2002), *The Genius Within: Discovering the Intelligence of Every Living Thing* (New York: Harcourt).

Shaun Gallagher

Moral Agency, Self-Consciousness, and Practical Wisdom[1]

Abstract: This paper argues that self-consciousness and moral agency depend crucially on both embodied and social aspects of human existence, and that the capacity for practical wisdom, phronesis, is central to moral personhood. The nature of practical wisdom is elucidated by drawing on rival analyses of expertise. Although ethical expertise and practical wisdom differ importantly, they are alike in that we can acquire them only in interaction with other persons and through habituation. The analysis of moral agency and practical wisdom is framed by Dennett's proposal that moral personhood requires satisfaction of six conditions, including self-consciousness.

To have the status of moral personhood means two things: first, that one has the ability to take responsibility for one's actions, and second, that one ought to be treated in a certain way. One way to put this latter concept is to say that a person has certain rights and must be treated

Correspondence:
Shaun Gallagher, Philosophy and Cognitive Sciences, Colbourn Hall 411, University of Central Florida, Orlando, FL 32816-1352, USA. *gallaghr@mail.ucf.edu*

[1] This paper was presented as part of a series of lectures at the University of Jyväskylä, Finland, in September 2006. A slightly earlier version was presented as part of a seminar with Hubert Dreyfus and Sean Kelly at the Norwegian School of Sports Sciences, in Oslo in June 2006. An even earlier version of this paper was published in French: 'Les conditions corporéité et d'intersubjectivité de la personne morale.' *Theologiques*, **12** (2004), pp. 135–64. The present version is substantially revised from earlier ones. I have greatly benefited from comments by Dreyfus, Kelly, Ejgil Jespersen, Arto Laitinen, Michael Quante, and an anonymous referee, as well as numerous participants in the seminars at Oslo and Jyväskylä. I have also benefited from a more formal comment by S. Mansour-Robaey (2004).

with respect. Moral personhood therefore involves the ability to take responsibility on the one hand and moral rights and obligations on the other. For purposes of this paper I want to separate these two aspects, and to do so I will distinguish between the *moral agent* who must be capable of taking responsibility for his or her own action, and the *moral subject* who has rights and is owed respect. I set aside the question of whether someone can be one without being the other, and I focus almost exclusively on the question of moral agency.

One way to think about moral agents, that is, persons who are capable of being responsible for their actions, whether their actions are moral or immoral, is to consider what conditions must be met to attain moral agency. Dennett, in an influential essay (1978), proposed that six conditions must be met to attain moral personhood, and I will take these to apply to the moral agent. First, the entity to whom we would attribute moral agency must have rationality. Second, we must be able to take the intentional stance toward it– that is, we must be able to attribute states of consciousness or intentions to it. Third, it must be the target of a certain kind of attitude (we have to treat it as a person, for example, with respect or, as the case may be, hostility). Fourth, it must be capable of reciprocity and thereby return that attitude. Fifth, it must be capable of communicating with others. The second, third, fourth and fifth conditions explicitly and importantly involve social dimensions, although, for Dennett, the precise nature of these social dimensions is still an open question. Finally, these first five conditions are necessary ones for the sixth: the entity must be capable of self-consciousness. Self-consciousness is here understood to be a higher-order reflective mental process, of which, as Dennett and others (Frankfurt, 1971; Wilkes, 1988) suggest, young children are incapable. In a variety of other contexts, however, Dennett suggests that a brain in a vat or a computer might be able to have this kind of self-consciousness (e.g., 1982; 1991). This implies that these conditions do not depend on embodiment in any strong sense, and at the same time it raises questions about the social dimensions that are involved in some of these conditions.

My intention is to explicate precisely how moral agency depends on both embodied and social aspects of human existence. The approach will be broadly Aristotelian in two senses. First, consistent with Aristotle's idea that the soul is the form of the body, I will argue that the agent who is capable of moral action is fully embodied, and this embodiment shapes the very nature of moral agency. I will also suggest that the form of human embodiment makes certain demands upon others. Second, Aristotle contends that without *phronesis* (practical wisdom) moral virtue and the excellence of moral action are impossible. I will argue that someone has the capacity for moral agency only if they are *capable* of having (practising) *phronesis*. I don't mean that they actually have to have or practice *phronesis* — the only thing required is the capacity for *phronesis*. Furthermore, having the capacity for something is different from having the potential to obtain it. One has the capacity for X when one meets all the conditions necessary for X, although one might not meet the sufficient condition for X. When I've worked this out in terms of *phronesis* I want to return to take a more detailed look at Dennett's six conditions.

Although my argument is broadly Aristotelian, my approach will depend on contemporary studies — I will frame the argument in terms of a contemporary debate, and I will appeal to recent empirical science to support my conclusions. The contemporary debate to which I will appeal will first look like an odd detour on the way to a discussion of moral agency (but see Dreyfus and Dreyfus 1990, 2004 for precedent), but it has a point. The debate in question is about expertise and the nature of expert knowledge. I will not argue that *phronesis* is a kind of expertise, and indeed, I will argue that it is distinct from expertise; but I will suggest that the correct way to think about expertise will throw some light on the nature of *phronesis*. Specifically, through this detour, I want to suggest that *phronesis* involves an implicit self-relation that is both embodied and *endogenously* intersubjective. The notion that the self is *endogenously* intersubjective means that it is not just constrained or conditioned from the outside by its social environment, but is social *from the inside out*. And only by being intersubjective from the inside out, in a primary way, is it possible for it to be significantly social *from the outside in*, and subject to the constraints and conditions of social life.

The Debate On Expertise

What is expertise? What does it mean to have expert knowledge? A number of authors point to the relevance of the epistemological questions about the nature of expert knowledge to issues of intentionality, rationalist and representational notions of consciousness, and intersubjectivity (Pappas, 1994; Selinger and Crease, 2002). These questions are also directly related to the possibility of artificial intelligence and the creation of expert systems. One of the central questions that arise in this context is whether expert intelligence can be disembodied.

Hubert Dreyfus is well known for entering the debate just on this point. For him, expert judgment and behaviour are instances of embodied human performance on a continuum with basic life-world practice.

> We are all experts at many tasks and our everyday coping skills function smoothly and transparently so as to free us to be aware of other aspects of our lives where we are not so skillful. (Dreyfus and Dreyfus 1990).

The target of Dreyfus's analysis is any account of expertise explained in purely cognitive terms — expert knowledge reduced to a set of explicable rules or propositional knowledge. For Dreyfus expertise is best characterized as a set of skills, and appealing to Dewey's (1922) distinction, expert knowledge is a matter of practical reasoning, of 'knowing how' rather than 'knowing that'. Knowing how, in contrast to propositional knowledge, involves embodied practice rather than cognitive deliberation — the exercise of skills of which one cannot fully give an account or fully articulate.[2]

Dreyfus relies on Heidegger's notion of pragmatic contexts as our primary way of engaging in the world — just those contexts in which expertise is practised. Again, following Heidegger, higher order reflection on how one does what one does only occurs when things or procedures fail to work effectively. Thus, in Heidegger's example, the hammer in the carpenter's hand is something like an extension of her body schema and is not a piece of the objective world until it breaks and reflective regard is turned toward the instrument rather than toward the project that involves hammering (Heidegger, 1968, §15).

One way to summarize Dreyfus's position is to say that expertise is a matter of intuition, not intellectualization: 'Action becomes easier and less stressful [as the expert] simply sees what needs to be done rather than using a calculative procedure to select one of several possible alternatives' (Dreyfus, 2002, p. 371). The expert not only *sees* what needs to be done, but also how to achieve it *without deliberation*, immediately — non-reflectively recognizing new situations as similar

---

[2] Dreyfus appeals to Merleau-Ponty's (1962) notion of the lived body and the concepts 'intentional arc' (a rapport between the embodied agent and the world which allows the agent to respond to the solicitations of the current situation) and 'maximal grip' ('the body's tendency to respond to these solicitations in such a way as to bring the current situation closer to the agent's sense of an optimal gestalt' [Dreyfus, 2002, p. 367]). Such aspects of embodiment depend on practiced activities controlled by body schematic adjustments that operate as the basis for expert practices (Dreyfus, 2002). Basic motor skills are obviously essential for many kinds of expertise, and more generally, expert knowledge concerns how to make moves in whatever game (profession) one is playing. The understanding required for making such moves can be traced to embodied (sensory-motor) practices that provide a basis for learning and smooth interaction with the surrounding world.

to previously encountered ones, and intuiting 'what to do without recourse to rules'. The expert recognizes important features as contextually sensitive (Dreyfus and Dreyfus 1986). Thus, expertise is *in the practice*, and the expert is primarily a practitioner.

Dreyfus is here arguing against a position taken by Doug Lenat and his colleagues (see Lenat and Guha, 1990; Hayes-Roth *et al.*, 1983), who take a more traditional approach that conceives of expertise as possessing a body of propositional knowledge. Lenat considers expertise to be reducible to rational (computational) rules and information. As such, expertise can be rationally reconstructed as primarily a mental intellectual phenomenon. Lenat argues for a kind of expertise that Dreyfus rules out — an expert who is rich in propositional facts about X, but has never done or experienced X. The expert need not be a practitioner, and as a result it seems that this kind of expertise can be disembodied and instantiated in a computer.

In contrast to both Dreyfus and Lenat, Harry Collins (1996; 1998; 2000; 2004) develops a social explanation of expertise. Collins distinguishes between interactive expertise and contributory expertise. Interactive expertise consists in the kind of knowledge that we can pick up through association and sufficient communication with experts giving us the ability to enter into their language games. In contrast, contributory expertise consists of the kind of know-how that the expert has, and that one gets only through practice (see Giles, 2006). In agreement with Lenat, Collins thinks that Dreyfus overemphasizes embodiment, and in agreement with Dreyfus, he thinks that Lenat overemphasizes propositional knowledge. Both Dreyfus and Lenat, however, ignore the importance of social interaction. In an account that takes social dimensions seriously, expertise is thought of as 'distributed' — embedded in social practices and localized settings (laboratories and social networks), reflected in standard technologies, and promoted in specific rhetorical means of recruiting professional experts (Mialet, 1999).

Collins (2004), pursuing this path, thus argues for a different kind of expertise that Dreyfus rules out, interactive expertise — the kind of expert knowledge that someone may attain via social learning procedures — specifically, linguistic and communicative processes. But, in contrast to Lenat's interpretation, this expertise is not based on propositional knowledge — it is the result of a socialization process that requires conversational interaction with another.

> What I am saying is that it is possible to learn to say everything that can be said about bicycle-riding, car-driving, or the use of a stick by a blind

man, without ever having ridden a bike, driven a car, or been blind and used a stick. One could learn to pass the corresponding Turing Tests purely by spending enough time talking with the practitioners of the relevant domains without actually practicing the practices. But that is not the same as being able to make the knowledge explicit or to be able to encode it in a computer program (Collins, 2004, p. 127).

Collins offers himself as an example. As a sociologist of science he has to have some kind of expertise in the science that he studies, gravitational wave physics. Collins gains this expertise, not by learning a set of scientific propositions, and not by becoming a practitioner of the science, but by hanging out with the scientists, conversing with them, seeing what they do, etc., to the point that he becomes proficient in the language of gravitational waves and not only can hold up his side of a conversation, but can make scientifically productive suggestions — even though he is not a practitioner. Collins, Evans, Ribeiro, and Hall (2006) provide empirical evidence that this is the case. Collins is able to provide written answers to technical questions in the field of gravitational wave physics that cannot be distinguished by a group of gravitational wave physicists from answers provided by other gravitational wave physicists.

For Collins, expertise is like a language or language-game. He cites Wittgenstein's example of a talking lion. From Dreyfus's perspective, even if the lion spoke a familiar language, we would not understand the lion because it carves up the world in a way that does not correspond to the human world. For example, for us, a chair offers a different kind of affordance than for the lion. Dreyfus would say that unlike the lion we have a body that can use a chair to sit, so 'chair' if it were in the lion's vocabulary, would mean something different. Collins' point against Dreyfus, however, is the claim that if the lion hung around with humans long enough, the lion would come to know the meaning of chair, despite differences in embodiment. Thus, 'the language of a community embodied in one way can be acquired by individuals with different shaped bodies, and who, therefore, cannot participate in the activities of that community' (Collins, 2004, p. 130; see Collins, 1996; 2000). On his account, even a computer, if it were somehow connected to a social-linguistic 'form of life' could acquire interactive expertise. His conclusion, then, is that embodiment contributes little to the acquisition of expertise.

The criticism of Dreyfus for ignoring the social aspects of expertise has been made in a different way. Both Iris Young (1998) and Maxine Sheets-Johnstone (2000) emphasize the cultural embeddedness of the body and criticize Dreyfus for assuming that the body, which acquires skill, has no relevant biography, gender, race, or age. This approach nicely explicates the *external limitations* on expertise that cultural factors impose, and has much to say about social and political factors that limit embodied processes, but in itself it does not provide any positive account of how expertise develops except by adding these external limitations to Dreyfus's account. Moreover, Selinger and Crease (2002) point out that Dreyfus does have a place for the idea that 'cultural styles' affect how skills are learned (Dreyfus, 2000), but that this notion is simply not developed.

> From Dreyfus's perspective, one develops the affective comportment and intuitive capacity of an expert solely by immersion into a practice; the skill-acquiring body is assumed to be able, in principle at least, to become the locus of intuition without influence by forces external to the practice in which one is apprenticed (Selinger and Crease 2002, pp. 260–1).

This way of putting it, however, suggests that we need to consider social forces that are only external to embodied practice; I'll suggest that there are also important intersubjective factors that are implicit or endogenous to embodied practice, and that considerations of this endogenous intersubjectivity are important for a full account of expertise.

In summary, Lenat rules out any important role for embodiment and emphasizes a cognitive–computational model consistent with traditional views of expertise as a mentalistic or intellectual phenomenon. This approach is rejected by both Dreyfus and Collins. Collins, however, like Lenat, also rules out any important role for embodiment and emphasizes a socially contextualized model of expertise. This model is primarily a linguistic-communicative one. Dreyfus critiques traditional and computational models, but ignores social dimensions and emphasizes pre-reflective embodied skills as the basis for expertise.

Some Necessary Conditions for the Acquisition of Practical Reason

My intention is not to equate the concept of *phronesis*, practical wisdom, as characterized by Aristotle (350 BCE), with the concept of expertise. But let me set aside the question of how they relate to each other for now (I will return to this question), and consider them both as instances of practical reason. In this sense, *phronesis* is like expertise in certain ways. Moreover, a discussion of the notion of *phronesis* can follow the lines drawn in the debate about expertise. For example,

Aristotle makes it clear that *phronesis* is not the same as *theoria* — that is, a theoretical knowledge that is propositional and learnable in a purely intellectual way. *Phronesis* cannot be programmed into a computer.[3] It is, rather, as Dreyfus says of expertise, a kind of 'know-how'. It is not reducible to a set of rules, however, and should also be distinguished from *techne*. The good person, the person with *phronesis*, *sees* what to do in an immediate way, and does the good thing in a close to automatic way, as if it were second nature.

One of the most important questions about *phronesis* for Aristotle is how precisely one acquires it. On this score, Aristotle takes a position that is similar to Collins' position on expertise. According to Aristotle, one acquires *phronesis* through a good upbringing, and this means hanging around with the right people – good people who provide good examples of good actions. Yet this is not sufficient. To attain *phronesis*, one must also *act* in a good way. It would not be enough simply to watch, or to converse with good people. One needs to imitate them, to act as they do and to do the kinds of things that they do. This seems closer to Dreyfus' emphasis on being a practitioner. It suggests that for a correct understanding of *phronesis*, and perhaps for a correct understanding of expertise, it is not necessary to eliminate embodiment, and the practical action that it allows, in order to make room for a social dimension. Nor is it necessary to eliminate social dimensions in order to make room for the role played by embodiment.

I want to propose here an alternative model that relies on an *interactive* conception of embodied intersubjectivity.[4] This model recognizes an intersubjectivity that is *endogenous* to the embodied practices that constitute practical knowledge. It takes account of the social, not just as a communicative-linguistic phenomenon, and not just as a social-cultural external limitation on embodied practices, but as a dimension that is already built into embodied action. This model looks to evidence

---

[3] Here I mean the emphasis to be on the term 'programmed' — if we understand programming in a traditional way. Of course that's closely tied to the notion of a present day computer. So I wouldn't rule out the idea that an artificial learning system that is not programmed but that moves around the world and can interact with others could get *phronesis* — e.g., some kind of sophisticated social robot which we do not yet know how to build. I would think that this kind of system would have to replicate embodied experience. Thanks to Evan Selinger for helping me to clarify this point.

[4] Collins terms his model of expertise an 'interactive' model, highlighting the communicative interaction that is requisite for acquiring expertise. My use of the term 'interactive' is drawn from a debate in theory of mind. Interaction in that context refers to the ability we have to understand others perceptually, based on their embodied behaviour, movements, gestures, facial expressions, and context-related action. Interaction theory is proposed as an alternative to either 'theory theory' or simulation theories of social cognition. See Gallagher (2001; 2004b,c).

in three relevant areas: neuroscience, developmental psychology, and phenomenology.

Neuroscience

If we think of acquiring practical reason (*phronesis*, expertise) as involving action and the imitation of action, then recent work in brain imaging has shown what is clearly a neural basis for gaining practical knowledge. Specific brain areas (in the pre-frontal, pre-motor areas, the inferior parietal cortex, and other areas) have been shown to be activated not only when a subject *acts*, but also when a subject *perceives* another person doing an intentional action. These overlapping areas of 'shared neural representations' are also activated when the subject *imagines* doing an action and when she *prepares to imitate* the action presented by another (Decety and Grézes, 2006; Decety and Sommerville, 2003; Grézes and Decety, 2001; Jeannerod, 1997). These and similar studies supplement and expand the research on mirror neurons — neurons found in the premotor cortex of the macaque monkey and the human, that are activated both when we perform certain intentional actions (e.g., reaching, grasping) and when we observe others engaging in such actions (Rizzolatti *et al.*, 1996; Gallese *et al.*, Fadiga *et al.*, 1995).

> Whenever we are looking at someone performing an action, beside the activation of various visual areas, there is a concurrent activation of the motor circuits that are recruited when we ourselves perform that action. … Our motor system becomes active as if we were executing the very same action that we are observing (Gallese, 2001, p. 38).

When we see another person act our own motor system reverberates with that action. To what extent this neural activity is the basis for empathy is an open question. But it seems clear that these kinds of neuronal processes are involved in imitating, learning from, and understanding others. These activities involve neural processes that are implicit and endogenous to the motor system of the embodied self as it enters into intersubjective relations with others.

Developmental Psychology

There is corroborating evidence to be found in the field of developmental psychology. Colwyn Trevarthan's (1979) notions of primary and secondary intersubjectivity are directly relevant to questions about the acquisition of practical reason. The notion of primary intersubjectivity refers to embodied processes that are emotional and perceptual, that constitute our primary and continuing ability to understand others, and that characterize human behaviour from infancy (Gallagher, 2001). It includes the infant's ability to perceive meaning in the other's behaviour. Before the age of three, children already have a sense of what it means to be an experiencing subject, and that certain kinds of entities (but not others) in the environment are indeed such subjects. Evidence for this is found in instances of neonate imitation. Infants are able to distinguish between inanimate objects and people (agents), and can respond in a distinctive way to human faces, that is, in a way that they do not respond to other objects (see Legerstee, 1991; Johnson, 2000; Johnson *et al.*, 1998). This sense of others is already implicit, at least in a primitive way, in the behaviour of the newborn. Experiments by Meltzoff and Moore (1977; 1994) demonstrate that from birth the action of the infant and the perceived action of the other person are coded in the same 'language', an intermodal system that is directly attuned to the actions and gestures of other humans (Gallagher and Meltzoff, 1996).

As the infant develops, a number of other early interactive capabilities enhance primary intersubjectivity. These include the ability to detect the intentions of others.[5] Infants also show affective and temporal coordination between their own gestures and expressions and those of the other person. Infants 'vocalize and gesture in a way that seems "tuned" [affectively and temporally] to the vocalizations and gestures of the other person' (Gopnik and Meltzoff 1997, p. 131).

Trevarthan's notion of *secondary intersubjectivity* acknowledges that children do not simply observe others; they interact with others, and in doing so they develop a further capability for shared or joint attention beginning around 9–14 months (Trevarthan and Hubley, 1978). The child alternates between monitoring the gaze of the other and what the other is gazing at, checking to verify that they are

---

[5] Baldwin and colleagues have shown that infants at 10–11 months are able to parse some kinds of continuous action according to intentional boundaries (Baldwin and Baird, 2001; Baldwin *et al.*, 2001). Eighteen-month-old children can comprehend what another person intends to do. They are able to re-enact to completion the goal-directed behaviour that an observed subject does not complete (Meltzoff, 1995; Meltzoff and Brooks, 2001). Infants also learn to track eyes, and it is likely that various movements of the head, the mouth, the hands, and more general body movements are perceived as meaningful or goal-directed. Such perceptions are important for an understanding of the intentions and dispositions of other persons as well as for social reinforcement (Allison *et al.*, 2000), and they are operative by the end of the first year (Baldwin, 1993; Johnson, 2000; Johnson *et al.*, 1998). At 5 to 7 months infants are able to detect correspondences between visual and auditory information that specify the expression of emotions (Walker 1982). Infants pick up on the emotional nature of human movement and can perceive it even in the outline of point-lights attached to various body joints (Moore *et al.*, 1997). As early as five months of age infants show preferential attentiveness to human shape and movement in such displays (Bertenthal *et al.*, 1984).

continuing to look at the same thing. Infants between 9–18 months look to the eyes of the other person to help interpret the meaning of an ambiguous event (Phillips *et al.*, 1992). Thus, around the age of one year, the infant goes beyond person-to-person immediacy and enters contexts of shared attention — shared situations — learning what things mean and what they are for.

Just these kinds of activities, which seem basic, not only for understanding and imitating others, but for learning how to act and how to feel about that action, and thus for the embodied and social acquisition of practical reason, do not disappear in later development, but remain active and are enhanced across the variety of human intersubjective-social experiences.

Phenomenology

Trevarthan's developmental concept of *secondary intersubjectivity* was already foreshadowed by the phenomenological analyses of Heidegger (1968) and Gurwitsch (1931), and these are analyses that have also been taken up by Dreyfus. Understanding the meaning of something is dependent on pragmatic contexts. Aron Gurwitsch, following Heidegger's analysis of equipment and circumspective engagement with the surrounding environment, and the larger action contexts of human existence, indicates that our understanding of the other's expressive movements depends on meaningful instrumental/pragmatic contexts. Things and situations provide scaffolds for understanding the actions of others — and in those pragmatic contexts we see and come to learn and imitate what they do.

For both Heidegger and Gurwitsch, our encounters with others are primarily through these pragmatic contexts. In effect, they overlook the effects of primary intersubjectivity which give us a more direct, perception-based relationship with others. Accordingly, they give priority to the pragmatic as a basis for the social — other people appear with meaning only on the basis of pragmatic contexts. As Gurwitsch puts it, 'we continuously encounter fellow human beings in a determined horizon. …' (1931, p. 36). 'In these horizontal situations the "co-included" others appear. That they *come to light in this situation*, and are not "near by" or "merely beside" it, signifies that they appear as belonging to the situation in their specific roles and functions' (p. 97). Here Gurwitsch suggests that our understanding of others is from the beginning framed in terms of the roles that they play in relation to our projects. 'But it is always a matter of a person *in his role*.

Understanding is yielded here by virtue of the situation and is, therefore, limited to what is inherent in it' (p. 114).[6]

For Trevarthan, and for several phenomenologists (other than Heidegger and Gurwitsch), however, secondary intersubjectivity is dependent upon the development of primary intersubjectivity. Primary intersubjectivity characterizes infancy but continues to be primary in terms of how we interact with others. We perceive the intentions of others — their meaning — in the embodied expression of movements, gestures, facial expression, and so forth. These primary intersubjective processes are based on what Merleau-Ponty (1962) calls *intercorporeality* — a natural interaction of bodies that generates meaning in so far as we see the intentions of others in their expressive movements.

> I live in the facial expressions of the other, as I feel him living in mine ... (Merleau-Ponty, 2003, p. 218).

> The very first of all cultural objects, and the one by which all the rest exist, is the body of the other person as the vehicle of a form of behavior (Merleau-Ponty, 1962, p. 348).

Primary and secondary intersubjectivities together give us access to a shared world, and allow us to enter into its meaning in a pragmatic way.

> Insofar as I have sensory functions ... I am already in communication with others .... No sooner has my gaze fallen upon a living body in the process of acting than *the objects surrounding it immediately take on a fresh layer of significance* (Merleau-Ponty, 1962, p. 353).

Husserl (1973) explains how this intercorporeality can happen in phenomenological terms that correlate well with the neuroscience of shared representations. He describes a kinaesthetic (motoric) reverberation in our own bodies as we observe the comportment of others, which helps us to understand what they are doing and experiencing. These interactive or intercorporeal aspects of embodiment indicate an *endogenous intersubjective* dimension of embodiment that should not be ignored in the analysis of the acquisition of practical reasoning, whether that be expertise or *phronesis*.

These intercorporeal aspects are thus both *embodied and intersubjective* in a primary way — and specifically in a way that allows for the secondary contextualization of action in pragmatic and

---

[6] For a critique of Gurwitsch and Heidegger on this point, see Gallagher (2004; 2005).

social settings, which, I suggest, is necessary for both the development of expertise and the acquisition of *phronesis*.[7]

The Differences Between *phronesis* and Expertise

In the previous section we discussed some capacities that likely operate as enabling conditions for the acquisition of expertise and *phronesis*. The interaction model developed here is one that requires both embodiment and intersubjectivity to allow for the capacities to act in socially and pragmatically contextualized settings. Indeed, embodiment and intersubjectivity are not disparate issues since embodiment already involves an endogenous intersubjectivity. Acquiring an understanding of actions and a capacity to act in the kinds of contextualized settings that help to define expert knowledge or skill requires those intersubjective (intercorporeal) capacities for understanding and interacting with others. Although something similar can be said of *phronesis*, still, something more must be said about the difference between *phronesis* and expertise.

Is *phronesis* equivalent to expertise? Is the acquisition of *phronesis* best explained on a skills-acquisition model? In regard to acquisition, we noted, Collins's model of expertise is consistent with an Aristotelian model of *phronesis*: one acquires *phronesis* by hanging around with good people.[8] But on the Collins model of expertise, there is no guarantee that one's social interaction with experts will necessarily make one an expert, or lead to expert practice. This is reminiscent of Plato's complaint in the *Meno*: a son who is raised by good parents and given the best education amongst the best of society still may turn out bad. To attain *phronesis*, as Aristotle insists, one must also *act* and *interact* in a good way. It would not be enough simply to watch, or to converse with good people. One needs to imitate them, to act as they do and to do the kinds of things that they do: *phronesis*, like expertise, is *in the practice* — and in this regard only some combination of the Dreyfus and the Collins models could add up to Aristotle's model.

But let's look at the Dreyfus model more closely. In every case (according to Dreyfus, for expertise and for *phronesis*) Dreyfus outlines a multi-step acquisition process: novice to advanced beginner to competence to proficiency to expert. In each case the novice stage

---

[7] A fuller account that would go in a direction distinct from the standard theory-of-mind approaches would require some consideration of the importance of narrative. For this more developed account see Gallagher and Hutto (in press); Gallagher (2006); Hutto (2006; 2007).

[8] In contrast to a position like Lenat's, one certainly does not get *phronesis* by simply taking an ethics course.

starts like this: 'Normally, the instruction process begins with the instructor decomposing the task environment into context-free features that the beginner can recognize without benefit of experience. The beginner is then given rules ...' (Dreyfus and Dreyfus, 2004). Seemingly we start with rules and/or theory, and then work our way out of dependency on these mentalistic beginnings to gain a non-mentalistic expertise through practice. But is this the way it works in all cases? It seems that it may work for learning to drive or to play chess. But what about learning first language or learning to walk? In the case of language, I think we learn the rules (grammar) only after we learn to speak; in terms of walking — are there any rules? These are things we learn by pure practice, where, by 'pure' I mean without applying a rule. How do we learn our everyday coping skills? Not by working our way through theory or a set of rules. Again, how do we come to understand others and gain our 'people skills'— *not by theory*. We are not given rules, we are given people, and we start to interact with them and imitate them (as indicated in the explanations of primary and secondary intersubjectivity). Not theories, not rules, but pure *doings*.[9]

How do we gain *phronesis*? Aristotle suggests, by hanging out with the right people. Learning from example. Imitating. In contrast, although Dreyfus, who equates *phronesis* with ethical expertise, clearly supports the idea that practice is key, he also seems to be a friend of theory or rule-based learning in the acquisition stages.

> On analogy with chess and driving, it would seem that the budding ethical expert would learn at least some of the ethics of his or her community by following strict rules, would then go on to apply contextualized maxims, and, in the highest stage, would leave rules and principles behind and develop more and more refined spontaneous ethical responses (Dreyfus and Dreyfus, 2004, p. 254).

Still, Dreyfus is not a friend of theory in the actual practice of expertise or *phronesis*. Thus, he argues against Habermas and Benhabib's implicit moral theory, and the idea that persons of practical wisdom are ethical cognitivists, relying on rules and principles; and in this regard he favours aspects of Gilligan's emphasis on care over over-rational justice (Dreyfus and Dreyfus, 2004).

If *phronesis* is similar to expertise in some ways, in other ways it is not. I say this not only in regard to questions of acquisition, but also in regard to what these practices are. Accordingly, I want to avoid talking about 'ethical expertise', or equating ethical 'know how' with

---

[9] We learn by doing, but also, in the longer term we learn by narratives. See note 7.

expertise (in contrast to Dreyfus and Dreyfus, 1990; 2004; but also Varela, 1999). We can start to see the difference between *phronesis* and expertise in Aristotle's distinction between *phronesis* and cleverness, as well as in his distinction between virtuous action and *techné*.

> There is a faculty which is called cleverness; and this is such as to be able to do the things that tend towards the mark we have set before ourselves, and to hit it. Now if the mark be noble, the cleverness is laudable, but if the mark be bad, the cleverness is mere smartness; hence we call even men of practical wisdom clever or smart. *Practical wisdom is not this faculty, but it does not exist without this faculty.* ... practical wisdom is to cleverness — not the same, but like it .... it is impossible to be practically wise without being good (Aristotle, 350, 1144a22).

It seems to me that a similar distinction should be clearly made between *phronesis* and expertise. Just as one could be a clever criminal, so one could be an expert terrorist. In neither case, however, could we talk about *phronesis* or any sort of practical moral wisdom. Dreyfus is right and properly Aristotelian in characterizing *phronesis* as non-mentalistic and as not relying on rules or maxims; the *phronimos* (the good person) copes case-by-case, attending to differences in situations. But this is not the complete picture of *phronesis* — something more is required.

Consider the following characterizations made by Dreyfus (2004), following Heidegger. The *phronimos* is the 'master of his or her culture's practices' (p. 266). Ethical experts are 'experts capable of responding appropriately to a wide range of interpersonal situations in their culture. Such social experts could be called virtuosi in living .... This is obviously Aristotle's *phronimos*' (p. 268). And summarizing Heidegger: 'people have skills for coping with equipment, other people, and themselves' (p. 266). The question is whether *phronesis* is reducible to people skills or virtuosity in interpersonal dealings? Is virtuosity equivalent to virtue? Just as I can be a clever criminal, I can be a virtuoso in selling used cars, managing an organization, convincing people to vote for me, or managing a classroom, etc. But none of this requires that I do the right thing — the good thing. A person could know and have the *know how* for how to do exactly the right thing, to act morally — and in this respect perhaps we could say that they have ethical expertise — and they may even be inclined to act that way — but they nonetheless decide not to act ethically, but to use their knowledge to act in a way that is not ethical. Such a person might have ethical expertise, but would not have *phronesis*.

Having said this, one comes to a very difficult philosophical point. What exactly is it that makes *phronesis* so different from expertise? Is it just that the practice of *phronesis* leads to the moral good, and expertise does not necessarily do so? Why not say, for example, that *phronesis* is expertise in what constitutes the moral life? One might claim that to have *phronesis* is to have expert practical knowledge and skill in how to live the good life in the company of others. One might claim that the expertise of an expert in human affairs, for example a marriage councilor, is really a kind of *phronesis*. The problem that doesn't go away is that one might remain an expert marriage councilor and for whatever perverse reasons, intentionally deliver advice that will undermine the marriage of your clients when, in fact, the best thing would be to preserve the marriage. The expertise used to improve lives, which may be the same as that used to destroy lives, simply cannot be equated with *phronesis*. Rather, *phronesis* is precisely the thing that would prevent you from using your expertise for bad purposes.

On the Dreyfus model of expertise, one would have to practice one's skill, and that seems quite consistent with the notion of *phronesis*. But what precisely is the skill that one practices when one has *phronesis*?

What makes *phronesis* different from expertise, and even expertise in how to live the good life (if there is such an expertise) is, I suggest, the particular object or target involved. The particular target of *phronesis* is one's self — and specifically one's self in various but very particular situations, and in respect to how these situations can be integrated into the whole of one's life. Thus, Aristotle says: 'Practical wisdom also is identified especially with that form of it which is concerned with a man himself — with the individual; and this is known by the general name "practical wisdom"' (1141b28). Moreover, the target is not one's self as an object; but oneself as situated agent, moral practitioner. And we can note that while there are textbooks on different areas of expertise (rule books for driving and playing chess), there is no textbook on one's own self or on the unique situations in which one finds oneself.[10] Regardless of who you are, or the kind of person you are, you can read a textbook on chess, and then practice, practice, practice to the point that you become the intuitive expert. This gives you a skill and makes you an expert, but it doesn't necessarily change the kind of person you are. In contrast, for Aristotle, it is not the character of the actions that make them virtuous, but the character of the agent:

---

[10] So-called 'self-help' books are not about you or me in the particular situations of our lives, but supposedly about everyone in general (what Heidegger would call *Das Man* — everyone and no one at the same time).

The agent also must be in a certain condition when he does them; in the first place he must have knowledge, secondly he must choose the acts, and choose them for their own sakes, and thirdly his action must proceed from a firm and unchangeable character (1105a31).[11]

Phronesis, in contrast to expertise, involves making decisions about my own actions, and what is genuinely best for the situation defined as including myself.

Phronesis is practical (not theoretical or propositional) self-knowledge that we gain as we live through our situated and embodied actions. *Phronesis* involves a practical knowledge about oneself *from the inside out*, and from within the particular situation in which one exists. Yet, even if *phronesis* is about the self, in the way discussed, we are not entirely alone in our *phronesis*. The basis for the practical knowledge of oneself required for *phronesis* is found precisely in the embodied and intersubjective capacities that we discussed above. Although this is a know-how gained from the inside out, it is not a purely subjective knowledge, since from the inside (endogenously), and from birth, we are intersubjectively involved with others, and our self is shaped by these encounters.

Phronesis, Moral Agency, and Self-Consciousness

With this clarified concept of *phronesis* I would like to return to our starting point and revisit the conditions for moral agency as outlined by Dennett, and offer the following qualifications.

The kind of *rationality* (condition 1) involved in moral agency is not the sort that can be captured in computational models, but the kind of practical rationality that is involved in *phronesis*. Even if it were possible to reduce expertise to a set of rules and a disembodied body of propositional knowledge (and I think that Dreyfus is right, it is not), this is not possible for *phronesis*. The kind of rationality required for *phronesis* is at once embodied and intersubjective, and we begin to pick it up from our earliest encounters with others.

We must be able to take the *intentional stance* toward the person who would be a moral agent (condition 2). Dennett cites Strawson on this. He 'identifies the concept of a person as "the concept of a type of entity such that *both* predicates ascribing states of consciousness *and* predicates ascribing corporeal characteristics" are applicable'

---

[11] Dreyfus and Dreyfus (1990) take the second condition to be problematic because it suggests abstract reflection on action rather than a pre-reflective embeddedness of action. I am in agreement with them, however, that a non-intellectualist interpretation of this is possible. For a conception of embedded or situated reflection that is not the kind of detached intellectualism Dreyfus and Dreyfus want to avoid, see Gallagher and Marcel (1999).

(Dennett, 1978, p. 177). This says something about all of us, both 'ascribers' and 'ascribees'. Our ability to do this, which is the ability to recognize an entity in the environment as another person, and thus also to be a person to whom ascriptions of agency are made (because interaction goes two ways — see condition 4), exists from infancy. The ability to parse intentional action can be found in very young infants and is an aspect of primary intersubjectivity that is enhanced in the contextualized situations of secondary intersubjectivity. This capacity is clearly a condition for the development of *phronesis* to the extent that it is the beginning point for an understanding of others that involves our own motoric (action) reverberations, and therefore provides the basis for understanding and forming our own intentions.

In the intersubjective and richly affective interaction that characterizes primary intersubjectivity (and this is also true of the more developed and nuanced intersubjectivity that is built upon it) it is clearly possible for infants (as well as adults) to be the target of certain emotional attitudes (condition 3). Faces, and more generally, human forms of embodiment, in a certain manner, demand our attention, if not our respect. This is a point that could be developed further in support of the notion of obligation that goes along with moral personhood. That we are called to respond to others with some kind of moral sense and comportment is, as Levinas (1969) has pointed out, determined to some extent simply by the human form, and especially by the face and what the face expresses.[12] Insofar as the development of *phronesis* involves our social interactions this condition also plays an important role for moral agency.

It is also clear that normal infants (and some non-human animals) emotionally reciprocate (condition 4). This emotional interaction shapes our sense of self in an intersubjective mirroring that forms a necessary basis for social life and the possibility of moral practice. Gallese (2001), for example, seeks to extend the neural mirror system to include emotion and the possibility of empathy. Phenomenologists like Scheler (1970), who emphasizes the perceptual nature of intersubjective understanding, speak of our ability to 'see' the joy in the face of the other. It is also the case that infants look to their mothers' gestures for reassurance when they encounter a new object or situation (see Hobson [2002] for review). These emotional interactions are clearly part of what Aristotle identified as the source of *phronesis*; not only being with and observing others, but acting with their

---

[12] To what degree this may extend to non-human animals is a good question. My daughter, who is vegetarian, has a simple rule. She doesn't eat anything with a face.

emotional confirmation or caution, and coming to know what actions are good and what are bad.

Dennett's fifth condition involves the ability to communicate with others. The communication necessary for attaining moral agency, however, involves not just the verbal or signed transference of propositional knowledge, but the capacity to pick up on and understand the non-verbal expression of others. The communication of intentions and feelings is accomplished not simply in verbal discourse, but through embodied and perceptually informed interactions. Moreover, the kind of knowledge that results from such communication cannot always be summarized in propositional form. Again, it may be something that reverberates in an intuitive way in one's own action system, and as such form the basis of the intuitive sense of what the other expects or approves.

Dennett's final condition is self-consciousness. Self-consciousness in Dennett's sense, involves the ability to take a second-order volitional attitude toward oneself, as if from the outside – that is, as if I were acting upon another person (Dennett, 1976, p. 193). If, however, a higher-order reflective self-consciousness is necessary for making explicit moral decisions, it is not clear that on Aristotle's conception of *phronesis* responsible moral action always involves this kind of self-consciousness. *Phronesis*, to the extent that it involves something of a second nature, often leads to action that is intentional, but also close to automatic. The good person intuitively knows what to do and does it without much deliberation.

Such intentional action, however, is not done unknowingly or unconsciously. Phenomenologists like Husserl and Merleau-Ponty suggest that intentional action is always accompanied by a pre-reflective self-consciousness — a self-awareness that is implicit to experience itself. On this view, we could say that the person with *phronesis* knows what they are doing on an implicit level which is best expressed not by reflective or theoretically abstract propositions, but by descriptions on the highest pragmatic level of discourse (Gallagher and Marcel 1999). The person who is acting morally will not describe their action in self-conscious abstractions, nor as an exercise of muscles or motor programs. If I am asked, 'What are you doing right now', I don't respond by saying 'I am doing a morally good action'. Nor do I describe my action in terms of muscles moving or neurons firing (see Gallagher, 2006). Rather, I respond in contextually embedded terms — 'I'm driving my daughter to school'. This kind of situated self-consciousness develops within the dimensions defined by primary and secondary intersubjective interaction where our motor systems reverberate with the actions of others, and the right or appropriate thing to do is reinforced in narratives that we begin to hear and understand at a very early age. I'm doing the kind of thing that I've seen others do, and that makes intuitive sense to me as appropriate action in this context. To explain what makes it appropriate may require some further self-conscious deliberation, and it may be difficult to express or justify, but prior to such self-conscious, reflective deliberation the person with *phronesis* has an embodied and intersubjective self-surety about the rightness of the action. In principle, this is not the kind of thing that could be instantiated in a disembodied machine or brain in a vat.

There is more to be said about self-consciousness. Dennett's characterization of self-consciousness as a higher-order cognitive act involving multiple orders of intention seems appropriate if we find ourselves in situations that require deep deliberation and the kind of Herculean and lonely internal struggles described in Kantian moral philosophy. For the most part, however, the Aristotelian *phronimos* is not victim to such struggles. His or her reflection is self-situated, shaped by a self-knowledge that has been honed to something close to an intuitive level. In either of these cases, the Aristotelian or the Kantian, one might argue that what gives moral significance to self-consciousness is nothing intrinsic to self-consciousness itself. This seems clear from Dennett's discussion. What gives self-consciousness its moral significance is its function in moral deliberation. It allows us to stand back from our proposed action and ask whether this is appropriate or not. It gives us a perspective on ourselves that allows us to deliberate about our planned actions.

In contrast to this functional understanding of self-consciousness, José Bermúdez (1995; also Gallagher, 1996) has argued in a way that suggests that self-consciousness may have intrinsic moral significance. Bermúdez employs what he terms the 'principle of derived moral significance', which states that 'if a particular feature or property is deemed to confer moral significance upon a life that has it, then any primitive form of that feature or property will also confer moral significance, although not necessarily to the same degree' (1995, p. 383). On this basis he argues that a kind of self-consciousness that is something less than the sort described by Dennett should still have moral significance. This minimal form of self-consciousness is characterized by three features: first, a primitive proprioceptive sense of one's body; second, the capacity to differentiate between self and non-self; and third a recognition that the other is of the same sort as oneself. Bermúdez cites evidence from experiments on neonatal imitation to show that this sort of self-consciousness can be found in very young infants. Whatever moral significance this minimal self-consciousness has, however, it is not due to the sort of function that Dennett is interested in. So Bermúdez seems to be suggesting that it has some kind of intrinsic moral significance simply because it is a form of self-consciousness.

I want to stake out a middle position between these two extremes. If an embodied (proprioceptive), minimal self-consciousness cannot serve the same function as reflective, higher-order self-consciousness in moral deliberation, it can nonetheless serve a variety of purposes that are morally significant. First, just this kind of minimal self-consciousness may be involved in monitoring my own action in a way that allows me to know what I am doing without having to reflect on it. In this regard, this pre-reflective self-consciousness is the basis for the kind of situated reflection that is involved in the intuitive responses that constitute action guided by *phronesis*. As such, it helps to contribute to the capacity for *phronesis*. Second, it plays an essential role in intersubjective interaction from the very beginning. The proprioceptive-kinaesthetic aspects of this self-awareness are involved in and may be activated by our perception of others. Insofar as it is part and parcel of the earliest form of imitation, it likely continues to play a role in our ability to learn from others. In that respect too, it contributes to the capacity for *phronesis*.

Let me add that with respect to the aspect of moral personhood that involves rights and obligations, one can argue that just this sort of pre-reflective self-awareness is necessarily involved in the experience of pain, whether this is emotional or physical pain.[13] This is not an unusual way to think about the mutual obligation we have towards one another: *Primum non nocere*. If we recognize the other as someone who can experience pain, then we have a moral obligation to behave in a certain way towards him. In part, at least, that intuition is included in knowing what constitutes good action towards another.

I have argued that it is possible to define moral personhood in the sense of moral agency in terms of the capacity for *phronesis*. Someone who has the capacity for *phronesis* (whether it is actualized or not) is someone who is capable of moral agency. On this definition, moral agency depends on an embodied and intersubjective existence in which the rationality at stake is practical rather than theoretical, and is characterized by a situated self-consciousness, emotionally informed

---

[13] For an argument that pre-reflective self-awareness is required for phenomenal experience, for the "what it is like" of experience, and therefore for the phenomenal experience of pain, see Gallagher and Zahavi (in press).

by an intersubjectivity that is endogenous to our own action systems. One's capacity to act as a moral agent (that is, to act morally or immorally, responsibly or irresponsibly), and to act morally towards others, is just this capacity to act on an intuitive insight into one's own self in a way that is not divorced from but rather fully implicated in our relations with others.

This view suggests that one may fail to meet the conditions of moral agency and thereby to be responsible for one's actions if certain aspects of one's social development or embodied neurobiology are compromised.

References

Allison, T., Puce, Q., and McCarthy, G. (2000), 'Social perception from visual cues: Role of the STS region', *Trends in Cognitive Science*, **4** (7), pp. 267–78.
Aristotle (350), *Nicomachean Ethics*. Trans. W. D. Ross. In R. McKeon (ed.). *The Basic Works of Aristotle* (New York: Random House).
Baldwin, D. A. 1993. Infants' ability to consult the speaker for clues to word reference. *Journal of Child Language* 20: 395-418.
Baldwin, D. A. and Baird, J. A. 2001. Discerning intentions in dynamic human action. *Trends in Cognitive Science* 5 (4): 171-78.
Baldwin, D.A., Baird, J. A., Saylor, M. M. and Clark, M. A. 2001. Infants parse dynamic action. *Child Development*, 72: 708-717.
Bermúdez, J. 2005. The moral significance of birth. *Ethics* 106: 378-403.
Bertenthal, B. I. Proffitt, D. R. and Cutting, J. E. 1984. Infant sensitivity to figural coherence in biomechanical motions. *Journal of Experimental Child Psychology* 37: 213-30.
Collins, H. M. 2004. Interactional expertise as a third kind of knowledge. *Phenomenology and the Cognitive Sciences* 3 (2): 125-43.
Collins, H. M., 1996. Embedded or embodied: Hubert Dreyfus's *What Computers Still Can't Do*. *Artificial Intelligence* 80 (1) 99-117.
Collins, Harry, Robert Evans, Rodrigo Ribeiro, and Martin Hall. 2006. Experiments with Interactional Expertise. *Studies in History and Philosophy of Science* 37a (4).
Collins, H. M., & Kusch, M. 1998. *The Shape of Actions: What Humans and Machines Can Do*. Cambridge, MA: MIT Press.
Collins, H. M. 1990. *Artificial Experts: Social Knowledge and Intelligent Machines*. Cambridge, MA: MIT press.
Collins, H. M. 1995. Humans, machines, and the structure of knowledge. *Stanford Humanities Review* 4 (2): 67–83.
Collins, H. M. 2000. Four kinds of knowledge, two (or maybe three) kinds of embodiment, and the question of artifical intelligence. In J. Malpas, and M. A. Wrathall, (eds.), *Heidegger, Coping, and Cognitive Science: Essays in Honor of Hubert L. Dreyfus*, vol. 2 (179-195). Cambridge, MA: MIT Press.
Decety, J. and Grézes, J. 2006. The power of simulation: Imagining one's own and other's behavior. *Brain Research* 1079: 4-14.
Decety, J. and Sommerville, J. A. 2003. Shared representations between self and other: a social cognitive neuroscience view. *Trends in Cognitive Sciences* 7 (12): 527-533.

Dennett, D. 1976. Conditions of personhood. In A. Rorty (ed). *The Identities of Persons* (175-96). Berkeley: University of California Press.

Dennett, D, 1982. Where am I. In Hofstadter, D. R., & Dennett, D. R. (eds.), *The Mind's I: Fantasies and Reflections on Self and Soul* (217-229). London: Penguin.

Dennett, D. 1991. *Consciousness Explained*. Boston: Little, Brown, and Company.

Dewey, J. 1922. *Human Nature and Conduct: An Introduction to Social Psychology*. London: George Allen and Unwin.

Dreyfus, H. 1991. *Being-in-the-World: A Commentary on Heidegger's Being and Time*. Cambridge: MIT Press.

Dreyfus, H. 1992. *What Computers Still Can't Do: A Critique of Artificial Reason*. Cambridge: MIT Press.

Dreyfus, H. 2000. Could anything be more intelligible than everyday intelligibility? Reinterpreting Division I of *Being and Time* in the light of Division II. In J. Faulconer and M. Wrathall (Eds.), *Appropriating Heidegger* (155–170). Cambridge: Cambridge University Press.

Dreyfus, H. 2002. Intelligence without representation Merleau-Ponty's critique of mental representation: The relevance of phenomenology to scientific explanation. *Phenomenology and the Cognitive Sciences* 1: 367-383.

Dreyfus, H. and Dreyfus, S. 1985. From Socrates to expert systems: The limits of calculative rationality. In C. Mitcham and A. Huning (Eds.), *Philosophy and Technology II: Information Technology and Computers in Theory and Practice*. Boston: D. Reidel Publishing Company, pp. 111–130.

Dreyfus, H. and Dreyfus, S. 1986. *Mind Over Machine: The Power of Human Intuition and Expertise in the Era of the Computer*. New York: Free Press.

Dreyfus, H. and Dreyfus, S. 1990. What is Morality? A Phenomenological Account of the Development of Ethical Expertise. In D. Rasmussen (Ed.), *Universalism vs. Communitarianism: Contemporary Debates in Ethics*. Cambridge: MIT Press, pp. 237–264.

Dreyfus, H. L. and Dreyfus, S. E. 2004. The ethical implications of the five-stage skill-acquisition model. *Bulletin of Science, Technology and Society* 24 (3): 251-64.

Fadiga, L., et al. 1995. Motor facilitation during action observation: a magnetic stimulation study. *Journal of Neurophysiology* 73: 2608-2611.

Frankfurt, H. 1971. Freedom of the will and the concept of a person. *Journal of Philosophy* 68: 5-20.

Gallagher S. 2006. The narrative alternative to theory of mind. *Consciousness and Emotion* 7: 223-229.

Gallagher, S. 2005. Phenomenological contributions to a theory of social cognition. *Husserl Studies* 21: 95–110.

Gallagher, S. 2001. The practice of mind: Theory, simulation, or interaction? *Journal of Consciousness Studies* 8 (5–7): 83–107.

Gallagher, S. 2004a. Les conditions corporéité et d'intersubjectivité de la personne morale. *Theologiques* 12 (1-2): 135-64.

Gallagher, S. 2004b. Understanding interpersonal problems in autism: Interaction theory as an alternative to theory of mind. *Philosophy, Psychiatry, and Psychology* 11 (3): 199-217.

Gallagher, S. 2004c. Situational understanding: A Gurwitschean critique of theory of mind." In L. Embree (ed.), *Gurwitsch's Relevancy for Cognitive Science* (pp. 25-44). Dordrecht: Kluwer.

Gallagher, S. 1996. The moral significance of primitive self-consciousness: A response to Bermúdez. *Ethics* 107 (1): 129-140.

Gallagher, S. and Hutto, D. (in press). Primary interaction and narrative practice. In: Zlatev, Racine, Sinha and Itkonen (eds). *The Shared Mind: Perspectives on Intersubjectivity*. Amsterdam: John Benjamins.

Gallagher, S. and Marcel, A. J. 1999. The self in contextualized action. *Journal of Consciousness Studies* 6 (4): 4-30.

Gallagher, S. and Meltzoff, A. 1996. The earliest sense of self and others: Merleau-Ponty and recent developmental studies. *Philosophical Psychology* 9: 213-236.

Gallagher, S. and Zahavi, D. (in press). *The Phenomenological Mind*. London: Routledge.

Gallese, V. 2001. The 'shared manifold' Hypothesis: From mirror neurons to empathy. *Journal of Consciousness Studies* 8 (5-7): 33-50.

Giles, J. 2006. Sociologist fools physics judges. *Nature* 442 (8). Online publication 6 July 2006.

Gopnik, A. and Meltzoff, A. N. 1997. *Words, Thoughts, and Theories*. Cambridge, MA: MIT Press.

Grézes, J. and Decety, J. 2001. Functional anatomy of execution, mental simulation, observation, and verb generation of actions: A meta-analysis. *Human Brain Mapping* 12: 1–19.

Gurwitsch, A. 1931. *Die mitmenschlichen Begegnungen in der Milieuwelt*. Berlin: Walter de Gruyter, 1977; *Human Encounters in the Social World*. Trans. F. Kersten. Pittsburgh: Duquesne University Press, 1978.

Hayes-Roth, F., Waterman D.A. & Lenat, D.B. 1983. An overview of expert systems. In Hayes-Roth, F., Waterman, D., and Lenat, D. (Eds,) (1983). *Building Expert Systems*. Addison-Wesley.

Heidegger, M. 1968. *Being and Time*, trans. J. Macquarrie and E. Robinson. New York: Harper and Row.

Hobson, P. 2002. *The Cradle of Thought*. London: Macmillan.

Husserl, E. 1973. *Ding und Raum* (Husserliana XVI). Den Haag: Nijhoff.

Hutto D.D. 2006. "Narrative Practice and Understanding Reasons: Reply to Gallagher." *Consciousness and Emotion: Special Issue on Radical Enactivism*, ed. R Menary.

Hutto D.D. 2007. "The Narrative Practice Hypothesis." In *Narrative and Understanding Persons*, Hutto, D. D. (ed.). Royal Institute of Philosophy Supplement. Cambridge: Cambridge University Press.

Jeannerod, M. 1997. *The Cognitive Neuroscience of Action,* Oxford: Blackwell Publishers.

Johnson, S. C. 2000. The recognition of mentalistic agents in infancy. *Trends in Cognitive Science* 4: 22-28.

Johnson, S. et al. 1998. Whose gaze will infants follow? The elicitation of gaze-following in 12-month-old infants. *Developmental Science* 1: 233-238.

Legerstee, M. 1991. The role of person and object in eliciting early imitation. *Journal of Experimental Child Psychology* 51: 423-433.

Lenat, D. B. and Guha, R. V. 1990. *Building Large Knowledge Based Systems*. Reading, Massachusetts: Addison Wesley.

Levinas, E. 1969. *Totality and Infinity*. Trans. A. Lingis. Duquesne University Press.

Mansour-Robaey, S. 2004. Le corps, ses représentations et le statut de la personne morale. *Theologiques* 12 (1-2): 156-59.

Meltzoff, A.N. 1995. Understanding the intentions of others: Re-enactment of intended acts by 18-month-old children. *Developmental Psychology* 31: 838-850.

Meltzoff, A. N. and Brooks, R. 2001. "Like Me" as a building block for understanding other minds: Bodily acts, attention, and intention. In B. F. Malle, et al. (eds.), *Intentions and Intentionality: Foundations of Social Cognition* (171-91). Cambridge, MA: MIT Press.

Meltzoff, A. and Moore, M. K. 1977. Imitation of facial and manual gestures by human neonates. *Science* 198: 75-78.

Meltzoff, A. and Moore, M. K. 1994. Imitation, memory, and the representation of persons. *Infant Behavior and Development* 17: 83-99.

Merleau-Ponty, M. 1962. *Phenomenology of Perception*, trans. C. Smith. London: Routledge and Kegan Paul.

Merleau-Ponty, M. 2003. *Nature: Course Notes from the College de France*, D. Seglard, ed. R Vallier, trans. Evanston: Northwestern University Press.

Mialet, H. 1999. Do angels have bodies? Two stories about subjectivity in science: The cases of William X and Mister H. *Social Studies of Science* 29 (4): 551–582.

Moore, D. G., Hobson, R. P. and Lee, A. 1997. Components of person perception: An investigation with autistic, non-autistic retarded and typically developing children and adolescents. *British Journal of Developmental Psychology* 15: 401-423.

Pappas, G. 1994. Experts. *Acta Analytica* 9 (12): 7-17.

Phillips, W., Baron-Cohen, S. and Rutter, M. 1992. The role of eye-contact in the detection of goals: Evidence from normal toddlers, and children with autism or mental handicap. *Development and Psychopathology* 4: 375-383.

Rizzolatti, G., et al. 1996. Localization of grasp representations in humans by PET: 1. Observation versus execution. *Experimental Brain Research* 111: 246-252.

Selinger, E. 2003. The necessity of embodiment: The Dreyfus-Collins debate. *Philosophy Today* 47 (3): 266-279.

Scheler, M. 1970. *The Nature of Sympathy*. Trans. P. Heath. Hamden, CN: Archon Books. Original: *Wesen und Formen der Sympathie*. Bonn: Verlag Friedrich Cohen, 1923; Fifth edition, 1973 in *Collected Works VII*. Bern: Francke Verlag.

Selinger, E. M. and Crease, R. P. 2002. Dreyfus on expertise: The limits of phenomenological analysis. *Continental Philosophy Review* 35: 245-79.

Sheets-Johnstone, M. 2000. Kinetic tactile-kinesthetic bodies: Ontogenetical foundations of apprenticeship learning. *Human Studies* 23: 343–370.

Trevarthen, C. 1979. Communication and cooperation in early infancy: A description of primary intersubjectivity. In M. Bullowa (ed.), *Before Speech* (321-347). Cambridge: Cambridge University Press.

Trevarthan, C. and Hubley, P. 1978. Secondary intersubjectivity: Confidence, confiding and acts of meaning in the first year. In A. Lock (ed). *Action, Gesture and Symbol: The Emergence of Language* (183-229). London: Academic Press.

Walker, A. S. 1982. Intermodal perception of expressive behaviors by human infants. *Journal of Experimental Child Psychology* 33: 514-35.

Wilkes, Kathleen V. 1988. *Real People: Personal Identity without Thought Experiments*. Oxford: Clarendon Press; New York: Oxford University Press.

Young, I. 1998. Throwing like a girl. In D. Welton (Ed.), *Body and Flesh: A Philosophical Reader* (259–273). Oxford and Malden, MA: Blackwell Publishers.

Heikki Ikäheimo

Recognizing Persons

Abstract: In this article a wide range of candidates for features that are defining of personhood are conceived of as interrelated, yet irreducible, layers and dimensions of what it is to be a person in the full-fledged sense of the word. Three layers of personhood — consisting of person-making psychological capacities, person-making interpersonal significances, and person-making institutional or deontic powers — are distinguished. Running through the layers there are then two dimensions — the deontic and the axiological — corresponding to the recognitive attitudes of respect and love. These recognitive attitudes of 'taking something/-one as a person' are responses to the psychological layer and directly constitutive of the interpersonal layer of the respective dimensions of personhood. The multiplicity of ways to understand what 'personhood' means is only apparently chaotic and reveals, on a closer look, a well-ordered and dynamic internal structure.

Introduction

The concept of a person, or of personhood, is arguably of central importance for understanding and organizing our lives and position in the order of things. Yet personhood is also a very slippery concept, in that it is far from obvious how exactly the distinction between persons and non-persons is to be drawn. In light of the various philosophical, theological and juridical definitions of personhood the extension of 'us persons' may, or may not — in addition to you and me — include such things as anencephalic human embryos, intelligent Martians or the Wal-Mart-company. To put it politely, personhood is an essentially contested concept. To put it less politely, 'personhood' is a

Correspondence:
heanik@yfi.jyu.fi

battleground for proponents of different religious and ethical world views, not to mention corporate lawyers, each of whom try to draw the line in ways which best fit their personal convictions or interest groups. All in all, it is hard or impossible to imagine what it would be like *not* to distinguish between persons and non-persons, but finding one's way among the various and often mutually incompatible ways of making the distinction is not particularly easy either.[1]

What I want to do in this article is to outline a holistic conceptual model which is *both* faithful to the central importance of the concept of personhood, *and* takes seriously the fact that there are a wide variety of intuitions and proposals as to what is defining of personhood. In trying to reconcile many different intuitively central elements into a synthetic whole, the article takes a broadly speaking Aristotelian approach to the topic. In trying to grasp systematically the relationships of the different elements as layers and dimensions of the whole, it tries to follow the footsteps of the greatest of modern Aristotelians, namely Hegel. The approach taken in this paper is also Hegelian in the sense that it uses, as the synthesizing principle, one of Hegel's central concepts: *recognition*. For Hegel, recognition, or *Anerkennung*, was something through which animals sublate (*Aufheben*) their merely natural way of existing into spirit (*Geist*), or, in other words, develop from mere animals into persons with a life-world that is radically differently structured than the environment of mere animals. Although this much is relatively clear,[2] it is not particularly easy to say what exactly 'recognition' in the Hegelian sense is. Hegel nowhere gives a definition for the concept, and uses the word in ways which are hard or impossible to subsume under a simple definition. In this article I will follow a proposal according to which recognition, in a specifically interpersonal sense, consists of attitudes of 'taking something as

---

[1] Thus, for instance, anencephalic human embryos can be included in the category of persons by saying that all members of the biological species *homo sapiens* are persons, but then intelligent Martians and the Wal-Mart-company will be excluded. Or one can include intelligent Martians in the category by saying that all creatures with relevant kinds of psychological capacities are persons, but then anencephalic embryos and the Wal-Mart company will be excluded. Or, finally, one can include Wal-Mart by saying that being a person (in a particular, juridical, sense) is having a particular juridical status, but then anencephalic human embryos and intelligent Martians might be excluded. If these are examples of mutually incompatible definitions of personhood, examples of mutually compatible definitions would be ones where the proposed *differentia specifica* of persons can be understood as more or less the same thing, as aspects of the same, or as necessarily implying each other (take 'reason', 'self-consciousness', 'first person perspective' and the like).

[2] My textual reference is primarily Hegel's 1830 Berlin *Encyclopaedia of the Philosophical Sciences*. For some of the relevant details, see Ikäheimo (2004).

a person'; and I will show how this is, in certain ways, both responsive to and constitutive of personhood.

Before starting, I should point out one more respect in which what I attempt in this paper is broadly speaking Hegelian: it presupposes what, following Robert Brandom, we could call the Hegelian 'autonomy-thesis of the spirit' (Brandom, 1999, p. 170). According to this thesis, the essentially distinguishing features of the realm that Hegel called *Geist* — that is, of personhood and of the basic structures characteristic of the life-world of persons — are, on the one hand, not reducible to natural facts or processes, nor, on the other hand, do they flow from any transcendent source or authority called 'God'. On this view, in important senses we persons bootstrap ourselves into personhood and maintain personhood simply by taking each other as persons — that is, through interpersonal recognition.[3]

1. Recognition, Preliminary Distinctions and Questions

Let us start with some basic conceptual clarifications and questions in order to have a preliminary grasp of what recognition, in the Hegelian sense, is. First of all, in discussing the topic in English it is necessary to distinguish between three broad families of meanings that the term 'recognition' has, which are easily confused with each other.

A. There is, first of all, 'recognition' in the sense of *'identification'*. In this sense we can recognize, i.e. identify *anything* (a) *numerically* as a distinct individual, (b) *qualitatively* as having particular features and (c) *generically* as falling under a genus.

B. Secondly, there is 'recognition' in the sense in which it is, at least roughly, synonymous with *'acknowledgement'*. In this sense we can recognize, i.e. acknowledge, *normative or evaluative entities or facts*, such as values, reasons, norms, rights, responsibilities, institutions, claims, facts, guilt etc.

C. Thirdly, we have 'recognition' in the specific sense in which, to state the case approximately, it only makes sense to recognize *persons*. To avoid unnecessary ambiguity, I will use the term 'recognition' *only*

---

[3] For accounts of 'the spirit' which emphasize its independence from nature as well as from any supposed transcendent sources see Brandom (1999; 2007) as well as Pippin (2000). That my account of personhood follows this general 'enlightenment' conception of spirit (Brandom, 1999, p. 170) means of course that it too is, to some extent, partisan. See Spaemann (1996), Sturma (1997) and Rovane (1998) for alternative accounts to mine each of which highlights the close relationship of personhood to 'recognition' or *Anerkennung*. A comparison with these accounts would require first clarifying what exactly is meant by 'recognition' or *Anerkennung* in each of them; an undertaking which will have to be left to another occasion.

in this third, specifically interpersonal sense and reserve the term 'identification' for (A) and 'acknowledgement' for (B).

Hegel used the German word '*Anerkennung*' for B. and C., but not for A.[4] Even though B. and C. are clearly in many ways intertwined with each other as well as with A., when we talk of interpersonal (or 'intersubjective') recognition in the Hegelian sense, we should understand ourselves as talking primarily of C. and not confuse it with A. and B.

What is it then to recognize something/-one in the interpersonal sense? I take as my working hypothesis Axel Honneth's reconstruction of the concept (C), according to which Hegelian interpersonal recognition has three forms: respect, love and esteem (*Liebe, Achtung/Respect* and *Wertschätzung*; see Honneth, 1995). To put it more exactly, these are species of the genus 'recognitive attitude'. Elsewhere I have proposed 'taking something as a person' as a definition for the genus (see Ikäheimo 2002, and Ikäheimo & Laitinen, 2007). Following this proposal, to recognize, or to have the interpersonal recognitive attitude of respect, love or esteem, is thus — in some sense — to take something as a person. The proposal is of course not much more than vaguely suggestive until it is made clear in which sense 'taking' and 'person' are meant;[5] nor is it particularly clear until the relevant concepts under which the different species are to be thought of as falling have been spelled out. In this article I will restrict myself to discussing only the species respect and love.

The first point to make in this regard is that 'taking' is *not* meant here in the sense of the epistemic act or attitude of (A.c) *identifying* something as a person generically — this is clearly not what respect or love are. Both of these, in the relevant senses, are rather some kind of a practical attitude towards something/-one. (Preliminarily, think of Wittgenstein's 'attitude towards a soul'; Wittgenstein ,1953, part II, paragraph IV). The second point relates to a question raised in the recent discussions on recognition: this is whether recognitive attitudes should be understood as responses to something pre-existing or rather

---

[4] With a CD-ROM-version of the Suhrkamp edition of Hegel's *Werke* nowadays available anyone with enough patience will be able to examine the claim. Compare also Ricoeur 2005, who, following French dictionaries, distinguishes between 16 meanings of the French word *reconnaissance*. As far as I can see, these can rather handily be ordered under A, B and C.

[5] Since 'taking' and 'person' allow for readings that are not meant, 'taking something as a person' fails as a strict definition. Its's value is rather in preliminarily delimiting the semantic sphere inside of which a more informative characterization is to be sought.

as bringing about something.[6] As I see it, they clearly have to be understood in both ways, and the question is only how, exactly.[7] As regards personhood, recognition seems to be both responsive to and constitutive of it. To grasp this responsive-constitutive relation of recognition to personhood we need to distinguish, however, between different senses of 'personhood'.

2. Three Concepts of Personhood

There are some standard ways to distinguish between different types of concepts of personhood, but for the purposes of this paper the following three-fold distinction should be useful.[8] To begin with, there is, on the one hand, what we may call the *psychological* concept of personhood, and, on the other hand, what we may call the *status*-concept of personhood. Further, on a closer look, the status-concept of personhood can be seen to comprise of two more closely defined concepts: what we may call the *interpersonal* (status-) concept of personhood on the one hand, and what we may call the *institutional* (status-) concept of personhood on the other hand. Let me explain.

Psychological concept of personhood

According to a psychological concept of personhood, something's being a person is its having particular *psychological person-making capacities or characteristics*, which distinguish it essentially from

---

[6] See Markell (2000), Laitinen (2002), Honneth (2002) and Markell (2007). My answer to this question is meant to be generally complementary to that of Laitinen (2002), even if not all the details are wholly compatible.

[7] According to the final version of Hegel's illustration of the theme in the chapter 'Self-consciousness' of the 1830 *Encyclopedia of Philosophical Sciences* the merely animal desiring subjects face each other as something that, simply by being what they are, resist being subsumed under the significances that mere desire attributes to them within the desiring viewpoint. The emancipation from the egocentric point of view of desire takes place in a 'consciousness of a free object' (*Werke*, 10, § 429), in confronting and experiencing another subject 'as an I that is an absolutely independent other object against me' (*Werke*, 10, § 430). Here recognition as a harmonious solution to the potentially conflictual situation ensuing from this primary encounter is clearly somehow a response to what the other subject is independently. That according to Hegel recognition brings about something is also clear: basically it brings about the realm of spirit (see, for instance, Pippin, 2000; Brandom, 1999; 2005). I should mention that the account of recognition and personhood given in this paper does not follow in any detail Hegel's own way of discussing the themes. For instance, I will not try to track exactly how Hegel himself uses 'personhood' (or its closest equivalence 'Persönlichkeit'), but intend my usage to resonate with a wide variety of classic and contemporary ways of using the term.

[8] The more standard ways of distinguishing between different types of concepts of personhood include distinguishing between 'metaphysical' vs. 'moral' concepts, or between 'descriptive' vs. 'normative' concepts. See Sturma (2002) for an overview of philosophical discussions on personhood.

non-persons (such as lower animals or computers). In principle, there are as many psychological concepts of personhood, as there are proposals as to which psychological characteristics or capacities, exactly, are defining of persons. Usual candidates in the literature include such things as rationality, the capacity for happiness and misery, some specific forms of self-relation, self-consciousness or first-person-perspective, communicative competences, social or cooperative capacities etc.

Status-concept of personhood

According to a status-concept of personhood, on the other hand, something's being a person is its having some particular status or statuses, which distinguish it essentially from non-persons (say, the 'human tools' of antiquity). But what is a status in the relevant sense? Often the word 'status' is used in a very general and vague sense to refer to something's situation, state or position in relation to whatever other things or order of things. Hence, also the expression 'the status of a person' is, without further explication, not at all clear as to its meaning. Here I want to be more precise. What I mean by 'statuses' are statuses in a specifically *intentionality-dependent* and *social* sense. The intentionality-dependent and social concept of status may allow for further variations, but there are two that are important now. These are what we may call the *interpersonal* concept and the *institutional* concept of status.[9] Think of the similarities and differences between being dear to someone, on the one hand, and being a priest, on the other hand. Both are statuses in an *intentionality-dependent* sense, in that having them is dependent on the relevant *attitudes or modes of intentionality* of one or more persons. Both, further, are statuses in a *social* sense, in that they are dependent on the relevant attitudes or modes of intentionality *of other persons* than the one having the status. (Assume that the one who is dear and the one to whom she is dear are two different persons.)

What about the differences? Whereas having the status of being dear to someone else is nothing else than being an object of the relevant 'dear-making' attitudes (of liking, caring etc.) of that someone, having the status of a priest is more complex. That is, while being dear

---

[9] See Ikäheimo & Laitinen (2007), subsection 2.6. Compare also the definition of 'status' in a recent sociology handbook: 'a recognized social position that an individual occupies' (Macionis & Plummer, 1998, p. 156). This definition is ambiguous between the interpersonal and the institutional meanings of status that I distinguish here. This distinction might also be useful for pinning down exactly the conceptual commitments of Nancy Fraser's usage of 'status' in her contributions to Fraser & Honneth (2003).

to someone is an interpersonal state of affairs, being a priest is an institutional state of affairs. As an institutional state of affairs, being a priest is — to put it roughly — dependent on, firstly, some kind of *collective* acknowledgement of the institution of priesthood and, secondly, some kind of *collective* attribution of the status of a priest to the person in question. A concise way to spell out the difference is to say that whereas being dear to someone is being a bearer of particular kinds of *significances* for one or more persons, being a priest is being a bearer of collectively instituted and attributed *deontic powers* — namely the *rights and duties* of a priest.[10]

Let us reserve the term *interpersonal status* for statuses consisting of relevant kinds of significances for another person or within another person's viewpoint, and the term *institutional status* for statuses consisting of collectively acknowledged and attributed — or in short, collectively administered — deontic powers. Coming back to personhood, understood as an *interpersonal status* personhood consists then of *person-making significances* for someone or within someone's viewpoint, whereas understood as an *institutional status* personhood consists of collectively administered *person-making deontic powers* such as rights, duties, entitlements, protections etc. Let me explain this in more detail.

Institutional (status-) concept of personhood

A few words about the institutional (status-) concept of personhood are enough at this point since I will return to it below. As I have already said, according to the institutional concept personhood is a collectively administered (and thus) institutional status. This is roughly what personhood meant in Roman law: the difference between persons and slaves was a difference in collectively administered deontic powers. Or think of the sense in which corporations can be juridically defined as 'persons'. Again, being a person in this juridical sense is having collectively administered person-making deontic powers. Finally, take Michael Tooley's proposal according to which 'being a person' is (the same thing as) 'having a serious right to life'. If one understands 'having a serious right to life' as having a collectively administered deontic power, then Tooley's proposal, too, treats personhood as an institutional status.[11] Just as with the psychological concepts of personhood, there are, in principle, as many institutional

---

[10] On conceiving institutions or institutional facts in terms of 'deontic powers', see Searle (1995).

[11] See Tooley (1972). For my heuristic purposes it is inconsequential whether Tooley himself understands deontic powers in this 'enlightenment' sense (to borrow Brandom), or in

concepts of personhood as there are proposals as to which deontic powers exactly are defining of personhood.

Interpersonal (status-) concept of personhood

What about the interpersonal (status-) concept of personhood according to which being a person is being a bearer of person-making significances to someone or within someone's viewpoint? Does such a curious concept capture something important in the real world? I believe it does indeed. Negatively speaking, there seem to be phenomena that can meaningfully be described as losses of personhood, which are reducible neither to loss of relevant psychological capacities nor to loss of deontic powers (rights, duties etc.), but which are rather to be understood in terms of loss of personhood in the sense of not being seen in terms of personifying significances by relevant others. This has at least three general types, which I will call (A) *interpersonal invisibility,* (B) *reification* and (C) *animal eroticisation.*[12]

(A) Imagine being a homeless person living on the streets of an anonymous metropolis without a single friend. Assume that your psychological person-making capacities are in perfect order and that in principle you bear the same fundamental rights as anyone else in that city. In other words, in terms of the psychological as well as the institutional concept of personhood, you are a person like anyone else. Yet no one pays any attention to you or attaches any significance to you: were you to die in the cardboard box where you live, not a single soul would feel anything of any importance was missing. It seems that in being socially or *interpersonally invisible* in this sense you lack some essential component of what it is to be a person in the full-fledged sense of the word.

(B) Take another cruel example. You are in a concentration camp undergoing medical experiments where only your biological make-up as *homo sapiens* is relevant for the scientific purposes in question and where nothing hangs on the fact that you are psychologically a person. You are certainly not interpersonally invisible, since you are the focus of intensive scientific scrutiny. That you have been stripped of all

---

some more straightforwardly 'realist' sense according to which rights or other deontic powers are 'simply there', in nature, independently of intentionality of persons. Saying that they are there in the 'second nature' or in 'the space of reasons' (following McDowell, 1994), is, as far as I can see, admitting that they are not independent of intentionality, and so is saying that (basic or human) rights are claims which it would be impossible rationally not to accept or acknowledge (see e.g. Forst, 1999).

[12] On 'invisibility' see Honneth (2001), on 'reification' (of persons) Honneth (2005), on 'erotic significances' Brandom (2007). I conceive of invisibility and reification slightly differently than Honneth, but here it is not possible to discuss the differences.

rights and therefore excluded from personhood institutionally is certainly terrible enough, yet this is not the total extent of your predicament. Rather, what is truly critical are the kinds of significances in light of which you are seen: they are significances that do not distinguish you from other types of laboratory animal. To the extent that you are seen purely as an object of scientific observation or as a living instrument, you are not being seen in light of person-making or 'personifying' significances, but rather of, to use a well-worn expression, 'reifying' significances. And to the extent that you are being so *reified* by the relevant others, you clearly, it seems, suffer from the loss of some essential component of what it is to be a person in the full-fledged sense of the word.[13]

(C) The third and last example. Imagine being chased by a hungry pack of wolves in a frozen Siberian landscape without any other human beings anywhere near. You are in perfect psychological order and a well-respected member of your community with the full rights and responsibilities of a legal and moral person. Thus psychologically and institutionally, you are certainly a person. To the blood-thirsty wolves you are, similarly, not invisible, nor are they capable of reifying you in the way in which the Nazi doctors are. The problem is rather that you are being seen by the only other intentional beings anywhere that matter at the present, exclusively in terms of the significance that their immediate animal desire for nourishment attaches to you: *as food*. To mark this purely animal desire-determined form of significance with a technical term, let us say that you are being seen thoroughly in the light of animal erotic significances, or are being *animally eroticized*. To the extent that this is so, there is probably a very concrete sense in which you feel yourself, in these circumstances, as having lost some essential component of what it is to be a person in the full-fledged sense of the word.[14]

---

[13] Conceived of in this way, reifying (psychological) persons, or having reifying attitudes towards them comes in many variations: think of seeing them as aesthetic objects, as objects of scientific observation, as objects of engineering or manipulation, as machines, as instruments, as animals, as raw-material, as labour-force, as investment, as commodity, as pest, dirt, cancer, etc. All these are different ways of seeing (psychological) persons in terms of significances that are not personifying or person-making, and thus different forms of taking (psychological) persons as (interpersonal) non-persons. For the many senses in which the term 'reification' has been used in social philosophy, see Pitkin (1987). Compare Margalit (1996), chapter 6.

[14] Of course the wolves do not acknowledge any of your rights either, but conceiving the situation as a violation of your rights as a person would be somewhat off the point. I am not perfectly happy about using the term 'eroticization' or 'erotic significance' in the way that I do here for a purely animal phenomenon, but for reasons of terminological consistency (and not having come up with a better term) I follow Brandom (2007) who uses 'erotic

Each of the three examples above are meant to be examples of what it is *not* to be seen in terms of personifying or person-making significances, and thus to suffer from a lack or loss of personhood in the interpersonal sense. Eyes that look through you, eyes that look at you attentively but without the slightest hint of the warmth of normal personal response, or eyes that look at you with the feverish lust of a predator, are directly constitutive of such lack or loss. In the interpersonal sense you are a person only to the extent that you are taken as a person by relevant others in that they have personifying attitudes towards you and thereby see you in light of personifying or person-making significances. But what are such person-making significances? My suggestion is that they are significances that *recognitive* attitudes attribute to objects. This is to say that 'personifying attitude' and 'recognitive attitude' are synonyms. It is hence precisely the lack or negation of recognitive attitudes (or more informally 'lack of recognition') that unites interpersonal invisibility, reification and animal eroticization.

3. Recognitive Attitudes and the Layers and Dimensions of Personhood

Having now, as a preliminarily step, distinguished between three concepts of personhood — the psychological, the institutional and the interpersonal — the next question to ask is what to make of this plurality of concepts. I cannot see that any one of them could be ignored in discussing personhood — it seems that lack or loss conceived in terms of any of them can meaningfully be understood as a lack or loss of full personhood. Neither can I see that any of them could reasonably be reduced to any of the others. In order to do justice to this apparently irreducible plurality in an orderly way I suggest that we should think of the three concepts as identifying three respective elements, or as I will say, *layers* of full or full-fledged personhood.

At the end of chapter 1 I said that recognition is both responsive to and constitutive of personhood. In terms of the above distinctions, the point was to say that recognitive attitudes are very specific kinds of responses to psychological person-making capacities — namely responses of a kind that attribute to their object personifying or person-making significances. In other words, recognitive attitudes are

---

significance' as a general term for significances that the desiring animal intentionality (which in Hegel's conception precedes recognition (see e.g. *Werke* 10, § 426-9)) attaches to objects. It is important to distinguish this animal phenomenon of 'eroticization' from the phenomenon of 'reification', which only persons are capable of.

responsive to the psychological layer and directly *constitutive of the interpersonal layer* of the recognizee's personhood.

What I want to do next is to show that we can informatively distinguish between two species of the recognitive attitude, which correspond in the way just mentioned to two intuitively central components of psychological person-making capacities or features (or the psychological layer of personhood), as well as to two intuitively central components of interpersonal person-making significances (or the interpersonal layer of personhood). Thus, I will talk of two *dimensions* of full or full-fledged personhood, corresponding to the two recognitive attitudes and running through the two (or, including personhood in the institutional sense, three) layers of personhood. I will call these recognitive attitudes *respect* and *love* (freely following Honneth's analysis of Hegel's concept of recognition), and the dimensions corresponding to these, the *deontic* and the *axiological* dimension of personhood respectively [see Table.][15]

	Deontic dimension of personhood	**Axiological dimension of personhood**
Recognitive attitude	*Respect*	*Love*
Psychological layer of personhood	capacity for rational authority or deontic co-authorship	capacity for valuing intrinsically
Interpersonal (status-) layer of personhood	the significance/status of deontic co-authority	the significance/status of someone whose happiness is intrinsically valuable, or an end in itself
Institutional (status-) layer of personhood	person-making deontic powers (rights, duties etc.)	

Respect and the deontic dimension of personhood

Historically probably the most widely-held view on what distinguishes humans from animals, or more recently (roughly, as it has dawned that also humans are an animal species with a natural history) persons from non-persons, has to do with their rational capacities. One way to formulate this difference is to say that persons are rational

---

[15] I believe that a roughly analogical account could be given of the recognitive attitude of esteem or cooperative valuing (*Wertschätzung*) of Honneth's three-dimensional analysis of recognition. but for reasons of space I will leave it out of the discussion in this article.

beings in a way that is different from the more simple ways in which 'mere' animals or computers can be said to be rational. Mere animals can be said to be rational in the sense that their instinctual or desire-oriented behaviour is functionally in tune with their physiological needs and environment, and computers can be said to be rational in the sense that they run on the pre-given rules which their programmes consist of. But mere intelligent behaviour or running on pre-given rules does not fully encompass how we normally conceive of the rationality of our actions and thoughts as persons.[16]

To distinguish our distinctive way of being 'rational', it is more accurate to say that persons as persons are *autonomously* rational creatures, in that they administer their thoughts, actions and interactions by means of norms which they themselves, implicitly or explicitly, institute or authorize. Following Robert Brandom and, in his reading, Hegel, instituting and authorizing — or administering — norms is a collective (as it were meta-) practice, which requires that the relevant individuals 'recognize' each other as co-authorities or co-administrators of deontic powers.[17] There is no private norm-administration (as Wittgenstein also emphasized), nor is there collective norm-administration without the relevant individuals forming an administrative collective or 'we' by mutually recognizing each other as co-administrators or co-authorities.[18]

The word *'respect'* has various meaning in everyday and philosophical parlance (see Feinberg, 1975; Darwall, 1979; Dillon, 2003), but starting from Immanuel Kant it has been associated with a basic attitude between 'law-givers in the kingdom of ends'. Generalizing this line of thought and word-usage by following Hegel and Brandom, we can call 'respect' the basic interpersonal recognitive attitude that is constitutive of the interpersonal practice of administering, not only moral norms and deontic powers, but *any* social norms and deontic powers. For any social norms to exist there have to be individuals who

---

[16] See Pirmin Stekeler-Weithofer's contribution to this volume on the difference between 'mere rationality' and 'reason' (*Vernunft*).

[17] See Brandom (1994; 1999; 2007). Brandom does not distinguish at all between different recognitive attitudes, as Honneth does, but in terms of the multi-dimensional analysis of these attitudes that I am working on Brandom talks of what I call respect. My account of respect differs from that of Honneth (see Honneth, 1995, pp. 107–21) in that I distinguish more sharply between, on the one hand, respecting someone as an author or *co-author* of deontic powers (such as of rights), and, on the other hand, 'respecting' someone as a *bearer* of deontic powers (such as rights).

[18] This formulation should not be read as presupposing fully-developed persons who get together and start legislating norms. Rather, the coming-about of norm-structures, norm-administrating 'we's and persons (as persons) are moments of the same process. I thank the anonymous referee for prompting me to be explicit on this issue.

have *both* the psychological capacities needed for norm-administration (whatever these may be exactly) *and* the significance of co-authority or co-administrator for each other. Whereas the capacity for norm-administration, and thus for regulating actions and thoughts (of oneself as well as of others) with self-given norms seems to be one of the essential dimensions of the *psychological capacities* that distinguish (what we call) persons from non-persons, being *respected* in the sense of being taken as a co-authority with regard to these norms seems to be one of the essential dimensions of being taken as a person by others and thus of the *interpersonal status* of being a person.

Love and the axiological dimension of personhood

Even if one accepts that the deontic account of the defining features of persons identifies something undeniably important about personhood, it also seems to leave out something important. For example Harry Frankfurt and Charles Taylor have argued for an alternative account of personhood in which axiological concepts such as 'second order desires', 'love' (Frankfurt, 1971; 2004) or 'strong valuing' (Taylor, 1985) are used for conceptualizing that which distinguishes persons from non-persons.

Philosophers dispute how deontic and axiological concepts relate to each other or what is the relationship of norms and values. But personhood is not only a technical philosophical concept and, intuitively, both the deontic and the axiological approaches seem to articulate important components of what defines persons. It seems equally reasonable to say that, on the one hand, unlike mere animals, we persons are autonomously rational creatures, and that, on the other hand, unlike for them, for us persons things, events and states of affairs have values of a kind that cannot be reduced to functions of mere animal desire, or of pleasure and pain. Therefore, it seems reasonable to include both views by saying that personhood has, alongside a deontic dimension, an axiological dimension.

In axiological terms, an economical way to put the difference between persons and mere animals that are not persons is to say that whereas mere animals desire something, persons, in addition, value or care about something. What persons desire, on the one hand, and what they value or care about, on the other hand, are often not the same thing, and for persons as persons the latter takes precedence. In other words, whereas mere animals follow their desire immediately, persons as persons are moved by their sense of what is good, for themselves or for others. Or, to put it yet differently, whereas mere animals see objects, events or states of affairs in light of immediate 'erotic significances', for persons things have, in addition, positive or negative value.

To value anything or to care about anything in the sense distinctive of person seems to presuppose that one values or cares about something *intrinsically*, or 'for its own sake'. This is so because anything's being *instrumentally* valuable for a subject is its being instrumental to something else. Assuming that the chain of instrumental valuings of a subject is not infinite, it has to end in something that the subject takes as valuable, not instrumentally or not for the sake of something else, but intrinsically or 'for its own sake'.

I suggest that whereas valuing something — and thus eventually valuing something intrinsically — is an essentially important component of the psychological layer of personhood, being valued by others in a certain way is an equally important component of the interpersonal layer of personhood. What is this way? Clearly, being valued in the sense of being taken as instrumentally valuable to something else — say, to the well-being or wealth of the valuer or some other persons — cannot be it. Slave-owners may value their slaves as good instruments, but being valued as a good instrument is not being seen in the light of a personifying significance — it is not being taken as a person, or being personified, but, rather, being reified.

Being valued in a personifying way seems rather to be something that Aristotle grasped well in his reflections about what he thought of as the 'core sense' of *philia* or *love*. In this core sense, loving, according to Aristotle, is wanting 'the good or what one takes to be good for someone for her own sake'.[19] Or in other words, loving in this sense is valuing or caring about someone's subjectively good life, happiness or well-being ('good *for* someone'), not instrumentally, but intrinsically ('for her own sake'). Being valued in this specific sense intrinsically, or being taken as someone whose good life or happiness is intrinsically valuable (or, if you like, an end in itself) seems clearly a personifying way of being valued or attached significance by others. Whereas the capacity for intrinsic valuing, or for seeing the world in light of values that transcend mere immediate erotic significance, hence seems to be one of the essential dimensions of the *psychological capacities* that distinguish persons from non-persons, being *loved*

---

[19] I am following Gregory Vlastos' (1981) reading of Aristotle on *philia*. This core sense of *philia*, of which Aristotle talks in *Nicomachean Ethics*, *Rhetoric* and *Eudemian Ethics* is not to be confused with the three more famous forms of *philia* in Aristotle: pleasure-*philia*, utility-*philia* and *philia* between the virtuous. Whereas these are different forms of concrete interpersonal relationships, *philia* in the core sense ('pros hen legomenon') is a single attitude.

in the sense of being taken as someone whose happiness or well-being is intrinsically valuable seems to be one of the essential dimensions of being taken as a person by others and thus of the *interpersonal status of being a person*.[20]

Recognitive attitudes as responsive to and constitutive of personhood

Let us next take a closer look at how, exactly, recognitive attitudes are responsive to and constitutive of personhood. Starting from the first question: how, more precisely, should we see the recognitive attitudes of respect and love as *responsive to* the corresponding dimensions of the psychological layer of personhood? Elsewhere I have proposed that having recognitive attitudes of 'taking something as a person' can be understood as 'acknowledging claims of personhood' (Ikäheimo & Laitinen 2007). The point of this formulation is to say that a creature's having enough of the right kind of psychological capacities, simply as such, presents suitably equipped others encountering it/him with claims. These claims of psychological personhood will *move* the suitably equipped other subject or person (in suitable circumstances) into seeing the object in light of personifying significances and thus in light of an interpersonal status of a person.

Think of demanding or judging eyes presenting a claim for co-authority over the rules or norms in terms of which their bearer is treated; or of the forms of interaction in which it/he takes part. Or think of vulnerable, suffering, fearful or hopeful eyes presenting a claim for their bearer to be taken as someone whose life and happiness has intrinsic value.[21] The point is to say, that the claims of psychological personhood in question are just those the acknowledgement of which is respecting someone as a co-author, or loving her in the sense of seeing her happiness as intrinsically valuable, respectively.[22]

---

[20] Honneth discusses the recognitive attitude of love mainly in a developmental psychological context (from which I abstract here in favor of a merely structural description), but I do not see my account to be in any clearly articulated substantial disagreement with his account. See especially Honneth (1995), pp. 95–107.

[21] One can find useful tools for this kind of phenomenology of *primary claims of personhood* — preceding institutionalized norms as well as established patterns of value and reasoning — in Sartre's notion of the 'look' and Levinas' notion of the 'face'. Both are inspired by readings of Hegel, even if, in both cases, by rather simplifying ones. On the influence and simplification of the Hegelian account of the interpersonal recognitive encounter in Sartre and Levinas, see Williams, 1992, chapter 12, and Williams, 1997, chapter 15.

[22] In bio-ethics it is often simply taken for granted that persons have 'intrinsic value' and that this is something they have independently of anyone's valuing (see e.g. Lee, 1996;

What about the *constitutive* role of recognitive attitudes? In addition to being directly creative of the interpersonal layer of personhood, there are still two further ways in which recognitive attitudes are constitutive of personhood. The second way is that *the capacity for recognitive attitudes towards others* seems to be an important component of the person-making *psychological* features or capacities of the recognizer.[23] On the deontic dimension this is rather clear — it is impossible to be autonomously rational in the sense of thinking and acting on collectively self-authorized norms without respecting others as co-authorities with oneself. There is no purely private authorization of norms and there is no collective authorization of norms without respect. On the axiological dimension the constitutive role for personhood of being a recognizer may be somewhat less clear. Yet there seems to be a quite distinctive sense in which the capacity to love others is an important component of having the normal psychological make-up of a person, and in which incapacity for loving is regarded as a deficiency of personhood.

Consider the following proposal. It is because of their relative incapacity for recognitive attitudes towards others, that we can think of *psychopaths* as limiting cases of personhood on the psychological layer. A subject who is relatively incapable of respecting others as authoritative on norms is relatively incapable of having social norms in his view. Similarly, a subject who is relatively incapable of seeing the happiness of others as intrinsically valuable is relatively incapable of seeing facts, events and actions in general in light of the complex evaluative or axiological significances that they have for normal persons who love some others. In brief, psychopaths are relatively unbound by social norms and relatively unmoved by considerations of value not reducible to desirability or self-interest, and this is because their world, or the world for them, is relatively devoid of significances that distinguish some beings in the world as person from non-persons. Clearly, it would be wrong to say that psychopaths are not psychological persons at all — after all, they are not mere animals or machines —

Stretton, 2000; Lee, 2004). I take it that there are no values without valuing viewpoints, and that being valuable is being valuable to someone. As 'erotic significance' exists only in a desiring viewpoint, 'intrinsic value' — and thus also instrumental value — exists only in an intrinsically valuing viewpoint. That persons (or, which I take to be the same thing, their good life or happiness) have intrinsic value, is a function of their being subjects who value themselves and each other intrinsically, that is, a function of their being self- and other-loving beings. Note that for an *axiological theist* the road is open for grounding intrinsic value on *God's love for the world*. For others this road is not open.

[23] Abstracting from differences in details and terminology, Dennett (1976) and Rovane (1998) agree on this. Italo Testa (manuscript) talks here of 'recognitive capacities'.

but it makes perfectly good sense to say that the psychological layer of their personhood is seriously deficient or diminished on the deontic and axiological dimensions because of their incapacity for recognitive attitudes.

There is still a third way in which recognitive attitudes are constitutive of personhood. This is the way in which being taken as a person by others, and thus having the status of a person in the *interpersonal* sense, seems to be empirically an important or even necessary condition for the actualization, full development and maintenance of the *psychological* layer of personhood of the recogni*zee*. As Axel Honneth has extensively argued, the experience of being recognized by others is a precondition for the development of a healthy practical self-identity or self-relation (Honneth, 1995).[24] Moreover, it is common sense that the experience of being recognized by others is also in some ways a precondition for one's own capacity and propensity to recognize others: having little experience of being an object of genuine respect or love by others is at least not favourable for the actualization and development of one's own capacity to respect and love others. In many ways, being recognized is thus causally linked to the development of the psychological layer of personhood of the recogni*zee*.[25]

All in all, I want to make no claim of exhaustiveness, but it seems that at least a lot of the intuitively central elements of what it is to be a person in a full-fledged sense are already covered by the four components of personhood discussed (consisting of the deontic and the axiological dimensions of the psychological and the interpersonal layers of personhood) — if not explicitly, then by implication[26] — and that at least some useful ways for conceiving their interrelations have

---

[24] How various kinds of self-relations are involved in the deontic and axiological dimensions of the psychological layer of personhood cannot be discussed here, but it should be obvious that they are.

[25] In Brandom's terms, not being respected *at all* as a co-authority of linguistic norms means being excluded from linguistic practices, and thus from the necessary requirement for the development of propositional thinking. But isn't there some circularity involved in saying that recognitive attitudes are both responses to the psychological person-making capacities and a condition for their actualization or development? Perhaps, but this does not seem particularly vicious. For one thing, we are capable of responding, not only to the claims of actual personhood, but also to the claims of *potential* personhood. In starting to personify an infant adults are not simply imagining or projecting something that is not yet really there, but rather responding to the potentialities that are really there from the beginning.

[26] For instance from the complete off-hand list of the usual candidates for person-making psychological capacities or features presented earlier — rationality, the capacity for happiness and misery, forms of self-relation, self-consciousness or first-person-perspective, communicative competencies, social or cooperative capacities — everything seems to be covered directly or by implication.

been opened. Yet one important phenomenon that is typically meant in describing something or someone as a person still needs to be accounted for. This is what I called, above, personhood according to the institutional concept, or in terms of the outlined model, *the institutional layer of full or full-fledged personhood*.

4. Institutional Personhood Revisited

In Table institutional personhood is placed under the deontic dimension. This should be obvious, since being a person in the institutional sense is having some particular deontic powers. Which deontic powers exactly are constitutive of personhood on the institutional layer of the deontic dimension is a matter of stipulation and legislation — *we* stipulate which deontic powers are the ones that comprise being a 'person' in this sense and legislate which entities have them, both juridically and morally.

An important point to note about the institutional layer of personhood is that it is ontologically secondary to, or less fundamental than, the psychological and the interpersonal layers of personhood. That anything has *any* deontic powers within the life-world of persons, or within a collective, is dependent on the necessary conditions of deontic administration being in place: only creatures with the basic capacities for co-authorship, as well as mutually attributed statuses of co-authority, form a collective or 'we' who can come up with and maintain any social norms and deontic powers.[27] This also holds for the deontic powers comprising of institutional personhood — whatever they are according to different philosophical or other stipulations,[28] or in the actual practices of a given culture or society.

---

[27] In bio-ethics it is often taken simply for granted that persons have rights as a natural fact, or that rights somehow naturally 'emerge from', 'arise from', 'flow from' or 'result from' their person-making features (see Lee, 2004; Stretton, 2000; 2004). Without further explanation, this is hardly anything else than simply bluffing one's way over the Humean gulf between descriptive and prescriptive talk. (Sturma, 2002, reminds s that the gulf still needs to crossed with conceptual caution.) Note that for a *deontological theist* the road is open for grounding deontic powers like rights and duties on God's authority. For others this road is not open. A further point: even if the model presented in this article has no place for moral (or other) deontic powers of persons that are independent of collective legislation, it does not imply that all morally relevant facts or claims depend on legislation. For instance, it does not imply that the existence of values, even if it is dependent on the existence of valuing viewpoints, is somehow dependent on collective legislation.

[28] Compare for instance the similarities and differences of Tooley's stipulation according to which being a person is 'having a serious right to life' and Hegel's concept of ('abstract') personhood, according to which being a person is being an owner and thus a bearer of property rights. (See Hegel, 1952, § 34–104, and for relevant secondary literature Honneth, 2000, and Schmidt am Busch, 2007, chapters 7 and 8).

In order to distinguish the different layers of the deontic dimension of personhood clearly, it is important to distinguish between two senses of 'respecting a person', which are very easily confused with each other. They are easily confused since both refer to the deontic dimension of personhood, but they are different since they refer to different layers of it. Let us call these *respect* and *respect**. Whereas respect is respecting someone as a *co-authority* with regard to deontic powers, respect* is respecting* someone as a *holder* of deontic powers. The first refers to the psychological layer, the second to the institutional layer of personhood. Often respect* comes first. For instance, in democratic societies human infants are usually attributed some basic rights — the possession of which can be called personhood in the institutional sense — and respected* as their bearers before they are respected as co-authorities or co-authors of these rights. Or think of colonialist systems where the colonized people are granted some rights by the colonial masters but are not respected by them as having any, or at least much, authority with regard to these rights — not to mention the rights of the masters.

Having rights is certainly better than not having rights, but merely having rights without being respected as a co-authority with regard to one's rights is to remain excluded from, and thus subjected to, the constitutive or authoritative community. To put the difference between respect and respect* more formally: whereas respecting is acknowledging claims of psychological personhood, which someone's having the relevant psychological capacities, as such, presents us with, respecting* is acknowledging claims of institutional personhood, which the authority of the authoritative collective creates. Strictly speaking, respecting* someone as a person in the institutional sense is not respecting him as an individual at all, but rather having due regard to the norms and deontic powers constitutive of institutional personhood, as they are stipulated and legislated by the authoritative community.[29]

5. Two Basic Question Concerning Personhood

After having sketched, in broad outlines, the multilayered and multidimensional model of personhood in its relation to recognition, let me now take up two standard questions concerning personhood to see

---

[29] That *political rights* can be conceived of as rights to take part in co-authorship complicates the picture somewhat, but, as far as I can see, does not compromise it. Note that whether having rights of any kind, *including political rights,* is a state of passive dependence on others or not depends on the extent that one is included — interpersonally and/or institutionally — in the legislative community of the rights in question.

what kind of answers the model implies. These are, *first*, the question of whether all, and only, humans are persons, and, *secondly*, the question whether personhood comes in degrees or is rather a matter of 'all or nothing'. To both the general answer is 'it depends.' That is, it depends on which of the layers of personhood one has in mind.

More exactly, as to the *first* question, limiting personhood on the *psychological and interpersonal layers* conceptually to all and only members of the species *Homo sapiens* is not a live option. On the one hand, there is no way to rule out the possibility that other existing or possible species may have some degree of the relevant psychological capacities, or some degree of recognitive attitudes and thus of the interpersonal person-making significances to each other (and/or for humans). Talking of 'mere animals' as non-persons is, in principle, indifferent to the distinction between *Homo sapiens* and other animal species. On the other hand, there are clearly humans that are not persons on the psychological or interpersonal layers — think of anencephalic embryos. Whether intelligent animals of other species or seriously deficient humans are then persons on the *institutional layer of personhood* is wholly up to legislation by persons with the required deontic-psychological capacities. (Were we humans to meet members of other species demonstrably equipped with these capacities, their claim to co-authorship of the norms of the inter-species interaction would be no less than ours.)

Similarly, whether corporations such as Wal-Mart are persons on the institutional layer is wholly up to the constitutive community to legislate. That they are not persons on the psychological or interpersonal layer should be clear: they do not have the relevant person-making psychological capacities, which shows in the fact that they do not qualify as appropriate objects of respect and love (even if figures like Ronald McDonald are designed to try to make you think differently).[30]

Often the personhood of corporations is called a 'legal fiction', but it is not obvious that this is particularly illuminating. On the one hand, there is nothing fictitious about rights and other collectively administered deontic powers, and thus nothing fictitious about institutional personhood. On the other hand, claiming that Wal-Mart is psychologically or interpersonally a person is simply false, and it is unclear why

---

[30] Of course philosophers can stipulate the required person-making capacities as they like in their theories, but my suggestion is that the default commonsense concept of psychological personhood is constrained by the appropriateness of objects to be loved and or respected: only psychological persons present claims, the appropriate acknowledgement of which is loving and respecting (in the senses spelled out above).

we should accept a clear falsehood as part of our juridical systems by calling it a 'legal fiction'. One approach would be to insist that institutional personhood should have a reasonable relation to psychological and interpersonal personhood, and to point out that this has not been the case in the sophistries of corporate lawyers according to which corporations are persons.[31]

As to the *second* question, of whether personhood comes in degrees or is a matter of 'all or nothing', on *the psychological and interpersonal layers* personhood clearly comes in degrees. As to the *institutional* layer, it is, again, up to us to legislate. If we stipulate the deontic contents of institutional personhood in a simple enough way — say, by stipulating that it consists of 'a serious right to life', and interpreting this in such a way that having it allows no degrees — we can make institutional personhood a simple either-or-state-of-affairs. Something either has it or it does not have it, depending on whether we give it to it or not. But there is no conceptual necessity to resort to this simple strategy. Following a proposal by Ludwig Siep (1993, p. 44), we can alternatively stipulate institutional personhood as consisting of several deontic components, and give some beings (say, the great apes) some of them, and others (say, people like you and me) the whole packet. Which deontic powers it is reasonable to give to which entities is an open question, but clearly differing needs or interests should be taken into account. What anencephalic human embryos, intelligent members of other species, or people like you and I need are hardly the same thing, and calibrating the deontic components of institutional personhood solely to suit the needs of one group may lead to odd or unwanted results in the case of some other group.

Another strategy is to say, in a certain way, *both* that personhood comes in degrees *and* that it is a matter of 'all or nothing' by stipulating personhood as a 'threshold-concept' or 'range-property'.[32] This is saying that the relevant person-making capacities or features come in degrees, but that when they surpass some 'threshold-level' or reach a certain 'range', their bearer is a person fully, without degrees. What is

---

[31] According to the (fifth and) fourteenth amendment of the American constitution 'no person shall be [...] deprived of life, liberty, or property without due process of law'. This seems to imply that persons in the sense meant in the constitution are creatures with 'life' and therefore capable of being deprived of it. I believe it is reasonable to assume that the relevant legislative authorities were mainly thinking of life in the sense in which persons such as you and me — having the capacities of autonomous rationality and valuing intrinsically our own lives — have or lead lives.

[32] See Michael Quante's contribution to this volume on conceiving personhood as a threshold-concept, and Rawls' discussion of moral personhood as a range-property in Rawls 1999, chapter 77.

striking about this strategy is that it seems to involve talking about personhood in more than one sense: on the one hand in the psychological or interpersonal sense in which there is no clear culmination point or limit to the development or degree of personhood, and on the one hand in the institutional sense in which such a limit can be created simply by the will of the authoritative collective. Talking of personhood as a threshold-concept or as a range-property is thus an indication of how these different senses form interrelated (and therefore also easily confused) layers of what it is to be a person in the full-fledged sense of the word.

Conclusion

The concept of a person is clearly of central importance for understanding and organizing our lives and position in the order of things. I have tried to show above that even if this concept is very complex, it has a well-ordered internal structure: we can conceive of a broad range of intuitively defining features of persons as interrelated layers and dimensions of what it is to be a person in the full or full-fledged sense of the word. I have also tried to substantiate the claim that these layers and dimensions relate in systematic ways to recognitive attitudes. It is in more than one way that we persons bootstrap ourselves into and maintain personhood by taking each others as persons — or in other words, through interpersonal recognition.[33]

References

Aristotle (2001), *The Basic Works of Aristotle* (New York: The Modern Library).
Brandom, Robert (1994), *Making It Explicit: Reasoning, Representing and Discursive Commitment* (Cambridge, MA: Harvard University Press).
Brandom, Robert (1999), 'Some pragmatist themes in Hegel's Idealism: Negotiation and administration in Hegel's account of the structure and content of conceptual norms', *European Journal of Philosophy*, 7 (2), pp. 164–89.
Brandom, Robert (2007), 'The structure of desire and recognition: Self-consciousness and self-constitution', *Philosophy and Social Criticism*, **33**, pp.127–50.
van den Brink, Bert & Owen, David (ed. 2007), *Recognition and Power* (New York: Cambridge University Press).
Darwall, Stephen (1977), 'Two kinds of respect', *Ethics,* **88**, pp. 36–49.

---

[33] My work on recognition and personhood is part of a cooperative effort with Arto Laitinen and other members of the Finnish Academy project 'The Limits of Personhood'. For comments on earlier versions of this paper, I am especially grateful to the participants of the philosophical seminar in Leipzig in 12.4.2006, Michael Quante's research seminar in Köln 23.6.2006, Dieter Sturma's Hauptseminar in Essen 30.10.2006, as well as to Axel Honneth, Arto Laitinen, Haeng-Nam Lee, Ming-Chen Lo, Michael Peacock, Christian Schmidt, Hans-Christoph Schmidt am Busch, Pirmin Stekeler-Weithofer, Henning Tegtmeyer, Titus Stahl, Brunela Vincenzi and the anonymous referee.

Dennett, Daniel (1976), 'Conditions of personhood', in A. Rorty (ed)., *The Identities of Persons* (Berkeley: University of California Press), 175–96.
Dillon, Robin S. (2003), 'Respect', *Standford Encyclopaedia of Philosophy*, retrieved Jan 02, 2007, http://plato.stanford.edu/entries/respect/
Feinberg, Joel (1975), 'Some conjectures on the concept of respect', *Journal of Social Philosophy*, **4**, pp. 1–3.
Forst, Rainer (1999), 'The basic right to justification: Toward a constructivist conception of human rights', *Constellations*, **6** (1), pp. 35–60.
Frankfurt, Harry (1971): 'Freedom of the will and the concept of a person', *Journal of Philosophy*, **68**, pp. 5–20.
Frankfurt, Harry (2004), *Reasons of Love* (Princeton: Princeton University Press).
Fraser, Nancy & Honneth, Axel (2003), *Redistribution or Recognition? A Political-Philosophical Exchange* (London: Verso).
Hegel, G.W.F. (1977), *Phenomenology of Spirit*, translated by A.V. Miller (Oxford: Oxford University Press).
Hegel, G.W.F. (1986–), *Werke in 20 Bänden* (Frankfurt am Main: Suhrkamp). [Werke]
Hegel, G.W.F. (1952), *Hegel's Philosophy of Right*, translated by T.M. Knox, (London: Oxford University Press).
Honneth, Axel (1995), *The Struggle for Recognition — The Moral and Political Grammar of Social Conflicts* (Cambridge: Polity Press).
Honneth, Axel (2000), *Suffering from Indeterminacy. An Attempt at Reactualization of Hegel's Philosophy of Right* (Amsterdam: Van Gorcum).
Honneth, Axel (2001): 'Invisibility: On the epistemology of "recognition"', *Proceedings of the Aristotelian Society: Supplementary Volume*, **75**, pp. 111–26.
Honneth, Axel (2002): 'Grounding recognition: A rejoinder to critical questions', *Inquiry*, **45**, pp. 499–520.
Honneth, Axel (2005), *Verdinglichung. Eine anerkennungstheoretische Studie* (Frankfurt am Main: Suhrkamp).
Ikäheimo, Heikki (2002), 'On the genus and species of recognition', *Inquiry*, **45** (4), pp. 447–62.
Ikäheimo, Heikki (2005), 'On the role of intersubjectivity in Hegel's encyclopaedic phenomenology and psychology', *The Bulletin of the Hegel Society of Great Britain*, **49/50**, pp. 73–95.
Ikäheimo, Heikki & Laitinen, Arto (2007), 'Analysing recognition: Identification, acknowledgement and recognition between persons', in van den Brink & Owen (ed. 2007).
Laitinen, Arto (2002), 'Interpersonal recognition: A response to "Value or a precondition of personhood?"', *Inquiry*, **45** (4), pp. 463–78.
Lee, Patrick (1996), *Abortion and Unborn Human Life* (Washington, DC: Catholic University of America Press).
Lee, Patrick (2004), 'The pro-life argument from substantial identity: A defence', *Bioethics*, **18** (3), pp. 249–63.
Macionis, John J. & Plummer, Ken (1998), *Sociology; A Global Introduction* (New York: Prentice Hall).
Margalit, Avishai (1996), *The Decent Society* (Cambridge, MA: Harvard University Press).
Markell, Patchen (2000), 'A recognition of politics: Comments on Emcke and Tully', *Constellations*, **4**, pp. 496–506.
Markell, Patchen (2007), 'The potential and the actual: Mead, Honneth, and the "I"', in van den Brink & David Owen (ed. 2007).
McDowell, John (1994), *Mind and World* (Cambridge, MA: Harvard University Press).

Pitkin, Hanna Fenichel (1987), 'Rethinking reification', *Theory and Society*, **16** (2), pp. 263–93.
Rawls, John (1999), *A Theory of Justice*, Revised Edition (Oxford: Oxford University Press).
Ricoeur, Paul (2005), *The Course of Recognition* (Cambridge, MA: Harvard University Press).
Rovane, Carol (1998), *Bounds of Agency* (Princeton: Princeton University Press).
Schalhorn, Christoph (2000), *Hegels enzyklopädischer Begriff von Selbstbewusstsein*. Hegel-Studien Beiheft 43 (Hamburg: Felix Meiner).
Schmidt am Busch, Hans-Christoph (2007), *Religiöse Hingabe oder soziale Freiheit. Die Saint-Simonische Theorie und die Hegelsche Sozialphilosophie*, Hegel-Studien, Beiheft 48 (Paderborn: Mentis).
Searle, John (1995), *The Construction of Social Reality* (London: Penguin Books).
Siep, Ludwig (1993), 'Personenbegriffe und angewandte Ethik', in C.F. Gethmann & Peter L. Oesterreich (eds.), *Person und Sinneserfahrung. Philosophische Grundlagen und interdisziplinären Perspektiven* (Darmstad: Wissenschaftliche Buckgesellschaft).
Spaemann, Robert (1996), *Personen* (Stuttgart: Klett-Cotta).
Stretton, Dean (2000), 'The argument from intrinsic value: A critique', *Bioethics*, **14** (3).
Stretton, Dean (2004), 'Essential properties and the right to life: A response to Lee', *Bioethics*, **18** (3).
Sturma, Dieter (1997), *Die Philosophie der Person* (Paderborn: Schöningh).
Sturma, Dieter (2002), 'Person und Menschenrechte', in Dieter Sturma (ed.): *Person. Philosophiegeschichte — theoretische Philosophie — Praktische Philosophie* (Paderborn: Mentis).
Taylor, Charles (1985), 'The concept of person', *Human Agency and Language: Philosophical Papers vol. 1* (Cambridge: Cambridge University Press).
Testa, Italo (manuscript), 'Social space and the ontology of recognition'.
Tooley, Michael (1972), 'Abortion and infanticide', *Philosophy and Public Affairs*, **2** (1).
Williams, Robert R. (1992), *Recognition: Fichte and Hegel on the Other* (Albany: State University of New York Press).
Williams, Robert R. (1997), *Hegel's Ethics of Recognition* (Berkeley: University of California Press).
Wittgenstein, Ludvig (1953), *Philosophical Investigations* (Oxford: Blackwell).
Vlastos, Gregory (1981), 'The individual as an object of love in Plato', in his *Platonic Studies* (New York: Princeton University Press).

Arto Laitinen

Sorting Out Aspects of Personhood
Capacities, Normativity and Recognition

Abstract. *This paper examines how three central aspects of personhood — the capacities of individuals, their normative status, and the social aspect of being recognized — are related, and how personhood depends on them. The paper defends first of all a 'basic view' that while actual recognition is among the constitutive elements of full personhood, it is the individual capacities (and not full personhood) which ground the basic moral and normative demands concerning treatment of persons. Actual recognition depends analytically on such pre-existing normative requirements: it is a matter of responsiveness to them. The paper then discusses four challenges. The challenges claim that pace the basic view, the relevant capacities depend on recognition, that recognition seems to have normative relevance, and that the basic view cannot as such explain the equality either of persons, or of humans. Responding to these challenges amounts to refining the basic view accordingly.*

Although in everyday usage 'person' can be used as a synonym for 'human being', in philosophy it has a special usage. In this usage, persons are standardly taken to be beings with various capacities, who also have a moral or normative status dependent on those capacities:

> Where it is more than simply a synonym for 'human being', 'person' figures primarily in moral and legal discourse. A person is a being with *a certain moral status*, or a bearer of rights. But underlying the moral status, as its condition, are *certain capacities*. A person is a being who

Correspondence:
Arto Laitinen *armala@yfi.jyu.fi*

has a sense of self, has a notion of the future and the past, can hold values, make choices; in short, can adopt life-plans. At least, a person must be the kind of being who is in principle capable of all this, however damaged these capacities may be in practice. (Charles Taylor 1985a, 97, italics added)

Ever since Boethius's classical characterization of persons as 'individual substances of rational nature', most concepts of a person have taken personhood to be dependent solely on the capacities of individuals. I will below call such views *monadic*. But various philosophers defend social conceptions of personhood, which can be called *dyadic*, as they assume that personhood is essentially relational:

[W]hether something counts as a person depends in some way on an *attitude taken* toward it, a *stance adopted* with respect to it. ... [I]t is not the case that once we have established the objective fact that something is a person, we treat him or her or it in a certain way, but that our treating him or her or it in this certain way is somehow and to some extent *constitutive* of its being a person. (Dennett 1981, 270, last italics added)[1]

This article asks how these aspects of personhood are to be combined. What is the relation between the *capacities* of individuals, the basic *moral or normative status* that persons have, and the putatively constitutive social existence or *recognition* from others that persons typically enjoy?

In the first section, the nature of these aspects will be briefly clarified. After that, the paper tries to combine the view that persons have an unconditional moral status (not dependent on contingent responses by others), with the view that recognition from others has direct relevance in the ontology of persons. At first blush, these views seem to be in conflict: if recognition is a necessary condition of full personhood then *not being recognized by others* makes it the case that one is not a full person, and thus is presumably not entitled to the moral status of persons either. Consistent patterns of racism or sexism would mean that some agents are not recognized, and therefore not full persons, and presumably not entitled to a moral status. And even those who happen to be recognized, have the moral status only conditionally on such contingent responses by others, and thus the moral status fails to be unconditional in the right way. I call this line of thought a 'moral objection' against some ways of sorting out the

---

[1] Dennett refers to a whole host of others who have claimed something similar (MacKay, Strawson, Rorty, Putnam, Sellars, Flew, Nagel, Van de Vate, for references see Dennett, 1981, p. 270). The Hegelian tradition seems to agree. See Hegel (1991) and Quante's and Ikäheimo's essays in this volume.

aspects of personhood. Various seemingly natural and straightforward ways of combining the aspects of personhood fail this test.

One view that clearly passes the moral test is one according to which the moral status, and full personhood, is based simply on the capacities of the individuals and not on recognition. So perhaps we should drop the idea that recognition could be constitutive of full personhood? I try to show that we can have it both ways: *the basic moral and normative requirements are based on the capacities alone, but recognition is also ontologically constitutive of full personhood.* I will argue that full personhood is not only a matter of having sufficiently of the capacities, but also of having sufficiently secure and sufficiently adequate social existence consisting of recognition, where adequacy is determined as responsiveness to normative and moral requirements based on the capacities.

That at least is the *basic view* to be defended here, but it needs to be refined and qualified in various ways. In the latter half of the paper I will discuss four challenges to the view. The challenges are that *pace* the basic view, (i) capacities depend on recognition, and (ii) recognition creates normative requirements. Furthermore, the basic view does not as such explain (iii) the equality of all persons, or (iv) the equality of all humans. The defenders of the basic view may disagree on whether the last two are problems at all, but I try to find out whether the basic view can be refined so that it can solve them.

1. Aspects of Personhood: Initial characterization

Using the abbreviation 'P' for the property 'being a person', 'C' for the property of having the relevant capacities, 'N' for normative significance and 'R' for the status of being recognized by others, the paper will examine the relations between P, C, N and R. This section gives an initial characterization of these aspects.

Person–making capacities C

This paper assumes that beings of any species can be persons. Having enough of the relevant capacities and other necessary features is sufficient to make one a person. Typical persons are human beings, but membership in the species *homo sapiens* is not necessary. Other kinds of animals, or Martians, will be persons once they have the relevant capacities to the sufficient degree.[2] Indeed, it is not necessary that persons are animals or biologically living things at all, as long as they are

---

[2] It has been claimed, for example, that there are currently at least five non-human persons, trained linguistically by humans (DeGrazia, 2005, p. 7, fn. 14).

so sophisticated agents or subjects that they qualify as persons.[3] Further, I simply assume that the things that are persons are not *necessarily* persons; 'person' is not a substance sortal picking up an ontological kind, which determines the persistence conditions of the beings that are persons.[4] Rather, like 'student' or 'child', 'person' is a phase sortal which might cease to apply to a being and yet the being could continue to exist.[5]

The least controversial issue concerning personhood is that it goes hand in hand with various capacities: the property 'being a person' depends directly at least partly on so called person–making capacities.[6] One may have some of the capacities without being a person, and one may conceivably be a person without having *all* of the capacities. For the purposes of this paper, we can think of personhood as depending on a cluster of features, and what matters is that one has sufficiently many of them to the sufficient degree.[7]

I will use the abbreviation 'C' for the feature of 'having sufficiently many person–making capacities to a sufficient degree', or for having the *capacities*, for short. We may have a long list of person–making capacities ($c_1, c_2, c_3, ...$) and C is the dependent property of having enough of those capacities. It is a threshold property, in that having the individual capacities to a sufficient degree is the basis of having the threshold property (see Rawls 1972, §77). Sufficient degree for what? Sufficient degree, which is *necessary* for instantiating the property 'being a person' P in what I will call a fully actual sense. What the

---

[3] Consider for example a living person, whose organs are one by one replaced by artificial ones. (For expressions of scepticism on whether such thought-experiments make sense, see Wilkes, 1988.) Such an agent could have a 'life' in some other sense, a life of self-directed activity which forms the material of biographical thinking (see Raz, 1986a, ch 12; Ricoeur, 1992), even though it would not be a life-process in the biological sense discussed by van Inwagen (1990), Thompson (1995) and Olson (1997).

[4] But *mutatis mutandis* the considerations put forward here may apply to views which hold that persons are necessarily persons. In that case, the relation between humans and persons would be that of constitution as defined by Baker. Taking recognitive relations to be constitutive could result in a view that persons are, like artefacts for Baker, what she calls socially dependent 'ID'-objects (see her essay in this volume).

[5] For the debate see e.g. Olson (1997); Baker (2000).

[6] This is denied by what will be called 'purely dyadic' notions (such as the one thematized by M.Thompson, 2004), or 'purely moral' notions of personhood (such as Tooley, 1972).

[7] Cf. DeGrazia (2005, pp. 5–6) 'Personhood appears to be associated with a cluster of traits without being precisely analyzable in terms of any specific subset: autonomy, rationality, self-awareness, linguistic competence, sociability, the capacity for intentional action, and moral agency. A being doesn't need all these traits, however specified, to be a person'. In his view, a person is roughly '*someone (of whatever species or kind) with the capacity for sufficiently complex forms of consciousness*'(2005, p. 6). A more structured view would point out a number of necessary and jointly sufficient features – the cluster account is more relaxed in not demanding that any single feature is necessary.

required level is, or what the required capacities are, will depend on the concept of a person. Note that there may be further conditions for fully actual personhood (related for example to social existence), but anyone who has the property C, has at least enough of the relevant capacities. After having passed the threshold, any further increases in the degree to which one has the capacities does not make one have 'more of C', because anyone who crossed the threshold possesses C fully. Perhaps we can say that once the threshold is more clearly passed, the property C is had more securely. Until the latter half of the paper, I will bracket the fact that each of the capacities develops gradually, and all human persons have started out as undeveloped persons. I will first focus on those who already have the capacities to the sufficient degree. People with different goals of self–realization, or with 'thick narrative selves' may differ in many practically important ways, but what they share is that they have the relevant person–making capacities to the sufficient degree.

What capacities, then, are the relevant 'person–making' capacities? For the purposes of this paper, a rough sketch will suffice. The capacities include sophisticated mental powers or sophisticated variants of subjectivity (intentionality, self–consciousness, reason and deliberation, rich emotional life including possible existential anxieties and fear of death, conceptions of value, free will, reflection and second order attitudes, conceptual thinking), as well as related sophisticated forms of agency and interaction (free action, giving and taking responsibility, responsiveness to moral requirements, norms and reasons of other kinds, joint action, communication).[8] On the other hand, sentience and intentional, motivated agency are not enough: there may be intentional agents, which are not sophisticated enough to be fit to be held responsible, and there may be sentient subjects, which are not sophisticated enough to count as sapient, rational thinkers.[9] Below the relevant threshold, such agents or subjects do not have C (that is, do not have the relevant capacities to the sufficient degree). Whether

---

[8] Note that the claims that persons have these capacities are not statistical: majority of persons may be female, and majority of persons may have dark hair, but it does not follow that statistically majority of persons are dark haired women. By contrast, if paradigmatic persons can understand justifications and if paradigmatic persons are self-conscious, it *does* follow that paradigmatic persons are both and. Thus, the logic involved is not statistical. See Thompson (1995) (who talks about the concept of 'life').

[9] This is critical of P.F. Strawson's view that 'the concept of a person is to be understood as the concept of a type of entity such that *both* predicates ascribing states of consciousness *and* predicates ascribing corporeal characteristics, a physical situation &c. are equally applicable to an individual entity of that type.' (1959, p.104). Harry Frankfurt (1971) and others have pointed out that this seems to include all sentient animals.

we should say instead that they have C 'to some degree' will be discussed below, but the basic view concerns those who have C (fully).

It is not uncommon to think that having the capacities to a sufficient degree equals being a person, or that having the capacities to a sufficient degree is the only necessary and sufficient condition for being a person. As will be explained presently, such views are monadic in that they do not take dyadic (or polyadic) relations to others as directly constitutive of personhood. That is, they do not take 'social existence' as a constitutive aspect of personhood. The concept of fully actual personhood that I try to develop in this paper does try to take social existence as constitutive, but it will be helpful to have a term for the being, who possesses C. Let us call it 'a monadic person' (P_M).

Personhood and recognition R

Is the notion of a person that of an individual with certain capacities, or is it always, at least implicitly, of the dyadic form 'X is a person in relation to Y', like 'sister', or 'father' are? When we state that X is a sister, this is just a de-relativized form of saying 'X is a sister of Y' (Thompson, 2004, p. 354). When we speak about personhood, do we have a similar structure in mind? Is 'person' for example by definition an actual participant in relations of recognition, a 'respondent' as Charles Taylor (1985a, p. 97) puts it?

While standard views concerning personhood (from Boethius to Strawson and Frankfurt) may indeed be 'monadic,' various theories suggest that personhood has also a 'dyadic' structure of personhood–for–others (from Hegel to Dennett, Taylor and Thompson).[10] The idea is that persons are necessarily participants in practices where they are regarded as persons. A crucial aspect of treating others as persons is to include them in normative practices, give them responsibility or to have such recognitive attitudes as gratefulness, blame, respect, concern or esteem towards them. By and large, the social philosophical interest in personhood focuses on such relations and on the ways in which they are simultaneously constitutive of the participants' standing as persons, and of the structures of the shared form of life (see, e.g., Honneth, 1995; Taylor, 1985a,b).

Typical persons are no doubt *in fact* persons in both monadic and dyadic senses. They have the capacities discussed above, and typically they are *in fact* objects of attitudes and bearers of positively granted, institutional or 'official' statuses (such as legal rights). This

---

[10] See e.g. Hegel (1991); Quante (2002); Gallagher (this volume); Ikäheimo (this volume); Dennett (1978); Thompson (2004).

factual predicament may partly explain the divergence of the rival concepts of personhood: the monadic ones stress the capacities, and the dyadic ones the relations. One option is to adopt a 'mixed view', and include dyadic structures among the necessary person-making features: a person is someone with certain capacities, *and* with certain relations to others. On the mixed view, overall personhood has both monadic and dyadic aspects as conditions of full personhood. For example Dennett (see the quote above) holds a mixed view — he lists both capacities and stances by others as necessary person-making features.

Interpersonal recognition (respect, esteem, care, etc.) can be understood in different ways, but here I will focus on recognition as more or less adequate normative responsiveness in one's attitudes and actions concerning the other individual.[11] Recognizing someone in the relevant sense goes beyond mere 'identification' or 'classification' as a person — it has a normatively responsive element to it.[12] One 'recognizes' others when one responds sufficiently adequately to the normative significance of their relevant capacities (even when not thematizing these as 'person–making' capacities, or even when not possessing a concept of a person). That is, responding adequately to the normative relevance of the other's self–consciousness, autonomy, rationality or freedom can be adequate recognition even when one possesses no single concept such as 'person', which would enable subsuming these properties ($c_1, c_2, c_3,...$) under an encompassing second–order property C. (To anticipate, another sense of 'recognition' will surface below. It consists in granting someone a positively created but normatively relevant institutional status, power or role – for example, granting someone a citizenship. For the time being, this latter sense of recognition can be bracketed.)

The basic normative status N

Persons are typically held to have a specific moral status, they are 'moral patients' or 'moral subjects' to whom others owe respect. They possess dignity and ought to be respected independently of their particular features, achievements, gender, birth and so on.[13] They possess various rights, such as a serious right to life, right to freedom from

---

[11] On the notion of interpersonal recognition, see Honneth (1995); Ikäheimo (2002; also in this volume and references given there); Laitinen (2002; 2006); Ikäheimo & Laitinen (2007).

[12] In Laitinen (forthcoming) I defend the Scanlonian view that the acknowledgement in question is 'taking wronging the other to be a normative consideration of special priority and importance'.

[13] The kind of respect in question is 'recognition respect', not 'evaluative' or 'appraisal respect' (Darwall, 1977).

interference in pursuit of their own goals (consistent with similar freedom of others), right not to be dominated *etc*. (see, e.g., Tooley, 1972). Others have duties that correspond to such rights. In addition to the narrowly 'moral' status, persons have a normative status more broadly, there is a variety of reasons that they give to others simply by being persons. There is a variety of recognitive attitudes (respect, esteem, care etc) that are called for by their different features, as well as a variety of patterns of possible interaction and interlocution (see Laitinen, 2002a, and references given there). We can use the abbreviation 'N' for the normative (including moral) reason-giving nature of personhood.

This normative status depends arguably on the various features that persons have (sentience, self-consciousness, autonomy, rationality *etc*). *Realists* (about morality or normativity) hold that such capacities are directly reason-giving, good-making, ought-making, whereas *constructivists* would hold that some 'source of normativity' must legislate that they are so. The legislative source may be autonomous individuals, communities or perhaps a divine source. I have argued against such constructivism elsewhere (Laitinen, 2003; 2006), and will here rely on a realist claim that person-making features are morally relevant independently of any moral legislation. (Those with constructivist sympathies are asked simply to plug in their favourite additional theory at this point).

There are two main ways in which such capacities can be directly normatively significant: first, through affecting what is *good or bad for* the persons, and second, through affecting what is impersonally 'good, period' (from the viewpoint of the universe, as it is sometimes said).[14] *First*, such capacities widen radically the scope of what can be good or bad *for* such beings — new ways of suffering and flourishing are opened for creatures with developed capacities.[15] There is a well-known variety of things (from injuries to insults) that we should do or omit 'for their sake', insofar as we respect and care about such beings.[16] And we have direct normative reasons to indeed respect such beings or care about them: they have so weighty interests that they

---

[14] There is also a third alternative: that person–making capacities are relevant in terms of what is good for others. This was pointed out to me by Ralf Stoecker. Presumably these 'others' include non-persons. This is an interesting option, relevant for example to a picture of human persons as shepherds of being — with duties and responsibilities to see to it that *all* beings fare well.

[15] The relevance of this is stressed by Margalit (1996).

[16] And have reasons to wish for ourselves: see Skorupski (2000) for discussion on the thought-experiment that you could choose between a life with what I have called person-making capacities, and a happier life without them.

create duties for us.[17] To put it bluntly, racists, sexists and so on are not excused from moral condemnation because they do not happen to care about others.

Second, insofar as there are impersonally valuable things at all, successful exercise of various person-making capacities is bound to be among the impersonally good things (such as understanding, deep personal relations, aesthetic creation, enjoyment and so on): agents with relevant capacities can 'realize' and appreciate impersonal value by engaging with valuable things and engaging in valuable activities. This provides others with reasons to engage with them in joint pursuits, and more importantly, gives others reasons to respect and protect both the agents and such valuable objects (Raz, 2000).

The first line of argument stresses the nature of persons (thanks to their relevant capacities) as 'wrongables' – they have a viewpoint, are capable of normative expectations, reactive attitudes and suffering, and can therefore be wronged in a way in which, say, plants (which also have interests) cannot be.[18] The second line sees persons (thanks to their relevant capacities) as special kind of agents and as deserving special kind of protection and respect, because of their unique dignity and role in engaging in worthwhile 'higher' activities (see Raz, 2001; Audi, 1997). Often the two lines of argument converge, the idea being roughly that doing worthwhile things (of impersonal value) is good for the agent. In any case, both arguments lead to the view that in virtue of their capacities, persons possess a significant normative or moral status N.

The nature of the property P: being a full–fledged person

The concept of a person, then, determines what features are necessary for being a person: whether interpersonal relations are necessary, what capacities are relevant, and to what degree are the relevant capacities to be had for someone to qualify as a fully actual person. The property of being a person is thus concept-dependent: changing the concept makes a difference in who has the property. (The property C of having sufficiently of the relevant capacities is in the same way dependent on the criteria included in the concept of a person).

If we accept that the property 'being a person' is not a substance sortal, providing persistence conditions for the beings that have the property, then we can accept that the property can be actualised in more or less full-fledged ways. The Hegelian ontological idea of

---

[17] See Raz (1986b) on how interests of others create duties for us.

[18] Strawson (1974); animals are a borderline case (see Scanlon, 1998, ch. 5; Thompson, 2004).

'actualisation' may be helpful here. This idea is that existing, empirical things can be more or less 'full' or 'complete' actualisations of some plan, idea or concept. To give a rough analogue, a building has to correspond to a plan that the architect made, in order to be an actualisation of *that* plan. Further, even though it would correspond perfectly with some other plan, it was in some sense *meant to be* an actualisation of precisely this plan. Although the plan is ontologically speaking just an idea, just a thought, it determines what kind of structures the actual building must have in order to be a proper actualisation of the plan. Such actualisations come in degrees, and thus the existing things may have more or less perfect correspondence with the plans or concepts. We can of course measure anything with any arbitrary criteria (say, their distance from Rome), but the ontological interest is related to criteria that some thing is by its nature 'meant' to meet, or something that it in some sense 'ought' to be.

Similarly, the concept of a person determines the structural features that persons must have in order to be fully actual persons. Because person-making capacities come in degrees, it is very deeply rooted to the debates on personhood that infants or embryos, who have not yet actualised their potentials, are not yet 'full-fledged' or 'complete' persons — they do not fully meet the criteria but are on their way there. This Hegelian idea of reality as 'corresponding to a concept' can be applied to other aspects of personhood as well. For example, to correspond fully to a dyadic concept of a person, the persons must have more or less adequate social existence.

The notion of 'actualisation' can be given a metaphysically heavyweight interpretation if the concept or 'plan' to which reality ought to correspond to, is taken as a Platonic Idea. On a more down-to-earth interpretation, all concepts of a person are human inventions for human purposes. As there are many such concepts of a person, there are equally many properties of 'being a person', so that we can strictly speaking distinguish the properties 'being a Strawson-person', 'being a Frankfurt-person' *etc*. For simplicity's sake, I will continue to speak of the property 'being a person' in an unqualified sense, but if you wish, the view defended here can be taken as an outline of what the property P of being a 'Laitinen–person' is like. In characterizing that property, I aim at a philosophically favoured way of sorting out the rival conceptions that tradition has handed down to us as aspects of overall personhood (individual capacities, normative significance, constitutive recognition). For example, some ways of combining these aspects threaten to be arbitrary (say, if the capacities play no role, and only actual recognition as a person matters, even stones could be included). In the next section I discuss whether some ways of combining these aspects are basically morally objectionable.

2. Sorting Out the Aspects: The Basic View

We can now turn from the initial characterization of the aspects to the question of how they are to be combined. I will defend the view that the morally unobjectionable way to sort out the aspects follows the sequence C → N → R. (In this paper I use the arrow symbol loosely to indicate the way in which the analysis moves: in the sequence above, we start from capacities, which ground normative requirements, which precede recognition). Various other ways of combining the aspects are morally dubious in making the moral status conditional on something that it ought not be conditional upon. One way to meet this moral objection is to give up the insight that recognition might be constitutive of personhood. By contrast, I try to show that we can also include the constitutive role of recognition to our theory in a morally unobjectionable way.

How (not) to meet the moral objection

Consider, first, an idea that morality, like all normativity, is a human construction, and is always in the making. As the authors of morality, we create and renew morality by applying it in the situation at hand. The moral or normative status of persons *just is* the social status of being recognized. To have a moral right is to be recognized to have a moral right. This is too simplistic, insofar as it does not draw an elementary distinction between how things *are* responded to and how they *ought to be* responded to. It would clearly rob morality and normativity of any point, if anything we in fact do in a situation would define what was the right thing to do — it would make requirements toothless and impossible to violate. Thus we must have a way of holding that *recognition* is responsive to pre-existing *normative requirements (R is responsive to N)*.

What about the slightly more plausible idea, that in any situation there are pre-existing normative requirements, which are created by our commitments and normative implications of our past acts? This would succeed in distinguishing requirements from responses: the ways in which we act here and now ought to be consistent with our past action. But reflection immediately shows that this is problematic: what if some of our past acts were bad or unideal? And what if we have not committed ourselves to consistency? Or if we are consistent racists or sexists, does it follow that we *ought to be* racists and sexists?

After all, not being so would be inconsistent with the requirements created by our past actions and commitments. Appeal to possible community-level agreement against racism and sexism is of no help, as it leaves us with the problem of consistently racist or sexist communities. As these are unattractive ideas to say the least, we must have a way of thinking that basic normative requirements are independent of actual social responses, or actual recognition. *(N is basically independent of R)*.

What then could the normative requirements depend on, if not actual recognition? The obvious candidate is the view discussed above that the capacities of individuals simply have moral significance and that they *ought to be* responded to, whether or not they are. Insensitivity to the significance of such capacities is a moral failure, even when consistent. As was pointed out above, we can say that the normative significance results from the capacities. *(N results from C)*.

Thus, the morally *unobjectionable* way of sorting out aspects of personhood is the sequence C → N → R. That is, capacities ground normative requirements and recognition is partly defined as responsiveness to such requirements. Basic normative demands are independent of actual recognition, and result from the capacities alone.

Recognition as constitutive of personhood?

Accepting the C → N → R progression does not yet fully determine any definition of personhood. We are still free to choose between monadic, dyadic or mixed views. One unobjectionable option is to define personhood monadically as an agent having the capacities (P_M=C). It seems right to say that such a monadic notion underlies the moral or more broadly normative standing of persons. But as we saw above, it is an appealing idea that recognition plays a constitutive role in the ontology of persons. Can we have this ontological view, without falling prey to the moral objection of not being able to condemn consistent racism?

Some versions of the dyadic theory of personhood are vulnerable to the moral objection. A purely dyadic theory of personhood (P_D) might for example hold that to be a person is to be recognized, and that the moral and normative status belongs to persons so understood, that is, ($R=P_D$) → N. But it follows that those who are not recognized do not have the moral status, so that consistent forms of sexism and racism are, again, off the hook. In the same vein, mixed views hold that both capacities C and recognition R are constitutive of personhood, that is C+R = P. Some variants of the mixed view additionally hold that moral status depends on personhood so understood: $[C+R = P] \to N$. This is for example Dennett's (1978) view, and is a *very* natural one: it first gives us various conditions of personhood and then states that persons, so defined, have a moral status (see also Quante, in this volume). But again it follows that unless someone is recognized, conditions of personhood are not met, and there is no moral requirement that they ought to be recognized. And again, consistent forms of racism or sexism are off the hook. Thus, the most straightforward applications of the idea that recognition is ontologically constitutive encounter moral objections.

We may, however, claim that the property 'being a person' depends on recognition, but nonetheless insist that the basic normative requirements depend on the relevant capacities alone. The individuals are not fully actual persons if they are not recognized, but they *ought to* be recognized because they have the relevant capacities. Thus the more complicated view holds that the moral status is indeed based on the capacities alone, and not on the fact of being recognized, but nonetheless, one is a person in a fuller, complete sense when recognized. Recognition is necessary for exemplifying the *complete* structure of personhood, or being *fully actual* person. That, at least, is the 'basic view' suggested here. It maintains that although it is morally objectionable to make normative requirements fully conditional on recognition, it need not be objectionable to make recognition ontologically constitutive of complete personhood.[19] (Whether it follows that personhood is normatively fully inert, will be discussed below).[20]

To sum up, the basic view is that the fundamental moral and normative status depends on the capacities alone. Being recognized cannot be the precondition of the moral status or basic moral requirements, and it should rather be a response to such requirements. And insofar as 'full–fledged personhood' includes other aspects than having the capacities, basic moral status is not dependent on them. (This is not to deny that such things, too, have normative significance, but even without them, a person with the requisite capacities has the basic moral status). To put this point with the help of the symbols, we hold first of all that $C \to N \to R$ and then add that both capacities and

---

[19] Another aspect of personhood concerns self–understandings and the proper exercise of the capacities. Like recognition, exercise should not be a condition of basic moral status, but it might be taken as ontologically relevant for full personhood: someone who fails to exercise the person-making capacities in adequate ways makes him- or herself metaphorically 'less than a person'. See Dillon's article in this volume.

[20] Alternatively, we could hold in the *purely dyadic* version, $C \to N \to (R=P_D)$, where P_D stands for dyadic personhood. The view defended in this paper holds that personhood is not purely dyadic, as it also depends on the capacities.

normatively responsive social recognition are needed for fully actual unqualified personhood; C+N+R = P.

3. Refining the Basic View

The basic view as presented above is not vulnerable to the moral objection, and it preserves the direct ontological relevance of recognition, but a number of other questions remain. In what follows, I will discuss four challenges to it. The challenges are that *pace* the basic view, (i) capacities depend on recognition, and that (ii) recognition creates normative requirements. Furthermore, the basic view does not as such show (iii) how the relevance of individual capacities is compatible with the equality of all persons, or (iv) how to defend the equality of all humans.

The first challenge: capacities depend on recognition

The first challenge is that the basic story given above (C → N → R) gets the relation between recognition and capacities the wrong way around. Quite obviously, our actual capacities depend on socialization, and thus (in various ways) on recognition by others, so shouldn't we accept that recognition precedes actual capacities?[21] The challenge, schematically put, is that we have reasons to accept 'R → C'. This claim does not presuppose the dyadic (or even mixed) thesis that personhood is (partly) a social status, granted by other persons, or that the attitudes of others would directly constitute personhood. The claim is rather that it is impossible for humans, in the lack of magic pills, to become rational, responsible, self-conscious *etc* animals without interaction with and recognition from others.

This is an empirical claim which comes in various forms. It can concern *developmental* dependence (we need social interaction to develop or actualise the person-making capacities) or *sustenance* dependence (we need social interaction to sustain our capacities) or actual *exercise* dependence: we can exercise the capacities only in a social context (say, exercising the capacities to interact respectfully with others demand the presence of others, like playing tennis demands the presence of others). Developmental dependence is uncontroversial concerning humans, but the other two may be too strong for many person-making characteristics: after all, one can sustain and exercise many of one's capacities on one's own on desert islands. So I will focus on the challenge posed by the developmental

---

[21] See Stekeler-Weithofer [this volume]. Compare to Charles Taylor's (1985b, p. 191) well known 'social thesis'. For discussion, see Laitinen (2002; 2003).

dependence (the other ideas could be accounted for in roughly similar ways).

The challenge is to make room for the observation that the development of the capacities presupposes recognition. We must have room somewhere in the story for 'R → C'. To meet this challenge, we need *not* reconsider anything that we have claimed so far about agents with C, that is, with sufficiently developed capacities to be full persons. We simply need an account of how they get there. And that account will in fact include the C→N→R structure twice: we start from someone's *potential* capacities C_P, which ground the potential persons' normative status N_P, responsiveness to which partly constitutes the social existence of such potential persons R_P, which in turn is a developmental precondition of having the capacities to the sufficient degree, i.e. having C. And that is the starting point for the basic view outlined above: such capacities ground normative demands N responsiveness to which counts as recognition R. The full progression is, schematically put, $C_P→N_P→R_P→ C→N→R$. And in this we have room for the idea that recognition precedes capacities, it is just that the recognition, which precedes the actually depeloped capacities, is recognition of the potentials, R_P.

Thus, having the relevant capacities in a potential form, (C_P), creates normative requirements (N_P) for others to respect the being, not to harm it, and to do one's due share in participating in its developmental process (and one's share may depend on one's position in relation to the potential person – whether one is a parent, a neighbour or living in the opposite end of the world).[22] More or less adequate responsiveness to such requirements constitutes recognizing (R_P) and giving social existence to the potential person, which is empirically speaking developmentally necessary for it ever to have the relevant capacities in a sufficiently developed, or actual, or unqualified form (C). And from then onwards, the basic story goes that having the capacities C of an actual person creates for others normative requirements N, responsiveness to which constitutes recognition of the actual person R. And such recognition is necessary for being a person in the complete or fully actual sense.[23]

---

[22] Mere potential to develop the capacities is different from actually having the capacities, but it is significant in its own right. It grounds different normative requirements, though: similarly, a prince does not have the rights, entitlements and duties of a king, even though he is a potential king (see e.g. Feinberg, 1994, pp. 45–51).

[23] Here we can coin terms for different partial notions of personhood. A *potential* person has the relevant capacities in a potential form. A *gradually developing* person has them in a more and more actualised and developed form. A fully developed (monadic) person has

The second challenge: normative significance of recognition

The second challenge points out that the normative requirements to which interpersonal recognition is responsive to, are not based (only) on the capacities of the individuals, but derive from various social practices. Various social practices, granted statuses, publicly adopted principles *etc* make a normative difference. *Insofar as granting such statuses is 'recognition'* (say, granting someone the rights of a citizen), and generates reasons and oughts (such citizenship–rights ought to be respected by others), we have reasons to think that *normative requirements depend on recognition* ($R \to N$), at least in some sense of 'recognition'. And the normative relevance of social practices and recognition may go very deep – even the norm of equality of persons may not depend on the capacities of the individuals alone, but on a socially acknowledged norm of equality. The basic view argues that recognition must to some extent be defined as responsiveness to normative requirements. But – so the challenge goes – recognition as granting statuses also *creates* normative requirements, and the basic story does not yet account for that.

I think the right way to respond to this challenge is to admit that the basic view concerns only *basic* normative requirements, and that there are additional normative requirements which flow from actual social practices with constitutive rules for various roles (such as 'client', 'salesperson', 'officer', 'priest', 'citizen', 'legal owner'). There is, so to speak, a second leg for the normative requirements concerning treatment of persons. It is important to see that this sense of 'recognition' as granting statuses, roles and powers, is different from recognition as responding to pre-existing normative features of the individual. (This sense of recognition as granting statuses was bracketed during the discussion above). Much more could of course be said about how social practices and recognition also create normative demands, but a minimal way of responding to the challenge is simply to point out that the challenge is based on a different sense of 'recognition', which can enrich the basic story. Nonetheless, we may stress that the *basic* normative and moral status of persons is based on their capacities C, and that social practices concern mostly the distribution of additional roles.

---

them to the sufficient degree. But even though one is 'fully developed' one is not 'fully actual' person, because the other structural element, that of social existence, may still be missing.

The third challenge: normative relevance of capacities and the equality of persons?

A third challenge is really a demand for more specificity. Is it the individual capacities such as self–consciousness or autonomy, that are normatively relevant, or is it really the property C (of having *sufficiently* of the capacities to be a person) that is relevant?

In my view, there is room for a reasonable debate here, although the question may not have been widely noticed. Here, two more or less novel alternative accounts can be formulated, both of which are consistent with the basic view. A 'buck-passing account' holds that personhood as such is not morally relevant over and above the moral relevance of the person-making capacities taken individually. A second view appealing to the notion of 'exclusionary reasons' holds that a norm of *equality* of persons does add something, which cannot be based on the person-making capacities individually.

The normative significance which depends directly on each of the person-making capacities ($c_1, c_2, c_3, \ldots$), does not yet give any justificatory role to monadic personhood, or the property C (as opposed to the plural capacities that it depends on). Reasons and oughts generated this way would be at place *even without* a concept of a person, or without any other unified concept in its place. Imagine a community which does not have a single unified concept of a person, but several concepts for all the capacities, and separate notions for agents possessing them (one concept for a self-conscious agent, another concept for a rational agent *etc*). Members of such a community might treat and regard each others more or less adequately in the light of the moral significance of each capacity individually (self-consciousness, autonomy etc.). Call the moral status that results from such capacities, a *clustered moral status*. Capable agents could be to a great extent adequately 'recognized', respected and loved even in the absence of any classification of self-conscious, autonomous *etc* beings under any single classificatory term such as 'person'. The rights and duties of beings with certain kinds of capacities could even be coded in laws, institutions and so on, without the concept of a person.

Is this the whole story? What can be called a 'buck-passing account' of the moral relevance of personhood would claim so.[24] The normative relevance of personhood depends in its entirety on such individual features, whether or not we classify the possessor with the

---

[24] To my knowledge, such a 'buck-passing' analysis of personhood has not been suggested, although buck-passing analyses of value (Scanlon, 1998) and welfare (Darwall 2002) have been suggested. The term comes from Scanlon (1998, ch 2). A related 'buck-passing' analysis could analyse the value-concept 'dignity' in terms of reasons of respect.

help of the concept of a person. This view claims that monadic personhood does not add to the reasons and oughts that make up the clustered moral status, it merely indicates the presence of individual reason-giving features on which the reasons and oughts depend (and is merely a handy way of unifying various concepts whose extensions are more or less identical). This buck-passing account bites the bullet and agrees that personhood as such does not make a moral difference, only the person-making capacities do.

A second view claims that this is not the whole story. When a community comes up with a concept of a person, this allows them to adopt a fresh moral norm or principle that *all persons* are to be treated *as equals* in some further respects. This goes beyond the uninformative universalistic meta-view that every entity ought always to be treated right, or that only morally relevant differences should matter. The substantive moral norm of equality makes a difference to what *is* morally relevant (based on considerations of justice, for example.)[25] Insofar as the capacities of individuals are the sole determinants of the moral significance, any differences in the degree to which these capacities are had seem morally relevant differences. But the norm of equality will neutralize the relevance of some differences (above some relevant threshold). This enables a move from the clustered moral status to the *equal moral status of persons.*

If there is a basic package of equal rights and entitlements that are owed to all persons who are above a certain threshold of capacities, then from that viewpoint, any further intelligence, rationality and self-consciousness do not make a moral difference. At some point, the beings in question already have full rights of persons, and any further differences are not normatively relevant. Technically speaking, such a norm of equal moral status of persons is a second-order 'exclusionary reason' (Raz, 1990), which not only gives a (first-order) normative reason to act, but at the same time is a second-order consideration excluding some other (first-order) reasons from consideration. Typical exclusionary reasons are promises (which provide a reason to do what is promised, and exclude from consideration further reasons to do or not to do it), and authoritative commands by higher ranking officers (such commands provide a reason to do what was commanded,

---

[25] Cf. Rawls 1972, p. 508: 'Now whether there is a suitable range property for singling out the respect in which human beings are to be counted as equal is settled by the conception of justice.' Lloyd Thomas (1979, p. 594) comments: 'in other words, it appears that the conception of justice as fairness *requires* that ' moral personality' should be regarded as a range property. This may be so, but then it can hardly be said that equal justice is founded on equal natural attributes. Rather, the conception of justice imposes this equality.'

and a reason not to consider other reasons for and against acting — the officer's choice may not be the wisest but it is his or her call) (Raz 1990). Although it has not been noted before in the literature, the norm of equal moral status of persons seems to have a similar structure: it provides a reason for acting in a certain way, and for excluding from consideration certain kinds of differences in individual capacities, which might be relevant otherwise (say, the norm of equality demands that extra intelligence makes no moral difference to the basic respect of persons). Thus the concept of a person does help us to form a new moral opinion (which according to realists may be a case of understanding a moral truth, or a true demand of justice, which we have previously missed).[26] My hunch is that most of those who accept the basic view will find this latter option more appealing, but I think both versions are defensible.

The fourth challenge: the equality of all humans – a trilemma and a promissory note

Is that, then, the whole story? There is a widespread (but also widely contested) intuition that all humans are entitled to equal respect, to basic human rights, and to a life consistent with human dignity (see e.g. Margalit, 1996; Nussbaum, 2006). Thus, in addition to the norm of equality of *persons*, the community in our example may adopt an even broader concept of moral equality, which covers *all humans*: all humans can be taken to be entitled to the basic moral rights (of persons, or of humans). The challenge is to do this in a way which avoids frank 'speciesism' (arbitrary favouritism towards one's own species — see Singer, 1978). The challenge is to come up with a justification that in some way refers to *the person-making features*, but nonetheless ends up defending the intuitively appealing view that *all humans are equal*. Many philosophers seem to find it simply obvious that this cannot be done.[27] Whatever relevant features we focus on, it will unfortunately turn out that it is not the case that all humans will have them.[28]

Thus, any attempt to ground human equality this way faces a problem, a trilemma of three mutually incompatible claims:

---

[26] It could further be argued that this requirement is disabled in communities without a concept of a person, where people cannot have apprehended the requirement. Compare Thompson 2004, 368: 'deontic truth of a given type is not there to be apprehended or to bind until ignorance of it among those whom it binds is rendered exceptional.'

[27] See e.g. the discussions summarized in Wong (1984, ch 13).

[28] See Margalit 1996. His negative strategy focussing on the capacity to suffer does not work either — seriously cognitively impaired humans lack some of the capacities to suffer that person-making capacities (for better or worse) enable.

1) All humans are entitled to equal respect and equal moral status (often expressed in terms of human dignity and human rights),

2) The moral status is based on the individual's having relevant person-making features F,

3) Not all humans have these features F.

All three theses cannot be true. One must drop at least one of them. Perhaps (1) can be simply dropped, and indeed some do not feel the force of this premise, perhaps taking it to be a historical remnant from earlier worldviews. But suppose our moral intuitions speak for it. In that case, we must try to articulate them and perhaps end up accepting, rejecting or adjusting them in a reflective equilibrium (in such a process of reflection we should exercise also some hermeneutics of suspicion and reflect on explanations which could repudiate the intuition). But how should we articulate those intuitions? Most approaches conclude, understandably, that features F cannot figure in the articulation, and they turn to other kinds of considerations. But that may be too hasty. One promising answer to this trilemma is to reformulate (2), and make corresponding slight changes to (3). What can be called the 'suitable relation approach' does it in the following way:

2') The moral status is based on the individual's having *a suitable relation to* the relevant person-making features F.

Actually having the person–making features is one such suitable relation, which means that whatever species a being belongs to, if it has the features, it has the moral status. Thus we do not have frank speciesism. But there may be other suitable relations: for example, having the features in a potential form, or having had them in the past (e.g. children, old people or unborn people who do not at the moment have the actual capacities). And one such suitable relation to the capacities might be that of 'belonging to a biological species whose normal members have them, even though not having the capacities oneself'. If that relation is normatively relevant, then *all* members of all those species whose normal members are persons will be included to the equal basic status. But is that species-relation really normatively relevant? (If not, then we just have a kind of speciesism again, which admittedly favours not only humans, but members of any species whose normal members are persons).

Now it does seem that species-membership has at least some kind of normative relevance. For example, it makes a difference to what full-fledged participation in one's form of life consists of. Accordingly, not having the person-making capacities is a loss for humans, but not a loss for frogs, who can live a full-fledged frog-life in the absence of such capacities. Thus even those humans who do not have the relevant capacities themselves, have *some kind of a normative relation* to the capacities. *If* this normative relation is of the right kind to ground equal respect and equal moral status, then the trilemma can be solved accordingly:

1) All humans are entitled to equal respect and equal moral status (often expressed in terms of human dignity and human rights).

2') The moral status is based on the individual's having *a suitable relation to* the relevant person-making features F.

3') All humans may in fact have *a suitable relation* to the relevant person-making features F.

Whether all humans in fact have such a relation is a matter of moral argument and empirical claims.

Very much depends of course on the details of what the varieties of the 'suitable relation' are taken to be. It is a place-holder, which can be filled in differently in different cases (persons with fully developed capacities; foetuses without any brain structures yet to sustain consciousness; severely disabled members of a species whose normal members are persons etc.).[29] Whether such an argument will succeed, remains to be seen. The challenge is to come up with detailed arguments concerning the various cases, and that is beyond my powers, and aims in this essay.[30]

---

[29] On 'active' potentials, see Quante (2002, pp. 92–118); Wilkes (1988, chapter 2). See Bermudez (1996) & Gallagher (1996) on the debate about the relevance of primitive forms of self-consciousness. On foetuses without developed brains, see McMahan (2003). One step forward in trying to give an adequate analysis of the moral status of the unfortunate fellow humans, who do not have the specific potentials to become persons, is the idea of an 'Aristotelian loss' articulated by Kathleen Wilkes (1988, 62). Severely disabled persons have some relation to the person-making capacities, although not that of actually possessing them. But it is a misfortune that they do not possess them. (It is no misfortune that members of other species do not possess them — they can interact with similar species members as full participants even without such person-making features).

[30] I wish to thank Robin S. Dillon, Ralf Stoecker, Valerie Hardcastle, Heikki Ikäheimo, Jari Kaukua, Jussi Kotkavirta, Pessi Lyyra, Petteri Niemi, Mimosa Pursiainen, Michael Quante, Juhana Toivanen and Mikko Yrjönsuuri for comments on different versions of the paper. Work on the topic of this paper and this edited collection have been supported by research projects funded by the Academy of Finland ('Limits of personhood', 'Persons, reasons and realism').

References

Audi, R. (1997), *Moral Knowledge and Ethical Character* (Oxford: OUP).
Baker, L.R. (2000), *Persons and Bodies: A Constitution View* (Cambridge: Cambridge University Press).
Bermúdez, J. (1996), 'The moral significance of birth', *Ethics*, **106** (2), pp. 378–403.
Boethius, A.M.S (1973), *The Theological Tractates: The Consolation of Philosophy* (Loeb Classical Library).
Dancy, J. (2004), *Ethics Without Principles* (Oxford: Clarendon Press).
Darwall, S. (1977), 'Two kinds of respect', *Ethics*, **88**, pp. 36–49.
Darwall, S. (2002), *Welfare and Rational Care* (Princeton, NJ: Princeton UP).
DeGrazia, D. (1996), *Taking Animals Seriously* (Cambridge: CUP).
DeGrazia, D. (2005), *Human Identity and Bioethics* (Cambridge: CUP).
Dennett, D. (1981), 'Conditions of personhood', in *Brainstorms* (Cambridge, MA: MIT Press; orig.1978).
Feinberg, J. (1994), *Freedom and Fulfilment: Philosophical Essays* (Princeton, NJ: Princeton UP).
Frankfurt, H. (1971), 'Freedom of the will and the concept of a person', *Journal of Philosophy*, **lxvii**, pp. 5–20.
Gallagher, S. (1996), 'The moral significance of primitive self-consciousness: A response to Bermudez', *Ethics*, **107** (1), pp. 129–40.
Gallagher, S. (2005), *How the Body Shapes the Mind* (Oxford: OUP).
Hegel, G.W.F.(1991), *Elements of the Philosophy of Right*, ed. Allen W. Wood, trans. H.B. Nisbet (Cambridge: CUP; orig.1821).
Honneth, A. (1995), *The Struggle for Recognition: The Moral and Political Grammar of Social Conflicts* (Cambridge: Polity Press).
Ikäheimo, H. (2002), 'On the genus and species of recognition', *Inquiry*, **45** (4), pp. 447–62.
Ikäheimo, H. & Laitinen, A. (2007), 'Analysing recognition: Identification, acknowledgement and recognition between persons', in *Recognition and Power*, ed. van den Brink & Owen (New York: Cambridge University Press), pp. 33–56.
Laitinen, A. (2002), 'Interpersonal recognition: A response to value or a precondition of personhood?', *Inquiry*, **45** (4), pp. 463–78.
Laitinen, A. (2003), *Strong Evaluation Without Sources* (Jyväskylä: University of Jyväskylä).
Laitinen, A. (2006), 'Interpersonal recognition and responsiveness to relevant differences', *Critical Review of International Social and Political Philosophy*, **9** (1), pp. 47–70.
Laitinen, A. (forthcoming), 'Recognition, needs and wrongness: Two approaches'
Lloyd Thomas, D.A. (1979), 'Equality within the limits of reason alone'. *Mind*, New Series, **88** (352), pp. 538–53.
Lowe, E.J. (1996), *Subjects of Experience* (Cambridge: CUP).
Margalit, A. (1996), *Decent Society* (Cambridge, MA: Harvard UP).
McMahan, J. (2003), *Ethics of Killing* (Oxford: OUP).
Nussbaum, M. (2006), *Frontiers of Justice* (Cambridge, MA: Harvard UP).
Moore, G.E. (1993), *Principia Ethica. Revised Edition* (Cambridge: CUP; Orig. 1903).
Nagel, T. (1986), *The View from Nowhere* (New York: OUP).
Olson, E. (1997), *The Human Animal: Personal Identity Without Psychology* (Oxford: OUP).
Parfit, D. (1984), *Reasons and Persons* (Oxford: Clarendon Press).
Pettit, P. (2001), *A Theory of Freedom* (Cambridge: Polity).

Quante, M. (2002), *Personales Leben und menschlicher Tod* (Frankfurt: Suhrkamp).
Rawls, J. (1972), *A Theory of Justice* (Oxford: OUP).
Raz, J. (1986a), *Morality of Freedom* (Oxford: OUP).
Raz, J. (1986b), 'Right-based moralities', in *Theories of Rights*, ed. J. Waldron (Oxford: OUP), pp. 182–200.
Raz, J. (1990), *Practical Reason and Norms*. 2nd ed. (Oxford: OUP)
Raz, J. (1999), *Engaging Reason: On the Theory of Value and Action* (Oxford: OUP).
Raz, J. (2001), *Value, Respect and Attachment* (Cambridge: CUP).
Ricoeur, P. (1992), *Oneself as Another* (Chicago, IL: The University of Chicago).
Rorty, A.O. (1976), 'A literary postscript: Characters, persons, selves, individuals', in *The Identities of Persons*, ed. A.O Rorty, pp. 301–23.
Rovane, C. (1998), *The Bounds of Agency. An Essay in Revisionary Metaphysics* (Princeton, NJ: Princeton University Press).
Scanlon, T.M.(1998), *What We Owe To Each Other* (Cambridge, MA:Harvard University Press).
Skorupski, J. (2000), 'Quality of well-being: Quality of being', in *Well-Being and Morality. Essays in Honour of James Griffin*, ed. Crisp and Hooker (Oxford: Clarendon Press).
Searle, J. (1995), *Construction of Social Reality* (New York: The Free Press).
Singer, P. (1979), *Practical Ethics* (Cambridge: CUP).
Strawson, P.F (1959), *Individuals. An Essay in Descriptive Metaphysics* (London: Routledge).
Strawson, P.F. (1974), *Freedom and Resentment and other Essays* (London: Methuen).
Taylor, C. (1985a), *Human Agency and Language: Philosophical Papers vol. 1* (Cambridge: CUP).
Taylor, C. (1985b), *Philosophy and Human Sciences: Philosophical Papers vol. 2* (Cambridge: CUP).
Taylor, C. (1985c), 'The person', in *The Category of the Person: Anthropology, Philosophy, History*, ed. M. Carrithers, Steven Collins and Steven Lukes(New York: Cambridge University Press), pp. 257–81.
Thompson, M. (1995), 'The representation of life' in *Virtues and Reasons: Philippa Foot on Moral Theory* (New York: Clarendon Press).
Thompson, M. (2004), 'What is it to wrong someone?', in *Reason and Value, ed.* R.J Wallace et al (Oxford: OUP).
Tooley, M. (1972), 'Abortion and infanticide', *Philosophy and Public Affairs*, **2** (1), pp. 37–65.
van Inwagen, P. (1990), *Material Beings* (Ithaca, NY: Cornell University Press).
Wiggins, D. (1976), 'Locke, Butler, and the stream of consciousness', in *The Identities of Persons*, ed. A. Rorty, pp. 301–23.
Wiggins, D. (2001), *Sameness and Substance Renewed* (Cambridge: CUP).
Wilkes, K. (1988), *Real People* (Oxford: Clarendon Press).
Wong, D. (1984), *Moral Relativity* (Berkeley, CA: University of California Press).

Index

Allison, Truett, 208n5
Anscombe, Elizabeth, 85n8
Aristotle, 89, 125, 200, 205-6, 211-14, 216-17, 237
Armstrong, David, 164
Audi, Robert, 256
Augustine, 77, 82, 192
Ayer, Alfred, 81n4, 82

Baillie, James, 56n1
Baird, J. A., 208n5
Baker, Lynne Rudder, 11-12, 46-8, 166, 251n4, n5
Baldwin, Dare A., 208n5
Barresi, John, 56n1
Bartels, Martin, 135n24
Baumeister, Roy, 117n13
Beck, Lewis White, 122n15
Benhabib, Seyla, 212
Bentham, Jeremy, 7
Bermúdez, José Luis, 218-19, 268n29
Bernecker, Sven, 162
Bernheim, Hyppolyte, 140-1, 144-5
Bertenthal, B. I., 208n5
Bieri, Peter, 130n7, 131n10, 133n13
Block, Ned, 154, 170
Boethius, 249, 253
Boghossian, Paul, 161
Brandom, Robert, 177, 226, 228n7, 230n11, 231n12, 232n14, 235, 240n25
Brentano, Franz, 18n4, 159-60, 162
Breuer, Josef, 127, 135n23, 139
Brooks, D.H.M., 57n6
Brooks, Rechele, 208n5
Burge, Tyler, 161
Burke, Michael B., 51

Campbell, John, 167-9
Carter, William R., 45

Castañeda, Hector-Neri, 26n17, 90n17, 152, 154-5, 157, 159, 167n17
Cavell, Marcia, 140n35
Chalmers, David J., 38, 162n12
Chisholm, Roderick, 41, 90n17, 94, 154n5, 155, 157, 159-60
Churchland, Patricia, 88
Clark, Andy, 38
Collins, Harry, 203-6, 211
Condillac, Étienne Bonnot de, 174
Coopersmith, Stanley, 117n13
Crease, Robert P. , 201, 205

Darwall, Stephen, 110n7, n8, 235, 254n13, 264n24
Darwin, Charles, 7, 78
Davidson, Donald, 90
De Caro, Mario, 89n15
Decety, Jean, 207
DeGrazia, David, 250n2, 251n7
Dennett, Daniel, 14, 30, 57n6, 71n27, 80n3, 88-9, 200-1, 215-19, 239n23, 249, 253-4, 260
Descartes, René, 77, 80-85, 87, 92-3, 97, 158, 167, 192
Dewey, John, 178, 202
Dillon, Robin S., 13, 235, 260n19,
Dornes, Martin, 130n8
Dretske, Fred, 132n11
Dreyfus, Hubert, 201-6, 209, 211-15
Dreyfus, Stuart, 201-3, 212-13, 215n11

Erikson, Erik, 62
Evans, Robert, 204

Fadiga, Luciano, 207
Feigl, Herbert, 89, 90n16, n19
Feinberg, Joel, 235, 262n22
Fichte, Johann Gottlob, 14, 78n1, 157-9, 164, 169, 177-9, 187, 194

INDEX

Flew, Antony, 249n1
Forst, Rainer, 231n11
Foucault, Michel, 78
Frank, Manfred, 13-14
Frankfurt, Harry, 94, 200, 236, 252n9, 253, 257
Fraser, Nancy, 229n9
Frege, Gottlob, 193
Freud, Sigmund, 13, 78, 127-151
Friebe, Cord, 134n19, 135n24
Frith, Christopher D., 167-8

Gadamer, Hans-Georg, 197
Galilei, Galileo, 33
Gallagher, Shaun, 14, 167-8, 253n10, 268n29
Gallese, Vittorio, 207, 216
Gallup, Gordon G., Jr., 27n19
Geach, Peter, 154
Gilligan, Carol, 212
Glover, Jonathan, 56n1
Goldie, Peter, 170
Gopnik, Alison, 28n21, 208
Grézes, Julie, 207
Guha, Ramanathan V., 203
Gurwitsch, Aron, 209-10

Habermas, Jürgen, 212
Hall, Martin, 204
Harman, Gilbert, 163
Harris, John, 9
Hayes-Roth, Frederick, 203
Hegel, G.W.F., 14, 56, 71n27, 72n31, 78n1, 79, 81, 89, 174-98, 225-7, 228n7, 233n14, 234-5, 238n21, 241n28, 249n1, 253, 256-7,
Heidegger, Martin, 80, 96-7, 178, 202, 209-10, 213, 214n10
Henrich, Dieter, 157
Heraclitus, 180-1
Herder, Johann Gottfried, 174, 195
Hobbes, Thomas, 174, 195
Hobson, Peter, 216
Hoffman, Joshua, 49
Hölderlin, Friedrich, 194
Honneth, Axel, 11n6, 227,228n6, 229n9, 231n12, 234, 235n17, 238n20, 240, 241n28, 253, 254n11
Horgan, Terence, 170
Hubley, Penelope, 208
Hudson, Hud, 40
Hudson, Stephen D., 110n8
Hume, David, 40, 78, 83-4, 86, 174, 187-8, 195

Hurley, Susan, 7n1
Husserl, Edmund, 83, 161n10, 164n14, 170, 210, 217
Hutto, Daniel D., 211

Ikäheimo, Heikki, 14-15, 249n1, 253n10, 254n11

James, William, 84n6, 178
Jeannerod, Marc, 207
Johnson, S.C., 208

Kagan, Jerome, 28n21
Kant, Immanuel, 13-14, 78, 80, 84, 86-7, 89-91, 93, 97-8, 101-26, 134, 152-3, 158, 169, 174-98, 235
Kaplan, David, 167n17
Kenny, Anthony, 80n3, 85n8
Knapp, G., 134n18
Korsgaard, Christine M., 57n6, 58n9, 112, 125
Kripke, Saul, 162

Laitinen, Arto, 15, 227, 228n6, 229n9, 238
Lee, Patrick, 238n22, 241n27
Legerstee, Maria, 208
Leibniz, G.W., 77, 89, 158
Lenat, Doug, 203, 205, 211n8
Levinas, Emmanuel, 216, 238n21
Lewis, David, 154
Locke, John, 42, 64-5, 67n21, 77, 92-3, 97, 160, 174, 180
Löw-Beer, Martin, 142n36
Lowe, Jonathan, 38

MacArthur, 89n15
Mach, Ernst, 156-7, 161
Macionis, John J., 229n9
Malcolm, Norman, 85n8
Marcel, Anthony J., 215n11, 217
Margalit, Avishai, 232n13, 255n15, 266
Markell, Patchen, 228n6
Martin, Raymond, 56n1, 58n9
Marx, Karl, 178
McDowell, John, 89, 90n17, 95n27, 175n1, 231n11
McGinn, Colin, 89-90, 97
McMahan, Jeff, 268n29
Meinong, Alexius, 18n4, 160, 161n10
Mellor, David Hugh, 164-5
Meltzoff, Andrew N., 28n21, 208
Merian, Johann Bernard, 157n6

INDEX

Merleau-Ponty, Maurice, 202n2, 210, 217
Mialet, Helene, 203
Mittelstaedt, Horst, 167
Moore, M. Keith, 208
Moran, Richard, 154, 159n7, 165
Mruk, Christopher J., 117n13.

Nagel, Thomas, 90n16, 94, 97, 249n1
Neisser, Ulrich, 28
Nietzsche, Friedrich, 78, 127, 178-9
Noonan, Harold W., 46, 56n1, 63n15
Novalis, 14, 169-70
Nozick, Robert, 44, 159, 169n18
Nudds, Matthew, 7
Nussbaum, Martha, 266

Olson, Eric, 12, 66n20, 251n3,5

Pappas, George, 201
Parfit, Derek, 44, 88-9, 94n24, n25
Penelhum, Terence, 56n1
Perry, John, 56n1, 57n5, 90n17, 167
Phillips, W., 209
Pinkard, Terry, 175n1
Pippin, Robert B., 175n1, 226n3, 228n7
Pitkin, Hanna Fenichel, 232n13
Plato, 181, 183, 192, 195, 211
Plummer, Ken, 229n9
Polanyi, Michael, 130n9
Putnam, Hilary, 161, 249n1

Quante, Michael, 12, 244n32, 249n1, 253n10, 260, 268n29

Rawls, John, 94, 97, 244n32, 251, 265n25
Raz, Joseph, 251n3, 256, 265-6
Reichenbach, Hans, 167
Ribeiro, Rodrigo, 204
Ricoeur, Paul, 227n4, 251n3
Rizzolatti, Giacomo, 207
Rochat, Philippe, 28
Rorty, Amelie, 56, 249n1
Rorty, Richard, 88-9, 133n14, 185
Rosenberg, M., 117n13
Rosenkrantz, Gary S., 49
Rosenthal, David M., 165-6
Rousseau, Jean-Jacques, 89, 96n29
Rovane, Carol, 58n9, 64n16, 67n21, 226n3, 239n23
Ryle, Gilbert, 78, 84, 85n7, 92, 97

Sandler, Joseph, 135n24, 140

Sartre, Jean-Paul, 96-7, 158-9, 162-3, 165, 238n21
Scanlon, Thomas, 256n18, 264n24
Schechtman, Marya, 57n6, 58n9, 67n21
Scheler, Max, 216
Schelling, F.W.J., 78n1, 89, 152-3, 169
Schiller, Friedrich von, 194, 195n9
Schleiermacher, Friedrich, 152, 169
Schmalenbrach, Hermann, 159
Schmid, Hans Bernard, 70, 71n28
Schmidt am Busch, Hans-Christoph, 241n28
Schopenhauer, Arthur, 78, 127
Searle, John, 18n5, 32, 230n10
Selinger, Evan, 201, 205, 206n3
Sellars, Wilfrid, 9-10, 80, 89, 91, 94-5, 97, 249n1
Sheets-Johnstone, M., 204
Shoemaker, Sydney, 44, 46, 152, 159-61, 162n11, 163-4, 167
Sider, Theodore, 52
Siep, Ludwig, 56n1, 244
Siewert, Charles P., 170
Singer, Peter, 266
Singer, Wolf, 191, 193-4
Skorupski, John, 255n16
Sommerville, Jessica A, 207
Spaemann, Robert, 226n3
Sperry, Roger W., 167
Spinoza, Baruch, 79, 89
Stekeler-Weithofer, Pirmin, 14, 235n16, 261n21
Stoecker, Ralf, 255n14, 268n30
Strawson, Peter, 89, 152, 215, 249n1, 252n9, 253, 256n18
Stretton, Dean, 238n22, 241n27
Sturma, Dieter, 12, 56n1, 226n3, 228n8, 241n27
Swinburne, Richard, 40, 94n23

Taylor, Charles, 94, 95n28, 96n29, 97, 236, 249, 253, 261n21
Taylor, Gabriele, 101
Testa, Italo, 239n23
Thiel, Udo, 157n6
Thomas, Lloyd, 265n25
Thompson, Michael, 191n7, 251n3, n6, 252n8, 253, 256n18, 266n26
Thomson, Judith Jarvis, 48
Tiberius, Valerie, 103n3
Tienson, John, 170

Tooley, Michael, 10, 230, 241n28, 251n6, 255
Trevarthan, Colwny,, 207-10
Tugendhat, Ernst, 160n9, 164n14
Tye, Michael, 163

Unger, Peter, 40, 43-4

van de Vate, Dwight Jr., 249n1
van Inwagen, Peter, 38, 51, 251n3
Varela, Francesco, 213
Velleman, J. David, 67n21
Vertosick, Frank Jr., 191n7
Vesey, Godfrey, 56n1
Vlastos, Gregory, 237n19
von Holst, Erich, 167
Walker, Arlene S., 208n5
Walker, John D., 103n3
Wiggins, David, 61n12, 94n24
Wildt, Andreas, 13
Wilkes, Kathleen V., 57n4, 200, 251n3, 268n29
Williams, Bernard, 94n24
Williams, Robert R, 238n21
Wittgenstein, Ludwig, 80, 85, 89, 97-8, 176, 184, 195, 204, 227, 235
Wollheim, Richard, 94n25
Wong, David, 266n27
Wood, Allen, 112, 115n12
Young, Iris, 204

Zahavi, Dan, 219n13
Zimmerman, Dean W., 34, 40